Learning Patterns in Higher Education

Learning Patterns in Higher Education brings together a cutting edge international team of contributors to critically review our current understanding of how students and adults learn, how differences and changes in the way students learn can be measured in a valid and reliable way, and how the quality of student learning may be enhanced.

There is substantial evidence that students in higher education have a characteristic way of learning, sometimes called their learning orientation (Biggs 1988), learning style (Evans et al. 2010) or learning pattern (Vermunt and Vermetten 2004). However, recent research in the field of student learning has resulted in multifaceted and sometimes contradictory results which may reflect conceptual differences and differences in measurement of student learning in each of the studies. This book deals with the need for further clarification of how students learn in higher education in the 21st century and to what extent the measurements often used in learning pattern studies are still up to date or can be advanced with present methodological and statistical insights to capture the most important differences and changes in student learning.

The contributions in the book are organized in two parts: a first conceptual and psychological part in which the dimensions of student learning in the 21st century are discussed and a second empirical part in which questions related to how students' learning can be measured and how it develops are considered.

Areas covered include:

- Cultural influences on learning patterns
- Predicting learning outcomes
- Student centred learning environments and self-directed learning
- Mathematics learning

This indispensable book covers multiple conceptual perspectives on how learning patterns can be described and effects and developments can be measured, and will not only be helpful for 'learning researchers' as such but also for educational researchers from the broad domains of educational psychology, motivation psychology and instructional sciences who are interested in student motivation, self-regulated learning, effectiveness of innovative learning environments, as well as assessment and evaluation of student characteristics and learning process variables.

David Gijbels is an Associate Professor of Learning and Instruction at the Institute for Education and Information Sciences of the University of Antwerp, Belgium.

Vincent Donche is an Associate Professor of Research Methods in Education at the Institute for Education and Information Sciences of the University of Antwerp, Belgium.

John T. E. Richardson is Professor of Student Learning and Assessment in the Institute of Educational Technology at The Open University, UK.

Jan D. Vermunt is Professor of Education at the Faculty of Education, University of Cambridge, UK.

New Perspectives on Learning and Instruction

 **Earli**

New Perspectives on Learning and Instruction is published by Routledge in conjunction with EARLI (European Association for Research on Learning and Instruction). This series publishes cutting edge international research focusing on all aspects of learning and instruction in both traditional and non-traditional educational settings. Titles published within the series take a broad and innovative approach to topical areas of research, are written by leading international researchers and are aimed at a research and post-graduate student audience.

Also available:

Learning Patterns in Higher Education

Dimensions and research perspectives

Edited by David Gijbels,
Vincent Donche,
John T. E. Richardson and
Jan D. Vermunt

Routledge
Taylor & Francis Group

LONDON AND NEW YORK

First published 2014
by Routledge
2 Park Square, Milton Park, Abingdon, Oxon OX14 4RN

Simultaneously published in the USA and Canada
by Routledge
711 Third Avenue, New York, NY 10017

Routledge is an imprint of the Taylor & Francis Group, an informa business

British Library Cataloguing in Publication Data
A catalogue record for this book is available from the British Library

Library of Congress Cataloging in Publication Data
A catalog record for this book has been requested

ISBN: 978-0-415-84251-8 (hbk)
ISBN: 978-0-415-84252-5 (pbk)
ISBN: 978-1-315-88543-8 (ebk)

Typeset in Bembo
by Swales & Willis Ltd, Exeter, Devon

Contents

Figures

Tables

Contributors

Marlies Baeten obtained a PhD in Educational Sciences at KU Leuven, Belgium. Her research interests lie in the field of teaching methods, assessment and students' learning in higher education and teacher education. Currently, she is working as a Post-Doctoral Researcher at the University of Antwerp, Belgium.

Julien Balasse is a PhD student in the Department of Psychology and Educational Sciences at Université catholique de Louvain-La-Neuve, Belgium. His areas of research include team learning and learning environments.

Ana Belén García Berbén, PhD, is an Assistant Professor in the Department of Developmental and Educational Psychology at Granada University, Spain. Her areas of research include learning in higher education, learning approaches and self-regulated learning.

Larike H. Bronkhorst works as a Post-Doctoral Researcher at the Center for Educational Development and Training at Utrecht University in The Netherlands. She also teaches general pedagogy and practice-based research at the university's teacher education programme. Her areas of research include deliberate practice and learning across multiple contexts.

Francisco Cano studied Educational Psychology at the Sorbonne in Paris and obtained a PhD in Psychology from Granada University, Spain, in 1990. He is Associate Professor in the Department of Educational Psychology at Granada University and is a member of the European Association for Research on Learning and Instruction (EARLI). His research focuses on students' learning experience (learning approaches, achievement goals and learning patterns) and his articles have been published in many prestigious academic journals.

Eduardo Cascallar is a Guest Professor at the Centre for Research on Professional Learning & Development, and Lifelong Learning, University of Leuven, Belgium. He is also the Managing Director of Assessment Group International (USA/Belgium). His areas of expertise include psychometrics, large-scale assessments, cognitive abilities, cognitive processing, and the application of automated systems for the predictive classification of individuals and complex outcomes using advanced learning algorithms such as neural networks and support vector machines.

Liesje Coertjens is a Researcher at the Institute of Education and Information Sciences of the University of Antwerp. Her PhD research in progress focuses on the longitudinal change in learning strategies during higher education and during the transition from secondary to higher education on the one hand and on methodological issues in modelling this growth on the other hand.

Mikaël De Clercq is a PhD student at the Univesité catholique de Louvain. His research interests focus on the predictors of academic achievement among first year students at the university, and on the impact of motivation on students' learning processes.

Sven De Maeyer is an Associate Professor at the Institute for Information and Educational Sciences, University of Antwerp, Belgium, who teaches methodology and statistics. His areas of research include multilevel modelling, longitudinal analysis and educational measurement.

Filip Dochy is a Professor at the Centre for Research on Professional Learning & Development, and Lifelong Learning, University of Leuven, Belgium. In his research he concentrates on new learning and training environments, new modes of assessment on teaching, team learning and trainers' lifelong learning in teacher training and corporate training settings. He is a former president of the European Association for Research on Learning and Instruction (EARLI, www.earli.org).

Vincent Donche is an Associate Professor of Research Methods in Education at the Institute for Education and Information Sciences of the University of Antwerp, Belgium. His current research interests include student learning, teacher learning and educational measurement.

Maaike D. Endedijk, PhD, is an Assistant Professor in Educational Science at the University of Twente, The Netherlands. She is teaching in the domain of human resource development. Her areas of research include learning to teach, regulation of learning and workplace learning

Carol Evans is an Associate Professor in the College of Social Sciences and International Studies at the University of Exeter, UK; a visiting fellow at the Institute of Education, and she has a visiting professor fellowship at Trinity College, Dublin. She is a Principal Fellow of the Higher Education Academy and President of the Education, Learning, Styles, Individual differences Network (ELSIN). Her research interests include cognitive styles, assessment feedback and student learning transitions.

Mariane Frenay is a Professor at the Université catholique de Louvain, Belgium (Faculty of Psychology and Education) and received her PhD in Instructional Psychology in 1994. She is an active researcher in the field of higher education teaching and learning and faculty development and, since 2001, she has been part of the UNESCO Chair of university teaching and learning of her university. She has been teaching for several years in the master's and the doctoral programme in psychology and in education.

Benoît Galand obtained a PhD in Psychology from the University of Louvain in 2001. He is a Professor at the Department of Psychology of UCL. His research interests focus on the effects of instructional practices on student motivation, learning and psycho-social adaptation. He lectures in educational psychology, pedagogy, and research methodology for graduate and undergraduate students.

David Gijbels is Associate Professor of Learning and Instruction at the Institute for Education and Information Sciences of the University of Antwerp. His research and development interests focus on the relationship between learning and assessment in higher education and on workplace learning.

Anne Jacot is a PhD student at the Psychology and Educational Sciences Department of the Université catholique de Louvain (UCL), Belgium. She is part of the Psychological Sciences Research Institute (IPSY). Her research interests focus on learning and transfer processes in adult education.

Eva Kyndt is a Post-Doctoral Researcher at the Institute of Education and Information, University of Antwerp, Belgium, and the Centre for Research on Professional Learning & Development, and Lifelong Learning, University of Leuven, Belgium. Her research focuses on human resource development, workplace learning, approaches to learning, learning climate and higher education. She is currently assistant editor of *Educational Research Review.*

Sari Lindblom-Ylänne, PhD, is Professor of Higher Education and Director of the Helsinki University Centre for Research and Development in Higher Education. Her research focuses on student learning and teaching at university, for example on approaches to learning and teaching, self-regulation, self-efficacy beliefs, motivation to studying, assessment practices and quality enhancement in higher education.

J. Reinaldo Martínez-Fernández, PhD, is a Senior Lecturer in the Department of Cognitive, Developmental and Educational Psychology at Autonomous University of Barcelona, Spain, and he also teaches in sciences educational master's and doctoral programmes in Colombia, México and Venezuela. His areas of research include Latin American learning processes and research training.

Caroline Meurant is a PhD student in the Department of Educational Psychology at Université catholique de Louvain, in Belgium. Her main areas of research include learning in the workplace among older workers and the pursuit of work-related learning goals.

Ida Oosterheert, PhD, is a Senior Advisor and Lecturer at HAN University of Applied Sciences in Nijmegen, The Netherlands. Her areas of interest and expertise include learning to teach, transformational learning in higher education and assessment.

Anna Parpala, PhD, is a Senior Researcher and Project Manager in Learn – a research project in the Helsinki University Centre for Research and Development of Higher Education, Finland. She is responsible for developing a research-based quality system, Learn, at the University of Helsinki and she also teaches university pedagogy. Her research focuses on student learning and quality enhancement at the university.

Liisa Postareff, PhD, is an Assistant Professor of Higher Education at the Centre for Research and Development of Higher Education at the University of Helsinki, Finland. Her research areas include student learning in higher education, university teachers' approaches to teaching and teacher development, assessment of student learning and academic emotions. She also teaches pedagogical studies for university teachers and supervises master's and doctoral theses.

Linda Price, PhD, is a Senior Lecturer in the Institute of Educational Technology at The Open University, UK and a Guest Professor of Engineering Education in LTH, Lund, Sweden. She researches students' learning and teachers' teaching with new technology and uses this research to design educational development that engenders scholarly approaches to teaching and learning with digital technologies.

Isabel Raemdonck, PhD, is Professor in Adult Education and Learning at the Faculty of Psychology and Educational Sciences at the Université catholique de Louvain in Louvain-la-Neuve, Belgium. Her areas of research include workplace learning, self-directed learning, motivational processes in adult learning, employability and ageing at work.

Richard Remedios, PhD, is an Honorary Fellow at the School of Education at Durham University in England. His research focuses on individual differences in student motivation. He is particularly interested in methodological approaches for assessing student motivation and engagement, such as implicit association tests and eye-tracking.

John T. E. Richardson, DPhil, is Professor in Student Learning and Assessment in the Institute of Educational Technology at The Open University, Milton Keynes, United Kingdom. He is also responsible for institutional research on the evaluation of both courses and programmes of study at The Open University.

Katrien Struyven is Assistant Professor at Brussels' VUB (Vrije Universiteit Brussel) in the Educational Sciences Department. Her research focuses on student-activating and cooperative teaching methods and new modes of assessment in higher education and teacher education in particular. She teaches introductory and advanced courses on teaching and assessment within the bachelor-master programme of (adult) educational sciences and within the academic teacher training programme.

Tine van Daal is Researcher at the Institute for Education and Information Sciences at the University of Antwerp. Her research interests include teacher learning, learning in higher education and measurement issues related to these fields.

Peter Van Petegem is full Professor at the Institute of Education and Information Sciences of the University of Antwerp. He is chair of the research group EduBROn (www.edubron.be) and of the Center of Excellence in Higher Education (www.ua.ac.bc/ccho). His research interests focus on the level of learning and teaching strategies, external and internal evaluation of school policies and evaluation of educational policies.

Gert Vanthournout is a Post-Doctoral Researcher at the Institute of Education and Information Sciences of the University of Antwerp. His research interests focus on the development of learning patterns throughout higher education, on the relationship between motivation and learning patterns and on individual and contextual influences in learning pattern development.

Jan D. Vermunt is a Professor of Education at the University of Cambridge, Faculty of Education. He is an educational psychologist whose research interests have evolved from student learning and teacher learning as separate domains to include the way teacher learning and professional development affects processes and outcomes of student learning and vice versa.

Chapter 1

Students' learning patterns in higher education and beyond

Moving forward

David Gijbels, Vincent Donche, John T. E. Richardson and Jan D. Vermunt

The idea for this book originated at the first meeting of the 'learning patterns in transition' network in December 2011 in Antwerp. This research network sponsored by the Scientific Research Network of the Research Foundation Flanders (FWO) enables 12 international research units to foster a collaborative network and develop a joint research agenda of which the first results are presented in this book. For the name of the network and also for the title of the book, we have deliberately chosen for the term 'learning patterns' to include the wide range of theoretical perspectives that describe individual differences in student learning (e.g. Biggs 1993; Entwistle and McCune 2004; Meyer, 1995; Prosser and Trigwell 1999; Rayner and Cools 2010; Richardson 2011; Sadler-Smith 1996; Vermunt 2005).

The term *learning patterns* refers broadly to students' habitual ways of learning described in terms of how students cognitively process information and/ or the metacognitive, motivational and affective strategies they use (Vermunt and Vermetten, 2004). Research has indicated that a large number of person- and environment-related factors are linked to students' learning patterns. In the past decade a multitude of empirical studies have shown that how students cope with learning in specific learning situations is not solely determined by their general preferences but is the result of an interaction between their perceptions of the learning context, their disposition and other learner characteristics (Baeten et al. 2010; Entwistle et al. 2003; Vermunt and Vermetten 2004). Research has also shown that some learning pattern characteristics are to some degree variable across course contexts and throughout time in higher education settings (Donche et al. 2010; Vermetten et al. 1999). Inducing changes within students' learning patterns has, however, proven to be difficult in studies that took place in learning environments designed for that aim (Gijbels and Dochy 2006; Vermunt and Minnaert 2003). Part of the explanation for conflicting results in this latter domain of research may be generated by the conceptual base and measurement of student learning in these studies (Dinsmore and Alexander 2012; Donche and Gijbels 2013). Recent empirical contributions in the domain of learning pattern research stress the need for further clarification of vital components of students' learning patterns such as learning conceptions (Richardson 2011) and learning strategies (Vermunt and Endedijk 2011) and how these patterns develop in higher education in the 21st century (Vanthournout et al. 2011). This also brings in important questions concerning how differences and changes in student learning can be validly measured (Coertjens et al. 2013) and which future research perspectives are needed to increase our present understanding of student learning and development (Richardson 2013).

Against this background, the aim of this book is twofold: to further deepen our current understanding of (1) the dimensionality of student learning patterns in higher education and (2) how differences and changes within learning patterns can be measured in a valid and reliable way. The chapters in the first part of the book, 'Dimensions of learning patterns', provide theoretical perspectives aiming to broaden, deepen and integrate the present knowledge base on dimensions and patterns of student learning. The second part of the book, 'Measuring learning patterns and development', provides a range of research perspectives to further examine core measurement issues raised in previous learning pattern research regarding the nature or construct of a learning pattern and its development in higher education contexts and beyond.

We have to acknowledge that not all of the included chapters put emphasis on only one of these two vital research perspectives. Some chapters could be classified in both parts as research took place on important junctions (for instance, studies aiming to increase more conceptual understanding through using alternative measurement analysis techniques). To ensure that this book is intended not only for researchers but also for practitioners interested in student learning and enhancement, all authors were encouraged to pay attention to the relevance of the empirical research or developed theories for educational practice in their chapter. In the rest of this introduction we will briefly introduce the two parts that structure the book and the chapters within each part.

Part I: Dimensions of learning patterns

The first perspective concerns the quality of the learning pattern constructs under study and recent research is detailed in Chapters 2–6. Over the last few decades, a lot of research effort has been invested in exploring the ways in which students learn in higher education (Vermunt and Vermetten 2004). This research stems from a variety of research traditions and has evolved in different directions. A large number of studies have been carried out in diverse areas, such as: cognitive aspects of learning (Sadler-Smith 1996); learning conceptions or beliefs about learning and teaching (Säljö 1979); specific learning strategies (Marton and Säljö 1976); aspects of self-regulation (Boekaerts 1997); metacognition (Flavell 1987); and motivational aspects (Entwistle 1988). A shared feature of many of these studies is the search for relationships between various aspects of learning and an attempt to arrive at integrative models of student learning. In the domain of research on students' approaches to learning and learning patterns, models developed by researchers such as Biggs, Entwistle and Vermunt stress various key components and dimensions of student learning which show to some extent conceptual similarities but also point to different views on how components such as student motivation and processing strategies are situated and further elaborated in different sub-dimensions.

As the grounding knowledge base was developed two decades ago, there is a need to revise the theoretical components, especially against the background of 21st-century learning environments and learning demands in higher education. In particular, as new developments have been demonstrated within the fields of cognitive psychology, motivation psychology and educational sciences on the level of regulative aspects of learning, conceptions and motivation, theoretical and empirical validation studies are needed to investigate the possibilities of integration of these advanced theoretical perspectives within more fine-grained models of student learning patterns. This not only requires more in-depth research into the dimensions of student learning and interrelationships but also the relationship with the contexts and cultures in which student learning is investigated. In the following five chapters of Part I, this is thoroughly discussed.

In Chapter 2 the need for more theoretical and empirical investigation of dimensions of student learning is further addressed by Vanthournout, Donche, Gijbels and Van Petegem. In the first part of their chapter central theoretical concepts in two main theoretical models are clarified and compared: the concepts in the approaches to learning model (e.g. Biggs 2003; Entwistle et al. 2003) and the learning pattern model as developed by Vermunt (2005). In the second part of the chapter two alternative empirical research perspectives are explored: (1) a person-oriented perspective aimed at identifying subgroups of students with similar learning profiles, and (2) a longitudinal perspective interested in the complex growth trajectories in student learning in higher education.

In Chapter 3, Vermunt, Bronkhorst and Martínez-Fernández compare students' learning patterns from various countries and continents around the globe, and present empirical evidence from studies in different cultures using the same research instrument. Six underlying dimensions of learning patterns could be identified, representing an important extension compared to previous studies. They argue that research in this domain should go beyond Western countries only, and that universities should develop induction measures to help international students adapt to foreign learning cultures.

In Chapter 4, Price presents a heuristic model of student learning based on four other theoretical models: Dunkin and Biddle's (1974) model, Biggs' (1987) Presage-Process-Product model, Prosser and Trigwell's (1999) research on teaching and Price and Richardson's (2004) 4P model. The latter has four main groups of factors: presage, perceptions, process and product.

In Chapter 5, Raemdonck, Meurant, Balasse, Jacot and Frenay stress the need for a theory to understand learning patterns across the lifespan. Since characteristics of adult learning patterns have been connected with self-directedness in learning, the paper describes the concept of self-directedness in learning from the adult education research area.

Chapter 6 by Endedijk, Donche and Oosterheert closes the first research perspective on dimensions of learning patterns. Based on the results of a series of studies using the Inventory Learning to Teach Process (ILTP) a theoretical framework is provided on student teachers' learning patterns in relationship with personal, contextual and time-related variables.

Part II: Measuring learning patterns and development

In the second part of this volume, we present a selection of research perspectives to further examine core measurement issues often raised in the literature but scarcely investigated in the context of student learning in higher education, in particular regarding the nature or 'construct' of a learning pattern and development in higher education contexts and beyond. As we will illustrate below, several chapters explicitly deal with the question of how student learning patterns can be measured through self-report questionnaires and to what extent student learning patterns are related with personal and contextual variables as well as attainment or academic achievement in various educational contexts. Another important issue concerns the development of learning patterns and the need for more attention to change or development within and between crucial transitional phases in students' study career, such as the entry phase into higher education and the transition phase from higher education to work or transitions during professional life as an adult. Several chapters in this part also aim to increase our understanding of the flexibility and/or adaptability of learning patterns in educational contexts in and beyond higher education.

In Chapter 7, Richardson and Remedios administered two questionnaires, the Achievement Goal Questionnaire (AGQ) and the AGQ-Revised, in two separate studies to adult learners taking courses by distance education. The results showed that the achievement-goal framework is appropriate for understanding influences on attainment in adult learners. The chapter argues that the notion of 'learning patterns' might usefully be extended to include students' achievement goals and other indicators of motivation.

In Chapter 8, de Clercq, Galand and Frenay investigate the impact of motivational and cognitive processes on students' achievement. The results highlighted that final examination scores are essentially modulated by motivational factors, whereas the performance on the test is related to cognitive factors. The chapter discusses the results in the light of the relation between learning processes and academic achievement.

Chapter 9 by Cano and Berbén further explores the interplay between achievement goals and students' approaches to learning by detecting, using clustering procedures of acknowledged validity, patterns of motivation and learning constituted by the core variables of each of these research perspectives.

The chapter argues that students' approaches to learning and achievement goals are intertwined with aspects of students' experience of learning at university and should both be included in comprehensive models of how students learn.

In Chapter 10, Evans uses a phenomenological approach to explore the relationship between individual-difference and contextual variables in order to better understand the factors affecting a student's adoption of a deep approach. Evans argues that in the context of learning to teach it is important to consider approaches to learning in more complex and broader ways that acknowledge the relational dimensions of a deep approach.

In Chapter 11, Donche, Coertjens, van Daal, De Maeyer and Van Petegem present a study that explored the explanatory value of an integrated research perspective to understand differences in student learning and academic achievement in first year higher education. Two cohorts of first-year students from eight different professional bachelor programmes of a university college participated. Structural equation modelling reveals that, after control for students' socio-economic and linguistic ethnic background, having more academic self-confidence as well as being more autonomously motivated seems to be an important lever for more academic performance in terms of more active use of learning strategies as well as higher academic achievement.

In Chapter 12, Lindblom-Ylänne, Parpala and Postareff explore the stable versus contextual and dynamic nature of students' approaches to learning and studying by using a multi-method research design. Analyses took place of follow-up inventory data on the development of approaches to learning and studying of bioscience and veterinary medicine students. The results presented in the chapter warrant that quantitative group-level analyses should be critically evaluated and complemented by qualitative methods in order to identify students' individual learning paths.

In Chapter 13, Kyndt, Dochy and Cascallar report on the findings of a series of studies focusing on contextual and personal factors that are related to how students' approach their learning within higher education. More specifically, perceived workload and task complexity, motivation, working memory capacity and attention are examined. The chapter shows that students with a high working memory capacity and average motivation use less desirable approaches to learning than students who are autonomously motivated and possess an average working memory capacity.

In Chapter 14, Baeten, Struyven and Dochy compare students' approaches to learning, motivation and achievement in four learning environments: a lecture-based learning environment, a case-based learning environment, an alternated learning environment consisting of lectures and case-based learning, and a gradually implemented learning environment in which lectures gradually made way for case-based learning. The results of the study indicate that it is difficult to enhance the deep approach to learning and that students' motivational and learning profiles matter in explaining their perceptions of the learning environment.

We acknowledge that not all new or ongoing research perspectives have been taken into account, but we have selected research perspectives that are, at the time of writing, at the core of our research network. In this way, we are convinced that this book offers an important slice of the ongoing body of research that is being carried out in the field. The chapters in this book also provide further insights into issues regarding the dimensionality and under-standing of learning pattern development that have also been recently raised in other contributions regarding student learning in higher education (e.g. Donche and Gijbels 2013; Endedijk and Vermunt 2013; Richardson 2013).

In the final chapter of this book, we as editors critically look back and forward and present our challenges for the field. We hope in this way to inspire new or senior researchers in how further advances in learning pattern research can be made by considering these research perspectives and further developments.

References

Baeten, M., Kyndt, E., Struyven, K., and Dochy, F. (2010) 'Using student-centred learning environments to stimulate deep approaches to learning: Factors encouraging or discouraging their effectiveness'. *Educational Research Review, 5*: 243–260.

Biggs, J. (1987) *Student approaches to learning and studying.* Melbourne: Australian Council for Educational Research.

Biggs, J. (1993) 'What do inventories of students' learning processes really measure? A theoretical review and clarification'. *British Journal of Educational Psychology, 63*: 3–19.

Biggs, J.B. (2003) *Teaching for quality learning at university* (second edition). Buckingham: Open University Press/Society for Research into Higher Education.

Boekaerts, M. (1997) 'Self-regulated learning: A new concept embraced by researchers, policy makers, educators, teachers and students'. *Learning and Instruction, 7*: 133–149.

Coertjens, L., van Daal, T., Donche, V., De Maeyer, S., Vanthournout, G., and Van Petegem, P. (2013) 'Analysing change in learning strategies over time: A comparison of three statistical techniques'. *Studies in Educational Evaluation, 39*: 49–55.

Dinsmore, D.L., and Alexander, P.A. (2012) 'A critical discussion of deep and surface processing: What it means, how it is measured, the role of context, and model specification'. *Educational Psychology Review, 24*: 499–567.

Donche, V., and Gijbels, D. (2013) 'Understanding learning pattern development in higher education: A matter of time, context and measurement'. *Studies in Educational Evaluation, 39*: 1–3.

Donche, V., Coertjens, L., and Van Petegem, P. (2010) 'The development of learning patterns throughout higher education: A longitudinal study'. *Learning and individual differences, 20*: 256–259.

Dunkin, M.J. and Biddle, B.J. (1974) *The study of teaching.* New York: Holt, Rinehart and Winston.

Endedijk, M.D., and Vermunt, J.D. (2013) Relations between student teachers' learning patterns and their concrete learning activities. *Studies in Educational Evaluation, 39* (1): 56–65.

Entwistle, N. (1988) 'Motivational factors in students' approaches to learning'. In R.R. Schmeck (Ed.) *Learning strategies and learning styles* (pp. 21–51). New York: Plenum Press.

Entwistle, N., and McCune, V. (2004) 'The conceptual bases of study strategy inventories'. *Educational Psychology Review, 16*: 325–346.

Entwistle, N., McCune, V., and Hounsell, J. (2003) 'Investigating ways of enhancing university teaching-learning environments: Measuring students' approaches to studying and perceptions of teaching'. In E. De Corte, L. Verschaffel, N. Entwistle, and J. van Merriënboer (Eds.) *Powerful learning environments: Unravelling basic components and dimensions* (pp. 89–107). Amsterdam/Boston, MA/London: Pergamon.

Flavell, J.H. (1987) 'Speculations about the nature and development of metacognition'. In F.E. Weinert and R.H. Kluwe (Eds.) *Metacognition, motivation and understanding* (pp. 21–29), Hillsdale, NJ: Erlbaum.

Gijbels, D., and Dochy, F. (2006) 'Students' assessment preferences and approaches to learning: Can formative assessment make a difference?' *Educational Studies, 32*: 401–411.

Marton, F., and Säljö, R. (1976) 'On qualitative differences in learning: I. Outcome and process'. *British Journal of Educational Psychology, 46*: 4–11.

Meyer, J.H.F. (1995) 'A quantitative exploration of conceptions of learning'. *Research and Development in Higher Education, 18*: 545–550.

Price, L. and Richardson, J.T.E. (2004) 'Why is it difficult to improve student learning?' In C. Rust (Ed.) *Proceedings of the 11th Improving Student Learning Symposium, Improving Student Learning: Theory, Research and Scholarship* (pp. 105–120). Oxford: The Oxford Centre for Staff and Learning Development.

Prosser, M. and Trigwell, K. (1999) *Understanding learning and teaching: The experience in higher education*. Buckingham: SRHE and Open University Press.

Rayner, S., and Cools, E. (2010) *Style differences in cognition, learning and management: Theory, research and practice*. New York: Routledge.

Richardson, J.T.E. (2011) 'Approaches to studying, conceptions of learning and learning styles in higher education'. *Learning and Individual Differences, 21*: 189–203.

Richardson, J.T.E. (2013) 'Research issues in evaluating learning pattern development in higher education'. *Studies in Educational Evaluation, 39*: 66–70.

Sadler-Smith, E. (1996) 'Approaches to studying: Age, gender and academic performance'. *Educational Studies, 22*: 367–379.

Säljö, R. (1979) 'Learning about learning'. *Higher Education, 8*: 443–451.

Vanthournout, G., Donche, V., Gijbels, D., and Van Petegem, P. (2011) 'Further understanding learning in higher education: A systematic review on longitudinal research using Vermunt's learning pattern model'. In S. Rayner and E. Cools (Eds.) *Style differences in cognition, learning and management: Theory, research, and practice* (pp. 78–96). New York: Routledge.

Vermetten, Y., Vermunt, J., and Lodewijks, H. (1999) 'A longitudinal perspective on learning strategies in higher education: Different viewpoints towards development'. *British Journal of Educational Psychology, 69*: 221–242.

Vermunt, J.D. (2005) 'Relations between student learning patterns and personal and contextual factors and academic performance'. *Higher Education, 49*: 205–234.

Vermunt, J.D., and Endedijk, M.D. (2011) 'Patterns in teacher learning in different phases of the professional career'. *Learning and individual differences, 21*: 294–302.

Vermunt, J.D., and Minnaert, A. (2003) 'Dissonance in student learning patterns: When to revise theory?' *Studies in Higher Education, 28*: 49–61.

Vermunt, J.D., and Vermetten, Y. (2004) 'Patterns in student learning: Relationships between learning strategies, conceptions of learning and learning orientations'. *Educational Psychology Review, 16*: 359–384.

Part I

Dimensions of learning patterns

Chapter 2

(Dis)similarities in research on learning approaches and learning patterns

Gert Vanthournout, Vincent Donche, David Gijbels and Peter Van Petegem

The students' approaches to learning tradition

Over the last few decades, a lot of research effort has been invested in exploring the ways in which students learn in higher education. This research stems from a variety of research traditions (Lonka et al., 2004; Richardson, 2007b) and has evolved in different directions. A large number of studies have been carried out in diverse areas, such as: cognitive aspects of learning (Moskvina and Kozhevnikov, 2011); learning styles (Kolb, 1984); intellectual styles (Zhang and Sternberg, 2005); learning conceptions (Van Rossum and Schenk, 1984), approaches to learning (Marton and Säljö, 1997); aspects of self-regulation (Boekaerts et al., 2000); study orientations (Nieminen et al., 2004; Richardson, 1997); meta-cognition (Flavell, 1987); and motivational aspects of learning (Boekaerts and Martens, 2006). A shared feature of many of these studies is the search for relationships between various aspects of learning and an attempt to arrive at integrative models of learning (Biggs, 1993; Entwistle and McCune, 2004; Meyer, 1998; Vermunt and Vermetten, 2004).

One of the research traditions interested in student learning in higher education is the Students' Approaches to Learning tradition (the SAL tradition; Lonka et al., 2004). It is founded on the phenomenographical studies by Marton and Säljö in the 1970s (Marton and Säljö, 1976). Research in this tradition generally focuses on the different ways students engage in learning or handle learning tasks as reported by the students themselves (Biggs, 2001; Entwistle et al., 2006; Schmeck, 1988). Representatives of this tradition mostly concur on the viewpoint that there are qualitatively different ways in which students go about learning and that these differences in learning approaches are associated with qualitatively different learning outcomes (Biggs, 1979; Entwistle et al., 1991; Richardson, 1997; Vermunt, 2005). How students approach their learning is viewed as being influenced by factors in the learning environment, students' perceptions of these factors and student characteristics (Figure 2.1) (Baeten et al., 2010; Biggs, 2003; Donche and Van Petegem, 2006; Vermunt, 2005).

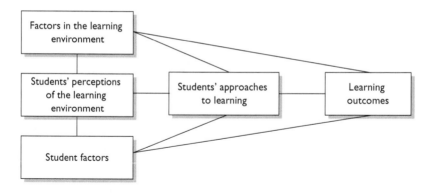

Figure 2.1 General model of the SAL tradition

Source: Based on Baeten et al., 2010; Biggs, 2003; Vermunt, 2005.

Exemplary models within the SAL tradition

Despite a general agreement on the basic assumptions mentioned above, a multitude of models can be discerned within the SAL tradition, placing emphasis on different aspects of learning, using a variety of different but related concepts, and using a multitude of self-report questionnaires to empirically measure their concepts (Coffield et al., 2004; Entwistle and McCune, 2004; Richardson, 2000). The field encloses frameworks and inventories by, amongst others, Schmeck and colleagues (Revised Inventory of Learning Processes (ILP-R); Schmeck et al., 1991), Weinstein and colleagues (Learning and Study Strategy Inventory (LASSI); Weinstein et al., 1987) or Meyer and colleagues (Reflections on Learning Inventory (RoLI); Meyer and Boulton-Lewis, 1999).

In this chapter we discuss two acclaimed and frequently used models within this tradition, namely the student approaches to learning model, albeit in two variants, and the learning pattern model (Desmedt and Valcke, 2004; Entwistle and McCune, 2004; Richardson, 2000). The first models were simultaneously and independently developed by John Biggs and colleagues in Australasia (Biggs, 1987, 2003) and by Noel Entwistle and colleagues in the United Kingdom (Entwistle et al., 2006; Entwistle and Ramsden, 1983). Their respective models were operationalized in two inventories, the Study Process Questionnaire (SPQ; most recent version R-SPQ-2F) (Biggs et al., 2001) and the Approaches to Studying Inventory (ASI; most recent version ALSI) (Entwistle et al., 2003). The learning pattern model was more recently devised by Jan Vermunt and colleagues in The Netherlands. As will be demonstrated during this chapter, it builds on the models mentioned above, but also expands them by incorporating additional components and contemporary insights from educational psychology (Vermunt and Vermetten, 2004). Vermunt and colleagues developed the Inventory of Learning Styles (ILS) (Vermunt, 1992; Vermunt and Van Rijswijk, 1988) to measure their model. The conceptual framework of each of these models is explained in more detail in the subsequent sections.

SAL models

The theoretical approaches to learning models generally distinguish between a deep and a surface approach to learning (Biggs, 2001; Entwistle et al., 2001). An approach is in each case conceived as the combination of a specific motive (Biggs, 1993) or intention (Entwistle, 1988b) and congruent learning strategies (Biggs, 1993) or learning and study processes (Biggs, 1993; Entwistle, 1988b). Therefore an approach is said to combine and integrate both a motivational and a strategy component (Entwistle, 1988a). A deep approach to learning is associated with students' intentions to understand and to appropriately engage in meaningful learning, focusing on the main themes and principles and using strategies that are appropriate for creating such meaning. The surface approach to learning, on the other hand, refers to students selectively memorizing, based on motives or intentions that are extrinsic to the real purpose of the task, such as fear of failure or keeping out of trouble.

Initially the models also incorporated a third approach, called a strategic approach (Entwistle and Ramsden, 1983) or an achieving approach (Biggs, 1987). Students adopting the latter approach try to maximize their grades by effectively using space and time. However, a conceptual difference separates the deep and surface approach from the achieving/strategic approach. Whereas the first two approaches describe ways in which students engage in learning, the latter deals with how students organize their learning (Kember et al., 1999). In addition, researchers have put question marks as to its validity as a separate construct. For instance Richardson (1994), based on a literature review on the cultural speci-ficity of learning approaches, stated that there is no unambiguous evidence for the existence of a separate achieving approach, whereas there is ample evidence of the existence of a deep and surface approach across various research contexts. He proposed viewing the achieving approach as being part of a deep approach to learning (Richardson, 2000). Research on the underlying structure of the SPQ (Biggs, 1987), an inventory aimed at measuring the three approaches to learning, also demonstrated that a model in which the achieving subscales were incorporated as indicators of the deep and surface approach fitted the data better than a model in which the achieving approach was conceived as a sepa-rate factor (Kember and Leung, 1998; Zeegers, 2002). Similarly, Entwistle and McCune (2004) also did not incorporate a separate strategic approach in the most recent version of their questionnaire, although they retained some of the ideas behind this approach in two separate scales, namely organized studying and effort management. Overall, however, following both conceptual and empirical argu-ments, the most recent theoretical models in approaches to learning distinguish only between a deep and a surface approach.

The learning pattern model

The learning pattern model, originally called the learning style model, was developed in the early 1990s in an attempt to provide a more comprehensive and integrated account of learning by bringing together four different learning components, namely: cognitive processing strategies, regulation strategies, conceptions of learning, and orientations to learning (Vermunt, 1996; Vermunt and Vermetten, 2004). Processing strategies refer to those thinking strategies and study skills that students possess and apply to process subject matter. Regulation strategies are those activities students use to steer their cognitive processing. The combination of processing and regulation strategies is sometimes referred to as learning strategies (Vermunt, 1998). Students' conceptions of learning can be defined as their beliefs with regard to what learning is, while students' orientations to learning can be conceived as their personal goals, intentions, motives, expectations, attitudes, concerns and doubts with regard to their studies. Each learning component encompasses several learning dimensions as Table 2.1 shows. The learning pattern model theorizes that some aspects of learning, such as learning conceptions and learning orientations, are more resilient to change, and partially influence or regulate the more changeable learning strategies (Vermunt, 1998, 2005).

Using factor analysis, Vermunt (1992) identified four recurring patterns based on students' scores on each of the learning components. He labeled these patterns as 'learning styles' distinguishing between an undirected style, a reproduction-directed style, a meaning-directed style, and an application-directed style (see Table 2.2). He theorized that these styles represented students' general preferences in learning for a specific period of time (Vermunt, 1996). However, as the notion of learning styles is mostly associated with invariant personality characteristics and a more trait-like view on learning, Vermunt and his colleagues recently suggested the use of the more neutral term 'learning patterns' in order to take the modifiability of students' learning into account (Vermunt, 2003; Vermunt and Minnaert, 2003; Vermunt and Vermetten, 2004). In accordance with this, the term 'learning patterns' will be used throughout this chapter.

(Dis)similarities in learning approaches and learning patterns

It can be argued that, to a degree, the learning pattern model builds on the historical heritage from the original studies by Marton and Säljö (1976) and the approaches to learning models (Biggs, 1987; Entwistle and Ramsden, 1983). However, the framework also expands, refines and updates these models in various ways.

Similar to approaches to learning, learning patterns include and integrate motivational and cognitive aspects of learning, in the form of learning orientations and cognitive processing strategies. However, the latter model also adds additional learning components to the mixture that are not included in

Table 2.1 Learning components, learning dimensions and their meaning in the learning pattern model

Learning component	Learning dimension	Meaning
Processing strategies	Deep processing – Relating and structuring	 The extent to which students actively relate aspects of the content
	– Critical processing	The extent to which students adopt a critical angle
	Stepwise processing – Analyzing	 The extent to which students methodically process the learning content
	– Memorizing	The extent to which students memorize the learning content
	Concrete processing	The extent to which students attempt to apply the content to concrete situations
Regulation strategies	Self-regulation	The extent to which students actively steer their own learning process
	External regulation	The extent to which students rely on teaching staff or the learning material to steer their learning process
	Lack of regulation	Lack of clarity on how to steer their learning process
Conceptions of learning	Intake of knowledge	The extent to which students regard learning as the absorption of knowledge
	Construction of knowledge	The extent to which students see learning as the construction of knowledge
	Use of knowledge	The extent to which students see learning as the application of knowledge
	Cooperative learning	The extent to which students see learning as a cooperative process
	Stimulating education	The extent to which students see learning as being stimulated by teachers or the learning environment
Orientations to learning	Personally interested	The extent to which students are intrinsically motivated to learn
	Self-test oriented	The extent to which students are motivated to learn by a drive to prove themselves
	Certificate oriented	The extent to which students are motivated to learn by a desire to test themselves or acquire a certificate
	Vocation oriented	The extent to which students are motivated to learn by a profession
	Ambivalent	The extent to which students experience problems with motivation

Table 2.2 Learning patterns and their constituting learning dimensions

Learning component	Learning pattern			
	Undirected	Reproduction oriented	Meaning oriented	Application oriented
Processing strategies	Hardly any processing	Stepwise processing	Deep processing	Concrete processing
Regulation strategies	Lack of regulation	External regulation	Self-regulation	Both external and self-regulated
Learning conceptions	Cooperation and being stimulated	Intake of knowledge	Construction of knowledge	Use of knowledge
Learning orientations	Ambivalent	Certificate or self-test oriented	Personally interested	Vocation oriented

Source: Based on Vermunt, 1996.

the original approaches to learning models, such as meta-cognitive regulation strategies and learning conceptions (Entwistle and McCune, 2004; Vermunt and Vermetten, 2004). Although the importance of meta-cognition is generally acknowledged by authors of the original approaches to learning models (Biggs, 1987; Entwistle et al., 2003), the component was not included by Biggs and colleagues, according to them to keep the amount of items and constructs in their instrument limited as its primary aim was to provide a quick diagnostic tool (Biggs et al., 2001). Entwistle and colleagues (2003) did not add a separate meta-cognitive component to their concept of approaches to learning for reasons of clarity of concepts and simplicity. However, they did include a separate scale that describes meta-cognitive aspects of learning, called monitoring study effectiveness, in the final version of their instrument. They conceive this scale as being distinct from, but related to, a deep approach to learning (Entwistle and McCune, 2004).

However, more recently, studies in the field have increasingly acknowledged the importance of regulatory strategies in contemporary higher education and have described them as crucial strategies for being successful in education and the working life (Gijbels et al., 2010; Lonka et al., 2004). Therefore studies have started investigating these strategies in unison with traditional approaches to learning models (e.g. Heikkilä and Lonka, 2006; Lonka and Lindblom-Ylänne, 1996).

A similar tendency is noticeable for learning conceptions, where research has provided evidence that indicates that 'how students conceive learning' is related to 'the way they actually engage in learning' (Edmunds and Richardson, 2009; Lindblom-Ylänne and Lonka, 1999; Meyer and Boulton-Lewis, 1999; Nieminen et al., 2004). Therefore, it has been argued that students' learning conceptions, to a degree, regulate their approaches to learning (Richardson, 2011), as these ideas provide a framework for students on how to interpret their own learning (Lonka et al., 2004). In addition, in the early 1990s learning conceptions were recognized as one of the three important aspects of students' study orchestration, together with students' approaches and their perceptions of the learning context (Lindblom-Ylänne, 2003; Meyer, 1991). A study orchestration is defined as a contextualized study approach adopted by individual students or groups of students (Meyer, 1998; Meyer et al., 1990). The concept was developed as a way of exploring individual differences in the quality of learning approaches by incorporating relevant influencing factors and analyzing their dynamic interrelations from a 'whole-person' perspective (Meyer, 1998, 1999; Meyer et al., 1990). To sum up, it can be concluded that, in contrast to the learning pattern model, regulation strategies and learning conceptions are not incorporated as explicit learning components in the approaches to learning models. However, their importance and their relations to learning approaches are generally acknowledged in the SAL field (Entwistle and McCune, 2004), and, therefore, they have increasingly been studied together.

In addition, a conceptual comparison between the approaches to learning models and the learning pattern model suggests that both frameworks use different, but also somewhat related, concepts and dimensions to describe student learning. This is also acknowledged by Vermunt (1998) himself. Some authors have explicitly drawn conceptual lines between the deep learning approach and (parts of) Vermunt's meaning-oriented and application-oriented patterns (Vermetten et al., 2002). Others have pointed to theoretical similarities between the surface approach on the one hand and the reproduction-oriented (Vermunt and Minnaert, 2003) or undirected patterns on the other hand (Hoeksma, 1995). Richardson (2004), however, warns that conceptual similarities do not necessary result in significant empirical links between instruments designed to measure these models.

The incorporation of the application-oriented pattern and its constituting learning dimensions potentially provides a valuable addition to the traditional distinction by covering more concrete or applied ways of thinking and studying, and could therefore be instrumental in describing differences in learning quality in professional courses in higher education (Entwistle and McCune, 2004). However, the more refined view on learning in the learning pattern model is perhaps most clearly illustrated by the incorporation of a pattern that indicates problems with aspects of learning, such as a lack of regulatory skills (lack of regulation) or motivational difficulties (ambivalent learning orientation). In doing so, it acknowledges both 'different qualities in learning' and a lack thereof. The value of (aspects of) this undirected pattern has been demonstrated by its relation to a number of other negative factors in education such as low academic performance (Boyle et al., 2003; Donche and Van Petegem, 2011; Vermunt, 2005), neuroticism (Busato et al., 1999), fear of failure (Busato et al., 2000) or drop out (Vanthournout et al., 2011b). Therefore, it has the potential to provide valuable additional insights into (the negative sides of) the learning process.

Finally, with regard to context-specificity and changeability, the models take a similar but different viewpoint. In line with the general assumptions of the SAL tradition, all models acknowledge the fact that the ways in which students engage in learning are a result of the context on the one hand (Biggs, 1996; Vermetten et al., 2002) and students' personal factors and preferences on the other hand (Biggs, 2001; Vermunt, 2005). That is, they agree that learning can be 'changed'. However, their primary focus regarding the specificity of the context seems to differ. As a result, the time period in which developments in learning approaches can be expected also differs. The original phenomenographic studies on SAL by Marton and Säljö (1976) were situated at the task level. The theoretical models of Biggs and colleagues and Entwistle and colleagues seem to primarily situate at the level of the course or the learning environment (Biggs, 2001; Entwistle et al., 2006). However, these theoretical models also acknowledge that students have more general, context-independent and somewhat more stable preferences regarding learning. These are mostly referred to as students' general learning orientations (Honkimäki et al., 2004; Richardson, 1997). Conceptual links have been drawn between these general predispositions and students' learning patterns (Endedijk, 2010; Entwistle et al., 2006; Lonka et al., 2004). This seems in line with Vermunt's own description of learning patterns as 'general preferences' or 'being characteristic for student's learning for a certain period of time' (Vermunt, 1998). However, what constitutes this 'period of time' is not clearly specified and making hypotheses hereon is complicated by the fact that the model encompasses more stable as well as more changeable components (e.g. learning orientations and learning conceptions versus regulation and processing strategies). However, it seems to be the case that the learning pattern model's primary focus, as opposed to that of the approaches to learning models, is predominantly on more general, less context-specific preferences in learning. Changes in learning patterns might therefore be expected to take a longer period of time. As a result, changes in approaches to learning and learning patterns do not necessarily have to collide. This has led to some scholars hypothesizing a reciprocal relation between students' context-specific learning approaches and their general learning preferences (Vermetten et al., 2002; Wilson and Fowler, 2005). To provide an overview, Table 2.3 summarizes the most important similarities and differences.

Alternative perspectives in research on student learning

Research interest in the SAL tradition gradually evolved to exploring factors that influence the adoption of certain approaches (Baeten et al., 2010). Encouraging and discouraging factors were sought in characteristics of the context, in students' perceptions of this context and in students'

Table 2.3 Comparison of learning components and learning dimensions in the approaches to learning and learning pattern models (conceptually similar dimensions are linked by dotted lines)

	SAL tradition	
	Approaches to learning models (Biggs, 2003; Entwistle et al., 2003)	Learning pattern model (Vermunt and Vermetten, 2004)
Central concept:	Learning approach	Learning pattern
	Motive + strategy	Learning orientations + learning conceptions + regulation strategies + processing strategies
	Deep approach ----------	Meaning-directed pattern (A.)
	Surface approach ----------	Reproduction-directed pattern (B.) Application-directed pattern (C.) Undirected pattern (D.)
Motivational component:	Motives	Learning orientations
	Intention to understand ---- (intrinsic) (A.) Intention to get task done with minimal effort (extrinsic) (B.)	Personally interested (A.) Certificate oriented (B.) Self-test oriented (B.) Vocation oriented (C.) Ambivalent (D.)
Conceptual component:		Conceptions of learning
		Construction of knowledge (A.) Intake of knowledge (B.) Use of knowledge (C.) Stimulating education (D.) Cooperative learning (D.)
Meta-cognitive component:		Regulation strategies
	Monitoring study ---------- effectiveness (Approaches and Study Skills Inventory for Students (ASSIST) only)	Self-regulation (A. + C.) External regulation (B. + C.) Lack of regulation (D.)
Cognitive component:	Learning strategies	Processing strategies
	Deep strategies ---------- (A.)	Deep processing strategies (A.) Relating and structuring Critical processing

Table 2.3 continued

Cognitive component:	Learning strategies	Processing strategies
	Surface strategies ----------	Stepwise processing (B.)
	(B.)	Analyzing
		Memorizing
		Concrete processing (C.)
	Organized studying (ASSIST only)	
	Effort management (ASSIST only)	

characteristics (Biggs, 2003; Donche and Van Petegem, 2006; Richardson, 2007a; Vermunt, 2005). It has been clearly demonstrated that factors such as assessment practices or demands (Birenbaum, 1997; Dochy and McDowell, 1997), students' perceptions of the workload (Struyven et al., 2006), teaching quality (Trigwell et al., 1999) or students' perception of an innovation (Nijhuis et al., 2005) influence their learning approaches. In addition studies have established a link between conceptual, meta-cognitive, cognitive and motivational aspects of learning (Heikkilä and Lonka, 2006; Kyndt et al., 2011; Lucas and Meyer, 2005; Richardson, 2007a). However, our insights into (the developments of) approaches to learning and learning patterns are far from complete. For a detailed account on these factors, we refer to the review study of Baeten and colleagues (2010).

As of yet, there is *no full understanding on how student learning develops* within and across learning environments. While some studies found an increase in deep approaches to learning (Abraham et al., 2006; Dart and Clarke, 1991; Donche and Van Petegem, 2009), others reported a decline in the use of this approach, even when learning environments were designed to stimulate this approach (Nijhuis et al., 2005; Struyven et al., 2006; Volet et al., 1994; Watkins and Hattie, 1985). Studies have also demonstrated (unexpected) increases in surface learning (Baeten et al., 2008; Gijbels et al., 2008) or no significant developments at all in deep approaches (Gijbels et al., 2009; Gijbels and Dochy, 2006), surface approaches (McParland et al., 2004; Struyven et al., 2006) or stepwise processing strategies (Van der Veken et al., 2009). This has prompted the idea that stimulating a preferred deep approach to learning or a meaning-directed learning pattern is far from obvious (Marton and Säljö, 1997). However, advancing our understanding of the development of learning is somewhat hampered by the research design the majority of the studies have applied up till now, namely a pretest, post-test design across a time period of one academic year or less. Therefore, little is known about potential complex, long-term developments in learning in higher education (Donche and Van Petegem, 2009; Gordon and Debus, 2002).

In addition, there are *conceptual issues* regarding SAL that challenge us to expand, refine or at least critically question traditional models in the SAL tradition. For instance, deep and surface approaches to learning (or meaning-directed and reproduction-directed) have traditionally been viewed as dichotomous, or at least situated at opposing ends of a continuum (Kember et al., 1999). Therefore, at least theoretically, different approaches should exclude each other (Cano, 2005). However, various research findings have questioned this assumption (e.g. Lindblom-Ylänne, 2003; Lindblom-Ylänne and Lonka, 2000; Meyer and Shanahan, 2003; Vermunt and Minnaert, 2003). Based on an exploration of how students combine meaning-oriented and reproduction-oriented approaches, these studies have identified other ways in which students engage in learning besides these traditional approaches. By doing so they have demonstrated that the two traditional approaches should be regarded as orthogonal rather than dichotomous and that learning should be viewed as a multidimensional instead of a one-dimensional construct (Cano, 2005). Moreover, these studies have drawn attention to the fact that it does not only matter to what degree students use different learning strategies, but also 'why' and 'how' they combine these strategies. That is, they have pointed towards the importance of incorporating various learning components in approaches to learning or learning patterns and exploring their dynamic interrelations.

These research findings as well as conceptual questions not only urge more research on student learning, but also point towards the need to deepen our understanding by using additional research perspectives and applying different data-analysis techniques. Two such alternative research perspectives appear promising for broadening our insights and therefore constitute the backbone of the subsequent paragraphs of this chapter:

1   The use of *a longitudinal perspective*, incorporating multiple data-gathering points across longer periods of time in order to explore students' complex growth trajectories across higher education.
2   The use of a *person-oriented perspective*, aimed at identifying subgroups of students with similar learning profiles by taking into account various learning dimensions and their dynamic interrelations.

In the following paragraphs, we discuss these perspectives in more detail.

Studying the development in student learning using longitudinal research designs

Although questions about the degree of stability and variability in SAL have been posed for over 20 years (Watkins and Hattie, 1985), longitudinal research that looks into the developmental trajectories of learning approaches remains scarce. As mentioned earlier, research results on the developments of learning approaches within specific learning environments remain inconclusive (Gijbels et al., 2009) and call for further exploration. Questions can also be raised as to how students' preferences in learning change over a longer period of time and across several learning environments (Wilson and Fowler, 2005). A longitudinal study by Zeegers (2001) during a three-year period indicated that SAL changed as a result of the learning experiences they encountered. His research indicated an initial decline in the deep approach, followed by a subsequent increase of this approach. He also found that the surface approach increased during the first year of higher education, but changed little overall. In addition, a review study on longitudinal research using the learning pattern model indicated that students predominantly evolve towards a deeper, more concrete and more self-regulated way of learning (Vanthournout et al., 2011a). It was also found that some dimensions of learning such as stepwise processing, external regulation or learning conceptions show a high resilience to change. Undirected learning generally decreased throughout higher education. Differences in the specificity of the context and the time period under investigation might be one explanation as to why outcomes between studies using a different theoretical framework sometimes differ. Overall, however, studies adopting a long-term perspective on growth in learning remain scarce, limiting our understanding of how and why students develop in their learning.

Moreover, the advancement of our insights is hampered by the design the majority of the research has applied up till now, namely a pretest, post-test design with a research period equalling one academic year or less (Baeten et al., 2010). At least two caveats seem to be inherently related to these designs. First, there are questions as to what degree pre- and post-test designs can provide valid information on 'growth' or 'development' (Schmitz, 2006). Their response at least seems limited, as these models can only provide an affirmative or negative answer to the question as to whether change in learning took place (Weiss, 2005). Pretest, post-test models are unable to provide a clear indication on the shape or complexity of the growth trajectory however (Rogosa, 1988). Although significant differences in scores between a pre- and a post-test measure appear to represent a linear growth trajectory, drawing such a conclusion may be misleading or oversimplifying matters, as different or more complex growth patterns may in fact take place instead (Schmitz, 2006). These more complex growth trajectories can only be uncovered by incorporating additional measurement points. Authors have stated that at least three measurement points are needed to explore linear growth trajectories and four measurement points to investigate quadratic growth models (Singer and Willett, 2003). Therefore incorporating more data-gathering points over a longer period of time seems crucial if we want to investigate not only whether change exists, but also the complexity of how developments unfold. A few studies provide initial indications that developmental trajectories in approaches to learning (Zeegers, 2001) or learning patterns (Donche et al., 2010) are complex.

Second, the exploration of change has often been examined in terms of mean difference (Taris, 2000). This is especially true for research applying paired sample t-tests. Although this technique provides some valuable and useful initial indications on average growth, it does not do justice to the potential richness of a longitudinal data set (Weiss, 2005). For example, this data-analysis technique is limited to comparing mean scores and is therefore unable to provide information on individual variation in growth (Singer and Willet, 2003). Previous research in the SAL field has provided initial indications on the importance of incorporating individual differences, by relating initial scores on learning approaches or learning patterns to long-term developmental trajectories. Wilson and Fowler (2005) have demonstrated that students with a general preference for deep learning were more stable in their learning approaches compared to students with a typical preference for surface learning. Donche and Van Petegem (2009) also demonstrated that students with various learning profiles at the start of higher education follow different change trajectories. Using initial scores in predicting change has its own pitfalls, such as regression to the mean and ceiling effects (Taris, 2000), and only permits limited conclusions on the degree and the nature of individual variation. Several advanced longitudinal techniques, however, allow the explicit modelling of variation and provide interesting potential for investigating differences in growth trajectories.

Investigating learning profiles using a person-oriented perspective

A person-oriented approach, sometimes also referred to as a person approach (Magnusson, 2003) or a person-centered approach (Magnusson, 1998) is a theoretical concept that originally stems from developmental psychology and the holistic-interactionistic perspective on development within this field (Magnusson, 1999). One of the basic assumptions of this framework is that human behavior and human development is to a degree unique and is not 'caused' by one single factor or variable or even by the mere piling up of variables and components (Magnusson, 1998, 2003). Some sort of dynamic interplay and reciprocal interaction between various variables or components is at play and this 'pattern of interrelations' or 'profile' has to be taken into account when investigating behavior or individual development (Bergman and Magnusson, 1997). Moreover, the person-oriented framework states that the specific meaning of one of the factors in these patterns is derived from its relation to other factors in the pattern (Von Eye and Bogat, 2006). Translated to research on approaches to learning, this would mean that students' scores on a single learning dimension or learning approach could have a different interpretation, depending on its relative position to scores on other learning dimensions or approaches. At the extreme, this reasoning would necessitate a unique, personal model for each individual, as every individual will probably score somewhat different on various factors. However, when investigating groups of individuals, a relatively small, finite number of 'typical' subgroups with similar patterns can be discerned (Bergman and Magnusson, 1997).

Exploring these subgroups or profiles, instead of individual differences, reduces complexity and allows for generalization (Bergman and Trost, 2006). With regard to research design and data analysis this theoretical perspective seems to necessitate a two-step approach:

1   the identification of 'typical' subgroups of respondents with similar profiles;
2   the investigation of inter-individual or intra-individual differences in development of these patterns (Von Eye and Bogat, 2006).

The person-oriented perspective is often opposed to the more traditional variable-oriented technique in the aims of the research, unit of analysis, measurement model and data-analysis techniques (Bergman, 2001; Muthén and Muthén, 2000). Table 2.4 summarizes some of the most salient differences. However, most scholars insist that a person-oriented perspective and a variable-oriented perspective should be seen as providing complementary information, rather than as opposites (Bergman and Trost, 2006; Fortunato and Goldblatt, 2006).

Gradually ideas from the person-oriented perspective in developmental psychology seeped into other areas such as motivation psychology (e.g. Fortunato and Goldblatt, 2006; Hayenga and Henderlong Corpus, 2010) and educational psychology (Heikkilä et al., 2011; Parpala et al., 2010). During this process the original assumptions of the framework seem to have been broadened

Table 2.4 Comparison of person-oriented and variable-oriented perspectives in data analysis

	Person-oriented approach	Variable-oriented approach
Research interest	Identifying meaningful patterns Understanding short-term and long-term developmental processes and the mechanisms underlying them	Exploring relations between variables Predicting outcomes on the basis of variables
Unit of analysis	Individuals (Sub)Groups of individuals	Variable Groups of variables
Measurement model: An individual score on a single dimension derives its meaning from . . .	The scores that same individual has on various other dimensions	The scores other individuals have on the same dimension
Data-analysis techniques	Cluster analysis, latent class analysis, mixture modeling, . . .	Factor analysis, analysis of variance (ANOVA), regression analysis, structural equation modelling (SEM), . . .

Source: Based on Magnusson, 2003; Von Eye and Bogat, 2006.

somewhat and assumptions of this perspective appear to have been elucidated to a degree. For instance, most studies in motivation or education have been primarily concerned with identifying subgroups or profiles, omitting the idea of exploring differences in development (e.g studies by Vansteenkiste et al., 2009; Vermetten et al., 2002). While some scholars perceive this as a normal step in the development of this perspective, others warn against aligning the perspective to the use of specific data-analysis techniques such as cluster analysis, without referencing the conceptual models and urge scholars to clarify their theoretical stances (Bergman and Trost, 2006).

In our opinion, applying a person-oriented perspective on SAL or learning patterns can be valuable for both increasing our understanding of the complex and multidimensional nature of learning and for facilitating the translation of complex models into educational practice. After all, the ways in which most students engage in learning cannot be characterized by a single approach or learning strategy (Donche and Van Petegem, 2009). Students do not learn in solely a deep or a surface manner, but in most cases combine several strategies, typical for various approaches, but to a different degree. Therefore, one can state that the way students engage in learning is not solely the sum of the repertoire of learning strategies they have acquired, but also the interrelationship between these strategies. Consequently, it can be said that students have a relatively unique 'learning profile'. Identifying typical learning profiles within a student population and investigating the relation of these subgroups and other variables such as instructional methods or learning outcomes is likely to yield valuable information that is complementary to insights gained by a variable-oriented approach (Fortunato and Goldblatt, 2006). Moreover, using profiles to describe students' scores on various learning dimensions and their interrelation also reduces complexity, as a single (complex) construct replaces the influence of various factors and their interrelations (Von Eye and Bogat, 2006). It may therefore also be valuable for educational practice. A person-oriented approach could, for instance, be useful for identifying subgroup(s) of 'at risk' students, based on several learning (and/or motivational) dimensions (Entwistle et al., 1991) and thus be valuable for diagnosis or the design of remedial or coaching initiatives.

However, up till now, not that much attention has been devoted to this person-oriented perspective in the SAL field. Although they never used the term person-oriented approach, Meyer and colleagues (Meyer, 1991, 1999; Meyer et al., 1990) seem to have been harbingers of this perspective when they introduced their notion of 'study orchestration'. Orchestrations can easily be perceived as profiles based on students' learning conceptions, approaches to learning and perceptions of the learning environment. A small but increasing number of studies have demonstrated the existence of these orchestrations or profiles. For instance, Lonka and Lindblom-Ylänne (1995) used cluster analysis based on SAL to identify four different orchestrations or profiles (which they termed reproducing orchestration, both-low orchestration, both-high orchestration, and meaning orchestration). Rodríguez and Cano (2006) found similar profiles, while Long (2003) identified no less than 14 orchestrations, based on a large sample of university students. A number of authors have applied a similar person-oriented perspective using the Vermunt model. Wierstra and Beerends (1996), for instance, found three clusters of university students based on the ILS: a 'self-regulated/meaning oriented' cluster, an 'externally regulated/reproductive' cluster, and a 'flexible/versatile' cluster. Other researchers (Donche and Van Petegem, 2006; Vermetten et al., 2002) found similar clusters, but additionally also identified an 'inactive' cluster, consisting of students whose learning patterns are characterized by low levels of learning activities. Other studies have revealed that qualitative differences in the theoretical consonance of these orchestrations are related to various outcomes' measures, such as students' perceptions towards innovative courses (Honkimäki et al., 2004) or differences in academic learning outcomes (Lindblom-Ylänne and Lonka, 1999; Meyer et al., 1990; Rodríguez and Cano, 2006).

To conclude, two predominant models in research within the SAL tradition, the approaches to learning models by Biggs and colleagues and Entwistle and colleagues and the learning pattern model by Vermunt and colleagues, were illustrated. It was put forward that some alternative research perspectives might help to increase our understanding of (the developmental trajectories regarding) SAL and explain some unexpected research results. Two such perspectives were proposed and illustrated: (1) a person-oriented perspective aimed at identifying subgroups of students with similar learning profiles and (2) a longitudinal perspective, investigating growth trajectories across a longer period of time and taking into account data from multiple data-gathering points.

References

Abraham, R., Kamath, A., Upadhya, S. & Ramnarayan, K. (2006) Learning approaches to physiology of undergraduates in an Indian medical school. *Medical Education*, 40: 916–923.

Baeten, M., Dochy, F. & Sruyven, K. (2008) Students' approaches to learning and assessment preferences in a portfolio-based learning environment. *Instructional Science*, 36: 359–374.

Baeten, M., Kyndt, E., Struyven, K. & Dochy, F. (2010) Using student-centred learning environments to stimulate deep approaches to learning: Factors encouraging or discouraging their effectiveness. *Educational Research Review*, 5: 243–260.

Bergman, L. (2001) A person approach to adolescence: Some methodological challenges. *Journal of Adolescent Research*, 16: 28–53.

Bergman, L. & Magnusson, D. (1997) A person-oriented approach in research on developmental psychopathology. *Development and Psychopathology*, 9: 291–319.

Bergman, L. & Trost, K. (2006) The person-oriented versus the variable-oriented approach: Are they complementary, opposites or exploring different worlds? *Merill-Palmer Quarterly*, 52: 601–632.

Biggs, J. (1979) Individual differences in study processes and the quality of learning outcomes. *Higher Education*, 9: 114–125.

Biggs, J. (1987) *Student approaches to learning and studying*, Melbourne: Australian Council for Educational Research.

Biggs, J. (1993) What do inventories of students' learning processes really measure? A theoretical review and clarification. *British Journal of Educational Psychology*, 63: 3–19.

Biggs, J. (1996) Enhancing teaching through constructive alignment. *Higher Education*, 32: 347–364.

Biggs, J. (2001) Enhancing learning: A matter of style or approach. In Sternberg, R. J. & Zhang, L. (eds.) *Perspectives on thinking, learning, and cognitive styles.* London: Lawrence Erlbaum Associates.

Biggs, J. (2003) *Teaching for quality learning at university* (2nd ed.), Buckingham: SRHE & Open University Press.

Biggs, J., Kember, D. & Leung, D. (2001) The revised two-factor Study Process Questionnaire: R-SPQ-2F. *British Journal of Educational Psychology*, 71: 133–149.

Birenbaum, M. (1997) Assessment preferences and their relationship to learning strategies and orientations. *Higher Education*, 33: 71–84.

Boekaerts, M. & Martens, R. (2006) Motivated learning: What is it and how can it be enhanced? In Verschaffel, L., Dochy, F., Boekaerts, M. & Vosniadou, S. (eds.) *Instructional psychology: Past, present and future trends.* Amsterdam: Elsevier.

Boekaerts, M., Pintrich, P. & Zeider, M. (2000) *Handbook of self-regulation*, San Diego, CA: Academic Press.

Boyle, E., Duffy, T. & Dunleavy, K. (2003) Learning styles and academic outcome: The validity and utility of Vermunt's inventory of learning styles in a British higher education setting. *British Journal of Educational Psychology*, 73: 267–290.

Busato, V., Prins, F., Elshout, J. & Hamaker, C. (1999) The relation between learning styles, the Big Five personality traits and achievement motivation in higher education. *Personality and Individual Differences*, 26: 129–140.

Busato, V., Prins, F., Elshout, J. & Hamaker, C. (2000) Intellectual ability, learning style, personality, achievement motivation and academic success of psychology students in higher education. *Personality and Individual Differences*, 29: 1057–1068.

Cano, F. (2005) Consonance and dissonance in students' learning experience. *Learning and Instruction*, 15: 201–223.

Coffield, F., Moseley, D., Hall, E. & Ecclestone, K. (2004) *Learning styles and pedagogy in post-16 learning: A systematic and critical review.* London: Learning and Skills Research Centre.

Dart, B. & Clarke, J. (1991) Helping students become better learners: A case study in teacher education. *Higher Education*, 22: 317–335.

Desmedt, E. & Valcke, M. (2004) Mapping the learning styles 'jungle': An overview of the literature based on citation analysis. *Educational Psychology*, 24: 445–464.

Dochy, F. & McDowell, L. (1997) Assessment as a tool for learning. *Studies in Educational Evaluation*, 23: 279–298.

Donche, V., Coertjens, L. & Van Petegem, P. (2010) Learning pattern development throughout higher education: A longitudinal study. *Learning and Individual Differences*, 20: 256–259.

Donche, V. & Van Petegem, P. (2006) Learning patterns in higher education: The influence of personal and contextual factors. *British Educational Research Association Annual Conference.* Warwick: University of Warwick.

Donche, V. & Van Petegem, P. (2009) The development of learning patterns of student-teachers: A cross-sectional and a longitudinal study. *Higher Education*, 57: 463–475.

Donche, V. & Van Petegem, P. (2011) The relationship between entry characteristics, learning style and academic achievement of college freshmen. In Poulson, M. (ed.) *Higher education: Teaching, internationalisation and student issues*. New York: Nova Science Publishers.

Edmunds, R. & Richardson, J. T. E. (2009) Conceptions of learning, approaches to studying and personal development in UK higher education. *British Journal of Educational Psychology*, 79: 295–309.

Endedijk, M. (2010) *Student teachers' self-regulated learning*, Utrecht: IVLOS.

Entwistle, N. (1988a). Motivation and learning strategies. *Educational and Child Psychology*, 5: 5–20.

Entwistle, N. (1988b) Motivational factors in students' approaches to learning. In Schmeck, R. (ed.) *Learning strategies and learning styles*. New York: Plenum Press.

Entwistle, N. & McCune, V. (2004) The conceptual bases of study strategy inventories. *Educational Psychology Review*, 16: 325–345.

Entwistle, N., McCune, V. & Hounsell, D. (2003) Investigating ways of enhancing university teaching-learning environments: Measuring students' approaches to studying and perceptions of teaching. In De Corte, E., Verschaffel, L., Entwistle, N. & Van Merriënboer, J. (eds.) *Powerful learning environments: Unraveling basic components and dimensions*. Amsterdam: Pergamon.

Entwistle, N., McCune, V. & Scheja, M. (2006) Student learning in context: Understanding the phenomenon and the person. In Verschaffel, L., Dochy, F., Boekaerts, M. & Vosniadou, S.. (eds.) *Instructional psychology: Past, present and future trends*. Amsterdam: Elsevier.

Entwistle, N., McCune, V. & Walker, P. (2001) Conceptions, styles and approaches within higher education: Analytic abstractions and everyday experience. In Sternberg, R. & Zhang, L.-F. (eds.) *Perspectives on thinking, learning and cognitive styles*. London: Lawrence Erlbaum Associates.

Entwistle, N., Meyer, J. & Tait, H. (1991) Student failure: Disintegrated perceptions of study strategies and perceptions of the learning environment. *Higher Education*, 21: 249–261.

Entwistle, N. & Ramsden, P. (1983) *Understanding student learning*, London: Croom Helm.

Flavell, J. (1987) Speculations about the nature and development of metacognition. In Weinert, F. & Kluwe, R. (eds.) *Metacognition, motivation and understanding*. Hillsdale, NJ: Erlbaum.

Fortunato, V. & Goldblatt, A. (2006) An examination of goal orientation profiles using cluster analysis and their relationships with dispositional characteristics and motivational response patterns. *Journal of Applied Social Psychology*, 36: 2073–2336.

Gijbels, D., Coertjens, L., Vanthournout, G., Sruyf, E. & Van Petegem, P. (2009) Changing students' approaches to learning: A two year study within a university teacher training course. *Educational Studies*, 35: 503–513.

Gijbels, D. & Dochy, F. (2006) Students' assessment preferences and approaches to learning: Can formative assessment make a difference? *Educational Studies*, 32: 401–411.

Gijbels, D., Raemdonck, I. & Vervecken, D. (2010) Influencing work-related learning: The role of job characteristics and self-directed learning orientation in part-time vocational education. *Vocations and Learning*, 3: 239–255.

Gijbels, D., Segers, M. & Struyf, E. (2008) Constructivist learning environments and the (im)possibility to change students' perceptions of assessment demands and approaches to learning. *Instructional Science*, 36: 431–443.

Gordon, C. & Debus, R. (2002) Developing deep learning approaches and personal teaching efficacy within a preservice teacher education context. *British Journal of Educational Psychology*, 72: 483–511.

Hayenga, A. & Henderlong Corpus, J. (2010) Profiles of intrinsic and extrinsic motivations: A person-centered approach to motivation and achievement in middle school. *Motivation and Emotion*, 34: 371–383.

Heikkilä, A. & Lonka, K. (2006) Studying in higher education: Students' approaches to learning, self-regulation, and cognitive strategies. *Studies in Higher Education*, 31: 99–117.

Heikkilä, A., Niemivirta, M., Nieminen, J. & Lonka, K. (2011) Interrelations among university students' approaches to learning, regulation of learning, and cognitive and attributional strategies: A person oriented approach. *Higher Education*, 61: 513–529.

Hoeksma, J. (1995). *Learning strategy as a guide to career success in organizations*, Leiden: DSWO Press.

Honkimäki, S., Tynjälä, P. & Valkonen, S. (2004) University students' study orientations, learning experiences and study success in innovative courses. *Studies in Higher Education*, 29: 431–449.

Kember, D. & Leung, D. (1998) The dimensionality of approaches to learning: An investigation with confirmatory factor analysis on the structure of the SPQ and LPQ. *British Journal of Educational Psychology*, 68: 395–407.

Kember, D., Wong, A. & Leung, D. (1999) Reconsidering the dimensions of approaches to learning. *British Journal of Educational Psychology*, 69: 323–343.

Kolb, D. (1984) *Experiential learning: Experience as a source of learning and development*, Englewood Cliffs, NJ: Prentice Hall Inc.

Kyndt, E., Dochy, F., Cascallar, E. & Struyven, K. (2011) The direct and indirect effect of motivation for learning on students' approaches to learning, through perceptions of workload and task complexity. *Higher Education Research and Development*, 30: 135–150.

Lindblom-Ylänne, S. (2003) Broadening understanding of the phenomenon of dissonance. *Studies in Higher Education*, 28: 63–77.

Lindblom-Ylänne, S. & Lonka, K. (1999) Individual ways of interacting with the learning environment: Are they related to study success? *Learning and Instruction*, 9: 1–18.

Lindblom-Ylänne, S. & Lonka, K. (2000) Dissonant study orchestrations of high-achieving university students. *European Journal of Psychology of Education*, 15: 19–32.

Long, W. (2003) Dissonance detected by cluster analysis of responses to the approaches and study skills inventory for students. *Studies in Higher Education*, 28: 21–35.

Lonka, K. & Lindblom-Ylänne, S. (1995) Epistemologies, conceptions of learning and study-success in two domains: Medicine and psychology. *Bienniel Conference of the European Association on Learning and Instruction*. Nijmegen.

Lonka, K. & Lindblom-Ylänne, S. (1996) Epistemologies, conceptions of learning and study practices in medicine and psychology. *Higher Education*, 31: 5–24.

Lonka, K., Olkinuora, E. & Mäkinen, J. (2004) Aspects and prospects of measuring studying and learning in higher education. *Educational Psychology Review*, 16: 301–323.

Lucas, U. & Meyer, J. (2005) 'Towards a mapping of the student world': The identification of variation in students' conceptions of, and motivations to learn, introductory accounting. *The British Accounting Review*, 37: 177–204.

Magnusson, D. (1998) The logic and implications of a person-centered approach. In Cairns, R., Bergman, L. & Kagan, J. (eds.) *Methods and models for studying the individual*. Thousand Oaks, CA: Sage Publications.

Magnusson, D. (1999) On the individual: A person-oriented approach to developmental research. *European Psychologist*, 4: 205–218.

Magnusson, D. (2003) The person approach: Concepts, measurement models, and research strategy. In Peck, S. & Roeser, R. (eds.) *Person-centered approaches to studying development in context*. New York: Jossey-Bass.

Marton, F. & Säljö, R. (1976) On qualitative differences in learning - I: Outcome and process. *British Journal of Educational Psychology*, 46: 4–11.

Marton, F. & Säljö, R. (1997) Approaches to learning. In Marton, F., Hounsell, D. & Entwistle, N. (eds.) *The experience of learning: Implications for teaching and studying in higher education*. Edinburgh: Scottish Academic Press.

McParland, M., Noble, L. & Livingston, G. (2004) The effectiveness of problem-based learning compared to traditional teaching in undergraduate psychiatry. *Medical Education*, 38: 859–867.

Meyer, J. (1991) Study orchestrations: The manifestation, interpretation and consequences of contextualised approaches to studying. *Higher Education*, 22: 297–316.

Meyer, J. (1998) A medley of individual differences. In Dart, B. & Boulton-Lewis, G. (eds.) *Teaching and learning in higher education*. Melbourne: ACER-Press.

Meyer, J. (1999) Variation and concepts of quality in student learning. *Quality in Higher Education*, 20: 167–180.

Meyer, J. & Boulton-Lewis, G. (1999) On the operationalisation of conceptions of learning in higher education and their association with students' knowledge and experiences of their learning. *Higher Education Research & Development*, 18: 289–304.

Meyer, J., Parson, P. & Dunne, T. (1990) Individual study orchestrations and their association with learning outcomes. *Higher Education*, 20: 67–89.

Meyer, J. & Shanahan, M. (2003) Dissonant forms of 'memorising' and 'repetition'. *Studies in Higher Education*, 28: 5–20.

Moskvina, V. & Kozhevnikov, M. (2011) Determining cognitive styles: Historical perspective and directions for further research. In Rayner, S. & Cools, E. (eds.) *Style differences in cognition, learning, and management: Theory, research, and practice*. New York: Routledge.

Muthén, B. & Muthén, L. (2000) Integrating person-centered and variable-centered analyses: Growth mixture modeling with latent trajectory classes. *Alcoholism: Clinical and Experimental Research*, 24: 882–891.

Niemenen, J., Lindblom-Ylänne, S. & Lonka, K. (2004) The development of study orientations and study success in students of pharmacy. *Instructional Science*, 32: 387–417.

Nijhuis, J., Segers, M. & Gijselaers, W. (2005) Influence of redesigning a learning environment on student perceptions and learning strategies. *Learning Environment Research*, 8: 67–93.

Parpala, A., Lindblom-Ylänne, S., Komulainen, E., Litmanen, T. & Hirsto, L. (2010) Students' approaches to learning and their experiences of the teaching-learning environment in different disciplines. *British Journal of Educational Psychology*, 80: 269–282.

Richardson, J. T. E. (1994) Cultural specificity of approaches to studying in higher education: A literature survey. *Higher Education*, 27: 449–468.

Richardson, J. T. E. (1997) Meaning orientation and reproducing orientation: A typology of approaches to studying in higher education? *Educational Psychology*, 17: 301–311.

Richardson, J. T. E. (2000) *Researching student learning: Approaches to studying in campus-based and distance education*, Buckingham: SRHE/Open University Press.

Richardson, J. T. E. (2004). Methodological issues in questionnaire-based research on learning in higher education. *Educational Psychology Review*, 16: 347–358.

Richardson, J. T. E. (2007a) Motives, attitudes and approaches to studying in distance education. *Higher Education*, 54: 385–416.

Richardson, J. T. E. (2007b) Variations in student learning and perceptions of academic quality. In Entwistle, N. & Tomlinson, P. (eds.) *Student learning and university teaching*. Leicester: The British Psychological Society.

Richardson, J. T. E. (2011) Approaches to studying, conceptions of learning and learning styles in higher education. *Learning and Individual Differences*, 21: 288–293.

Rodríguez, L. & Cano, F. (2006) The epistemological beliefs, learning approaches and study orchestrations of university students. *Studies in Higher Education*, 31: 617–636.

Rogosa, D. (1988) Myths about longitudinal research. In Schaie, K., Campbell, D., Meredity, W. & Rawlins, C. (eds.) *Methodological issues in aging research*. New York: Springer Publishing Company.

Schmeck, R. (1988) An introduction to strategies and styles of learning. In Schmeck, R. (ed.) *Learning strategies and learning styles*. New York: Plenum Press.

Schmeck, R., Geisler-Brenstein, E. & Cercy, S. (1991) Self-concept and learning: The revised inventory of learning processes. *Educational Psychology*, 11: 343–362.

Schmitz, B. (2006) Advantages of studying processes in educational research. *Learning and Instruction,* 16: 433–449.

Singer, J. & Willett, J. (2003) *Applied longitudinal analysis: Modeling change and event occurence*, Oxford: Oxford University Press.

Struyven, K., Dochy, F., Janssens, S., Schelfhout, W. & Gielen, S. (2006) On the dynamics of students' approaches to learning: The effects of the teaching/learning environment. *Learning and Instruction*, 16: 279–294.

Taris, T. (2000) *A primer in longitudinal data analysis*, Thousand Oaks, CA: Sage Publications.

Trigwell, K., Prosser, M. & Waterhouse, F. (1999) Relations between teachers' approaches to teaching and students' approaches to learning. *Higher Education*, 37: 57–70.

Van der Veken, J., Valcke, M., De Maeseneer, J. & Derese, A. (2009) Impact of the transition from conventional to an integrated contextual medical curriculum on students' learning patterns: A longitudinal study. *Medical Teacher*, 31: 433–441.

Van Rossum, E. & Schenk, S. (1984) The relationship between learning conception, study strategy and learning outcome. *British Journal of Educational Psychology*, 54: 73–83.

Vansteenkiste, M., Soenens, B., Sierens, E., Luyckx, K. & Lens, W. (2009) Motivational profiles from a self-determination perspective: The quality of motivation matters. *Journal of Educational Psychology*, 101: 671–688.

Vanthournout, G., Donche, V., Gijbels, D. & Van Petegem, P. (2011a) Further understanding learning in higher education: A systematic review on longitudinal research using Vermunt's learning pattern model. In Rayner, S. & Cools, E. (eds.) *Style differences in cognition, learning and management: Theory, research and practice*. London: Routledge Studies in Management, Organizations and Society.

Vanthournout, G., Gijbels, D., Coertjens, L., Donche, V. & Van Petegem, P. (2011b) The relationship between motivational regulations, learning strategies and first year students' study persistence and study-success in a professional bachelor program. *Bi-annual Conference of the European Association for Research on Learning and Instruction*. Exeter.

Vermetten, Y., Vermunt, J. & Lodewijks, H. (2002) Powerful learning environments? How do students differ in their response to instructional measures. *Learning and Instruction*, 12: 263–284.

Vermunt, J. (1992) *Leerstijlen en sturen van leerprocessen in hoger onderwijs. Naar procesgerichte instructie in zelfstandig denken [Learning styles and the regulation of learning processes in higher education. Towards process-oriented instruction in self-regulation]*. Amsterdam/Lisse: Swets&Zeitlinger.

Vermunt, J. (1996) Metacognitive, cognitive and affective aspects of learning styles and strategies: A phenomenographic analysis. *Higher Education*, 31: 25–50.

Vermunt, J. (1998) The regulation of constructive learning processes. *British Journal of Educational Psychology*, 68: 149–171.

Vermunt, J. (2003) The power of learning environments and the quality of student learning In De Corte, E., Verschaffel, L., Entwistle, N. & Van Merriënboer, J. (eds.) *Powerful learning environments: Unraveling basic components and dimensions*. Oxford: Elsevier.

Vermunt, J. (2005) Relations between student learning patterns and personal and contextual factors and academic performance. *Higher Education*, 49: 205–234.

Vermunt, J. & Minnaert, A. (2003) Dissonance in student learning patterns: When to revise theory? *Studies in Educational Evaluation*, 28: 49–61.

Vermunt, J. & Van Rijswijk, F. (1988) Analysis and development of students' skill in self-regulated learning. *Higher Education*, 17: 647–682.

Vermunt, J. & Vermetten, Y. (2004) Patterns in student learning: Relationships between learning strategies, conceptions of learning and learning orientations. *Educational Psychology Review*, 16: 359–384.

Volet, S., Renshaw, P. & Tietzel, K. (1994) A short-term longitudinal investigation of cross-cultural differences in study approaches using Biggs' SPQ questionnaire. *British Journal of Educational Psychology*, 64: 301–318.

Von Eye, A. & Bogat, A. (2006) Person-oriented and variable-oriented research: Concepts, results, and development. *Merill-Palmer Quarterly*, 52: 390–420.

Watkins, D. & Hattie, J. (1985) A longitudinal study of the approaches to learning of Australian tertiary students. *Human Learning*, 4: 127–141.

Weinstein, C.-E., Schulte, A. & Palmer, D. (1987) *Learning and study strategy inventory (LASSI)*, Clearwater, FL: H&H Publishing.

Weiss, R. (2005) *Modeling longitudinal data*, New York: Springer.

Wierstra, R. & Beerends, E. (1996) Leeromgevingspercepties en leerstrategieën van eerstejaars studenten sociale wetenschappen. [Perceptions of the learning environment and learning strategies of first-year students in social sciences]. *Tijdschrift voor Onderwijsresearch*, 21: 306–322.

Wilson, K. & Fowler, J. (2005) Assessing the impact of learning environments on students' approaches to learning. *Assessment and Evaluation in Higher Education*, 30: 37–56.

Zeegers, P. (2001). Approaches to learning in science: A longitudinal study. *British Journal of Educational Psychology*, 71: 115–132.

Zeegers, P. (2002) A revision of the Biggs' Study Process Questionnaire (R-SPQ). *Higher Education Research and Development*, 21: 73–92.

Zhang, L. & Sternberg, R. (2005) A threefold model of intellectual styles. *Educational Psychology Review*, 17: 1–53.

Chapter 3

The dimensionality of student learning patterns in different cultures

Jan D. Vermunt, Larike H. Bronkhorst and J. Reinaldo Martínez-Fernández

Introduction

Teaching and learning in higher education are becoming ever more international. The number of students that spend (part of) their studies at a foreign university is increasing rapidly. Likewise, academic staff exchange programmes make it possible for university teachers to go abroad for a limited or longer period of time to form part of another academic community. The development of joint degree programmes, in which academic staff from two or more universities from different countries together develop and teach an academic programme to students from different countries, is increasing as well.

Although such foreign experiences may be enriching in many ways, adaptation to a new teaching and learning environment cannot be taken for granted. Cultures of teaching and learning may differ across countries and continents, being embedded in the more general culture of the country and its prevailing views on knowledge, learning, education and interpersonal relations. Hofstede's research (e.g. 2001) clearly shows that intimate ties exist between learning, education and culture. In the course of their studies, higher education students have developed certain approaches to learning, conceptions of learning and good teaching, and study motivations, in interaction with the prevailing study environment in their own country. Wierstra et al. (2003) studied international exchange students' learning patterns and perceptions of their learning environment in Europe. They found that these students perceived quite different educational cultures in Northern and Southern Europe, which were associated with differences in students' learning patterns. Studying abroad may mean that the learning patterns that students have developed in their home country are no longer adequate for studies at the new university. Biemans and Van Mil (2008), for example, studied the learning patterns of Chinese students who had started an undergraduate programme at an agricultural university in The Netherlands. The dominant teaching method at this university was project-based learning, in which students had to work a lot in small groups, collaborating on project work. The Chinese students, being accustomed to strong individual competition for foreign grants in which high marks were vital, had huge problems trying to cope with the collaborative demands and lack of precisely defined readings for the assessment at this university.

Several authors point to cultural factors in an attempt to explain possible differences in student learning patterns in different countries. For example, Marambe et al. (2012) note that in Sri Lankan culture it is the custom to respect, listen to, and not to criticize or challenge one's teacher. Martínez-Fernández and Vermunt (submitted) notice that, in general, lectures and final examinations based on reproduction of factual knowledge prevail in some Latin American countries. Trigwell and Prosser (2004) have shown that teachers' approaches to teaching are often closely related to their students' approaches to learning. The above studies show the importance of knowledge about students' patterns of learning when they go to study abroad. This knowledge may inform teachers and student counsellors about how to help students to cross the boundaries between studying in their home country and the demands posed by the new study environment. Although the recognition that 'there is a relationship between learning styles and culture is not new and has been discussed in scholarly research for a few decades' (Yoshitaka, 2005, p. 522), only a few arguments used in this discussion are based on empirical research. To fill this gap, during the last two decades some researchers have conducted qualitative studies on approaches to learning and conceptions of learning among students from different cultural backgrounds (e.g. Charlesworth, 2008; Dahlin & Watkins, 2000; Kennedy, 2002; Manikutty et al., 2007; Martínez-Fernández et al., 2004; Valiente, 2008). Some of these studies resulted in the characterization of students from certain cultural backgrounds in terms of dominant learning patterns. Kember (1996), for example, pointed to the existence of the 'Asian paradox', meaning that Asian students seemed to have a propensity for rote learning, but at the same time achieved highly on examinations. Studies with Australian, Japanese and Chinese students, however, pointed to the necessity to re-examine some of the beliefs about cross-cultural differences in student learning (Clark & Gieve, 2006; Kember, 2000; Marton et al., 2005; Purdie & Hattie 2002; Purdie et al., 1996; Sachs & Chan 2003).

The present study aims to re-examine some widely held beliefs about differences in learning between higher education students in various countries around the world. As a result, preparation for foreign exchanges for students and staff members, often based on those widely held beliefs, may need to be adapted. For these reasons it is necessary to analyse in depth the different factors linked to the way students learn and, based on that knowledge, to develop guidelines for good teaching and learning in an international university study context. The aim of this chapter is to contribute to the empirical knowledge base about student learning patterns in different cultures. Studies from different countries and continents using the same diagnostic instrument for student learning patterns will be compared and contrasted, and the dimensionality of student learning patterns in different countries will be identified. The ultimate aim is to foster the quality of international exchange experiences of university students and staff and of international collaborative degree programmes.

Patterns in student learning

In contemporary theories often four domains or components of student learning are discerned (see for example Entwistle & McCune, 2004; Lonka et al., 2004; Pintrich, 2004; Richardson, 2000; Vermunt & Vermetten, 2004): cognitive processing of subject matter, meta-cognitive regulation of one's own learning processes, conceptions of learning and learning orientations. Cognitive processing activities are those learning activities that students use to process the subject matter. They directly lead to learning outcomes in terms of knowledge, understanding, skills, etc. Meta-cognitive regulation activities are those learning activities that students use to regulate and steer their learning processes and lead therefore indirectly to learning outcomes. Conceptions of learning are the beliefs and views students have about learning and associated phenomena: how different learning tasks can be tackled, who is responsible for what in learning, what good teaching looks like, etc. Learning orientations refer to the whole domain of personal goals, motives, expectations, attitudes, worries and doubts students have with regard to learning and studying (Gibbs et al., 1984). Vermunt (1996, 1998) used the term 'learning style' as an encompassing concept in which the cognitive processing of subject matter, the meta-cognitive regulation of learning, conceptions of learning and learning orientations are united. Later on, because the term 'learning style' is often associated with invariant personality characteristics, he and his colleagues changed to using the more neutral term 'learning pattern' to denote this united phenomenon (Vermunt & Vermetten, 2004; Vermunt, 2005). In a series of studies with university students, they consistently found four such patterns: undirected, reproduction directed, meaning directed and application directed learning (see also, for example, Lindblom-Ylänne, 2003; Meyer, 2000).

First, an *undirected* learning pattern was found, in which students hardly came to process the subject matter, mainly because they had trouble with selecting what was more or less important within the huge amounts of study materials, showing lack of regulation in their studying, attaching much value to being stimulated by others (fellow students, teachers, study counsellors) in their learning, and having an ambivalent learning orientation showing many doubts about their study choice, own capacities, and the like. Second, a *reproduction directed* way of learning was identified, in which students often used a stepwise processing strategy (combining learning activities like memorizing, rehearsing, analysing the subject matter in a detailed way), let their learning be regulated by external sources such as teachers and directions in study materials, viewed learning mainly as the intake of knowledge from knowledgeable sources (such as books, teachers) and were certificate and self-test oriented in their learning orientation. The third pattern which emerged was a *meaning directed* way of learning, typified by the use of a deep processing strategy (relating, structuring, critical processing of the study materials), self-regulation in learning (planning, monitoring, evaluating, reflecting, reading 'around' the prescribed materials), a learning conception in which learning was seen as a personal construction of knowledge and one's own responsibility for learning was stressed, as well as personal interest in the subject matter as a learning orientation. Fourth, an *application directed* learning pattern was identified, in which students used a concrete processing strategy (trying to concretize the subject matter, thinking of possible applications), involved both self and external regulation strategies, attached much importance to learning to use the knowledge they acquired, and were vocation oriented in their learning motivation. Overall, meaning directed learning is mainly focused on relations *within* the subject matter of the studies; application directed learning is focused most on relations *between* the subject matter and the world around.

Whether one or the other way of learning is regarded as 'better' is a matter of perspective. Meaning and application directed learning are, in general, viewed as more appropriate for studies in higher education than is undirected learning (Baeten et al., 2010). Sometimes a distinction is made between university and higher vocational studies, in the sense that meaning directed learning is viewed as most appropriate for university studies and application directed learning as most appropriate for higher vocational studies. People often disagree on the value of reproduction directed learning. Some see this as an important route to basic factual knowledge, others argue that this basic factual knowledge can as well, or even be better acquired through meaning or application directed learning (Vermunt, 2007).

The Inventory of Learning Styles

As stated above, a learning pattern is conceived here as a coordinating concept in which the interrelationships between students' learning activities, regulation of learning, conceptions of learning and learning orientations are united (Vermunt & Vermetten, 2004). The Inventory of Learning Styles (ILS) was developed as an instrument to measure such learning patterns. It is based on interviews with university students about their way of learning, their views on learning, studying and good teaching, and their motives, concerns and personal goals in their studies (Vermunt, 1996). The interviews were analysed in a phenomenographic way, resulting in categories of description for the various elements of students' learning patterns. Subsequently, statements were selected from the interviews that were viewed to be typical for the various categories. These statements were included as items in the inventory and, if considered necessary, slightly adapted in phrasing. In various studies, the final version of the instrument was constructed, using factor, reliability, item, and test–retest analyses (see Vermunt, 1998).

Since its development, the ILS has been translated into several languages and used for research purposes in a variety of countries, at first in Northern European countries (e.g. Boyle et al., 2003; Lonka & Lindblom-Ylänne, 1996; Vanthournout, 2011). Research conducted with the ILS in higher education in these countries (e.g. The Netherlands, United Kingdom, Finland, Belgium) typically shows the existence of four distinct learning patterns: meaning directed, reproduction directed, application directed and undirected learning (described above). Subsequently, the ILS was translated for research outside Northern Europe as well. In the last decade, for example, large-scale studies with the ILS have been conducted on student learning patterns in Indonesia (Ajisuksmo, 1996), Argentina (Alves de Lima et al., 2006), Sri Lanka (Marambe, 2007), Thailand (Eaves, 2009), China (Chung-Sea Law, 2009), and Colombia, Mexico, Venezuela and Spain (Martínez-Fernández & García-Ravidá, 2012; Martínez-Fernández & Vermunt, submitted). These studies showed marked differences in many mean scale scores between students from different countries. These differences indicated differences in the way students from different countries reported to study the subject matter, to regulate their learning processes, to think about learning and teaching at university, and to be motivated towards their studies. However, differences did not only become manifest in mean scale scores, but also in the *interrelations* among the scales. For example, Dutch students showed strong relations between their study behaviour, conceptions and orientations, while this was much less the case for Indonesian students.

The final version of the ILS consists of 120 statements in 16 main scales, of which four scales can be divided into two subscales each. The items cover four learning components: processing strategies, regulation strategies, conceptions of learning and learning orientations. For the strategy items, students are asked to indicate on a five-point scale the degree to which they use the described learning activities in their studies. For the items on learning conceptions and learning orientations, students are asked to indicate on a five-point scale the degree to which the described views and motives correspond to their own views and motives. The ILS assesses five processing strategies, five regulation strategies, five conceptions of learning and five learning orientations. These ILS scales and their content are described in Table 3.1. A shorter, 100-item version has been developed as well, with the same scales but a few less items in some scales (Vermetten et al., 1999).

Marambe et al. (2012) compared student learning patterns in higher education across three countries: two Asian countries (Sri Lanka and Indonesia) and one European country (The Netherlands). They performed a meta-analysis on three large-scale studies that all had used the original or translated versions of the ILS. The researchers tested the differences in mean ILS-scale scores between the three groups and compared the factor structures of the ILS scales between the three studies. They found that most differences in student learning patterns existed between Asian and European students. On the other hand, many differences between students from the two Asian countries showed up as well. The authors concluded that one cannot speak of *the* Asian learner. Besides, since the Sri Lankan students scored lowest on memorizing strategies of all groups, the authors concluded that the view that Asian learners would have a tendency for rote learning was not supported by their findings. Moreover, they found that some patterns of learning were universal and showed up in all groups, while other patterns were found only among the Asian or the European students.

Table 3.1 Scales of the ILS and their content

Parts and scales of the ILS	Description of content
Processing strategies	
Deep processing	
Relating and structuring	Relating elements of the subject matter to each other and to prior knowledge; structuring these elements into a whole.
Critical processing	Forming one's own view on the subjects that are dealt with, drawing one's own conclusions, and being critical of the conclusions drawn by textbook authors and teachers.
Stepwise processing	
Memorizing and rehearsing	Learning facts, definitions, lists of characteristics and the like by heart by rehearsing them.
Analysing	Going through the subject matter in a stepwise fashion and studying the separate elements thoroughly, in detail and one by one.
Concrete processing	Concretizing and applying subject matter by connecting it to one's own experiences and by using what one learns in a course in practice.
Regulation strategies	
Self-regulation	
Learning process and results	Regulating one's own learning processes through regulation activities like planning learning activities, monitoring progress, diagnosing problems, testing one's results, adjusting and reflecting.
Learning content	Consulting literature and sources outside the syllabus.
External regulation	
Learning process	Letting one's own learning processes be regulated by external sources, such as introductions, learning objectives, directions, questions or assignments of teachers or textbook authors.
Learning results	Testing one's learning results by external means, such as the tests, assignments and questions provided.
Lack of regulation	Monitoring difficulties with the regulation of one's own learning processes.
Conceptions of learning	
Construction of knowledge	Learning viewed as constructing one's own knowledge and insights. Most learning activities are seen as tasks of students.
Intake of knowledge	Learning viewed as taking in knowledge provided by education through memorizing and reproducing; other learning activities are tasks of teachers.
Use of knowledge	Learning viewed as acquiring knowledge that can be used by means of concretizing and applying. These activities are seen as tasks of both students and teachers.

Stimulating education	Learning activities are viewed as tasks of students, but teachers and textbook authors should continuously stimulate students to use these activities.
Cooperative learning	Attaching a lot of value to learning in cooperation with fellow students and sharing the tasks of learning with them.
Learning orientations	
Personally interested	Studying out of interest in the course subjects and to develop oneself as a person.
Certificate oriented	Striving for high study achievements; studying to pass examinations and to obtain certificates, credit points and a degree.
Self-test oriented	Studying to test one's own capabilities and to prove to oneself and others that one is able to cope with the demands of higher education.
Vocation oriented	Studying to acquire professional skill and to obtain a(nother) job.
Ambivalent	A doubtful, uncertain attitude toward the studies, one's own capabilities, the chosen academic discipline, the type of education, etc.

The present study

The present study is meant as an extension of the Marambe et al. (2012) study. New studies using the ILS in various countries made it possible to include a new continent in the comparisons (Latin America with Venezuela, Colombia and Mexico as countries), to add a European country (Spain), and to add an Asian country (Hong Kong China). The present study is a review of different studies conducted with the ILS across the globe, aiming to clarify and discuss some of the currently held beliefs on cross-cultural differences in student learning patterns. Learning patterns of university students in Hong Kong, Colombia, Indonesia, Mexico, Spain, Sri Lanka, The Netherlands and Venezuela, all investigated with the same research instrument (the ILS), will be compared and contrasted.

The following research questions will be addressed:

1   To what extent do students from different countries and continents differ from each other in the learning strategies they report, the conceptions of learning they adhere to, and the learning orientations they have?

2   What underlying dimensions are exhibited in the interrelations among their learning strategies, conceptions of learning and learning orientations and how do these dimensions differ for students from different countries and continents?

Method

Samples

A review was performed on the results of five studies conducted in eight different countries from three different continents (Ajisuksmo, 1996; Law, 2009; Marambe, 2007; Martínez-Fernández & Vermunt, submitted; Vermunt, 1992). Thus, we analysed studies from Asia (Hong Kong N = 1572, Indonesia N = 888 and Sri Lanka N = 144), Europe (The Netherlands N = 795 and Spain N = 102), and Latin America (Colombia N = 115, Mexico N = 100 and Venezuela N = 139). All studies investigated the learning strategies, regulation strategies, learning conceptions and learning orientations of university students measured by validated versions of the same ILS questionnaire in the countries' respective languages.

In the five studies five different language versions were used: Dutch (ILS) for The Netherlands, Chinese (ILSC) for Hong Kong, Sri Lankan (ARPM) for Sri Lanka, Indonesian (ICB) for Indonesia, and Spanish (IEA) for Colombia, Mexico, Spain and Venezuela. In most studies, the equivalent 120-item version of the ILS has been used. Law's (2009) Hong Kong study, however, used a slightly shortened 100-item version based on Vermetten et al. (1999). In all analyses reviewed in this chapter, scale totals were divided by the number of items, so mean scores could be compared.

Procedure and data analysis

A big advantage of these primary studies was that they all had used very similar methods of data analysis, which made comparisons possible across the various studies. First, the reliabilities (internal consistencies) of scales and subscales were examined using Cronbach's alpha criteria (Peter, 1979). Subsequently, the mean scale scores of the eight groups of students were compared using analysis of variance. To this end, the mean scale scores and standard deviations as published in the original studies were used (Soper, 2011). Bonferroni corrections for significance levels were made to correct for the number of comparisons made (p = .05 divided by the number of comparisons). Scheffé post hoc analyses were run to identify which of the student groups differed from each other, in case of a significant overall F-value (Wendorf, 2004). Finally, we computed the Cohen (1977) size effect (d) in each of significant differences between means.

In our view it may be meaningful to compare mean scores on a validated instrument. This is in fact what most comparative studies do. However, in our view an important addition to this way of comparison is to compare the interrelationships between scales across students from different countries. Both perspectives may complement each other. Therefore, as a third part of our secondary data analyses the factor loadings of the inventory scales for the eight student groups, as published in the original studies, were inspected and compared. Exploratory factor analyses had been performed in each study, resulting in solutions of four rotated factors in all studies. In the Dutch, Sri Lankan and Indonesian samples a principal component analysis with Varimax rotation had been conducted; in the Spanish, Venezuelan, Mexican and Colombian samples a principal component analysis with oblique rotation had been performed; and in the Hong Kong study a maximum likelihood analysis with oblique rotation had been conducted. Since we only used the published factor loadings, and mostly loadings < .25 were omitted in those original publications, we were not able to quantify the similarity between the factor structures (e.g. Tabachnick & Fidell, 2007). Instead, the factor structures of the different samples were compared by analysing high positive and negative scale loadings on these factors.

Results

ILS scale reliabilities across countries

In Table 3.2 alpha values of ILS scales in the various studies are shown. Most alphas associated with processing strategies ranged above the critical level of .60, typically between .60 and .85 (31 out of 33 alpha values). One subscale, memorizing and rehearsing, showed somewhat lower alphas (.56 and .58) in the Indonesian and Sri Lankan samples. Alphas for regulation strategies typically ranged between .60 and .82 (30 out of 33 alpha values), with three exceptions. The Sri Lankan sample showed alphas of .50 and .49 in two subscales (self-regulation of learning content and external learning of learning process); in the Dutch sample one subscale's alpha was below .60 (external regulation of learning processes); and in the Indonesian sample the same was true for another subscale (external regulation of learning results).

The alphas of the conceptions of learning scales ranged between .63 and .89 (24 out of 25), with one exception: construction of knowledge in the case of Indonesian students (.53). The learning orientations component showed a slightly different picture, with alpha values showing more inconsistencies than the other three components mentioned above. Nine out of 25 alpha values below .60 were observed, for example .58 and .55 for the scale self-test orientation for Sri Lankan and Indonesian students, and .50 and .46 for the scale vocational orientation in Sri Lankan and Indonesian students. Finally, the personally interested scale showed alpha values below .60 in all samples.

All in all, alpha values in 101 of the 116 cases were good (87 per cent above .60; Peter, 1979). In particular, in the Indonesian and Sri Lankan samples some scales showed lower internal consistencies. The personally interested scale showed, however, below average values in all samples. Overall, these findings suggest that the ILS is a reliable measurement instrument across the countries involved.

Differences on learning pattern scales between students from different countries

Overall, on 22 of the 24 analysis of variance (ANOVA) scale comparisons between the countries significant differences were manifested (92 per cent). Only the main scales stepwise processing strategy and external regulation of

Table 3.2 Internal consistencies (Cronbach α) per ILS scale of Dutch (ILS, N = 795), Sri Lankan (ARPM, N = 144), Indonesian (ICB, N = 888), Spanish and Latin American (IEA, N = 456), and Hong Kong (ILSC, N = 1,572) samples

Inventory scales	ILS	ARPM	ICB	IEA	ILSC
Processing strategies					
Deep processing	.85	.83	.83	.85	
Relating and structuring	.83	.75	.76	.78	.78
Critical processing	.72	.73	.69	.74	.73
Stepwise processing	.78	.65	.73	.76	
Memorizing and rehearsing	.79	.56	.58	.75	.62
Analysing	.63	.60	.62	.72	.73
Concrete processing	.71	.77	.64	.69	.72
Regulation strategies					
Self-regulation	.79	.73	.78	.82	
Learning process and results	.73	.68	.74	.73	.75
Learning content	.73	.50	.68	.73	.73
External regulation	.68	.69	.68	.75	
Learning process	.48	.49	.68	.61	.62
Learning results	.65	.69	.59	.67	.66
Lack of regulation	.72	.66	.61	.69	.60
Conceptions of learning					
Construction of knowledge	.77	.73	.53	.81	.71
Intake of knowledge	.78	.66	.74	.79	.63
Use of knowledge	.70	.74	.66	.74	.71
Stimulating education	.88	.66	.82	.88	.75
Cooperative learning	.89	.67	.67	.82	.73
Learning orientations					
Personally interested	.57	.55	.22	.34	.50
Certificate oriented	.76	.63	.62	.61	.69
Self-test oriented	.84	.58	.55	.78	.75
Vocation oriented	.69	.50	.46	.72	.79
Ambivalent	.82	.68	.64	.69	.65

learning did not show a significant overall mean difference across the eight countries (see Table 3.3). Scheffé post hoc comparisons on the scales that showed significant overall mean differences resulted in a set of more specific significant differences between countries. Based on Bonferroni corrections all differences commented on below are significant (p < .001). In the following, we will only describe the most extreme differences and include the effect sizes d according to Cohen (1977). In the interpretation of these effect sizes we will follow Cohen's suggestions: a d of 0.2 represents a small effect size; a d of 0.5 a medium effect size; and a d of 0.8 a large effect size.

With regard to the *processing of study materials*, the Colombian students reported to use more deep processing strategies than Spanish students (3.55 vs. 2.94;

Table 3.3 Means (M) and standard deviation (SD) of ILS subscales

Inventory scale	Colombia N = 115		Hong Kong N = 1572		Indonesia N = 888		Mexico N = 100		The Netherlands N = 795		Spain N = 102		Sri Lanka N = 144		Venezuela N = 139		F	p
	M	SD	M	SD	M	SD	M	SD	M	SD	M	SD	M	SD	M	SD		
Processing strategies																		
Deep processing	3.55	.63					2.97	.74	3.16	1.21	2.94	.60			3.37	.80	7.04	***
Relating and structuring	3.60	.64	2.44	.67	2.56	1.61	2.92	.80	3.36	1.18	3.19	.64	3.17	.77	3.38	.81	81.80	***
Critical processing	3.50	.73	2.38	.74	2.18	1.34	3.03	.81	2.81	1.25	2.68	.77	2.32	.87	3.37	.96	59.50	***
Stepwise processing	3.04	.61					2.58	.56	2.78	1.29	2.91	.48			2.97	.78	3.43	***
Memorizing and rehearsing	2.68	.84	2.72	.64	3.33	1.69	2.27	.75	2.83	1.30	2.82	.76	2.41	.73	2.65	1.02	33.61	***
Analysing	3.40	.66	2.49	.64	2.92	1.57	2.89	.68	2.73	1.16	3.01	.61	3.02	.68	3.30	.85	29.08	***
Concrete processing	4.14	.57	2.77	.68	2.99	1.37	3.50	.74	2.81	1.17	3.55	.68	3.19	.87	3.89	.72	61.96	***
Regulation strategies																		
Self-regulation	3.45	.63			2.76	1.67	2.97	.66	2.30	1.19	2.91	.47	2.75	.67	3.50	.81	29.08	***
Learning process and results	3.54	.63	2.58	.66	2.97	1.83	3.03	.62	2.54	1.28	3.12	.57			3.67	.79	42.87	***
Learning content	3.36	.77	2.44	.75	2.39	1.40	2.90	.84	1.87	1.03	2.69	.65			3.33	1.04	42.32	***
External regulation	3.39	.54			3.19	1.53	3.03	.71	3.22	1.22	3.04	.41	3.11	.60	3.29	.72	1.35	***
Learning process	3.21	.54	2.71	.61	3.15	1.53	2.91	.75	3.08	1.21	2.84	.57			3.06	.76	22.88	***
Learning results	3.57	.66	2.82	.64	3.25	1.52	3.16	.79	3.38	1.23	3.24	.57			3.64	.85	40.23	***
Lack of regulation	2.90	.80	2.78	.64	2.65	1.36	2.52	.68	2.40	1.17	2.73	.71	2.84	.79	2.77	.83	13.51	***
Conceptions of learning																		
Construction of knowledge	4.38	.46	3.31	.63	4.12	.86	3.98	.72	3.53	1.10	3.97	.48	3.93	.50	4.11	.68	115.43	***
Intake of knowledge	3.55	.80	3.34	.64	4.14	1.04	3.28	.76	3.52	.99	3.28	.66	3.74	.45	3.60	.85	80.60	***
Use of knowledge	4.37	.54	3.50	.67	4.57	.46	4.01	.76	3.91	.91	4.19	.53	4.16	.47	4.11	.74	215.49	***
Stimulating education	3.49	1.09	3.35	.65	3.71	1.45	3.51	.78	3.13	1.13	4.03	.59	3.80	.77	3.87	.79	32.63	***
Cooperative learning	3.50	.88	3.05	.73	3.82	1.12	3.33	.69	3.01	1.20	3.40	.72	3.85	.91	3.69	.87	74.60	***
Learning orientations																		
Personally interested	4.27	.61	3.19	.59	3.33	1.30	3.77	.77	3.17	1.04	3.99	.65	3.44	.63	3.79	.91	42.18	***
Certificate oriented	2.96	.86	3.46	.75	3.96	1.23	2.95	.73	3.28	1.18	2.89	.65	3.39	1.18	3.12	.93	50.36	***
Self-test oriented	3.69	1.16	3.29	.74	4.12	1.09	3.91	.86	2.83	1.28	3.05	.90	3.41	.72	3.75	1.05	117.20	***
Vocation oriented	4.20	.70	3.70	.76	4.43	.75	4.28	.74	3.79	1.07	4.40	.62	4.10	.79	4.07	.93	75.35	***
Ambivalent	2.07	.92	2.99	.68	2.79	1.82	2.05	.82	2.07	1.12	2.33	.75	2.84	.77	2.32	1.08	61.32	***

*** p < .001 (with Bonferroni correction).

Note: F-values and significance levels of the differences between the means based on ANOVA.

$F = 52.99$; $p < .001$; $d = .99$). The Dutch students score remarkably higher on relating and structuring than students from Hong Kong (3.36 vs. 2.44; $F = 583.66$; $p < .001$; $d = .96$). Colombian students scored higher on several scales than Hong Kong students: first, on critical processing (3.50 vs. 2.38; $F = 245.99$; $p < .001$; $d = 1.52$), second, on analysing (3.40 vs. 2.49; $F = 215.72$; $p < .001$; $d = 1.40$) and third, on concrete processing (4.14 vs. 2.77; $F = 201.13$; $p < .001$; $d = 2.18$). Lastly, Indonesian students reported to use more memorizing strategies than the students from Hong Kong (3.33 vs. 2.72; $F = 163.37$; $p < .001$; $d = .48$).

In general, the largest differences with regard to the way students process learning materials, according to Cohen's d, showed up between Colombian (Latin America) and Hong Kong (Asia) students, Colombian students scoring higher on concrete processing, critical processing, and analysing. There were also large differences between European and Asian students (Dutch students scoring higher on relating and structuring than Hong Kong students), and Latin American and European students as well (Colombian students scoring higher on deep processing than Spanish students). Comparing within continents a medium but remarkable difference within Asia showed up: Indonesian students scoring higher on memorizing than Hong Kong students.

As for *regulation of learning*, Colombian students again showed higher mean scores on several scales. These students reported to self-regulate their learning much more than Dutch students (3.45 vs. 2.30; $F = 103.15$; $p < .001$; $d = 1.21$), and also had higher mean scores for self-regulation of learning processes and results (3.54 vs. 2.54; $F = 228.09$; $p < .001$; $d = .99$), and self-regulation of learning contents (3.36 vs. 2.44; $F = 160.66$; $p < .001$; $d = 1.21$) than Hong Kong students. Remarkably, Colombian students also used more external regulation of learning results than Hong Kong students (3.57 vs. 2.82; $F = 146.53$; $p < .001$; $d = 1.15$). Finally, Colombian students scored higher on lack of regulation than students from The Netherlands (2.90 vs. 2.40; $F = 19.66$; $p < .001$; $d = .50$).

Summarizing, with regard to regulation of learning, the largest differences showed up between students from Colombia (Latin America) on the one hand and students from Hong Kong (Asia) and The Netherlands (Europe) on the other. Colombian students scored higher than Hong Kong students on both self-regulation of learning scales, and on external regulation of learning results. Moreover, Colombian students scored higher than students from The Netherlands on self-regulation of learning and on lack of regulation.

With regard to *conceptions of learning*, Colombian students saw learning more as construction of knowledge than Hong Kong students (4.38 vs. 3.31; $F = 319.20$; $p < .001$; $d = 1.94$). Indonesian students viewed learning more as intake of knowledge than students from Spain (4.14 vs. 3.28; $F = 66.63$; $p < .001$; $d = .99$) and more as use of knowledge than students from Hong Kong (4.57 vs. 3.50; $F = 1,788.43$; $p < .001$; $d = 1.86$). In turn, Spanish students attached more value to stimulating education than Dutch students (4.03 vs. 3.13; $F = 62.47$; $p < .001$; $d = 1.00$). Sri Lankan students found cooperative learning more important than Hong Kong students (3.85 vs. 3.05; $F = 151.43$; $p < .001$; $d = .97$).

For the conceptions of learning component, the differences appeared to be located more within continents and less across them. In this respect, there were large differences within Europe: Spanish students scoring higher on stimulating education than Dutch students, and within Asia, Indonesian students scoring higher on use of knowledge than Hong Kong students, and Sri Lankan students scoring higher on cooperative learning than students from Hong Kong. Moreover, two large intercontinental differences showed up: Colombian students (from Latin America) scoring higher on construction of knowledge than Hong Kong students (from Asia), and Indonesian students (Asia) scoring higher on intake of knowledge than Spanish students (Europe).

As far as *learning orientations* are concerned, Colombian students reported to study more out of personal interest than students from The Netherlands (4.27 vs. 3.17; F = 122.48; p < .001; d = 1.29). Indonesian students were more oriented towards gaining certificates than Colombian students (3.96 vs. 2.96; F = 74.74; p < .001; d = .94). Compared to Dutch students, Indonesian students were more self-test oriented (4.12 vs. 2.83; F = 498.31; p < .001; d = 1.11), and they were more vocational oriented than Hong Kong students (4.43 vs. 3.70; F = 528.53; p < .001; d = .97). Finally, Hong Kong students appeared to be more ambivalent than Mexican students (2.99 vs. 2.05; F = 174.96, 1; p < .001; d = 1.25).

The differences for this learning orientations component were thus all large and can be found between Latin American countries (Colombia and Mexico) on the one hand and Asians countries (Indonesia and Hong Kong) and Europe (The Netherlands) on the other hand, but also between Asia (Indonesia) and Europe (The Netherlands). Colombian students scored highest on personal interest, Indonesian students on certificate orientation, self-test orientation and vocational orientation, and students from Hong Kong on ambivalent orientation.

In general, Colombian students scored highest on various features of meaning directed learning, while Indonesian students scored highest on different characteristics of reproduction directed learning. Hong Kong student scored lowest of all groups on features of application directed learning, and highest on ambivalent orientation. Colombian students showed the highest scores on lack of regulation, but low scores on ambivalence. Students from the other countries scored more in between on most scales. Remarkable exceptions are the low score of Mexican students on ambivalent orientation, the high score of Sri Lankan students on cooperative learning, the high score of Spanish students on stimulating education, and the low scores of Dutch students on both self-regulation and lack of regulation.

The dimensionality of learning patterns for students from different countries

In Table 3.4, factor loadings of ILS scales on four extracted and rotated factors are presented from all studies. The total percentage of explained variance (R^2) by these four factors in the various samples was 66.6 per cent (Mexico),

Table 3.4 Factor loadings of ILS subscales in 4-factor rotated solutions for Colombian (CO), Hong Kong (HK), Indonesian (IN), Mexican (ME), Dutch (NL), Spanish (SP), Sri Lankan (SL), and Venezuelan (VE) students

Inventory scale	Factor 1								Factor 2								Factor 3								Factor 4							
	CO	HK	IN	ME	NL	SP	SL	VE	CO	HK	IN	ME	NL	SP	SL	VE	CO	HK	IN	ME	NL	SP	SL	VE	CO	HK	IN	ME	NL	SP	SL	VE
Processing strategies																																
Deep processing																																
Relating and structuring	.89	.83	.82	.80	.73	.61	.85	.86																								
Critical processing	.78	.84	.72	.84	.71	.81	.78	.87																								
Stepwise processing																																
Memorizing and rehearsing		.34	.58								.41		.72		.58					.46			.56		.77	−.52						.75
Analysing													.73		.28						.34					−.36						
Concrete processing	.69	.60	.74	.74	.67	.85	.69	.75																								
Regulation strategies																																
Self-regulation																																
Learning process and results	.86	.75	.77	.85	.74	.81	.77	.83																								
Learning content	.76	.74	.68	.84	.71	.75	.50	.82																								
External regulation																																
Learning process	.34	.47	.78	.78		.55			.59		.59	.72	.72	.40	.69					.66			.63		.61	−.71						
Learning results	.33	.61	.68				.41	.59			.36	.57	.57		.54								.63		.58	−.67					.60	
Lack of regulation																.59		.34		.66			.79		.82	−.39	−.69	.74		.68		.64
Conceptions of learning																																
Construction of knowledge									.72	.82	.73	.78	.78			.42					.55		.75				.32					
Intake of knowledge									.83	.57	.54	.65	.60	.40	.56	.56			.52	.59		.46	.44					.39	.30		
Use of knowledge				.38			.36		.74	.81	.70	.66	.66	.69	.75	.51			.59		.74		.75				.28		.72		
Stimulating education		.26					.29		.75	.79	.80	.69	.69	.85	.68	.85			.62				.68				−.31	.72			
Cooperative learning							.41		.75	.37	.83	.57	.57	.75	.53	.75			.69				.53					.62			
Learning orientations																																
Personally interested				.52							.45	.50			.59		.59	.30	.55	.50			.25	.64			.35	.65		.30		
Certificate oriented				−.40							.67	.46	.46		.59	.60	.74	.30	.59	.71	.36	.33	.52					.30	.56	.37	−.59
Self-test oriented						.52					.47				.52	.58	.83	.35	.35	.36	.80	.36						.60	.60	.34	
Vocation oriented											.37			.58	.56		.76	.29		.80	.80			.80			.46	.51		.36	
Ambivalent				−.26									.37				.48	.80	.77			.61			−.67		.46	.65	.51		.76	.33

65.4 per cent (Venezuela), 61.9 per cent (Colombia), 56.7 per cent (Hong Kong), 54.7 per cent (The Netherlands), 54.7 per cent (Spain), 53.7 per cent (Indonesia), and 52.5 per cent (Sri Lanka). Thus, there is not a big difference between the samples in this regard.

The first dimension that shows up very clearly can be seen on the first factor. This factor groups a set of scales related to processing and regulation strategies typical for meaning directed learning. Relating and structuring, critical processing, concrete processing and self-regulation load on this first factor in all samples. In all groups but the Dutch, the analysing strategy also loads on this factor. In six cases (Colombia, Indonesia, Mexico, Spain, Sri Lanka and Venezuela), external regulation strategies show loadings on this factor as well. In the Dutch, Indonesian and Sri Lankan groups, construction of knowledge also shows a significant loading on this factor. The personally interested learning orientation loads on this factor in the Dutch and Sri Lankan groups. Noteworthy is that in five groups (Colombia, Mexico, Spain, Venezuela and Hong Kong) no conception and orientation scales show any loading on this meaning directed factor at all.

A second dimension that shows up is the grouping of all conceptions of learning on the second factor in five samples (Colombia, Hong Kong, Mexico, Spain and Venezuela) and on the third factor in two samples (Indonesia and Sri Lanka), with almost no loadings from scales of the other learning components. This dimension did show up in earlier research (Ajisuksmo, 1996) as well and can be interpreted as a passive–idealistic learning pattern, since it only contains ideas about learning and no learning activity. The Dutch sample is the only one that does not show a similar grouping of all conception scales on one factor.

A third dimension that stands out clearly is characterized by high loadings of memorizing and rehearsing, external regulation of learning, intake of knowledge as a learning conception, and certificate orientation. This pattern can be interpreted as a reproduction directed learning pattern and is clearly visible on the second factor in the Indonesian, Sri Lankan and Dutch samples and on the third factor in the Spanish sample. Colombian, Hong Kong and Venezuelan students show a 'bare' version of this pattern on the fourth factor, associating memorizing and rehearsing with external regulation of learning but not with intake of knowledge as underlying learning conception and certificate orientation as motivational component.

A fourth pattern that can be recognized clearly is the undirected learning pattern, typified by high loadings of lack of regulation and an ambivalent learning orientation. This patterns shows up on the third factor among the Mexican, Dutch and Hong Kong students and on the fourth factor among the Sri Lankan, Indonesian and Venezuelan students. Noteworthy is that lack of regulation is associated with different other aspects of learning patterns in different countries. Among Mexican, Spanish, Colombian, Venezuelan and Hong Kong students it is associated with aspects of reproduction directed learning (e.g. memorizing strategy, certificate orientation, intake of knowledge, external regulation), among Dutch students with finding stimulating education and cooperative learning important, among Indonesian students with a vocational orientation, and among Sri Lankan students with personal interest (inversely).

The application directed learning pattern that was identified among Dutch and Finnish advanced students in earlier studies (Vermunt, 1998) shows up here only in the Dutch sample: the combination of concrete processing, use of knowledge as learning conception and a vocational learning orientation. For all other groups, concrete processing is a part of the meaning directed learning pattern.

A sixth phenomenon that can be observed in Table 3.4 is the grouping of many or all learning orientations on one factor. The most clearly this can be seen is in the Colombian sample, where the five learning orientation scales all load on the third factor, with no loadings from other scales on this factor. But also among the Indonesian students (four orientation scales loading on factor 2) and Sri Lankan students (four orientation scales loading on factor 4) this phenomenon is manifested. In the Venezuelan and Mexican samples there is one factor with loadings of only orientation scales and no scales from other learning components (factors 3 and 4, respectively). Analogous to the second dimension, this pattern can be interpreted as a passive–motivated learning pattern.

Conclusions and discussion

In the context of internationalization trends in higher education, this study set out to identify the dimensionality in student learning patterns in different cultures and to re-examine some widely held beliefs on cross-cultural differences in university students' learning. Learning patterns of university students in Hong Kong, Colombia, Indonesia, Mexico, Spain, Sri Lanka, The Netherlands and Venezuela, all investigated with the same research instrument (the ILS), were compared and contrasted. In doing so, we aimed to answer two main research questions:

1   To what extent do students from different countries and continents differ from each other in the learning strategies they use, the conceptions of learning they adhere to and the learning orientations they have?
2   What underlying dimensions are exhibited in the interrelations among their learning strategies, conceptions of learning and learning orientations and how do these dimensions differ for students from different countries and continents?

As a preliminary step in our analyses, the internal consistencies of the scales in the five studies in terms of Cronbach alphas were compared. Overall, the scale alphas were satisfactory to excellent in three of the four main domains of the inventory: processing strategies, regulation strategies and conceptions of learning. The only exceptions were the subscales of the external regulation scale that proved to be somewhat less internally consistent than the other scales. However, the main scale external regulation had satisfactory alphas in all samples. In the fourth domain of the inventory, learning orientations, there were more scales that showed relatively low alphas. In particular, the scale 'personal interest' showed below average alphas in all samples. Obviously, in several of the samples in this study students' motivation or orientation to learn is not as differentiated as the scales of the ILS intend to cover. This was especially the case in the Indonesian and Sri Lankan samples. Probably these students' orientation to learning is not as multidimensional as in the original sample on which the ILS was developed (Dutch adult university students). In the Hong Kong and Spanish speaking samples, reliabilities of the orientation scales were more comparable to those of the original Dutch sample. Personal interest turned out not to be a unidimensional construct. Probably the scale contains items that measure different aspects of personal interest, especially in the Indonesian and Spanish speaking samples. Overall, it can be concluded that the ILS is a reliable measurement instrument across the countries involved.

With regard to the first research question, on almost all scales (22 out of 24) significant overall differences in mean scales' scores between the different student groups were revealed. Taking the effects' sizes into account, the largest differences were as follows. In terms of the original four learning patterns, Colombian students score highest on all features of meaning directed learning: deep processing, analysing, self-regulation, construction of knowledge and personal interest. Indonesian students score highest on different characteristics of reproduction directed learning: memorizing and rehearsing, intake of knowledge, and certificate and self-test learning orientations, while Colombian and Venezuelan students scored highest on external regulation of learning. With regard to the elements of the application directed learning pattern the picture was more varied: Colombian and Venezuelan students scored highest on concrete processing, Indonesian students on use of knowledge, and Indonesian and Spanish students of vocational orientation. This varied picture could also be observed regarding the undirected learning pattern: Colombian students showed the highest scores on lack of regulation, and Hong Kong students on ambivalent orientation. Finally, of all students Sri Lankan students attached most value to cooperative learning, and Spanish students to stimulating education.

These patterns of similarities and differences show that the differences between students from different countries in one continent are often larger than the differences between students from different continents. These outcomes do not support the existence of stereotypes like *the* Asian learner, or *the* European learner, or *the* Latin American learner. To be able to explain the similarities and differences found between the various studies and student groups in this study, a closer inspection of the educational cultures in the various countries seems necessary. Marambe et al. (2012), for example, point to the paternalistic attitudes of many parents in the Sri Lankan culture, who make choices for field of studies and subsequent careers for their children. They state that the high degree of ambivalent orientation among Sri Lankan students may be a consequence of this phenomenon. Similar explanations may be valid for the differences between Latin American countries in this study, for example in terms of academic traditions in some countries being more teacher-centred and individualistic (e.g. Spain and Mexico) and in other countries being more collaborative and student-centred (e.g. Colombia and Venezuela) (Urrero Peña, 2003; Triandis et al., 1990).

With regard to the second research question, six main patterns of dimensionality emerged from the analyses. In all samples, clearly a meaning directed pattern stood out as the first dimension in the factor analyses. There seem to be two variants of this pattern, however: one in which self-regulation of learning is the defining regulation characteristic (in the Hong Kong and Dutch samples), and one in which both self-regulation and external regulation of learning are part of this pattern (the other six samples). This may mean that for many students, particularly from Asia and Latin America, external regulation and self-regulation both are important as drivers for meaning oriented learning and co-exist together, or that external regulation is a relevant step to acquire self-regulation strategies later on.

In almost all samples, a second dimension showed up combining *all* conceptions of learning, with almost no loadings from other scales. This was interpreted as a passive–idealistic learning pattern, since it only contains ideas about learning and no learning activity. A third dimension clearly standing out in all samples can be interpreted as a reproduction directed learning pattern. In some samples, however, a 'bare' version of this pattern showed up, in the sense that no conception or orientation scales contributed to the definition of this pattern. In all samples an undirected fourth dimension also showed up, combining at least lack of regulation with an ambivalent learning orientation. Other aspects associated with this undirected pattern varied per country.

A fifth dimension showing up was interpreted as an application directed learning pattern. However, this dimension previously identified mainly among adult students only showed up here in the Dutch sample. Finally, in some samples many or all learning orientations clustered on one factor, with few or no loadings from other scales. This is a similar phenomenon to the clustering of all learning conception scales on one factor (see the second dimension above). This sixth dimension can therefore be interpreted as a passive–motivated pattern.

A remarkable difference between samples is that in some countries conception and orientation scales do not load on the same factors as learning strategy scales, while in other countries the factors are defined by loading of scales coming from all four components of the inventory: two behavioural components (the processing and regulation strategy scales), conceptual components (the conception scales) and motivational components (the orientation scales). In some countries what students do to learn is strongly associated with what they think about learning and what they want with their learning; in other countries what students do to learn is much less associated with what they think about and want with learning. For example, in the Dutch sample all factors were defined by loadings of at least three learning components, which may indicate that learning activities employed by the Dutch students were guided or regulated by their views on learning and their motives for studying. In terms of components, in the Dutch sample the learning strategies students used and their learning conceptions and orientations were associated with one another. In other cultures, these associations are not always present for all factors. As such, an important difference seems to be that in some countries relations between students' learning behaviour, conceptions and motives are stronger than in other countries. This brings an interesting nuance to the debate of whether study behaviour is predicted by study conceptions and motives. Often, this debate is polarized: some research finding evidence that study behaviour is predicted by learning conceptions and motives, while other research fails to do so. Based on our results, these contrasting findings might be partly explained by differences in the structure of learning patterns across different countries.

Another remarkable difference between student groups from different countries is the degree of differentiation within the various learning components. For example, in many countries all conceptions of learning cluster on one factor, indicating that these views about learning are highly interrelated. In some other countries, these views load in different factors, pointing to a more differentiated set of views about learning.

As was the case with the comparison of means, in the comparison of underlying dimensions the differences between student groups from countries from the same continent are also often larger than the differences between students from different continents. Again, the typical 'Asian', 'European' or 'Latin American' student does not seem to exist. These outcomes are in line with the outcomes found by Marambe et al. (2012) with a smaller sample of students from only three countries.

Implications for practice

Differences and similarities in the occurrence and dimensionality of student learning patterns such as identified in this study have important implications in the context of international student mobility and international cooperation, for example in joint degree programmes. As such, these programmes may be based on a better cross-cultural understanding of students' learning patterns and teachers' teaching patterns. A better understanding of how students from foreign countries learn, think and are motivated can help in developing better support for those students in adapting to a new study environment. This knowledge may be helpful for teachers and student counsellors to understand students from various backgrounds in their struggle to meet the demands posed by different assignments and assessments than they were used to in their home country. For example, assignments requiring students' critical judgement of theories and research findings may prove very difficult for students coming from countries where these thinking skills are hardly ever asked from students. Assignments requiring close collaboration in small student groups may be very alien to students coming from a competitive and individualistic academic culture. Fostering the quality of international student exchange experiences requires the explicit recognition of these differences and the provision of more explicit induction of foreign students into the educational culture of the host country. The development of joint degree programmes by institutions from different countries and continents can likewise benefit a lot by being mindful of the different implicit pedagogical and educational conceptions underlying the separate programmes in the different countries.

Suggestions for further research

A first set of important suggestions for follow-up research has to do with methodology. Analyses using all factor loadings will make it possible to quantify the similarity between factor structures much more than was possible in this review (Tabachnick & Fidell, 2007). Moreover, confirmatory factor analyses are needed to analyse in much more detail the power of the dimensions identified in this study.

In this review different studies were included that all had used the same research inventory, developed in a Western country. Future research should, in our view, also work the other way around. For example, interviews with Chinese students may reveal aspects of Chinese learning that were not captured by this Western inventory. This would mean developing an inventory based on interviews with Chinese students, translating that inventory into English, Spanish, etc., and administrating that inventory to European and American students. Or, better still, developing a real cross-cultural item pool based on interviews with students from a variety of countries and cultures, and developing a cross-cultural inventory based on that item pool.

A third research line is to study adaptation processes of students in international mobility programmes, and the development and evaluation of induction programmes aimed at helping students to make the transitions across the boundaries of their home study environment and the new foreign study environment.

References

Ajisuksmo, C.R.P. (1996). *Self-regulated learning in Indonesian higher education*. PhD thesis, Tilburg University, The Netherlands & Atma Jaya Catholic University, Indonesia.

Alves de Lima, A., Ines Bettati, M., Baratta, S., Falconi, M., Sokn, F., Galli, A., Barrero, C., Cagide, A., & Iglesias, R. (2006). Learning strategies used by cardiology residents: Assessment of learning styles and their correlations. *Education for Health, 19*, 289–297.

Baeten, M., Kyndt, E., Struyven, K., & Dochy, F. (2010). Using student-centred learning environments to stimulate deep approaches to learning: Factors encouraging or discouraging their effectiveness. *Educational Research review, 5*, 243–260.

Biemans, H., & Van Mil, M. (2008). Learning styles of Chinese and Dutch students compared within the context of Dutch higher education in life sciences. *The Journal of Agricultural Education and Extension, 14*, 265–278.

Boyle, E., Duffy, T., & Dunleavy, K. (2003). Learning styles and academic outcome: The validity and utility of Vermunt's Inventory of Learning Styles in a British higher education setting. *British Journal of Educational Psychology, 73*, 267–290.

Charlesworth, Z.M. (2008). Learning styles across cultures: Suggestions for educators. *Education & Training, 50*, 115–127.

Clark, R., & Gieve, S.N. (2006). On the discursive construction of 'the Chinese learner'. *Language Culture and Curriculum, 19*, 54–73.

Cohen, J. (1977). *Statistical power analysis for the behavioral sciences.* New York: Academic Press.

Dahlin, B., & Watkins, D. (2000). The role of repetition in the processes of memorising and understanding: A comparison of the views of German and Chinese secondary school students in Hong Kong. *British Journal of Educational Psychology, 70*, 65–84.

Eaves, M.J. (2009). *A mixed methods study of learning styles and adaptation issues of Thai postgraduate students in England.* PhD thesis, University of Birmingham, United Kingdom.

Entwistle, N., & McCune, V. (2004). The conceptual bases of study strategy inventories. *Educational Psychology Review, 16*, 325–345.

Gibbs, G., Morgan, A., & Taylor, E. (1984). The world of the learner. In F. Marton, D. Hounsell & N. Entwistle (Eds.), *The experience of learning* (pp. 165–188). Edinburgh: Scottish Academic Press.

Hofstede, G.H. (2001). *Culture's consequences: Comparing values, behaviours, institutions, and organizations across nations* (2nd ed.). Thousand Oaks, CA: Sage Publications.

Kember, D. (1996). The intention to both memorise and understand: Another approach to learning? *Higher Education, 31*, 341–354.

Kember, D. (2000). Misconceptions about the learning approaches, motivation and study practices of Asian students. *Higher Education, 40*, 99–121.

Kennedy, P. (2002). Learning cultures and learning styles: Myth – understandings about adult (Hong Kong) Chinese learners. *International Journal of Lifelong Education, 21*, 430–445.

Law, D.C. (2009). *The adaptation, validation and application of a research instrument for investigating the relationships between students' perceptions of the learning context and students' learning patterns in post-secondary education of Hong Kong.* EdD thesis, University of Durham, United Kingdom.

Lindblom-Ylänne, S. (2003). Broadening an understanding of the phenomenon of dissonance. *Studies in Higher Education, 28*, 63–78.

Lonka, K., & Lindblom-Ylänne, S. (1996). Epistemologies, conceptions of learning, and study practices in medicine and psychology. *Higher Education, 31*, 5–24.

Lonka, K., Olkinuora, E., & Mäkinen, J. (2004). Aspects and prospects of measuring studying and learning in higher education. *Educational Psychology Review, 16*, 301–323.

Manikutty, S., Anuradha, N.S., & Hansen, K. (2007). Does culture influence learning in higher education? *International Journal of Learning and Change, 2*, 70–87.

Marambe, K.N. (2007). *Patterns of student learning in Medical Education – A Sri Lankan study in a traditional curriculum.* PhD thesis, Maastricht University, The Netherlands.

Marambe, K., Vermunt, J.D., & Boshuizen, H.P.A. (2012). A cross-cultural comparison of student learning patterns in higher education. *Higher Education, 64*, 299–316.

Martínez-Fernández, J.R., & García-Ravidá, L. (2012). Patrones de aprendizaje en estudiantes universitarios del Máster en Educación Secundaria: variables personales y contextuales relacionadas [Patterns of learning in teacher education students: Personal and contextual variables related]. *Revista de Curriculum y Formación del Profesorado, 16*, 165–182.

Martínez-Fernández, J.R., & Vermunt, J.D. (submitted). A cross-cultural analysis on the patterns of learning and academic performance of Spanish and Latin-American undergraduates. Manuscript submitted for publication.

Martínez-Fernández, J.R., Villegas, M.E., & Martínez Torres, M. (2004). Concepciones de aprendizaje y estrategias metacognitivas en universitarios venezolanos y españoles [Conceptions of learning and metacognitive strategies in Spanish and Venezuelan undergraduates]. *Revista Latina de Pensamiento y Lenguaje, 12*, 21–35.

Marton, F., Wen, Q., & Wong, K.M. (2005). 'Read a hundred times and the meaning will appear . . .' Changes in Chinese university students' views of the temporal structure of learning. *Higher Education, 49*, 291–318.

Meyer, J.H.F. (2000). An empirical approach to the modelling of dissonant study orchestrations in higher education. *European Journal of Psychology of Education, 15*, 5–18.

Peter, J.P. (1979). Reliability: A review of psychometric basics and recent marketing practices. *Journal of Marketing Research, 16*, 6–17.

Pintrich, P. (2004). A conceptual framework for assessing motivation and self-regulated learning in college students. *Educational Psychology Review, 16*, 385–408.

Purdie, N., & Hattie, J. (2002). Assessing students' conceptions of learning. *Australian Journal of Educational & Developmental Psychology, 2*, 17–32.

Purdie, N., Hattie, J., & Douglas, G. (1996). Student conceptions of learning and their use of self-regulated learning strategies: A cross-cultural comparison. *Journal of Educational Psychology, 88*, 87–100.

Richardson, J.T.E. (2000). *Researching student learning.* Buckingham: SRHE and Open University Press.

Sachs, J., & Chan, C. (2003). Dual scaling analysis of Chinese students' conceptions of learning. *Educational Psychology, 23*, 181–193.

Soper, D. (2011). Statistics calculators. http://www.danielsoper.com/statcalc/calc43.aspx (accessed 8 May 2013).

Tabachnick, B.G., & Fidell, L.S. (2007). *Understanding multivariate statistics* (5th ed.). Boston, MA: Allyn and Bacon.

Triandis, H.C., McCusker, C., & Hui, C.H. (1990). Multimethod probes of individualism and collectivism. *Journal of Personality and Social Psychology, 59*(5), 1006–1020.

Trigwell, K., & Prosser, M. (2004). Development and use of the Approaches to Teaching Inventory. *Educational Psychology Review, 16*, 409–424.

Urrero Peña, G. (2003). From Madrid to Mexico: Spanish exiles and their impact on the thought, science, and educational system of Mexico. *Cuadernos Hispanoamericanos, 631*, 150–151.

Valiente, C. (2008). Are students using the 'wrong' style of learning? *Active Learning in Higher Education, 9*, 73–91.

Vanthournout, G. (2011). *Patterns in student learning: Exploring a person-oriented and a longitudinal research perspective.* PhD thesis, University of Antwerp, Belgium.

Vermetten, Y.J., Vermunt, J.D., & Lodewijks, H.G. (1999). A longitudinal perspective on learning strategies in higher education: Different viewpoints towards development. *British Journal of Educational Psychology, 69*, 221–242.

Vermunt, J.D.H.M. (1992). *Leerstijlen en sturen van leerprocessen in het hoger onderwijs – Naar procesgerichte instructie in zelfstandig denken* [*Learning styles and regulation of learning processes in higher education – Towards process-oriented instruction in autonomous thinking*]. Amsterdam: Swets & Zeitlinger.

Vermunt, J.D. (1996). Metacognitive, cognitive and affective aspects of learning styles and strategies: A phenomenographic analysis. *Higher Education, 31*, 25–50.

Vermunt, J.D. (1998). The regulation of constructive learning processes. *British Journal of Educational Psychology, 68*, 149–171.

Vermunt, J.D. (2005). Relations between student learning patterns and personal and contextual factors and academic performance. *Higher Education, 49*, 205–234.

Vermunt, J.D. (2007). The power of teaching-learning environments to influence student learning. *British Journal of Educational Psychology Monograph Series II, 4*, 73–90.

Vermunt, J.D., & Vermetten, Y.J. (2004). Patterns in student learning: Relationships between learning strategies, conceptions of learning, and learning orientations. *Educational Psychology Review, 16*, 359–384.

Wendorf, C.A. (2004). *Manuals for univariate and multivariate statistics.* http://www.uwsp.edu/psych/cw/statmanual/ (accessed 10 March 2011).

Wierstra, R.F.A., Kanselaar, G., Van der Linden, J.L., Lodewijks, H.G.L.C., & Vermunt, J.D. (2003). The impact of the university context on European students' learning approaches and learning environment preferences. *Higher Education, 45*, 503–523.

Yoshitaka, Y. (2005). Learning styles and typologies of cultural differences: A theoretical and empirical comparison. *International Journal of Intercultural Relations, 29*(5), 521–548.

Chapter 4

Modelling factors for predicting student learning outcomes in higher education

Linda Price

Background

Considerable time and attention has been spent understanding and theorising aspects of learning in higher education (Richardson 2000), yet predicting student learning still remains difficult. There has been some criticism of the student learning literature in its failure to adequately demonstrate how learning can be improved (Gibbs 2003). This appears to stem from uncertainty about what factors, or combination of factors, need to be investigated in order to predict student learning; see also Vanthournout et al. (this volume). Richardson's (2000) review has provided a corner stone in assembling and critiquing student learning research. It encompasses conceptions of learning, approaches to learning, orientations to study, and a variety of ways in which to measure these such as study processes, approaches to study, and learning styles. He concluded that all educational research 'needs to be subjected to a continuing process of critical scrutiny and evaluation' (p. 174). It is in this spirit that this chapter considers what factors might influence student learning and how interrelationships between them might be modelled in order to examine this in a holistic manner. The model is drawn from Price and Richardson's (2004) 4P model that considered factors in improving student learning. In this chapter I argue that the model can also be used to make predictions about student learning. It is structured by presenting the model and then illustrating the interrelationships by reviewing student learning, the influence of context, teaching, and the interrelationship of all of these with student learning outcomes. The chapter begins by establishing why such an approach is necessary.

Why do we need a model?

There are several reasons why we need to model student learning outcomes in higher education. These are related to variations in ideology, theory, the nature of evidence, quality of the research and in understanding the scope of what needs to be considered in making predictions. For example, in a recent review of the literature Price and Kirkwood (2011) examined claims that technology had improved student learning. However, the review illustrated that many studies lacked theoretical underpinning in their investigation and measurement of phenomena. The problems stemmed from a lack of understanding of what to examine, how to examine it, and how subsequent findings answered their research question. The review also showed that limited use was made of existing theories and models to drive the educational development and interpret the results. This example underscores that researchers and practitioners lack a holistic definition and understanding of what impinges upon investigating student learning. While real world teaching situations differ from theoretical abstractions it is still important to know *why* something works and not just *that* it works so that it might be applied to different contexts.

Hargreaves (1996, 1997) argues that teachers could benefit from adopting evidence-based practices similar to the field of medicine, as both professions are people-centred, and require not just scientific application of knowledge, but also require sophisticated professional judgement too. However, this approach to understanding and improving student learning is not without its criticism (Hammersley 1997; Hargreaves 1997; Elliott 2001; Oakley 2001). Hammersley (1997, pp. 144–145) argues that this privileges positivist experimental studies not easily replicable in education. Although pragmatic and ethical difficulties inherent in such experiments in schools and colleges could be overcome, historically they are not the kind of research that attracts funding. In the United States, meta-analyses and systematic reviews of quantitative studies have been used to summarise 'what works' from large-scale studies as the basis of 'evidence-based practice' (Hattie and Marsh 1996; Slavin 2008; Means et al. 2010; Slavin et al. 2011; Tamim et al. 2011). Clegg (2005) expresses concern about using largely quantitative research as the basis for evidence-based practice as it has implicit epistemological assumptions that favour positivist positions rather than, for example, critical realist perspectives. She argues that such approaches fail to provide insights and understanding about actual practices that impact on student learning. Hence there are ideological variations in the nature of research and what it contributes to our understanding of student learning.

Research quality is also variable. There has been a growing expectation that teachers should be aware of evidence and research relating to student learning to underpin scholarly approaches to improving teaching and learning practices (Kreber and Cranton 2000; Trigwell et al. 2000; Higher Education Academy 2007). This is in no small part due to concerns about the quality of the scholarship of teaching and learning outputs (Kanuka 2011) and the applicability of educational research to impact on educational outcomes (Higher Education Funding Council for England et al. 2009). The quality of research also lacks longitudinal data sets and cumulative research building, also noted by the last UK Research Assessment Exercise (Higher Education Funding Council for England et al. 2009).

Drawing on the educational technology literature as an example, where there is a large corpus of research into how variations in technological interventions impact upon student learning, the use of existing research to drive theoretically underpinned research is limited (Price and Kirkwood 2011). Evidencing what factors influence student learning is challenging, but it needs to be investigated holistically in order to incorporate the complexities involved in the whole educational enterprise (Oliver and Conole 2003; Kirkwood and Price 2005).

An important aspect of building knowledge about student learning has been the in-depth modelling and analysis of single dimensions, such as conceptions of learning, approaches to learning, learning development, and learning patterns. It is now time to reflect upon how this knowledge can be used as building blocks to examine student learning more holistically and model what factors might usefully be studied in combination. This too needs to encompass other components in the educational enterprise such as teaching and context. This could bolster the quality of student learning research as well as fostering cumulative research evidence to sustain and improve it. Arguably issues in relation to the quality of educational research could be understood in terms of the differences between researcher and practitioner traditions, where teachers are principally interested in what works while researchers are primarily interested in why (Hargreaves 1997). Nonetheless as a field we need to develop theoretical models that can be used to understand both the *what* and *why* of improving student learning.

The 4P model

The 4P model presented in this chapter draws upon existing research into student learning and teaching (see Figure 4.1). It is heuristic in nature and it gathers together salient factors from a range of research findings. It is an expression and an expansion of Dunkin and Biddle's (1974) model as well as an expansion of Biggs' (1985) original Presage-Process-Product model. It also incorporates research by Prosser and Trigwell (1999). The discussion of the model also takes account of other research in relation to factors that may encourage and discourage deep approaches to learning (Baeten et al. 2010). Price and Richardson (2004) originally presented the 4P model as a means to consider factors in improving student learning. In this chapter I argue that the model is also useful for predicting student learning.

The factors presented in the model are not limited to quantitative research given ideological positions discussed earlier in this chapter about varying traditions and their respective qualities. One of the challenges this highlights is the difficulty in effectively capturing qualitative changes in learning. Critics of quantitative research may doubt that questionnaires can adequately reveal qualitative changes in learning. Critics of qualitative research may equally question how effective interventions can be judged with small samples, more typical in qualitative studies. This chapter does not attempt to resolve this dilemma but merely acknowledges its existence and hence has included consideration of research using varying methods in the model.

While there may be some criticism of mixing a number of traditions to examining student learning, Lonka and Lindblom-Ylänne (Lonka and Lindblom-Ylänne 1996; Lindblom-Ylänne and Lonka 2000) have successfully

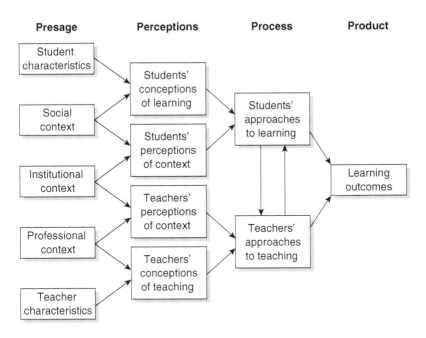

Figure 4.1 The 4P model

used Information Processing (IP) and Student Approaches to Learning (SAL) traditions together. They argue:

> Biggs (1993) pointed out that mixing constructs derived from the IP position with those derived from the SAL tradition leads to problems of interpretation. We found that, as long as we were asking the students about what they would do (rather than making assumptions of their actual processing) our results and measures showed conceptual coherence and also construct validity. For instance, students' suggestions for their comprehension resting on the basis of Weinstein and Mayer's (1986) classification matched their epistemological beliefs as we expected. Mixing Perry's (1968; 1970), Ryan's (1984), and Lonka and Lindblom-Ylänne (1994) measures in the same study with approaches to learning provided a chance to look at the interactions between different theoretical constructs.
>
> (Lonka and Lindblom-Ylänne 1996, p. 20)

This holistic position is one that Vermunt (2005) too has adopted in considering the role of context and personal factors in examining student learning through the ILS. Vermunt and Vermetten (2004) argue that investigating and improving student learning requires that 'all learning components should be addressed in the interventions, not just learning strategies' (p. 379). This heuristic model extends this idea by including some other factors that may be pertinent to predicting student learning. The model at this point makes no suggestions as to how such measurements would take place, although there are some clear indications from Lindblom-Ylänne, Lonka, Vermunt and Vermetten that using aspects of different inventories and research approaches can work.

The aim of the 4P model is to provide a way of articulating the scope and interrelationships of factors that may help us in predicting aspects of student learning. It is presented as a basis for engaging in future research in a holistic manner, that is to examine a number of factors in combination in order to model the interrelationships and effects they have on predicting student learning. The 4P model has four main groups of factors: presage, perceptions, process, and product (see Figure 4.1). Arrows have been drawn indicating some causal relationships that exist on the basis of existing research.

Presage factors encompass personological and situational factors. It is understood that both students and teachers have their own personal characteristics (Richardson 2000) and that these may influence conceptions of learning and conceptions of teaching, respectively. These include things such as age, gender, prior knowledge, ability, motivation, and personal attributes. The social context is personal to the students while the professional context is particular to the teachers (although teachers also have influential social contexts). The institutional context is considered to be within the domain of the institution and this too influences both learner and teacher. These presage factors are in place before learning and teaching begins. They are what the students and the teachers bring to the learning and teaching situation and typically are learner and teacher specific, respectively. These factors influence students' beliefs about learning and how they perceive the learning context. They also influence teachers' beliefs about teaching and how they interpret the teaching context.

Perceptions factors include students' beliefs about learning and teachers' beliefs about teaching. They also includes how students perceive the context in which they are learning and how teachers conceive the context in which they are teaching. Students' perceptions of the context encompass attributes such as assessment, workload, clarity of goals, student autonomy, quality of teaching, and discipline. Teachers' perceptions of the context include discipline, the dominant teaching paradigm, educational goals, appropriate student workload, institutional aspirations, and research/teaching emphasis. These are considered to be at the students' and teachers' levels of consciousness and are not directly observable. The conceptions-of-learning research (Perry 1970; Marton 1975; Marton and Dahlgren 1976; Marton and Säljö 1976a, 1976b; Dahlgren and Marton 1978; Laurillard 1979; Säljö 1979a, 1979b; Laurillard 1984; Marton et al. 1993) and conceptions-of-teaching research (Prosser et al. 1994; Prosser and Trigwell 1999) have largely been investigated through interviews. Marton (1981) argues that in using a qualitative phenomenographic approach to investigation, conceptions of phenomena can enable insights into how the learner experiences the world, which are not readily attainable via quantitative means. The perceptions group of factors are important because they influence how students approach learning and how teachers approach teaching.

Process factors encompass how students and teachers approach their tasks. This ranges from surface to deep approaches to learning in students and from teacher-centred to student-centred approaches to teaching in teachers. Students' experiences are determined by their perceptions of their social context, their perceptions of the institutional context, and their conceptions of learning. Studies have consistently shown that students' conceptions of learning relate to students' approaches to learning (Entwistle and Ramsden 1983; Van Rossum and Schenk 1984; Prosser and Millar 1989; Crawford et al. 1994; Marton and Säljö 1997). However Meyer et al. (1990) found that some students exhibit disintegrated perceptions and approaches to learning, where they adopt neither surface nor deep approaches. This is shown in the model as the interrelationships between the students' perceptions of the context, their conceptions of learning, and their approaches to study. This space can also be considered as where self-regulation strategies are in effect (Vermunt and Rijswijk 1988).

Teachers' conceptions of teaching and approaches to teaching are also important factors in this model. They too impact upon the students' approaches to learning (Trigwell et al. 1999). Figure 4.1 illustrates a relationship between teachers' approaches to teaching and students' approaches to learning. It also illustrates the inverse relationship. Teachers may change their approaches to teaching in response to the approaches that students display so as to engender more desirable approaches to learning. Desirable forms of study are understood to mean that students adopt a deep or meaningful approach to their studies (Richardson 1994). It is already well established that students' approaches to learning are related to their learning outcomes (Marton and Säljö 1997). However, the way in which students approach learning are in turn affected by all of the factors mentioned thus far. As Marton (1981) argues:

> We cannot gain knowledge about learning as such, nor about operatory structures as such and not even about a conception of price as such. (In other words, learning, operatory structures, conceptions as psychological entities are epistemologically unattainable independently of context and content.)
>
> (p. 194)

In the following sections factors in learning and teaching are discussed in a holistic manner given the interrelationship between them as illustrated in the model.

Student learning

Historically, research into learning had been predicated on an instructionist model where student learning was seen as a quantitative change in learning

Table 4.1 Interpretation of Perry's (1970) scheme of intellectual development

Dualism/received knowledge: student divides the world into right and wrong	1	*Basic duality*: student sees the world in polar terms where the task is to learn the right solution.
	2	*Full dualism*: student seeks to 'learn the right answer' for themselves.
Multiplicity/subjective knowledge: student accepts there are conflicting answers	3	*Early multiplicity*: the student accepts uncertainty – that is the solutions that are known and those that have yet to be found.
	4	*Late multiplicity*: the student legitimised uncertainty accepting that others have their opinions: however, right and wrong still prevail.
Relativism/procedural knowledge: student accepts there are disciplinary reasoning approaches	5	*Contextual relativism*: student perceives knowledge as contextually dependent.
	6	*'Pre-commitment'*: students orient themselves to a particular solution.
Commitment/constructed knowledge: student integrates knowledge learned from others with personal experience and reflection	7	*Commitment*: Student makes a commitment.
	8	*Challenges to commitment*: student experiences implications of commitment and explores issues of responsibility.
	9	*'Post-commitment'*: Student realises commitment is an ongoing, unfolding, evolving activity

encompassing the memorisation of facts and procedures (see Bransford et al. 2000). Around the 1970s higher education research recognised that when learners were engaged conceptually rather than through rote learning they could generalise and apply their learning better to a greater variety of circumstances (see Richardson 2000, for a full review). Perry (1970) conducted a longitudinal study during the 1950s and 1960s with students at Harvard University in the US on which he based his model of intellectual development. His scheme proposed nine stages of intellectual development ranging from a simplistic view of knowledge to complex and multiple perspectives that acknowledge uncertainty (see Table 4.1).

Later, in Sweden, Säljö (1979a) explored qualitative differences in the meaning and process of learning in higher education. He found that students described learning in different ways, which were categorised hierarchically into developmental conceptions of learning. These encompassed a qualitative change in the learner from

Table 4.2 Interpretation of Belenky et al.'s (1986) women's ways of knowing

Silence	Women experience being disconnected from knowledge, as being mindless and voiceless subject to authority.
Received knowledge	Women experience learning as receiving and repeating the knowledge of others, but not capable of creating knowledge independently.
Subjective knowledge	Women consider knowledge and truth as intrinsically personal.
Procedural knowledge	Women focus on critical analysis of knowledge and exclude personal feelings and beliefs.
Constructed knowledge	Women perceive knowledge as contextual. As creators of knowledge they value both objective and subjective approaches to knowledge.

- learning as the increase in knowledge
- learning as memorisation
- learning as the acquisition of facts and procedures
- learning as the abstraction of meaning
- learning as an interpretative process in understanding reality.

He argued that his scheme had parallels with Perry's. This was further confirmed by a study conducted in The Netherlands by Van Rossum and Schenk (1984) who investigated students' views of learning. Others have similarly confirmed this notion of development in learning (Hounsell 1987; Martin and Ramsden 1987; Vermunt and Rijswijk 1988). A sixth conception, learning as developing a person, was later added to Säljö's original scheme (Marton et al. 1993) presupposing a yet more sophisticated conception.

Although Belenky et al. (1986) and Baxter Magolda (1992) have researched conceptions of learning and come up with different schemes, they too are developmental. Belenky et al. (1986) focused on women's ways of knowing (see Table 4.2). Through interviewing 135 women, who were a mix of students, graduates, or patients at a health clinic, she developed an alternative, but broadly compatible scheme of intellectual development to Perry's based on five ways of knowing. Another model was developed by Baxter Magolda (1992) (see Table 4.3). This was an attempt to reconcile differences between Perry's developmental model and other subsequent theories (Richardson 2000). The scheme was based on interviews with 101 students that encompassed four ways of knowing. These too move through development stages of having absolute knowing through to contextual knowing.

Vermunt (1996) identified four conceptions of learning that he termed as mental models, which he identified through interviews with 35 Dutch students, 24 of whom were from a distance education university and the other 11 were from a traditional university. This formed the basis of his Inventory of Learning Styles (ILS) questionnaire that was used to measure different aspects of learning

Table 4.3 Interpretation of Baxter Magolda's (1992) epistemological reflection model (illustrating the role of the learner)

Absolute knowing	Students view knowledge as certain, but they don't have access to it: it is obtained from the teacher.
Transitional knowing	Students understand that not all knowledge is absolute: the focus is on understanding rather than acquiring knowledge.
Independent knowing	Students recognise that knowledge is mostly uncertain: teachers are expected to provide an environment where arguments and logic are presented and valued even if they differ from the teachers'.
Contextual knowing	Students recognise that the nature of knowledge is uncertain but the legitimacy of the claims about knowledge is contextual. The student still composes a point of view, but that perspective requires supporting evidence.

(Vermunt 1998). His study of 717 students confirmed the four learning dimensions of *undirected*, *reproduction-directed*, *meaning-directed*, and *application-directed*. Each of these was distinguished by four learning components: *cognitive processing, metacognitive regulation, mental learning models,* and *learning orientations.* He suggests that learning styles in the ILS are not used in the traditional sense of deeply rooted personality traits but represent a more neutral interpretation of learning pattern (Vermunt and Vermetten 2004). He argued that this integrated model can greatly reduce the overlap in learning conceptualisations while stressing the importance of process-oriented study as a means to improve the quality of student learning (Vermunt 1998). Although some researchers have shown that cluster analysis of ILS scores illustrate qualitatively different conceptions of learning, they found they were not hierarchical or developmental in nature (Lindblom-Ylänne and Lonka 1999, 2000; Vermetten et al. 2002; Richardson 2007; Donche and Petegem 2008). However, a strong relationship between students' scores on the mental models scales of the ILS and their approaches to studying has been demonstrated, indicating some kind of developmental pattern (Edmunds and Richardson 2009; Richardson 2010).

The conceptions of learning schemes provide explanatory sources for variations in the production of learning outcomes (Meyer 1997). This cumulative and developmental body of research provides reliable evidence that learning is *developmental* and hence is a factor that needs to be considered when examining student learning. However, this raises questions about how best to determine student development.

Approaches to learning

Marton and others carried out studies in Sweden, gathering accounts of how students approached their learning (Dahlgren 1975; Säljö 1975; Marton and

Table 4.4 Student conceptions of learning and students' approaches to learning

Student conceptions of learning	Student approaches to learning
Learning as the increase in knowledge	Surface
Learning as memorisation	Surface
Learning as the acquisition of facts, procedures etc., which can be retained and/or utilised in practice	Surface
Learning as the abstraction of meaning	Deep
Learning as the interpretative process aimed at the understanding of reality	Deep

Dahlgren 1976; Marton and Säljö 1976a, 1976b; Svensson 1976, 1977; Fransson 1977; Dahlgren and Marton 1978). These studies showed that students had qualitative differences in the process of learning. Marton and Säljö (1976a) described these as having two broad dimensions: surface-level and deep-level processing. Students oriented towards surface-level processing concentrated on the sign as in the content itself. Students oriented towards deep-level processing focused on what was signified and on comprehending what was being conveyed. Approaches to learning are important not only as a way of understanding how students go about their learning, but also because of their relationship with how students conceive of learning (Marton 1976). The mapping between these is illustrated in Table 4.4.

Approaches to studying have also been linked with attainment. The Approaches to Studying Inventory (ASI) was developed by Entwistle et al. (1979), to examine approaches to learning in higher education. This was revised by Entwistle and Ramsden (1983), and later developed into a shorter form as the Revised Approaches to Studying Inventory (Tait and Entwistle 1996) as an instrument to determine variations in study behaviour. Studies into approaches to learning have shown that students adopting deeper approaches to learning have higher quality learning outcomes. Comparatively those adopting surface approaches to learning have poorer learning outcomes (Svensson 1977; Entwistle and Ramsden 1983). So how students conceive of learning is important as it can affect how they approach their learning and their outcomes.

More recent research has also indicated that development in learning is neither linear nor in isolation of other factors:

> Learning is not to be looked upon as a linear process in which we first learn 'facts' ... and then try to understand these facts ... Rather learning is to be regarded as a simultaneous processing of these levels where the learner is continuously oscillating between [them] ... In the beginning ... both the understanding of the meaning of facts and the theoretical understanding are vague ... When we are trying to learn something entirely new, our point of departure can perhaps only be constituted by common speech

genre. However, when knowledge grows, the theoretical understanding as well as the ability to interpret empirical evidence become more articu-lated ... If instruction is linearly organised, or if the theoretical context is not made explicit ..., the learner has to invent higher order structures ... [from] a common-sense view of the world.

(Halldén 2001, pp. 64–65)

Hence context too is an important and interrelated factor in student learning.

The student context

Laurillard (1978, 1979, 1984) conducted a number of investigations into English university students' methods of studying. She found that students' approaches to study were also influenced by their overall orientation or conception of study and also by their perceptions of the demands of the task and the nature and style of the teaching. Hence task and context influence an individual's approach to learning (Laurillard 1978). They also impinge upon the approach that students adopt in different topic areas and these may vary not only between subjects but also within subjects.

Meyer et al. (1990) have shown that students' perceptions of the context can affect their learning outcomes. They introduced the notion of orchestration as a construct to represent an individual's approach to studying as a context-specific response that is influenced by a qualitative perception of key elements of learn-ing context. They concluded that successful students had a well defined meaning orchestration and a holistic perception of the learning context. Comparatively unsuccessful students had a disintegrated orchestration and perception of the learning context. Meyer and Boulton-Lewis (1997) developed the Reflections of Learning Inventory (RoLI), and presented the two categories 'accumulative' and 'transformative'. They argue that conceptions of learning do not operate in isolation of other aspects of learning. Hence in the RoLI, conceptions of learn-ing and other variants such as the context are analysed in relation to assessment and student learning outcomes (Meyer and Shanahan 2000).

Lonka and Lindblom-Ylänne (1996) developed an open-ended question booklet to examine the conceptualisations of learning that psychology students developed as they progress in their studies. The answers were classified into the three scales of *active epistemology, constructivity,* and *mental representation.* They found that the constructivist approach to knowledge and learning was common among psychology students but was rare among teachers and lay people. They argue that these conceptions are domain-specific and this suggests that con-text is influential. In further studies, Lindblom-Ylänne and Lonka (1999, 2000) show differences in orchestrations between medical students and psychology students. Vermunt (2005) also found that academic performance is influenced by contextual and personal factors. In a study of 1279 Dutch students he showed that personal and contextual factors, such as type of academic discipline, prior education, age, and gender influenced performance. This further confirms the role of context in influencing student learning.

Student learning outcomes

Perceptions of the task and context, as perceived through the demands of the task, have an impact on how students approach learning and indirectly on student learning outcomes. Marton and Säljö (1984) observed the 'technification' phenomenon where students' study approaches to a task reflected the requirements of the task. Scouller (1998) also found that the demands of the assessment were instrumental in cueing students to adopt particular approaches to their learning. Meyer (1999) has shown that conceptions of learning, perceptions of the context and the process of learning can influence learning outcomes. However, using assessment grades as a measure of successful student learning is contentious as they can be distorted by variations in assessment practices – which in themselves can cue students to adopt less desirable approaches to learning – and by the learning context (see Richardson 2000 for a full review). Price and Richardson (2003) argue that improvements in student learning should not solely be characterised by learning outcomes but should also include an examination of the learning process itself. Although associating study processes with academic attainment is not simple, better academic attainment tends 'to be positively related to desirable forms of study behaviour and negatively related to less desirable forms' (Richardson 2006, p. 869). Hence if students adopt a deep approach to their studies they are likely to have better academic attainment.

Biggs (1987) developed the Study Process Questionnaire (SPQ) to examine whether assessment and other contextual elements in the teaching and learning system are constructively aligned to promote deep approaches to learning. It aims to help teachers research the learning environment in their own classrooms (Biggs 1999; Kember 2000). This instrument too incorporates the notions of deep and surface learning. The SPQ, and the later Revised SPQ (Biggs et al. 2001), were based on Biggs' (1985) Presage-Process-Product, 3P model of student learning. The 3P model illustrates how students enter the learning environment with a variety of factors, that is, prior knowledge, ability, and their preferred approaches to learning and how these interact with the teaching context to culminate in student learning outcomes. This model brings together a number of important factors to consider when examining student learning outcomes.

However, there is another aspect that requires consideration: that is the role of teaching in influencing students' awareness of their learning environment and how this impacts upon their approach to learning. Ramsden (1992) illustrates that students' perceptions of their learning environment are related to their approaches to learning. Those who comprehend the nature of the assessment as fostering recall and memorisation, with a high workload, are more apt to adopting a surface approach. Comparatively students who perceive

Table 4.5 Relationships between teachers' conceptions of teaching and teachers' approaches to teaching

Teachers *conceptions* of teaching	Teachers *approaches* to teaching
Transmitting concepts of the syllabus	Teacher focused – transmission of information
Transmitting the teacher's knowledge	Teacher focused – transmission of information
Helping student acquire concepts of the syllabus	Teacher focused – students acquire discipline concepts
Helping students acquire teacher's knowledge	Teacher–student interaction – students gain teacher's knowledge through engaging
Helping students develop conceptions	Student centred – students develop their conceptions
Helping students change conceptions	Student centred – students change their conceptions

independence in their learning and clear perception of goals and standards, are more likely to be associated with deep approaches (Trigwell et al. 1994; Prosser and Trigwell 1999). Hence we need to also consider the role of teaching and its relationship with student learning.

Teaching

Similar categories to the research on student learning can be found in the literature about teaching (Vermunt and Vermetten 2004, p. 362). Dall'Alba (1991) interviewed 20 teachers in an Australian university and identified seven different conceptions of teaching ranging from *teaching as presenting information* to *teaching as bringing about conceptual change*. Kember (1997) conducted a review of the conceptions of teaching literature and found similar conceptions. In a similar vein to the research conducted on approaches to learning, Trigwell et al. (1994) conducted a phenomenographic study and identified five qualitatively different approaches to teaching.

Further research by Trigwell and Prosser (1996) found that these were related to teachers' conceptions of teaching and also to their commensurate conceptions of their student learning. These have broad parallels with the conceptions of learning literature. The relationships between teachers' conceptions of teaching and teachers' approaches to teaching are illustrated in Table 4.5. They argue that teachers' conceptions of teaching and teachers' conceptions of their students' learning represents the *what* and *how* of teaching. The *what* is the focus of the teaching intention and the *how* is the approach that a teacher adopts to addressing that perceived learning need. They found that teachers who conceive of learning as the accumulation of information also conceive of teaching as the transmission of information to students. Subsequently they approached their teaching in terms of teacher-focused strategies. Comparatively, those teachers who conceive of learning as developing and changing students' conceptions, conceive of teaching in terms of supporting students' development and approach their teaching in a student-focused manner (Trigwell and Prosser 1996, p. 281).

Furthermore, teachers' approaches to teaching are linked with SAL and this forms an important factor in considering influences upon student learning. Trigwell et al. (1999) conducted a study investigating the relationship between teachers' approaches to teaching and students' approaches to learning. The study showed that where teachers reported a teacher-centred approach to teaching aimed at transmitting knowledge, students correspondingly reported using surface approaches to learning. Contrastingly, where teachers adopted a student-centred approach to teaching aimed at changing the students' conceptions, students tended to report using deep approaches to learning, although to a lesser extent. Thus both teachers' conceptions of teaching and their subsequent approaches to teaching influences student learning. However, Richardson (2000) notes that

> Although a teacher's approach to teaching may constitute part of the institutional context that influences a student's approach to learning, it is equally possible that teachers modify their approaches to teaching to respond to the preferences or predispositions of their students.
>
> (p. 78)

The point of this comparison is that university teachers may have a view of teaching that is not commensurable with their students' view of learning. Hence it is not only important to consider students' conceptions of learning, their approaches to learning, and their influence upon learning outcomes, but also teachers' conceptions of teaching and their approaches to teaching, and their influence upon student learning.

The teaching context

Teachers too operate within a professional context and are subsequently subjected to those influences. Because of the strong associations between teachers' approaches to teaching and students' approaches to learning, the teaching context forms an important part of the whole teaching and learning system. It is also an area that we as educators have most control over and the greatest ability to change, hence its importance. The teaching context can have an influence upon teachers' approaches to teaching, or more precisely their teaching practices.

Norton et al. (2005) conducted a study into teachers' beliefs and intentions. They distributed a questionnaire measuring nine different aspects of teachers' beliefs and intentions at four institutions in the UK (N = 638). Although there was a high degree of overlap, differences were found between beliefs and intentions. They were able to classify 556 respondents into three broad academic disciplines: arts, science, and social science. These differed across institutions and between teachers and seemed to result from contextual factors. They found that disciplinary teaching differences remained significant even when institution, teaching experience, and gender were taken into account. They concluded that these differences appear to represent 'genuine differences in teaching conceptions across different disciplines' (p. 554). Teaching intentions thus reflect a compromise between teachers' conceptions of teaching and their academic and social contexts. Teachers in different disciplines and professional backgrounds may have undergone different processes of integration and adaptation. Furthermore, if teachers' conceptions of teaching are not aligned with the dominant culture of that discipline then teachers may feel marginalised. They may have to adapt their preferred modus operandi in order to be accepted or else remain in the margins. Their students too may question the value of the course they are studying if they perceive that the teaching of it is not aligned with the rest of the curriculum in that discipline.

Tormey and Henchy (2008) acknowledge the ideological challenges that the teaching context presents. They recognise clashes between teaching values and teaching practices. While teachers may feel committed to relational, socially and politically transformative student-centred teaching, these values are difficult to realise when teachers have to lecture to large groups. As Laurillard argues the traditional lecture is seldom an appropriate context within which to support and engage students in learning. The lecture model persists partly because of tradition and partly because it is a convenient model for higher education institutions to 'deliver' education to large numbers of students (Laurillard 2002, p. 94). Thus teaching context influences what teachers do. This suggests that teachers might have both *ideal* and *working* views about teaching. Thus the institutional context may constrain the teaching approach that teachers would actually prefer to use by affecting how teachers perceive the teaching situation and thus how they respond. Similarity it can affect students' perceptions of the teaching situation and how they respond.

As the model illustrates there are two main aspects – those of the student and those of the teacher. We have not yet managed to find an easy way in which to improve student learning in a consistently robust and convincing manner to any great magnitude. Hence the teaching context is important as this is the area that we as teachers have the most control over and the greatest ability to change.

The wider context for teachers and students

However, there are contexts other than institutional ones that can impact on students and teachers. In the case of students this is the social context and in the case of teachers this is the professional context (although they too will have social influences). Social context can influence students' conceptions where family, peer group, cultural values and expectations contribute to the views that students form. Tinto (1975, 1982, 1987) conducted research into student attrition rates in the US. He argued that it was necessary to take account of the social interactions beyond the classroom as family situations, peer groups, or local communities could impact upon whether students persisted with their studies. This is an especially important factor for students who may be studying part-time or are conducting their studies off-campus (Kember 1995). While the social context is one that will be difficult to measure it should still be taken into account as a factor that may indirectly affect student learning outcomes.

Conclusion

The 4P model provides a way of considering important factors in predicting student learning, and the interrelationships between them and hence what combination of factors might be important to measure in predicting student learning. It draws upon a wide body of literature to portray factors that have already been identified as pertinent in predicting student learning. Students' perceptions and their conceptions of learning and teachers' perceptions and their conceptions of teaching are important elements related to the whole concept of improving student learning. Furthermore it shows an interrelationship between the context in which learning takes place, the learner themselves, the teacher and the outcomes. Epistemological conceptions about the process of teaching and learning should be viewed as an interrelated set, as should predictions about student learning. The model does not argue for a particular approach to examining these factors but argues that in order to predict student learning it is important to consider a range of factors. This model is presented as a basis for engaging in future research in a holistic manner so we may add or heighten varying combinations of factors that prove effective in predicting student learning.

Limitations and future directions

The 4P model is limited in a number of ways. First it makes assertions about causal links (represented by the arrows in Figure 4.1). In practice these have yet to be demonstrated. Further, the causal direction on the arrows might be incorrect. Richardson (2006) conducted two studies that investigated the general theoretical link between students' perceptions of their academic environment and their study behaviour. He found that

> there exists a bi-directional causal relationship between variations in students' perceptions of the academic environment and variations in their study behaviour. The findings are both empirically and conceptually consistent between the two different data sets that were described in this paper.

From a practical point of view, they entail (a) that approaches to studying in higher education are driven in part by the students' perceptions of their academic environment, but (b) equally that students' perceptions of their academic environment are driven in part by the extent to which they are able to adopt congenial approaches to studying. Consequently, attempts to enhance the quality of student learning in higher education need to address both students' perceptions of their academic context and their study behaviour within that context.

(p. 890)

The model may also be limited by the factors articulated. If the model is to explain variation then perhaps it may not explain enough of the variation and other factors need to be included. The model is principally cognitive; however, affective and motivational factors may further explain variation and help us to effectively predict student learning. Additionally, the model only provides a 'snapshot' of the factors affecting student learning at a moment in time. So the model does not show student development and changes over time.

As we already know students may adopt different approaches to study for different tasks (Laurillard 1979) indicating that the context in terms of the nature of the task and the environment are important and interrelated influences. Baeten et al. (2010) have shown that there is a complex set of factors that influence student learning. These include *personological factors* such as motivation, self-confidence and self-efficacy, the *context of the learning situation, students' perceptions of the context*, and *students' approaches to learning*, all of which relate to the teaching context and the teacher's approach to teaching. Their research indicates not only that a range of factors need to be considered in tandem but also that some may be more influential than others. The 4P model presented here does not take account of the relative importance of particular factors compared with others, but this could be extended through further research.

Other aspects worthy of additional research are investigations into what combination of factors are most effective for predicting student learning. Future research should also investigate how development or qualitative changes in learning may be appropriately investigated. Can qualitative changes in learning be effectively measured through quantitative methods? And do qualitative changes in learning need to be investigated at varying points in time in the students' development in order to determine their effectiveness? Further, given that approaches to learning are context dependent, are more generic quantitative approaches appropriate for investigating such factors? Learning outcomes per se, which are judged in terms of end of programme assessment, are inextricably linked with the nature of the assessment itself. This makes the measurement of assessment an unreliable means for determining student development, particularly between independent studies, as they are context dependent particularly in higher education. Given this, researchers investigating predictions in student learning need to consider further what other means may be appropriate for capturing learner development and hence for predicting student learning.

References

Baeten, M., Kyndt, E., Struyven, K., and Dochy, F. (2010). Using student-centred learning environments to stimulate deep approaches to learning: Factors encouraging or discouraging their effectiveness. *Educational Research Review*, 5, 243–260.

Baxter Magolda, M.B. (1992). *Knowing and reasoning in college: Gender-related patterns in students' intellectual development*. San Francisco, CA: Jossey-Bass.

Belenky, M.F., Clinchy, B.M., Goldberger, N.R., and Tarule, J.M. (1986). *Women's ways of knowing: The development of self, voice and mind*. New York: Basic Books.

Biggs, J. (1987). *Student approaches to learning and studying*. Melbourne: Australian Council for Educational Research.

Biggs, J. (1993). What do inventories of students' learning processes really measure? A theoretical review and clarification. *British Journal of Educational Psychology*, 63, 3–19.

Biggs, J.B. (1999). *Teaching for quality learning at university*. Buckingham, UK: SRHE & Open University Press.

Biggs, J., Kember, D., and Leung, D.Y.P. (2001). The revised two-factor Study Process Questionnaire: R-SPQ-2F. *The British Psychological Society*, 71, 133–149.

Biggs, J.B. (1985). The role of metalearning in study processes. *British Journal of Educational Psychology*, 55, 185–212.

Bransford, J.D., Brown, A.L., and Cocking, R.R., eds. (2000). *How people learn: Brain, mind, experience, and school*. Washington, DC: National Academy Press.

Clegg, S. (2005). Evidence-based practice in educational research: A critical realist critique of systematic review. *British Journal of Sociology of Education*, 26, 415–428.

Crawford, K., Gordon, S., Nicholas, J., and Prosser, M. (1994). Conceptions of mathematics and how it is learned: The perspectives of students entering university. *Learning and Instruction*, 4 (4), 331–345.

Dahlgren, L.O. (1975). *Qualitative differences in learning as a function of content-oriented guidance*. Göteborg: Acta Universitatis Gothoburgensis.

Dahlgren, L.O., and Marton, F. (1978). Students' conceptions of subject matter: An aspect of learning and teaching in higher education. *Studies in Higher Education*, 3, 25–35.

Dall'Alba, G. (1991). Foreshadowing conceptions of teaching. *Research and Development in Higher Education*, 13, 293–297.

Donche, V. and Petegem, P. (2008). The development of learning patterns of student teachers: A cross-sectional and longitudinal study. *Higher Education*, 57, 463–475.

Dunkin, M.J., and Biddle, B.J. (1974). *The study of teaching*. New York: Holt, Rinehart and Winston.

Edmunds, R., and Richardson, J.T.E. (2009). Conceptions of learning, approaches to studying and personal development in UK higher education. *British Journal of Educational Psychology*, 79 (2), 295–309.

Elliott, J. (2001). Making evidence-based practice educational. *British Educational Research Journal*, 27 (5), 555–574.

Entwistle, N.J., and Ramsden, P. (1983). *Understanding student learning*. London & Canberra: Croom Helm.

Entwistle, N., Hanley, M., and Hounsell, D. (1979). Identifying distinctive approaches to studying. *Higher Education*, 8 (4), 365–380.

Fransson, A. (1977). On qualitative differences in learning IV: Effects of intrinsic and extrinsic motivation and test anxiety on process and outcome. *British Journal of Educational Psychology*, 47, 244–257.

Gibbs, G. (2003). Ten years of improving student learning. In C. Rust, ed. *Improving student learning: Theory and practice – ten years on*. Oxford: The Oxford Centre for Staff & Learning Development, 9–26.

Halldén, O. (2001). Social constructionism, constructivism and intentional analysis as a heuristic tool. In O. Halldén, M. Scheja, and H. Jacobsson-Öhm, eds. *Intentional analysis: Research bulletins from the department of education*. Stockholm: Stockholm University.

Hammersley, M. (1997). Educational research and teaching: A response to David Hargreaves' TTA lecture. *British Educational Research Journal*, 23 (2), 141–161.

Hargreaves, D.H. (1996). Teaching as a research-based profession: Possibilities and prospects. In *The teacher training agency annual lecture 1996*. The Teacher Training Agency, 1–12.

Hargreaves, D.H. (1997). In defence of research for evidence-based teaching: A rejoinder to Martyn Hammersley. *British Educational Research Journal*, 23 (4), 405–419.

Hattie, J. and Marsh, H.W. (1996). The relationship between research and teaching: A meta-analysis. *Review of Educational Research*, 66 (4), 507–542.

Higher Education Academy (2007). UK Professional Standards Framework (UKPSF). Available from: http://www.heacademy.ac.uk/ukpsf (accessed 16 Sep 2011).

Higher Education Funding Council for England (HEFCE), Scottish Funding Council (SFC), Higher Education Funding Council for Wales (HEFCW), and Department for Employment and Learning, Northern Ireland (DEL) (2009). Research Assessment Exercise RAE2008: RAE2008 subject overviews. RAE2008 Research Assessment Exercise. Available from: http://www.rae.ac.uk/pubs/2009/ov/ (accessed 15 Nov 2011).

Hounsell, D. (1987). Essay writing and the quality of feedback. In J.T.E. Richardson, M.W. Eysenck, and D. Warren Piper, eds. *Student learning: Research in education and cognitive psychology*. Milton Keynes, UK: SRHE and Open University Press, 109–119.

Kanuka, H. (2011). Keeping the scholarship in the scholarship of teaching and learning. *International Journal for the Scholarship of Teaching and Learning*, 5 (1), 1–12.

Kember, D. (1995). *Open learning courses for adults: A model of student progress*. Englewood Cliffs, NJ: Educational Technology Publications.

Kember, D. (1997). A reconceptualisation of the research into university academics' conceptions of teaching. *Learning and instruction*, 7 (3), 255–275.

Kember, D. (2000). *Action learning and action research: Improving the quality of teaching and learning*. London: Kogan Page.

Kirkwood, A.T., and Price, L. (2005). Learners and learning in the 21st century: What do we know about students' attitudes and experiences of ICT that will help us design courses? *Studies in Higher Education*, 30 (3), 257–274.

Kreber, C., and Cranton, P.A. (2000). Exploring the scholarship of teaching. *Journal of Higher Education*, 71, 476–495.

Laurillard, D. (1978). A study of the relationship between some of the cognitive and contextual factors in student learning. Unpublished doctoral thesis. University of Surrey, UK.

Laurillard, D. (1979). The processes of student learning. *Higher Education*, 8 (4), 395–409.

Laurillard, D. (1984). Learning from problem-solving. In F. Marton, D. Hounsell, and N. Entwistle, eds. *The experience of learning*. Edinburgh: Scottish Academic Press, 124–143.

Laurillard, D. (2002). *Rethinking university teaching: A framework for the effective use of learning technologies*. 2nd ed. London, UK: Routledge Falmer.

Lonka, K. and Lindblom-Ylänne, S. (1994). The effect of study strategies on learning from text. *Learning and Instruction*, 4 (3), 253–271.

Lonka, K. and Lindblom-Ylänne, S. (1996). Epistemologies, conceptions of learning, and study practices in medicine and psychology. *Higher Education*, 31, 5–24.

Lindblom-Ylänne, S. and Lonka, K. (1999). Individual ways of interacting with the learning environment – are they related to study success? *Learning and Instruction*, 9 (1), 1–18.

Lindblom-Ylänne, S. and Lonka, K. (2000). Dissonant study orchestrations of high-achieving university students. *European Journal of Psychology of Education*, 15 (1), 19–32.

Martin, E. and Ramsden, P. (1987). Learning skills, or skill in learning? In *Student learning: Research in education and cognitive psychology*. Milton Keynes, UK: SRHE and Open University Press, 15–167.

Marton, F. (1975). On non-verbatim learning. I: Level of processing and level of outcome. *Scandinavian Journal of Psychology*, 16, 273–279.

Marton, F. (1981). Phenomenography: Describing conceptions of the world around us. *Instructional Science*, 10, 177–200.

Marton, F., and Dahlgren, L.O. (1976). On non-verbatim learning: The outcome space of some basic concepts in economics. *Scandinavian Journal of Psychology*, 17, 49–55.

Marton, F., Dall'Alba, G., and Beaty, E. (1993). Conceptions of learning. *International Journal of Educational Research*, 19, 277–300.

Marton, F., and Säljö, R. (1976a). On qualitative differences in learning: I. Outcome and process. *British Journal of Educational Psychology*, 46, 4–11.

Marton, F., and Säljö, R. (1976b). On qualitative differences in learning: II. Outcome as a function of the learner's conception of the task. *British Journal of Educational Psychology*, 46, 115–127.

Marton, F. and Säljö, R. (1984). Approaches to learning. In F. Marton, D. Hounsell, and N. Entwistle, eds. *The experience of learning*. Edinburgh: Academic Press, 36–55.

Marton, F. and Säljö, R. (1997). Approaches to learning. In F. Marton, D. Hounsell, and N.J. Entwistle, eds. *The experience of learning: Implications for teaching and studying in higher education*. Edinburgh: Scottish Academic Press.

Means, B., Toyama, Y., Murphy, R., Bakia, M., and Jones, K. (2010). *Evaluation of evidence-based practices in online learning: A meta-analysis and review of online learning studies*. Washington, DC: US Department of Education Office of Planning, Evaluation, and Policy Development.

Meyer, J.H.F. (1997). Conceptions of learning: Interviews with black South African engineering students in their mother tongue. *Research and Development in Higher Education*, 20, 481–487.

Meyer, J.H.F. (1999). Variation and concepts of quality in student learning. *Quality in Higher Education*, 167–180.

Meyer, J.H.F., and Boulton-Lewis, G.M. (1997). The association between university students' perceived influences on their learning and their knowledge, experience, and conceptions, of learning. Presented at the 7th EARLI Conference, Athens.

Meyer, J.H.F., Parsons, P., and Dunne, T.T. (1990). Individual study orchestrations and their association with learning outcome. *Higher Education*, 20, 67–89.

Meyer, J.H.F. and Shanahan, M.P. (2000). Making teaching responsive to variation in student learning. Presented at the 7th Improving Student Learning Symposium, Manchester.

Norton, L., Richardson, T.E., Hartley, J., Newstead, S., and Mayes, J. (2005). Teachers' beliefs and intentions concerning teaching in higher education. *Higher Education*, 50, 537–571.

Oakley, A. (2001). Making evidence-based practice educational: A rejoinder to John Elliott. *British Educational Research Journal*, 27 (5), 575–576.

Oliver, M., and Conole, G. (2003). Evidence-based practice and e-learning in higher education: Can we and should we? *Research Papers in Education*, 18 (4), 385–397.

Perry, W.G. (1968). *Patterns of development in thought and values of students in a liberal arts college. A validation of a scheme.* US: Department of Health, Education, and Welfare, Office of Education, Bureau of Research, Final Report No. Project No. 5-0825, Contract No. SAE 8973.

Perry, W.G. (1970). *Forms of intellectual and ethical development in the college years: A scheme.* New York: Holt, Rinehart and Winston.

Price, L., and Kirkwood, A.T. (2011). Enhancing professional learning and teaching through technology: A synthesis of evidence-based practice among teachers in higher education. Higher Education Academy, York, UK. Available from: http://oro.open.ac.uk/30686/ (accessed 8 May 2013).

Price, L., and Richardson, J.T.E. (2003). Meeting the challenge of diversity: A cautionary tale about learning styles. In C. Rust, ed. *Proceedings of the 2002 10th International Symposium of Improving Student Learning, Improving Student Learning Theory and Practice – 10 Years On.* Oxford: The Oxford Centre for Staff & Learning Development, 285–295.

Price, L., and Richardson, J.T.E. (2004). Why is it difficult to improve student learning? In C. Rust, ed. *Proceedings of the 11th Improving Student Learning Symposium, Improving Student Learning: Theory, Research and Scholarship.* Oxford: The Oxford Centre for Staff and Learning Development, 105–120.

Prosser, M., and Millar, R. (1989). The how and what of learning physics. *The European Journal of Psychology of Education,* 4, 513–528.

Prosser, M. and Trigwell, K. (1999). *Understanding learning and teaching: The experience in higher education.* Buckingham, UK: SRHE and Open University Press.

Prosser, M., Trigwell, K., and Taylor, P. (1994). A phenomenographic study of academics' conceptions of science learning and teaching. *Learning and Instruction,* 4, 217–232.

Ramsden, P. (1992). *Learning to teach in higher education.* London: Routledge.

Richardson, J.T.E. (1994). Mature students in higher education: I. A literature survey on approaches to studying. *Studies in Higher Education,* 19 (3), 309–325.

Richardson, J.T.E. (2000). *Researching student learning: Approaches to studying in campus-based and distance education.* Buckingham: SRHE and Open University Press.

Richardson, J.T.E. (2006). Investigating the relationship between variations in students' perceptions of their academic environment and variations in study behaviour in distance education. *British Journal of Educational Psychology,* 76 (4), 867–893.

Richardson, J.T.E. (2007). Mental models of learning in distance education. *British Journal of Educational Psychology,* 77 (2), 253–270.

Richardson, J.T.E. (2010). Conceptions of learning and approaches to studying among White and ethnic minority students in distance education. *British Journal of Educational Psychology,* 80 (4), 535–556.

Ryan, M.P. (1984). Monitoring text comprehension: Individual differences in epistemological standards. *Journal of Educational Psychology,* 76 (2), 248–258.

Säljö, R. (1975). *Qualitative differences in learning as a function of the learner's conception of the task.* Göteborg: Acta Universitatis Gothoburgensis.

Säljö, R. (1979a). *Learning in the learner's perspective: I. Some common-sense assumptions.* No. Report No. 76. Göteborg: University of Göteborg, Institute of Education.

Säljö, R. (1979b). Learning about learning. *Higher Education,* 8, 443–451.

Scouller, K. (1998). The influence of assessment method on students' learning approaches: Multiple choice question examination versus assignment essay. *Higher Education,* 35 (4), 453–472.

Slavin, R.E. (2008). Perspectives on evidence-based research in education – what works? Issues in synthesizing educational program evaluations. *Educational Researcher,* 37 (1), 5–14.

Slavin, R.E., Lake, C., Davis, S., and Madden, N.A. (2011). Effective programs for struggling readers: A best-evidence synthesis. *Educational Research Review*, 6 (1), 1–26.

Svensson, L. (1976). *Study skill and learning.* Göteborg: Acta Universitatis Gothoburgensis.

Svensson, L. (1977). On qualitative differences in learning: III. Study skill and learning. *British Journal of Educational Psychology*, 47, 233–243.

Tait, H. and Entwistle, N. (1996). Identifying students at risk through ineffective study strategies. *Higher Education*, 31 (1), 97–116.

Tamim, R.M., Bernard, R.M., Borokhovski, E., Abrami, P.C., and Schmid, R.F. (2011). What forty years of research says about the impact of technology on learning: A second-order meta-analysis and validation study. *Review of Educational Research*, 81, 4–28.

Tinto, V. (1975). Dropout from higher education: A theoretical synthesis of recent research. *Review of Educational Research*, 45, 89–125.

Tinto, V. (1982). Limits of theory and practice in student attrition. *Journal of Higher Education*, 53, 687–700.

Tinto, V. (1987). *Leaving college: Rethinking the causes and cures of student attrition.* Chicago, IL: University of Chicago.

Tormey, R., and Henchy, D. (2008). Re-imagining the traditional lecture: An action research approach to teaching student teachers to 'do' philosophy. *Teaching in Higher Education*, 13 (3), 303–314.

Trigwell, K., Martin, E., Benjamin, J., and Prosser, M. (2000). Scholarship of teaching: A model. *Higher Education Research and Development*, 19, 155–168.

Trigwell, K. and Prosser, M. (1996). Changing approaches to teaching: A relational perspective. *Studies in Higher Education*, 21, 275–284.

Trigwell, K., Prosser, M., and Taylor, P. (1994). Qualitative differences in approaches to teaching in first year university science. *Higher Education*, 27, 75–84.

Trigwell, K., Prosser, M., and Waterhouse, F. (1999). Relations between teachers' approaches to teaching and students' approaches to learning. *Higher Education*, 37, 57–70.

Van Rossum, E.J., and Schenk, S.M. (1984). The relationship between learning conception, study strategy and learning outcome. *British Journal of Educational Psychology*, 54 (1), 73–83.

Vermetten, Y.J., Vermunt, J.D., and Lodewijks, H.G. (2002). Powerful learning environments? How university students differ in their response to instructional measures. *Learning and Instruction*, 12 (3), 263–284.

Vermunt, J.D. (1996). Metacognitive, cognitive and affective aspects of learning styles and strategies: A phenomenographic analysis. *Higher Education*, 31, 25–50.

Vermunt, J.D. (1998). The regulation of constructive learning processes. *The British Psychological Society*, 68 (2), 149–171.

Vermunt, J.D. (2005). Relations between student learning patterns and personal and contextual factors and academic performance. *Higher Education*, 49, 205–234.

Vermunt, J.D., and Vermetten, Y.J. (2004). Patterns in student learning: Relationships between learning strategies, conceptions of learning, and learning orientations. *Educational Psychology Review*, 16 (4), 359–384.

Vermunt, J.D.H.M., and Rijswijk, F.A.W.M. (1988). Analysis and development of students' skill in self regulated learning. *Higher Education*, 17 (6), 647–682.

Weinstein, C.E., and Mayer, R.E. (1986). The teaching of learning strategies. In M. Wittrock, ed. *Handbook of research on teaching.* New York: MacMillan, 315–327.

Chapter 5

Exploring the concept of 'self-directedness in learning'

Theoretical approaches and measurement in adult education literature

Isabel Raemdonck, Caroline Meurant, Julien Balasse, Anne Jacot and Mariane Frenay

Introduction

Understanding learning patterns across the lifespan

Given the increased importance of lifelong learning, adult students in higher education represent a growing population in the terrain of higher education. This increase in older students has brought with it a growth in student diversity and heterogeneity (Kasworm, 2003). Adults enrol in higher education for several reasons and with different prior educational experiences. Adult students' approaches to learning might also be somehow different from their younger colleagues because they are in a different life stage and perceive the world and their future time differently (Kasworm, 2003; MacKeracher, 2004; Richardson, 1994; Vermunt, 2005). Because of their complex lives and many different roles, these adults deliberately seek out educational settings that support their way of learning. Therefore, there is a need in theory and in higher education practice to understand learning patterns across the lifespan.

Learning patterns of the 21st century are characterised by self-directedness

Against the background of 21st century blended learning environments and increased learning demands in higher and continuing education and in workplaces, self-directedness in learning is perceived as the ideal approach to lifelong learning. The importance of the individual initiative and self-responsibility is emphasised and individuals are expected to play an active role in several domains of life (Jackson, 1996). In the field of adult education, self-directedness in learning has always been an important topic in research (Brockett et al., 2000; Owen, 2002). Therefore, approaches to self-directed learning in this discipline might produce knowledge and insights that offer new pathways for research on learning patterns in higher education. In line with the aim of this book, this paper describes assumptions and research about learning approaches of adults and clarifies the construct of self-directedness in learning from the adult education research area. An overview is given of the conceptual models and the measurement instruments developed within this field. Concepts and instruments are related to those commonly used in higher education.

Assumptions about adult learning approaches

How adults learn has been a central question in the field of adult education (Ellinger, 2004). One assumption about adult learning approaches in adult education literature is that adults have a natural preference for self-directedness in their learning as they are used to managing other aspects of their lives. When Knowles (1970) introduced the term 'andragogy' he described the adult learner as someone who (1) has an independent self-concept and who directs his or her own learning, (2) has accumulated a reservoir of life experiences that is a rich resource for learning, (3) has learning needs closely related to changing social roles, (4) is problem-centered and interested in immediate application of knowledge, and (5) is motivated to learn by internal rather than external factors. Tough (1971) found out that adult learners engage yearly in several self-directed learning projects initiated by the adults themselves as a response to their daily needs and problems. Rather than preplanning of learning experiences, it is often an 'organizing circumstance' in the lives of adults that serves as an impetus for engaging in self-directed learning (Spear & Mocker, 1984). Subsequently, Mezirow (1991) and Candy (1991) presented the adult learner as an autonomous person who is self-contained and does not need to respond to others. More recently, MacKeracher (2004) expressed a more nuanced view by stating that each adult has personally preferred strategies for learning and that different yet meaningful patterns are created from the same experiences by learning with different learning styles.

Learning patterns and the exercise of self-direction in learning occur within a specific context (Raemdonck, 2006). A second assumption about adult learning approaches is therefore that these approaches to learning differ depending on the type of context or situation. These learning contexts might be formal or informal in nature. Research demonstrated that in learning settings where adults had little control over their learning (i.e. time and instructional constraints set by external person) and where molecular learning (learning of relatively isolated and novel information in single training sessions) learning outcomes (such as performance) were less favorable (Schulz & Roßnagel, 2010). This is more often the case in formal classroom-based learning contexts. In informal learning settings adult learners demonstrate other learning patterns as learning is more often done on a voluntary basis and one has more opportunities to pace learning in accordance with one's capabilities and needs. Therefore, learners might choose learning formats which suit better their particular learning needs and which increase opportunities for the use of experience-based strategies and professional knowledge (Schulz & Roßnagel, 2010, p. 385). Especially for older adult learners, informal self-directed learning in the workplace might offer more opportunities to compensate for cognitive ageing effects (Schulz & Roßnagel, 2010). In formal learning settings differences in learning competence between adults of different ages were indeed found (e.g. Kubeck, Delp, Haslett & McDaniel, 1996 and Stine-Morrow, Shake, Miles & Noh, 2006).

Age-related research on learning approaches of adults

Learning patterns, learning orientations and learning styles have been extensively researched with children and young adults but very little is known about the learning patterns of older adults. It is only recently that age-related and developmental changes (over time) in learning patterns, styles and orientations of adults have been investigated in several contexts of learning (in higher education, training, at the workplace) and in different stages of adult life (during career life, during retirement). Schulz and Roßnagel (2010) explored age differences in learning competence in a sample of 470 employees from a major German mail order company. In measuring learning competence in informal self-directed work contexts, the authors distinguished the cognitive dimension (learning strategies such as elaboration, structuring and memorising of new learning material), the meta-cognitive strategies (control strategies such as organising, planning, monitoring, reflection) and the motivational strategies (learning and performance goal orientation). Three age groups were compared: 17–35 years, 36–50 years, and 50+ years. No age differences were found in learning competence.

Truluck and Courtenay (1999) determined the learning style preferences of older adults between 55 and 75+. Kolb's (1985) *Learning style inventory* was used to identify the preferred learning styles of 172 older adults in the United States. Results found the older adults in this study fairly evenly distributed across the styles of accommodator, assimilator and diverger, with fewer preferring the converger style, which involves thinking and doing while learning. Although no significant effects were found between learning style preferences and gender, age or educational level, there were some age trends noted. More of the 55 to 65 age group preferred the accommodator learning style (learning by feeling and doing), more of the 66 to 74 age group preferred the diverger style (learning by feeling and watching), whereas the 75 and older group preferred the assimilator style (learning by thinking and watching). Contrary to what is often suggested in adult education literature, not all older learners were active, but rather with age there was a tendency to become more reflective and observational in the learning environment.

Richardson (1995) compared 38 mature (aged between 23 and 50 years) and 60 non-mature students (aged between 18 and 22 years) taking the same course using a shortened form of the 'Approaches to Studying Inventory' (ASI-32). He found that mature students obtained significantly higher scores on meaning orientation (deep approach) and that they also tended to produce lower scores on reproducing orientation (surface approach). Three different reasons were put forward: the mature students are more motivated by intrinsic goals; the non-mature students acquire a surface approach to learning in the final years of secondary education; and the prior life experience of mature students promotes a deep approach towards studying in higher education.

Rønning (2009) also administered the 'Approaches to Studying Inventory' (ASI-32) to 1477 adult students attending flexible study programmes in higher education in Norway. The aim of the study was to investigate adult approaches to studying, taking into account their educational backgrounds and their present challenging study conditions (distance education and shortage of time due to work and family obligations). Rønning's study showed that adult students were primarily meaning oriented. The non-traditional (first time in higher education) adult students among them were, however, more reproducing oriented than students with prior higher education experience. Self-efficacy turned out to be more strongly associated with approaches than personal efforts. Obligations of everyday life did not have the expected impact.

The concept of self-directedness: approaches found in adult education literature

Self-direction and related concepts

Self-directedness in learning is a central concept in the study and practice of adult education and learning (Garrison, 1997). It is positioned at the junction of many different research fields. Related terms are 'self-management', 'self-regulation', 'self-control', 'self-education'. 'Self-directedness' is a term which is commonly used in the field of adult education and learning, 'self-regulation' is mostly used in higher education, educational and cognitive psychology and 'self-management' is a term mostly applied in work and organisational psychology and human resource development. In the field of adult education research the concept of self-directedness in learning is probably the most discussed issue (MacKeracher, 2004). Initially, the concept was only studied in formal and institutionalised contexts of adult education but more recently the workplace has also been investigated as a context for self-direction in learning (Ellinger, 2004; Marsick & Watkins, 1990).

According to Candy (1991) there are two approaches: when applied to the *learning process*, self-directedness refers to an instructional method in which the learner takes the primary responsibility or initiative in the learning experience for goal setting, implementation of appropriate learning strategies and evaluation of learning outcomes (Knowles, 1975). When applied to the *learner*, self-directedness can be either a general personal characteristic (not related to learning) or a characteristic with specific meaning to learning.

Self-direction as a personal characteristic

Some researchers have conceptualised a generalised sense of self-directedness. In that case, the term 'self-direction' is used to describe people in *general*

(MacKeracher, 2004). A self-directed person is a person who takes personal initiative in a broad range of activities and situations (Seibert, Kraimer & Crant, 2001). Similar constructs outside the field of adult education are Bateman and Crant's proactive personality (Bateman & Crant, 1993) and Frese's concept of personal initiative (Frese, Fay, Hilburger, Leng & Tag, 1997). Bateman and Crant (1993) defined proactive personality as a 'relatively stable tendency to effect environmental change' (p. 103). They described a proactive person as someone who is relatively unconstrained by situational forces and who effects environmental change. Frese et al. (1997, p. 140) defined the concept of personal initiative as 'a behavior syndrome that results in an individual taking an active and self-starting approach to work goals and tasks and persisting in overcoming barriers and setback'. In most of these general conceptualisations, self-directedness is more likely to be perceived as a personal trait, although as a general personal characteristic, self-directedness can be understood in three different ways: as a characteristic one is born with (a trait, disposition), as an acquired quality developing naturally with increased age or as a learned characteristic. If self-directedness is a learned characteristic it is amenable to the educational process (Mackeracher, 2004). Following the latter perspective, Raemdonck (2006) characterises self-directedness as characteristic adaptation. A characteristic adaptation is a psychological feature that is developed as the person encounters his or her environment, and it reflects the influences of traits, the social environment, and their interaction (McCrae & Costa, 1999, 2003). It is *characteristic* because it reflects the operation of enduring personality traits, and it is an *adaptation* because it is shaped in response to the demands and opportunities offered by the environment. A characteristic adaptation is acquired and can be more easily modified in comparison to a personality trait (De Fruyt et al., 2006). A characteristic adaptation varies across cultures, families and portions of the lifespan. Consequently, self-directedness is best viewed as a continuum or characteristic that exists to some degree in every person (Hiemstra, 1994; Long, 1991). Characteristic adaptations change over time and across circumstances in response to biological maturation, changes in the environment or deliberate interventions (McCrae & Costa, 2003). Self-directedness is thus described as a learned characteristic that is susceptible to the educative process and influenced by personal and environmental circumstances (MacKeracher, 2004).

'Self-direction' as a personal characteristic *with specific meaning to learning* is defined by Raemdonck, Plomp and Segers (2008) as 'a characteristic adaptation to take an active and self-starting approach to learning activities and situations and to persist in overcoming barriers and setbacks to learning'. Employees who are oriented towards self-directedness in learning identify learning opportunities, show learning initiative, undertake learning activities and persevere in overcoming barriers to learning. In contrast, people who are less oriented towards self-directed learning exhibit the opposite behaviour: they fail to identify learning opportunities, let alone seize opportunities to learn (Seibert et al., 2001). According to Taris and Kompier (2005, p. 153) taking a self-starting approach towards learning means that the goals of one's actions are not determined by someone else, but rather that one develops one's own goals. Having an active approach to learning implies that one acts proactively and one seeks opportunities for learning. Overcome barriers and setbacks implies that one tries to detect possible problems that may hinder learning and develops action plans to prevent such problems from occurring (Gijbels, Raemdonck & Vervecken, 2010). Brockett and Hiemstra (1991) defined self-direction as a personal characteristic as 'an individual's beliefs and attitudes that predispose one towards taking primary responsibility for their learning' (p. 29), and 'as a learner's desire or preference for assuming responsibility for learning' (p. 24). They conceptualised self-direction as a learner characteristic as behaviours relating to learner autonomous motivation (Deci & Ryan, 2000) and perceived self-efficacy for self-direction in learning (Bandura, 1997).

In line with Delahaye, Limerick and Hearn (1994) and Ponton, Derrick and Carr (2005), we argue that self-directedness is best understood as a domain-specific concept. That is, one can demonstrate different levels of self-directedness depending on the domain. An adult can show, for example, a high level of self-directedness in learning in order to master the various tasks involved in one's occupation. At the same time, the level of self-directness demonstrated in his/her career can be low because the employee is not looking for any career growth opportunities or has no intention to leave the organization he/she is working for.

Self-direction as an instructional method

In early perspectives on self-direction as an instructional method or process, self-direction refers to

> a process in which individuals take the initiative with or without the help of others, in diagnosing their learning needs, formulating learning goals, identifying human and material resources for learning, choosing and implementing appropriate learning strategies and evaluating learning outcomes.
>
> (Knowles, 1975, p. 18)

Another important influence in the conceptual development of this approach to self-directedness is Brockett and Hiemstra's (1991, p. 24) definition which is very similar to the one of Knowles: 'a process in which a learner assumes primary responsibility for planning, implementing and evaluating the learning process.' Both definitions describe a process of self-direction which is linear in nature. More recent models are interactive and reflect a constructivist framework (Stockdale, 2003). Within these frameworks, self-direction is a 'multi-component, iterative, self-steering process which modulates environmental, cognitive, affective and behavioral elements' (Boekaerts, 2006; Boekaerts & Minnaert, 1999). In relation to this approach, Garrison (1997) proposes a theoretical model which integrates self-management (environmental control, external management), self-monitoring (internal monitoring, cognitive responsibility) and motivational (entering motivation and staying on task and persisting) dimensions. Most of the research studies in adult education focus upon the external management of learning activities. However, Garrison (1997) sees *motivation* as the pivotal and pervasive dimension. Either research studies related to self-direction as an instructional method/process focus on the self-direction of single (or definable domain of) learning tasks (narrow or micro perspective) or on the self-direction of a learning project or learning trajectory across one's life and career (broader or macro perspective) (Raemdonck, 2006). If self-direction refers to the micro level, the construct is similar to the construct of self-regulated learning applied in higher education (Jossberger, 2011; Loyens, Magda & Rikers, 2008).

In self-directedness as an instructional method, it is the learner him/herself who steers the different components of the learning process instead of the teacher or instructor. The latter plays a facilitating role in the process (Stockdale & Brockett, 2011). This learning process consists of four main components: goal setting, choosing strategies, executing the strategy, and monitoring and evaluation (see Frese & Zapf, 1994; Knowles, 1975). First, the person diagnoses his needs. Once a goal is established, a person looks for strategies and human and material resources and, when dealing with dynamic systems, anticipates on future outcomes. The strategy choice leads to a plan which is then executed. During plan execution, appropriated strategies are applied and the action is monitored. In case of complexity and negative emotions, the person sticks to the plan. The person evaluates the (interim) outcomes and gathers information which helps him to adjust the process (goals, plans or the execution) (see Frese & Fay, 2001; Knowles, 1975). This process is not linear or sequential in nature which means that individuals do not necessarily follow a predefined set of steps (Merriam & Caffarella, 1991). At least each step will occur in the process. The steps are being constantly redefined during a process of self-direction (Raemdonck, 2006). The components of the learning process are described on the left-hand side of Table 5.1. For each component in the process, examples of self-directedness in the learning process are displayed.

Measurement of self-directedness

Measurement instruments in adult education literature

In adult education research, several measurement instruments have been developed over the years to measure self-directedness in learning (see Table 5.2 for a selection of research instruments). In the 1970s, the most significant contribution to the self-directed learning research field was Guglielmino's (1977) dissertation research about the development of the 'Self-directed Learning Readiness Scale' (SDLRS). This instrument measures self-directedness as a personal

Table 5.1 Examples of self-directedness categorised according to the components of the learning process

Components	Self-direction of the learning process
Goal setting	Anticipate on future learning needs
	Detect knowledge/skill gaps
	Diagnose personal learning needs
	Formulate learning goals
Choosing strategy	Collect information about learning opportunities
	Select appropriate strategy
	Develop a learning plan
	Identify human and material resources for learning
Execute strategy	Express learning interests
	Networking to create learning opportunities
	Ask advice to realise learning plan
	Explore learning market and work environment
Monitoring and evaluation	Reflect on the self as a learner
	Prioritise learning
	Overcome complexity and negative emotions
	Evaluate impact of strategy (result)
	Register progress
	Adjust goals, plan, implementation

Source: Based on Frese & Fay, 2001.

characteristic and is until now the most frequently used instrument for measuring self-directedness in learning and for examining correlations between self-directedness in learning and several characteristics (e.g. Chu & Tsai, 2009; Lai, 2011; Nikitenko, 2009). In spite of its popularity, the instrument has not been free from criticism. Subsequently, Oddi (1984) developed the 'Continuing Learning Inventory' (OCLI) to provide an instrument that measures personal characteristics related to self-directedness in learning. Oddi's measure is now the second most frequently used instrument (Confessore, Long & Redding, 1993).

In the 1990s new models of self-directedness in learning started to appear. The 'Staged Self-directed learning Model' from Grow (1991); the 'Two-shell Model of Motivated Self-directed Learning' from Straka and Nenniger (1996), Straka (1997) and Nenniger (1999); 'Garrison's Comprehensive Theoretical Model' (Garrison, 1997); and the 'Personal Responsibility Orientation (PRO) Model' from Brockett and Hiemstra (1991) are among the best known. The models share a strong emphasis on the teacher–learner interaction and the importance of students' perceptions of motivation and control (Stockdale, 2003). Some models, such as Brockett and Hiemstra's (1991) 'Personal Responsibility Orientation Model', integrated both views of self-directedness (instructional process and personal characteristic) and conceptualised them as complementary and interrelated. New instruments of self-direction that are informed by more recent conceptualisations of self-direction have been developed and empirically validated such as the `Personal Responsibility Orientation Model of Self-Direction in Learning' (PRO-SDLS) scale by Stockdale (2003) and Stockdale and Brockett (2011) and the 'Two-shell Model Scale of Motivated Self-directed Learning' (MOSLISB-BBS) by Nenniger and Wosnitza (1995) and Straka and Spevacek (1995) (see Table 5.2). In addition, at the turn of the century self-directedness in learning scales were developed for use in work environments. The 'Bartlett-Kotrlik Inventory of Self Learning' (BKISL) was developed for use in organisational settings (Bartlett & Kotrlik, 1999). This measurement is a 49-item seven-point Likert scale and contains 11 factors. According to the developers, social and environment variables, which are not included in the SDLRS or OCLI, were added to the scale alongside personal variables that may affect self-learning. The developers also reported the measurement had high estimates for internal consistency. However, no further studies reported BKISL's validity and reliability. Raemdonck, Plomp and Segers (2008) then developed the 'Self-directed Learning Orientation Scale' (SDLO). The SDLO scale contains 12 items and measures a person's tendency to take an active and self-starting approach towards learning goals, and to persist in overcoming barriers and setbacks to work-related learning (see Table 5.2). The scale is uni-dimensional and is developed on the basis of the short version of the 'Proactive Personality Scale' of Bateman and Crant (1993) and the 'Personal Initiative Scale' of Frese et al. (1997). Empirical evidence demonstrates that the SDLO scale measuring self-directedness in learning as a personal characteristic is a reliable ($\alpha > .80$) and valid instrument (see for example Gijbels, Raemdonck, & Vervecken, 2010; Gijbels, Raemdonck, et al. (2011) have developed the `Learner Self-Directedness in the Workplace Scale'. Similar to Raemdonck et al., the authors also focused on the personal characteristic approach and defined learner self-directedness as an internal disposition that motivates learners to take responsibility for their own learning. The 13-item scale contains items related to active learning, fun of work-related learning and motivation to learn at work. The scale is unidimensional and has, based upon the Rasch rating scale analysis, high reliability scores and construct validity. No replication studies have been reported.

(Dis)similarities in learning strategies' instruments developed in higher education and in adult education

We will now compare the measurement instruments developed in the field of adult education with the most frequently used instruments developed in higher education: Motivated Strategies for Learning Questionnaire (MSLQ), Approaches to Studying Inventory (ASI) and Inventory of Learning Styles (ILS). After a short description of the MSLQ, ASI and ILS, we point out the main similarities and differences.

Table 5.2 Measurement of self-directedness in learning in adult education literature

Instrument	Approach	Definition	Subscales	Validity	Limits
1 Self-directed Learning Readiness Scale (SDLRS) (Guglielmino, 1977) Also known as the Learning Preference Assessment (LPA).	The SDLRS aims to measure the extent to which individuals perceive themselves to possess the abilities, attitudes and characteristics associated with the notion of readiness, an internal state of psychological readiness for self-directed learning. As Guglielmino (1977) considers SDLR as a characteristic present in each person, this scale assesses self-directed learning as a personal characteristic.	The self-directed learner is a person choosing 'more learning objectives, activities, priorities and level of energy expenditure than others' (Guglielmino, 1977, p. 34). Measures characteristics of self-directed learners (derived from results of a Delphi study).	The 58-item and 34-item (short version) SDLRS contains eight factors using a five-point Likert scale (α = range .72 to .96). (1) Openness to learning opportunities (e.g. 'I'm not as interested in learning as other people seem to be'). (2) Self-concept as an effective learner (e.g. 'I am capable of learning for myself almost anything I might need to know'). (3) Initiative and independence in learning (e.g. 'I know what I want to learn'). (4) Informed acceptance or responsibility for one's own learning (e.g. 'If I don't learn, it's my fault'). (5) Love of learning (e.g. 'I admire people who are always learning new things'). (6) Creativity (e.g. 'I take more risks than most people').	Reliability (α > .80) and validity of the scale received substantial support in the literature (e.g. Brockett, 1985; Caffarella & Caffarella, 1986; Guglielmino, 1977). Validated in different countries (mostly US and Europe). Questionnaire has been translated into 21 languages.	Unrevised instrument: identical items since 1977, need for improved instrument (Brockett & Hiemstra, 1991). Problems have been reported with the negatively phrased items (Field, 1989, 1991). Not context free: measure self-directedness in school and book-oriented contexts (Brockett, 1985) while author stresses wide variety of situational use. Few applications of SDLRS in work setting contexts. Construct validity has been questioned: according to Bonham (1991), the scale measures a positive attitude towards learning in general (love and enthusiasm of learning) instead of an attitude towards learning described as self-directed.

Table 5.2 continued

Instrument	Approach	Definition	Subscales	Validity	Limits
			(7) Future orientation (e.g. 'I imagine I'll be learning as long as I'm living'). (8) Ability to use basic study skills and problem solving skills (e.g. 'I don't have any problems with basic study skills').		
2 Continuing Learning Inventory (Oddi, 1984)	In OCLI, self-directed learning is approached as a personal characteristic with specific meaning to learning. OCLI is aimed to identify some personal characteristic commonly associated with self-directed learning.	In Oddi's (1984) study, the self-directed continuing learning is defined as a psychological construct composed of three dimensions: (1) commitment to learning versus apathy or aversion to learning; (2) cognitive openness versus defensiveness;	The 24-item SDLRS contains three factors using a seven-point Likert scale ($\alpha = .88$) (1) Proactive versus reactive learning drive (e.g. 'I successfully complete tasks I undertake'). (2) Cognitive openness versus defensiveness (e.g. 'I read an average of one or more national news magazines each week'). (3) Commitment to learning versus apathy or aversion to learning (e.g. 'I am not comfortable with my performance on	Appropriate psychometric proprieties, tested extensively in research studies.	Not context free: measures self-directedness in school and book-oriented contexts (Brockett, 1985). Items are culturally biased (Candy, 1991). Scale relevant to adults who have spent little time in school?

3	Self-directed learning orientation (SDLO) scale (Raemdonck et al., 2008) Based on the short version of the Proactive Personality Scale (Bateman & Crant, 1993) and the Personal Initiative Scale (Frese et al., 1997).	Measures self-directedness in learning as a personal characteristic with specific meaning to learning (characteristic adaptation). Developed for assessing learners in work contexts.	(3) proactive versus reactive learning drive. This definition focuses on the personality characteristics related to self-directed learning. A tendency to take an active and self-starting approach to learning activities and situations and to persist in overcoming barriers and setbacks to learning.	an assignment until my supervisor says it's acceptable'). Twelve-item scale, unidimensional using a five-point Likert scale ($\alpha = .83$) 'I excel at identifying learning opportunities at work.' 'If I want to learn more for my job, no obstacle is going to stand in my way.' 'No matter what the odds, if I want to undertake a work-related learning activity I will make it happen.' 'A difficult work task does not stop me.'	Unidimensional structure was confirmed in all of the replication studies. High reliability scores ($\alpha > .80$) (see Gijbels et al., 2010; Habet, Segers, & Beausaert, 2012; Raemdonck, Croes, Van der Heijden, Segers, & Scheeren, 2011; Raemdonck, Tillema, De Kok, & Van der Wal, 2011). European samples only (Belgian, Dutch, UK).

Table 5.2 continued

Instrument	Approach	Definition	Subscales	Validity	Limits
4 The Two-shell Model Scale of Motivated Self-directed Learning (MOSLISB-BBS) (Nenniger & Wosnitza, 1995; Straka & Spevacek, 1995) Based on the static model (Knowles, 1975) and the Motivated Learning Strategies Questionnaire (MLSQ) (McKeachie & Pintrich, 1984; Pintrich & De Groot, 1990).	Measures self-directedness as an instructional process. Two-shell Model Scale of Motivated Self-directed Learning distinguishes between environmental circumstances (as a result of historical and social factors), internal circumstances (knowledge, values) and present events including learning needs, learning strategies, control and evaluation. Version for educational context (Nenniger & Wosnitza, 1995) and version for company context (Straka & Spevacek, 1995).	Self-directed learning is defined as a process in which a learner approaches the subject matter to be learned with interest (1), then the learner chooses strategies (2) to acquaint himself with the content, controls (3) the use of these strategies and assesses his/her results by means of an evaluation (4).	Constructs: Exterior shell of the model (1) Interest (1a) Content interest refers to the learner's personal interest in the subject matter. (1b) Procedural interest refers to the learner's anticipation of learning strategies in order to achieve the task. Interior shell of the model (2) Learning strategies include constructs such as resources management, sequencing and acquisition. (3) Control (3a) Meta-cognitive control refers to regulation and monitoring as elements of problem and goal oriented navigation.	The fit statistics from the LISREL procedure supported the correctness of the global model on the construct level in several validation studies in 171 US young adult students (Binder & Nenniger, 1998), 324 trainees of different professions (Straka, Nenniger, Spevacek & Wosnitza, 1996), 649 trainees at different vocational schools (Nenniger, Straka, Spevacek & Wosnitza, 1996) and 315 vocational trainees of different professions at vocational schools (Straka et al., 1996). Validated parts Constructs of both shells as well as parts of the postulated interrelations.	Tested in German samples. One study reported in US sample. More detailed analyses based on diverse cultural samples are needed to confirm this model.

Model	Theoretical basis	Concepts/definitions	Measurement	Evaluation/comments
5 Personal Responsibility Orientation Model of Self-Direction in Learning (PRO-SDLS) (Stockdale, 2003; Stockdale & Brockett, 2011)	Based on the PRO model (Brockett & Hiemstra, 1991), self-directed learning is viewed as a personal responsibility which integrates both (1) personality characteristics of the learner and (2) an instructional method process. Both components operating within the learner's social environment.	Learner's characteristics (LC) refers to personal beliefs and attitudes that predispose the learner toward taking primary responsibility for learning (self-efficacy) and assuming intrinsically responsibility for learning (motivation). Teaching–learning transaction (TLT) is a process in (3b) Motivational control seen as energising and goal directing of appetitive and aversive action tendencies. Interface from the interior to the exterior shell (4) Evaluation refers to diagnosis and attribution.	The 25-item PRO-SDLS contains four factors using a five-point Likert scale ($\alpha = .91$). (1) LC ($\alpha = .86$): (1a) Perceived self-efficacy for self-directed learning (six items; $\alpha = .78$) (e.g. 'I am very confident in my ability to independently prioritise my learning goals'). (1b) Learner autonomous motivation (seven items; $\alpha = .82$) (e.g. 'Most of the work I do in my courses is personally enjoyable or seems relevant	A highly reliable and valid measure of self-directed learning. Several validation analyses were conducted by Stockdale (2003). Content validation: Of the 25 items, 16 demonstrated inter-rater agreement at or above 90 per cent, 8 at 80 per cent. Congruent validity: r-value from the 187 participants who completed SDLRS (Guglielmino, 1977) and PRO-SDLS was .76 ($p < .001$) indicating a shared variance of 58 per cent. Criterion validity: Significant relationships	Only tested in American samples. Designed for use in a higher education context and not in other specific settings among different age groups (e.g. workplace, adult basic education). Because of the few studies that have used this scale, there is a need to further assess the reliability of the PRO-SDLS.

Table 5.2 continued

Instrument	Approach	Definition	Subscales	Validity	Limits
		which the learner demonstrates the ability and/ or willingness to take control and initiative for planning, implementing and evaluating the learning process.	to my reasons for attending college'). (2) TLT (α = .83): (2a) Exhibiting control of the learning situation (six items; α = .78) (e.g. 'I always effectively organise my study time'). (2b) Demonstrating initiative (six items; α = .81) (e.g. 'I often use materials I've found on my own to help me in a course'). PRO-SDLS's reliability has been consistent across studies (α = .91, Fogerson, 2005; α = .84, .87, Hall, 2011; α = .88, Holt & Brockett, 2012).	($ps < .01$) were found between PRO-SDLS scores and age, self-reported grade point average (GPA), previously completed semester hours, with a shared variance accounted for by PRO-SDLS total scores ranged from 21 per cent for GPA to 5 per cent for course performance. Convergent validity: No significant relationship between self-reported PRO-SDLS scores and professor ratings ($N = 22$). Significant relationship between initiative item scores and professor ratings ($r = .56$, $p < .05$). Incremental validity: PRO-SDLS added significant unique variance above and beyond scores from the SDLRS in predicting GPA (squared semi-partial $r = .14$, $p < .01$) and course performance (squared semi-partial $r = .03$, $p < .05$).	

The MSLQ (McKeachie & Pintrich, 1984; Pintrich & De Groot, 1990; Pintrich, Smith, Garcia & McKeachie, 1993) includes 81 items which refer to motivational (expectancy, value and affect), cognitive and meta-cognitive dimensions. This instrument served as the basis for the development of the MOSLISB-BBS for use in a company setting (Nenniger & Wosnitza, 1995; Straka & Spevacek, 1995). As a consequence, the two scales show high similarity. However, the MOSLISB-BBS contains specific aspects related to the work environment.

The ASI (Entwistle & Ramsden, 1983) has been one of the most widely used questionnaires on student learning in higher education. Since its development, the ASI has been revised several times to create the 'Revised Approaches to Studying Inventory' (RASI) (Tait & Entwistle, 1996) and more recently the 'Approaches to Learning and Studying Inventory' (ALSI) (Entwistle, McCune, & Hounsell, 2003). The ALSI questionnaire contains 36 items that covers five dimensions: deep approach, monitoring studying, surface approach, organised studying and effort management.

The ILS further builds on the first inventories developed in the 1970s and 1980s. These inventories incorporated motivational and cognitive aspects of learning. Vermunt (1996) provided a more comprehensive view of learning by integrating meta-cognitive regulation strategies and learning conceptions as dimensions (Entwistle & McCune, 2004; Vanthournout, Donche, Gijbels, & Van Petegem, 2013; Vermunt & Vermetten, 2004). The ILS contains 120 items and covers four learning dimensions: cognitive processing strategies, regulation strategies, conceptions of learning and orientations to learning (Vermunt, 1996).

Three important similarities can be pointed out between these instruments developed in higher education and those instruments in adult literature in which self-directedness is approached as an instructional process (and not as a personal characteristic). First, the majority of the instruments emphasise the meta-cognitive strategies in learning. Both MOSLISB-BBS and PRO-SDLS focus on the importance of personal control and strategies for self-directed learning. As Stockdale and Brockett highlight (2011), these concepts are related to constructs used in self-regulated learning literature (Schunk and Zimmerman, 2003). Second, if we compare ILS and MSLQ to MOSLISB-BBS and PRO-SDLS, we conclude that the motivational dimension is strongly highlighted. The learners' interest in the subject matter is viewed as an essential part of the learning process. We also notice that self-efficacy is included in both MSLQ and PRO-SDLS although in most instruments measuring learning strategies this competency perception is overlooked. Yet motivational and organisational literature clearly demonstrates the importance of self-efficacy in the process of self-regulation (Maurer, 2001). Finally, we observe that researchers in higher education and in adult education are interested in linking the measurement of learning strategies to the same outcome variables: (school or job) performance and (study or career) success.

We also observe dissimilarities. First, contrary to research in higher education, research in adult education emphasises the importance of the personal characteristics component in the measurement of self-direction. Measurement instruments in this field, which focus exclusively or partly upon the 'self-direction as a personal characteristic' approach (SDLRS, Continuing Learning Inventory, SDLO, PRO-SDLS), measure, in a more refined way, (several) aspects of the self-directed learner. Second, the measurement instruments in higher education often measure learning strategies on a different level from the measurement instruments developed in adult education. In higher education, the instruments generally measure learning strategies on the level of a course or study task. In that way, researchers are able to measure whether students' learning strategies vary by subject matter (e.g. mathematics, science), type of study task or across grade level. In adult education, instruments generally measure learning strategies from a broader scope (span of a learning trajectory, learning project) or measure learning strategies from a general perspective. Third, instruments developed in the field of higher education only tend to measure strategy use in school based, book oriented contexts (Vermunt & Vermetten, 2004) while the instruments in adult education measure learning strategies in more varied contexts of learning: formal adult education contexts and informal contexts (workplace, leisure time). Stockdale (2003) for example developed an instrument for use in formal adult education while Raemdonck et al. (2008) measure self-direction for use in a workplace context. Researchers in higher education do not take into account that students also learn in other then formal contexts and that the learning patterns outside formal settings might be characterised differently. Kirby, Knapper, Evans, Carty and Gadula (2003), for example, claimed that academic learning encourages learners to understand relatively abstract information from different disciplines and to make connections among them in a relatively well-structured context. Learning outside the context of formal learning might better encourage critical and creative thinking in response to ill-defined problems. Consequently, certain approaches to learning might be more necessary and desirable than in school while other approaches might be present in all contexts. Therefore, understanding the learning strategies of students in informal contexts might become more important for researchers in higher education in the light of 21st century learning environments. Instruments for measuring learning patterns in higher education should consider the diversity of contexts in which learning takes place by systematically including an 'environment perceptions' dimension.

Concluding remarks

Because people learn and develop throughout adulthood in settings that are formal and informal in nature, characteristics of adult learning patterns have been connected with self-directedness in this chapter. This chapter describes self-directedness in learning as a learning pattern preparing and strengthening people for continuous learning in the 21st century. We overviewed the various conceptualisations found in adult education literature and the different approaches and measurement instruments were examined.

What can higher education practice learn from these insights drawn up in adult education literature? How can the knowledge, models and instruments generate insights that inform us about the learning of adults entering into higher education in later life?

First, higher education settings should take into account the characteristics of adult learners. Boekaerts and Minnaert (1999, pp. 537–538) have drawn attention to the fact that the adult learner's appraisal of a specific learning environment may affect the quality of their learning process and their learning outcomes. Adult learners need to identify with the goals and instructional methods in each specific learning context. The same learning context might be interpreted differently by different adult learners. Moreover, as adults bring a lot of informal learning experiences into the classroom, we need to know the processes that make up self-direction in this type of learning setting and whether different learning patterns are demonstrated when learning in formal or informal contexts as this might affect their learning intention and engagement. This information is essential for the design of optimal learning environments for adult students in higher education. According to Boekaerts and Minnaert (1999) teachers should encourage adult students to apply the learning strategies they use with ease outside the context of higher education, instead of imposing ways of learning that are believed to be generally effective.

Second, other contexts of learning in adult life often give adults more freedom of choice, which is different from formal learning (Boekaerts & Minnaert, 1999). Self-directedness, in its true meaning, only occurs when the learner is able to set his own goals instead of entering into externally assigned goals (which is often the case in higher education). As stated previously in this paper, it is often a triggering event in the life course of the adult that serves as the impetus and motivational factor for engaging in self-directed learning (Spear & Mocker, 1984). Therefore, adult students have a better chance of developing their own goals in accordance with their true needs when they are able to learn in realistic contexts (Boekaerts & Minnaert, 1999, p. 542). Authentic learning contexts in higher education might prompt true self-directedness of adult students in that way.

Third, the models and related measurement instruments of self-directedness in learning developed in the field of adult education strongly emphasise the importance of 'motivation', either conceptualised as a dimension of the learning process or as a characteristic of the self-directed person. This strong emphasis is in line with the literature on self-regulated learning in educational psychology. Many researchers in that field (e.g. Boekaerts, 1999; Deci & Ryan, 1985; Winne, 2005) emphasised motivational control as a key element of self-regulation, although a lot of investigations have been restricted to the meta-cognitive control system. In the light of continuous lifelong learning, research on motivational control might be especially valuable to put on the future research agenda.

And finally, if we want to have an understanding of how learning patterns evolve over the lifespan and which learning components are resilient to change and which not (see Vanthournout, 2011), researchers need to come up with fine-grained measurement instruments that are able to grasp changes in learning patterns across time and learning contexts in a valid way. Cross-boundary research between disciplines such as educational psychology, educational sciences, adult education and neuroscience enhances the sharing of expertise on using and integrating different conceptual models, methodological approaches and research findings on learning patterns in transition. Only then can information on how learning patterns in the 21st century evolve within and between persons be gained.

References

Bandura, A. (1997). *Self-efficacy: The exercise of control.* New York, NY: Freeman.

Bartlett, J.E., & Kotrlik, J.W. (1999). Development of a self-directed learning instrument for use in work environments. *Journal of Vocational Educational Research, 24*(4), 185–208.

Bateman, T.S., & Crant, J.M. (1993). The proactive component of organizational behaviour: A measure and correlates. *Journal of Organizational Behavior, 14*, 103–118.

Binder, R., & Nenniger, P. (1998). *A structural model of motivated self-directed academic learning: Results of a validation study.* Paper presented at the 23th International Improving University Learning and Teaching Conference, Dublin, Ireland.

Boekaerts, M. (1999). Self-regulated learning: Where we are today. *International Journal of Educational Research, 31*(6), 445–457.

Boekaerts, M. (2006). How far have we moved toward the integration of theory and practice in self-regulation? *Educational Psychology Review, 18*(3), 199–210.

Boekaerts, M., & Minnaert, A. (1999). Self-regulation with respect to informal learning. *International Journal of Educational Research, 31*, 533–544.

Bonham, L.A. (1991). Gugliemino's Self-directed Learning Readiness Scale: What does it measure? *Adult Education Quarterly, 41*(2), 92–99.

Brockett, R.G. (1985). Methodological and substantive issues in the measurement of self-directed learning readiness. *Adult Education Quarterly, 36*, 15–24.

Brockett, R.G., & Hiemstra, R. (1991). *Self-direction in adult learning: Perspectives on theory, research, and practice.* London: Routledge.

Brockett, R.G., Stockdale, S.L., Fogerson, D.L., Cox, B.F., Canipe, J.B., Chuprina, L.A., et al. (2000, February). *Two decades of literature on self-directed learning: A content analysis.* Paper presented at the International Self-directed Learning Symposium. Florida (ERIC document No ED449348).

Buhl Conn, A. (2000). *Self-directed learning in the workplace.* Unpublished doctoral dissertation, University of Maryland.

Caffarella, R.S., & Caffarella, E.P. (1986). Self-directedness and learning contracts in adult education. *Adult Education Quarterly, 36*(4), 226–234.

Candy, P.C. (1991). *Self-direction for lifelong learning. A comprehensive guide to theory and practice.* San Francisco, CA: Jossey-Bass.

Chu, R.J., & Tsai, C.C. (2009). Self-directed learning readiness, Internet self-efficacy and preferences towards constructivist internet-based learning environments among higher aged adults. *Journal of Computer Assisted Learning, 25*(5), 489–501.

Confessore, G.J., Long, H.B., & Redding, T.R. (1993). The status of self-directed learning literature, 1966-1991. In H.B. Long & Associates (Eds.), *Emerging perspectives of self-directed learning* (pp. 45–56). Norman, OK: Oklahoma Research Center for Continuing Professional and Higher Education of the University of Oklahoma.

De Bruin, K., & De Bruin, G.P. (2011). Development of the Learner Self-Directedness in the Workplace Scale. *SA Journal of Industrial Psychology/SA Tydskrif vir Bedryfsielkunde, 37*(1), 1–10.

Deci, E.L., & Ryan, R.M. (1985). *Intrinsic motivation and self-determination in human behavior.* New York, NY: Plenum Press.

Deci, E.L., & Ryan, R.M. (2000). What is the self in self-directed learning? In G.A. Straka (Ed.), *Conceptions of self-directed learning: Theoretical and conceptual considerations* (pp. 75–92). New York, NY: Waxman.

De Fruyt, F., Bartels, M., Van Leeuwen, K.G., De Clercq, B., Decuyper, M., & Mervielde, I. (2006). Five types of personality continuity in childhood and adolescence. *Journal of Personality and Social Psychology, 91*(3), 538–552.

Delahaye, B.L., Limerick, D.C., & Hearn, G. (1994). The relationship between andragogical and pedagogical orientations and the implication for adult learning. *Adult Education Quarterly, 44*(4), 187–200.

Ellinger, A.D. (2004). The concept of self-directed learning and its implications for human resource development. *Advances in Developing Human Resources, 6*(2), 158–177.

Entwistle, N., & McCune, V. (2004). The conceptual bases of study strategy inventories. *Educational Psychology Review, 16*, 325–345.

Entwistle, N., McCune, V., & Hounsell, J. (2003). Investigating ways of enhancing university teaching-learning environments: Measuring students' approaches to studying and perceptions of teaching. In E. De Corte, L. Verschaffel, N. Entwistle, & J. van Merriënboer (Eds.), *Advances in learning and instruction series: Powerful learning environments: Unravelling basic components and dimensions* (pp. 89–107) Amsterdam: Pergamon.

Entwistle, N.J., & Ramsden, P. (1983). *Understanding student learning.* London: Croom Helm.

Field, L. (1989). An investigation into the structure, validity, and reliability of Guglielmino's Self-Directed Learning Readiness Scale. *Adult Education Quarterly, 39*(3), 125–139.

Field, L. (1991). Guglielmino's Self-Directed Learning Readiness Scale: Should it continue to be used? *Adult Education Quarterly, 41*(2), 100–103.

Fogerson, D.L. (2005). *Readiness factors contributing to participant satisfaction in online higher education courses.* Unpublished doctoral dissertation, University of Tennessee, Knoxville, TN.

Frese, M., & Fay, D. (2001). Personal initiative: An active performance concept for work in the 21st century. In B.M. Staw & R.M. Sutton (Eds.), *Research in organizational behavior* (pp. 133–187). Amsterdam: Elsevier Science.

Frese, M., Fay, D., Hilburger, T., Leng, K., & Tag, A. (1997). The concept of personal initiative: Operationalization, reliability and validity in two German samples. *Journal of Occupational and Organizational Psychology, 70*(2), 139–161.

Frese, M., & Zapf, D. (1994). Action as the core of work psychology: A German approach. In H.C. Triandis, M.D. Dunnette, & L. Hough (Eds.), *Handbook of industrial and organizational psychology* (Vol. 4, pp. 271–340). Palo Alto, CA: Consulting Psychologists Press.

Garrison, D.R. (1997). Self-directed learning: Toward a comprehensive model. *Adult Education Quarterly, 48*, 18–33.

Gijbels, D., Raemdonck, I., & Vervecken, D. (2010). Influencing work-related learning: The role of job characteristics and self-directed learning orientation in part-time vocational education. *Vocations and Learning, 3*(3), 239–255.

Gijbels, D., Raemdonck, I., Vervecken, D., & Van Herck (2012). Understanding work related learning: The case of ICT workers. *Journal of Workplace learning, 24*(6), 416–429.

Grow, G.O. (1991). Teaching learners to be self-directed. *Adult Education Quarterly, 41*, 125–149.

Guglielmino, L.M. (1977). Development of the Self-Directed Learning Readiness Scale. (Doctoral dissertation, University of Georgia, 1977). *Dissertation Abstracts International, 38*, 6467 A.

Habet, O., Segers, M., & Beausaert, S (2012). *Predicting employability: The role of employees' learning behavior and self-directed learning orientation.* Unpublished dissertation. University of Maastricht, Maastricht.

Hall, J. (2011). *Self-directed learning characteristics of first-generation, first-year college students participating in a summer bridge program.* Unpublished doctoral dissertation, University of South Florida, Tampa, FL.

Hiemstra, R. (1994). Self-directed adult learning. In T. Husen, & T.N. Postlethwaite (Eds.), *The international encyclopedia of education* (pp. 5394–5399). Oxford: Pergamon Press.

Holt, L., & Brockett, R.G. (2012). Self direction and factors influencing technology use: Examining the relationships for the 21st century workplace. *Computers in Human Behavior, 28*, 2075–2082.

Jackson, C. (1996). Managing and developing a boundaryless career: Lessons from dance and drama. *European Journal of Work and Organizational Psychology, 5*(4), 617–628.

Jossberger, H. (2011). *Toward self-regulated learning: Difficulties and opportunities.* Doctoral dissertation. Open University, Heerlen.

Kasworm, C.E. (2003). Setting the stage: Adults in higher education. In D. Kilgore, & P.J. Rice (Eds.), *Meeting the special needs of adult students: New directions for student services* (No.102, pp. 3–10). San Francisco, CA: Jossey-Bass.

Kirby, J.R., Knapper, C.K., Evans, C.J., Carty, A.E., & Gadula, C. (2003). Approaches to learning at work and workplace climate. *International Journal of Training and Development, 7*(1), 31–52.

Knowles, M.S. (1970). *The modern practice of adult education: Andragogy versus pedagogy.* New York, NY: Association Press.

Knowles, M.S. (1975). *Self-directed learning: A guide for learners and teachers.* New York, NY: Association Press.

Kolb, D. (1985). *Learning style inventory.* Boston, MA: McBer & Co.

Kubeck, J.E., Delp, N.D, Haslett, T.K., & McDaniel, M.A. (1996). Does job-related training performance decline with age? *Psychology and Aging, 11*, 92–107.

Lai, H.J. (2011). The influence of adult learners' self-directed learning readiness and network literacy on online learning effectiveness: A study of civil servants in Taiwan. *Educational Technology and Society, 14*(2), 98–106.

Long, H.B. (1991). Self-directed learning: Challenges in the study and practice of self-directed learning. In H.B. Long & Associates (Eds.), *Self-directed learning: Application and theory* (pp. 253–266). Athens, GA: Adult Education Department, University of Georgia.

Loyens, S.M.M., Magda, J., & Rikers, M.J.P. (2008). Self-directed learning in problem-based learning and its relationships with self-regulated learning. *Educational Psychology Review, 20*(4), 411–427.

MacKeracher, D. (2004). *Making sense of adult learning.* Toronto: University of Toronto Press.

Maurer, T.J. (2001). Career-relevant learning and development, worker age, and beliefs about self-efficacy for development. *Journal of Management, 27*, 123–140.

Marsick, V.J., & Watkins, K.E. (1990). *Informal and incidental learning in the workplace*. New York: Routledge.

McCrae, R.R., & Costa, P.T. (1999). A five-factor theory of personality. In L.A. Pervin, & O.P. John (Eds.), *Handbook of personality: Theory and research* (pp. 139–153). New York, NY: Guilford Press.

McCrae, R.R., & Costa, P.T. (2003). *Personality in adulthood: A five-factor theory perspective*. New York, NY: Guilford Press.

McKeachie, W.S., & Pintrich, P. (1984). *Motivated Learning Strategies Questionnaire (MLSQ)*. Unpublished manuscript. NCRIPTAL, The University of Michigan, Ann Arbor, MI.

Merriam, S.B., & Caffarella, R.S. (1991). *Learning in adulthood*. San-Francisco, CA: Jossey-Bass.

Mezirow, J. (1991). *Transformative dimensions of adult learning*. San Francisco, CA: Jossey-Bass.

Nenniger, P. (1999). On the role of motivation in self-directed learning: The 'two-shells-model of motivated self-directed learning' as a structural explanatory concept. *European Journal of Psychology of Education, 19*(1), 71–86.

Nenniger, P., Straka, G.A., Spevacek, G., & Wosnitza, M. (1996). Die Bedeutung motivationaler Einflussfaktoren für selbstgesteuertes Lernen. *Unterrichtswissenschaft, 3*, 250–265.

Nenniger, P., & Wosnitza, M. (1995). *Fragebogen zur Erfassung motivierten selbstgesteuerten Lerners in Schule und Betrieb. Version: Berufsbildende Schilen (MOSLISB-BBS)*. Landau: Zentrum für empriische pädagogische Forschung.

Nikitenko, G. (2009). *Correlational analysis of adult students' self-directed learning readiness, affective learning outcomes, prior electronic learning experience, and age in hybrid and online course-delivery formats*. Unpublished doctoral dissertation, University of San-Francisco, San Francisco, CA.

Oddi, L. (1984). Development of an instrument to measure self-directed continuing learning (Doctoral dissertation, Northern Illinois University). *Dissertation Abstracts International, 46* (01A), 49.

Owen, T.R. (2002). *Self-directed learning in adulthood: A literature review*. ERIC Document Reproduction Service No. ED461050.

Pintrich, P.R., & De Groot, E.V. (1990). Motivational and self-regulated learning component of classroom academic performance. *Journal of Educational Psychology, 82*(1), 33–40.

Pintrich, P.R., Smith, D.A.F., Garcia, T., & McKeachie, W.J. (1993). Reliability and predictive validity of the Motivated Strategies for Learning Questionnaire (MSLQ). *Educational and Psychological Measurement, 53*, 801–813.

Ponton, M.K., Derrick, M.G., & Carr, P.B. (2005). The relationship between resourcefulness and persistence in adult autonomous learning: *Adult Education Quarterly, 55*(2), 116–128.

Raemdonck, I. (2006). *Self-directedness in learning and career processes. A study in lower-qualified employees in Flanders*. Faculty of Psychology and Educational Sciences, Ghent University, Ghent.

Raemdonck, I., Croes, M., Van der Heijden, B., Segers, M., & Scheeren, J. (2011, May). *Employability of people working in education: Taking account of personal and organizational characteristics*. European Association of Work and Organizational Psychology 2011 conference, Maastricht, The Netherlands.

Raemdonck, I., Plomp, I., & Segers, M. (2008). Obsolete or up-to-date? The role of job characteristics and self-directed learning orientation. Paper presented at the 4th EARLI SIG 14 Learning and Professional Development Conference. 27–29 August, University of Jyväskylä, Finland.

Raemdonck, I., Tillema, H., De Kok, A., & Van der Wal, C. (2011, June). *Understanding occupational expertise of employees working in finance and in health care: Taking account of career phase, self-directed learning orientation and job characteristics*. ELSIN, Antwerp, Belgium.

Richardson, J.T.E. (1994). Mature students in higher education: I. A literature survey on approaches to studying. *Studies in Higher Education, 19*(3), 309–326.

Richardson, J.T.E. (1995). Mature students in higher education: II. An investigation of approaches to studying and academic performance. *Studies in Higher Education, 20*(1), 5–17.

Rønning, W.M. (2009). Adults, flexible students' approaches to studying higher education. *Scandinavian Journal of Educational Research, 53*(5), 447–460.

Schulz, M., & Roßnagel, C.S. (2010). Informal workplace learning: An exploration of age differences in learning competence, *Learning and Instruction, 20*, 383–399.

Schunk, D.H., & Zimmerman, B.J. (2003). Self-regulation and learning. In W.M. Reynolds & G.E. Miller (Eds.), *Handbook of psychology: Vol. 7. Educational psychology* (pp. 59–78). New York, NY: Willey.

Seibert, S.E., Kraimer, M.L., & Crant, J.M. (2001). What do proactive people do? A longitudinal model linking proactive personality and career success. *Personnel Psychology, 54*, 845–874.

Spear, G.E., & Mocker, D.W. (1984). The organizing circumstance: Environmental determinants in self-directed learning. *Adult Education Quarterly, 35*(1), 1–10.

Stine-Morrow, E.A.L., Shake, M.C., Miles, J.R., & Noh, S.R. (2006). Adult age differences in the effects of goals on self-regulated sentence processing. *Psychology and Ageing, 21*(4), 790–803.

Stockdale, S. (2003). *Development of an instrument to measure self-directedness. Dissertation Abstracts International, 59* (6A), 1969 (UMI No. 3092836).

Stockdale, S., & Brockett, R.G. (2011). Development of the PRO-SDLS: A measure of self-direction in learning based on the Personal Responsibility Orientation Model. *Adult Education Quarterly, 61*(2), 161–180.

Straka, G.A. (1997) Self-directed learning in the world of work. *European Journal of Vocational Training, 12*, 83–88.

Straka, G.A., & Nenniger, P. (1996) A conceptual framework for self-directed learning readiness. In H.B. Long & Associates (Eds.), *New dimensions in self-directed learning* (pp. 243–255). Norman, OK: Public Managers Center University of Oklahoma.

Straka, G.A., Nenniger, P., Spevacek, G., & Wosnitza, M. (1996). Motiviertes selbstgesteuertes Lernen in der kaufmännischen Erstausbildung – Entwicklung und Validierung eines Zwei-Schalen-Modells. *Zeitschrift für Berufs- und Wirtschafts-pädagogik, Beiheft, 13*, 150–163.

Straka, G.A., & Spevacek, G. (1995). *Fragebogen zur Erfassung motivierten selbstgesteuerten Lernens in Schule und Betrieb. Version Betrieb (MOSLISB-BET).* Bremen: Forschungsgruppe LOS, Universität Bremen.

Tait, H., & Entwistle, N. (1996). Identifying students at risk through ineffective study strategies. *Higher Education, 31*, 97–116.

Taris, T.W., & Kompier, M.A.J. (2005). Job characteristics and learning behavior: Review and psychological mechanisms. In P.L. Perrewé, & D.C. Ganster (Eds.), *Research in occupational stress and well-being: Exploring interpersonal dynamic* (Vol. 4, pp. 127–166). Amsterdam: JAI Press.

Tough, A.M. (1971). *The adults' learning projects.* Toronto: Ontario Institute for Studies in Education.

Truluck, J.E, & Courtenay, B.C. (1999). Learning style preferences among older adults. *Educational Gerontology, 25*(3), 221–236.

Vanthournout, G. (2011). *Patterns in student learning. Exploring a person-oriented and a longitudinal research-perspective.* Antwerp: Garant.

Vanthournout, G., Donche, V., Gijbels, D., & Van Petegem, P. (2013). (Dis)similarities in research on learning approaches and learning patterns. In D. Gijbels, V. Donche, J.T.E. Richardson, & J.D. Vermunt (Eds.), *Learning patterns in higher education: Dimensions and research perspectives*. London: Routledge.

Vermunt, J.D. (1996). Metacognitive, cognitive and affective aspects of learning styles and strategies: A phenomenographic analysis. *Higher Education, 31*, 25–50.

Vermunt, J.D. (2005). Relations between student learning patterns and personal and contextual factors and academic performance. *Higher Education, 49*, 205–234.

Vermunt, J.D., & Vermetten, Y.J. (2004). Patterns in student learning: Relationships between learning strategies, conceptions of learning, and learning orientations. *Educational Psychology Review, 16*(4), 359–384.

Winne, P.H. (2005). A perspective on state-of-the-art research on self-regulated learning. *Instructional Science, 33*(5/6), 559–565.

Student teachers' learning patterns in school-based teacher education programmes

The influence of person, context and time

Maaike D. Endedijk, Vincent Donche and Ida Oosterheert

Introduction

One of the key tasks of teacher education is to support student teachers to develop a way of learning that enables lifelong learning (Hagger et al. 2008). In order to design teacher education programmes to foster this development, scientific knowledge is needed about student teachers' learning patterns, the influencing factors and how student teachers' learning patterns develop over time. Previous research on learning patterns has focused predominantly on understanding individual differences in academic learning in higher education contexts (Vermunt and Vermetten 2004). In this way, 'academic' learning patterns have been widely investigated in first year higher education contexts and to some extent in teacher education programmes (Donche and Van Petegem 2009). The vast body of research has indicated that these learning patterns are relatively dynamic factors and are influenced by several personal and contextual factors, which to some extent can explain why students' learning patterns can be adaptive across time (Donche et al. 2010; Richardson 2011; Vermunt and Vermetten 2004). Further details on this body of research can also be found in the preceding chapters of this monograph on student learning in higher education (see also Vanthournout et al., this volume). In this chapter, we focus on students' learning patterns in teacher education programmes, which, in contrast with other university contexts and study programmes, have received far less attention.

In the past decade, evidence has been growing that student teachers' learning patterns are more diverse than what previous student learning models regarding academic learning were able to capture (e.g., Cassidy 2004; Lonka et al. 2004; Vermunt and Vermetten 2004). Many of these former student learning models have neglected the fact that many students in diverse higher education contexts not only learn by studying course materials but also learn, for instance, through experiential learning when involved in internships or practice placements – for example, in teacher education (Korthagen et al. 2006; Tryggvason 2009).

More than a decade ago, Oosterheert (2001) started all over again to question how student teachers learn, working on the assumption that student teachers could not only learn by studying course materials but also by being involved in internships in which many sources of regulation for learning can be distinguished, such as mentors, pupils and co-workers (Oosterheert and Vermunt 2001). Based upon phenomenography and subsequent survey research using the Inventory Learning to Teach Process (ILTP), a framework for studying individual differences in learning to teach during internships could be validated. Not only could different dimensions in student teacher learning be distinguished but the presence of learning patterns was also investigated. This study has led to a rich account of how student teachers learn and indicates the presence of different learning patterns, which we will discuss below.

In the last five years, multiple cross-sectional and longitudinal studies across different countries have been carried out using the same ILTP questionnaire. These studies have been partially replicating the original ILTP studies but have also expanded the explanatory framework regarding personal and contextual factors, as well as further investigating how variable these learning patters are across time. By describing, examining and comparing the results of these studies, we aim to present in this chapter an integrative framework for describing individual differences in how student teachers learn to teach and how their learning patterns are related to various personal and contextual variables and how these learning patterns develop over time.

All studies that are included in this overview have been selected based on three overarching criteria by which the comparability across studies can be increased: (1) the explicit use of the conceptual framework of Oosterheert regarding student teacher learning; (2) the use of the ILTP questionnaire as the main data collection tool to distinguish dimensions or patterns of student teacher learning; and (3) evidence that the scientific outcomes of these studies have been peer reviewed, either through publication in a scientific journal, presented as a conference paper or published as an academic dissertation. In Table 6.1, an overview can be found of these different studies, including details on the research contexts, designs, respondents and key variables and measurement instruments.

This chapter is organised as follows. In the first section, we describe the different dimensions and learning patterns found in the first ILTP studies carried out by Oosterheert (2001). In the second section, we focus on the development and characteristics of the instrument (ILTP) that is commonly used across all included studies to measure individual differences in learning to teach. In the following sections, we briefly describe the design and main outcomes of all recent ILTP studies. We first describe studies that have contributed to the further validation of the ILTP by describing the validation in Belgium, the concurrent validity by relating the outcomes of the ILTP to other measurements of learning and some studies contributing to the predictive validity by describing the relation between the outcomes of the ILTP and other measures. Second, we address ILTP studies in which changes over time in learning patterns were measured. Third, we provide an overview of relations between student teachers' learning patterns and person-related variables. Finally, we discuss the results of studies in which context-related variables were also included, such as the

Table 6.1 Overview of studies discussed in this chapter and their characteristics

Study	Context	Participants	Design	Other relevant variables included (instrument)
Oosterheert et al. (2002a)	Three programmes in The Netherlands: teacher education programmes for primary school teachers and secondary school teachers: professional bachelor and master's programmes	382 student teachers	One ILTP measurement: students with at least two months experience in independent teaching	Big Five (BSBBS-25), Self-esteem Scale II, Perception of learning environment (Constructive Communicative Press & Relating Conceptual Information), general background variables
Donche and Van Petegem (2005)	Pre-service teacher education programme, Belgium: professional bachelor education	366 third year (final year), pre-service student teachers (86 pre-primary/ kindergarten, 130 primary, 150 lower secondary)	One measurement: start of second semester, final year	Preferences for teaching environments (connectedness to pupils interests and experiences, constructive and cooperative learning environment, discovery-oriented learning environment)
Donche and Van Petegem (2007)	Pre-service teacher education programme, Belgium: professional bachelor education	254 third year (final year) pre-service teachers	Two waves: beginning and end of second semester	
Donche et al. (2009)	Pre-service and partly in-service teacher education programme, Belgium: academic initial teacher education programme	195 student teachers	Two cohorts, cross-sectional end of second semester of final year	Academic motivation through the lens of self-determination theory (Academic Self-Regulation Questionnaire and Academic Motivation Scale), self-efficacy and general background variables
Hooreman (2008)	Pre-service teacher education programme (professional bachelor) for lower secondary education in The Netherlands	60 student teachers	One measurement	Quality of the pedagogical action (Fontys' competence assessment inventory)
Endedijk (2010); Endedijk et al. (in press); Endedijk and Vermunt (2013)	Pre-service teacher education programme, The Netherlands: one-year postgraduate programme for upper secondary school teachers, all subjects (academic master's)	81 student teachers	Three waves: after three, six and nine months of the one-year (=10 months) programme.	Concrete learning activities measured from six learning experiences (Structured Learning Report), general background variables

perception of the learning environment and the influence of two different tracks of teacher education programmes.

Learning patterns of student teachers

Research into student learning over the last few decades has identified individual differences in how students learn in academic settings (Entwistle and McCune 2004; Richardson 2011). Reproduction-oriented learning and meaning-oriented learning have consistently been identified as the two main dimensions for describing these individual differences. In many teacher education programmes, student teachers learn from a combination of theoretical sources and sources in practice (professionals, their own teaching experience). Nowadays, teacher education programmes try to integrate learning in these two contexts as much as possible to overcome a theory–practice gap (Korthagen 2010). This means that qualitative differences in how student teachers learn are often related to how they are dealing with this combination of theory and practice (Buitink 2009; Hagger et al. 2008).

Oosterheert and Vermunt (2001) conducted three consecutive studies to develop a framework describing individual differences in learning to teach: one qualitative study followed by two quantitative studies. The studies took place in several Dutch dual pre-service teacher education programmes: these are teacher education programmes in which student teachers learn in parallel at the teacher education institute and in and from practice. This professional learning component is often designed as an internship but student teachers might also already have a (part-time) job as a teacher, including full teaching responsibilities. The framework describing individual differences in student teachers' learning is built from a combination of learning conceptions, learning activities and regulation activities, as well as emotion regulation. Student teachers' learning patterns were distinguished by using person-oriented data analyses on scales tapping individual differences in student teacher learning.[1] In the first study, in which student teachers' narratives were explored in a phenomenographic way, five qualitative different ways of learning to teach could be distinguished: survival oriented, closed reproduction oriented, open reproduction oriented, closed meaning oriented, and open meaning oriented. The survival-oriented learning pattern described student teachers holding tenaciously to their own field experience and scarcely being able to report on self-regulation. The other four learning patterns differed in whether they were meaning oriented or reproduction oriented and how they approached their problems: whether they acknowledged that they have a problem (open) or that the problem remains implicit (closed). In two follow-up studies, an inventory was developed (ILTP) to test these learning patterns on a larger scale (Oosterheert et al. 2002b). The existence of the initial learning patterns was confirmed, except for the open reproduction directed-oriented way of learning. In the cluster analysis, this learning pattern disappeared, since all students showed characteristics of this way of learning. Since the main distinction between the meaning-oriented patterns is whether student teachers are self-regulative in identifying and interpreting their problems and improving their teaching, or more dependent on others, the differences can be more clearly characterised with the distinction dependent versus independent meaning-oriented learning. This leads to the following description of four learning patterns (Oosterheert et al. 2002a).

1   *Inactive/survival-oriented learning pattern.* These student teachers stress that all one needs for learning to teach is a lot of teaching practice and experience. They do not appreciate the help of others in order to become aware of their teaching but also do not think that they should regulate their learning themselves. They rarely use the available sources in their learning environment and are very avoidant and not preoccupied with bad lesson experiences.

2   *Reproduction-oriented learning pattern.* These student teachers are focused on improving their teaching performance within their actual frame of reference. They are not directed at further developing this frame of reference, resulting in a limited use of available sources. They acknowledge bad lesson experiences and have serious worries about these.

3   *Dependent meaning-oriented learning pattern.* These student teachers try to extend their frame of reference and depend on external sources in doing so, which they highly value. They do not rely much on their own perceptions and thinking yet; others have to help them to interpret their experiences. They are extremely preoccupied with their bad teaching experiences.

4   *Independent meaning-oriented learning pattern.* These student teachers are most independent in learning to teach: they try to develop their frame of reference, make broad use of external sources and are highly self-regulative. They define problems of learning to teach not only as problems of performance, but also of meaning. On average, they are not very preoccupied with bad lesson experiences.

Measuring student teachers' learning patterns: the ILTP

Construction of the ILTP

An important starting point for the measurement of student teachers' learning patterns was the phenomenographic study conducted by Oosterheert and Vermunt (2001) in which 30 in-depth interviews were carried out. The study revealed a rich description of individual differences in learning to teach (Oosterheert and Vermunt 2001). In the next step, the interview statements of the student teachers were used to develop the items of the first version of a closed-ended and self-report questionnaire, resulting in a set of 103 items (Oosterheert et al. 2002b). In the pilot study, a total of 169 student teachers participated. Exploratory factor analysis on the survey data led to the removal of weak items and the identification of eight scales: one scale measuring a mental model; five learning activities scales; and two emotion regulation scales. Cluster analyses on the scores of these scales showed four clusters of learners (survival, closed reproduction, and dependent and independent meaning-orientated learning). In a subsequent survey study, a version of 67 items was administered to 382 student teachers. Exploratory factor analyses resulted in the removal of weak items. This time, a factorial structure of three factors describing different mental models was found in addition to five factors describing learning activities and two factors describing emotion regulation. The latter two were comparable with previous research findings. Cluster analysis showed the same outcomes as in the previous studies. Based upon these studies, the ILTP emerged and this version has also been used unaltered in the subsequent studies that are reported in this chapter.

Structure of the ILTP

The ILTP is a 52-item questionnaire with ten scales that cover learning conceptions, learning activities (including regulation activities and concerns) and emotion regulation. The reliability of these scales varied in the different studies but was satisfactory (Cronbach's alphas above .60). An overview of the scales and sample items are given in Appendix A. These scales will be described in more detail below (Oosterheert et al. 2002a).

Three scales measure different learning conceptions. *Practising and testing* consists of nine items. When student teachers score highly on this scale, they conceptualise learning to teach as practising while obtaining concrete teaching suggestions in practice, finding out what works and what does not. The primary role of teacher educators is to give them these practical suggestions. *Strong self-determination in performance improvement* is a three-item scale. This dimension reflects a high preference by student teachers for self-regulation in determining what they need to improve in their teaching. The last scale, *Raising consciousness under external control*, contains seven items. This scale mirrors the student teachers' desire that others help make them aware of their own teaching behaviour, how it might be improved and how teaching situations could be interpreted.

The learning activities, including cognitive and regulation activities, are measured with five different scales. *Proactive, broad use of the mentor* has six items and the scale measures the extent to which student teachers use their mentor not only for practical suggestions but also for interpreting teaching situations. The second scale, *Independent search for conceptual information*, uses five items to measure to what extent student teachers recognise a problem and are independent and proactive in their search for conceptual information. The next dimension, *Actively relating theory and practice*, contains five items and refers to the activities that student teachers undertake to use conceptual information from others to interpret their own practice. The scale *Developing views/ideas through discussion*, refers to the intentional use of experienced colleagues by the student teachers in developing their ideas and vision on teaching and to gain insights into alternative teaching methods (five items). The last scale in this domain is the three-item scale *Pupil-oriented evaluation criteria*, which refers to the criteria student teachers use to evaluate their teaching. It captures the extent to which student teachers use their pupils' well-being or learning outcomes as a reference.

Two scales measure emotion regulation. The two components are *Avoidance* (five items) and *Preoccupation* (four items). Avoidance is a recoded scale that refers to the extent to which student teachers avoid or approach the unpleasant experience of bad lessons. If they score low and, as a consequence, show less avoidance behaviour on this dimension, they use negative lesson situations as a vital source of information for meaning making and learning. *Preoccupation* measures the extent to which students experience long and intense periods of worrying about negative teaching experiences. Others can have a role in taking their worries and low self-confidence away.

Scale scores and cluster analyses

The ILTP questionnaire provides scale scores on ten different and important facets of student teacher learning within three components of learning patterns: students' learning conceptions; learning and regulation activities; and emotion regulation. Students' learning patterns are usually distinguished in the data after carrying out cluster analyses techniques on the ten separate ILTP scales. Across all former ILTP studies the most typical learning patterns found are the survival oriented, reproduction oriented, dependent meaning oriented and independent meaning oriented cluster, as described above.

Further validation of student teachers' learning patterns measured with the ILTP

After the publication of the ILTP questionnaire in 2002, the questionnaire has been further validated in subsequent research. In 2005, a cross-sectional study was carried out by Donche and Van Petegem in which 366 third year student teachers from one institution in Belgium participated and filled in the questionnaire at the time they were involved in a long internship period at a secondary school. Student teachers from kindergarten, primary and secondary education participated in this study. In order to be able to compare the results with previous findings, the same data analysis techniques were used, such as exploratory factor analyses to ascertain the dimensional structure of the ILTP and cluster analyses (Ward's method) to map differences in learning patterns. The study confirmed the expected dimensional structure in the data and enabled the assessment of individual differences in student learning along three components and ten dimensions, capturing mental models of learning, cognitive and regulative activities and emotion regulation. Also, differences in learning patterns could be distinguished. In general, three out of the four expected learning patterns could be replicated: dependent meaning oriented, reproduction oriented and survival oriented. The outcomes of the study further supported the external validity of the ILTP questionnaire.

Endedijk and Vermunt (2013) further investigated the validity of the ILTP questionnaire by examining the relationship between the learning patterns measured by the ILTP and the concrete learning activities of student teachers at the university and in practice. This study showed that relations exist between learning patterns and actual learning activities of students when taking multiple concrete learning experiences of student teachers into account. The results showed that survival oriented student teachers are more inactive in their learning, reproduction oriented student teachers learn most by 'learning by doing' to improve their teaching behaviour, dependent meaning oriented student teachers are strongly influenced by previous negative experiences and independent meaning oriented student teachers show the most deep and the most active way of learning. Overall, the typology as described by Oosterheert (2001) was resembled in the relations of the learning patterns with the concrete learning activities. However, all learning activities were found to some degree among student teachers with all different patterns, meaning that at the level of the individual, student teachers' dissonant relations (Lindblom-Ylänne and Lonka 2000; Vermunt and Verloop 2000) were found. This study provides evidence for the concurrent validity of the ILTP.

The outcomes of learning to teach are quite hard to measure. Standardised tests, such as the traditional multiple-choice paper and pencil test have proven to be irrelevant for measuring teachers' classroom effectiveness (Darling-Hammond and Snyder 2000). Different forms of multi-perspective authentic assessments are promising, but still face many problems (Tillema 2009). Therefore, the predictive validity of the ILTP is hard to assess. Nevertheless, we would like to mention three ILTP studies that have shed some light on this phenomenon.

A study (Hooreman 2008) in which the ILTP was used to explain differential effects of synchronous coaching of 60 student teachers showed that learning patterns could predict whether a student teacher was suitable for synchronous coaching. Student teachers with a survival-oriented learning pattern did not respond positively to synchronous coaching. They preferred ad hoc solutions to problems and disliked being steered through a synchronous intervention. Trainee teachers with a dependent meaning-oriented learning pattern benefited most from being prompted synchronously, followed by reproductive and independent meaning-oriented learners. A second study (Donche and Van Petegem 2005) examined the relation between the learning patterns of 366 student teachers and their preferences for their future teaching environments. Three preferences for learning environments were found to be related to student teachers' learning patterns: (1) a preference for a learning environment in which pupils' interests and experiences are taken into account; (2) a learning environment in which constructive and cooperative learning is centralised; and (3) a learning environment in which discovery-oriented learning takes place and in which self-regulated learning is supported. The results indicated that dependent meaning-oriented student teachers prefer more constructive and cooperative learning environments which indicates a similarity between student teachers' own ways of learning and which learning they find important to stimulate in future teaching practice. Similarity between student teacher learning and their preference for teaching practice was also found in the group of survival-oriented student teachers. These student teachers, who make very little use of different sources of regulation when learning to teach, were also found to express considerably less preference for taking the interests and experiences of pupils into account and fostering discovery-oriented learning in their future teaching practice. The study provides evidence that student teachers' learning patterns are associated with preferences for learning environments and might be a valuable influencing factor for explaining differences in teaching practice.

In another study, Donche et al. (2009) explored whether teachers' sense of self-efficacy regarding their own teaching as developed through teaching practice during their internship could be predicted by the separate ILTP scales. In the study, 195 students from a university teacher education programme participated. Regression analyses results show that up to 28 per cent of the variance in student teachers' self-efficacy could be explained by students' motivational drive and the component of emotion regulation within the ILTP framework. Higher levels of self-efficacy regarding own teaching practice were found among students showing less preoccupation and avoidance behaviour.

In their study, Oosterheert et al. (2002a) measured the concerns of the student teachers: the extent to which they were focused on 'pupil discipline/classroom management', 'pedagogy' and 'pupil learning and motivation' (cf. Oosterheert 2001). A preoccupation with pupil discipline/classroom management appears to be least indicative of a particular learning pattern. In contrast, concerns about 'pedagogy' and 'pupil learning and motivation' were clearly associated with a particular learning orientation. Student teachers with a meaning orientation were found to be most concerned with 'pedagogy' and 'pupil learning and motivation' whilst student teachers with a survival/inactive orientation were not. The question, then, is whether concerns determine the way of learning or the way of learning determines the (range of) concerns? The former implies an automatic shift of concerns in connection with a changed way of learning. The latter suggests that a shift of concerns may not occur automatically in all student teachers. Given the characteristics of the four learning patterns and our knowledge on learning to teach, we are inclined to think that learning habits – including emotion regulation – determine the (range of) concerns of student teachers. 'Survival', then, is a very fundamental concern shared by all student teachers, whereas a concern for 'pupil learning' may require changes to the self and therefore not emerge automatically (Oosterheert and Vermunt 2003).

The development of student teachers' learning patterns

Although the original conceptual base of the ILTP regards student teacher learning patterns as dynamic rather than stable characteristics, longitudinal studies were lacking in this domain of research. In 2001, Oosterheert hypothesised that – under the right circumstances – if student teachers change their learning orientation, this will probably occur from survival or reproduction oriented towards dependent meaning oriented and ending in independent meaning-oriented learning. To move forward with this hypothesis, Donche and Van Petegem's study (2007) investigated whether students' learning patterns were more variable or stable across two measurement points. In this repeated measurement study, 253 final year student teachers from three different teacher education programmes (kindergarten, primary education and secondary education) from one institution in Belgium completed the ILTP twice during the final semester of their teacher education programme, once in the first phase of their internship and once during the last phase of their internship. In order to assess the variability of student teacher learning across time, inspections of changes on the ILTP scales as well as within the learning patterns were further investigated using paired-sample t-tests. The findings confirmed the expected variability across time within most of the ILTP scales. In particular, the scales tapping vital aspects of meaning-oriented learning showed most variability and mean scores on those scales were found to generally increase between the two measurement points in time. Scales measuring dimensions of emotion regulation were also found to be variable, reflected in decreasing trends in self-reported aspects of preoccupation and avoidance behaviour. From these results it was inferred that the long internship period might be influencing these trends. In the next step, the study addressed whether some learning patterns of student teachers might be subject to more change than others. Paired-sample t-tests were carried out and were conducted on the cluster samples distinguished in the pretest phase of the study and calculation of effect sizes took place. The results showed that changes were, in a sense, more sporadic for the dependent meaning-oriented and reproduction-oriented learning pattern in comparison with the survival-oriented learning pattern, which was found to be most subject to change across time. Differences in changes within the learning patterns across time could also be distinguished. The empirical study also gave a first indication that student teachers' learning patterns are relatively variable constructs across time.

Endedijk et al. (in press) studied intra-individual changes on the ILTP scales and of the learning patterns. Their study included 81 student teachers who were completing a one year postgraduate teacher education programme in The Netherlands. The ILTP was administered three, six and nine months after entering the programme. Longitudinal multilevel analyses of the ILTP scales showed no change over time for six scales. The learning conception scale, *Raising consciousness under external control*, decreased in the first half year and then slightly increased afterwards. *Independent search for conceptual information* increased over time. *Developing views/ideas through discussion* increased during the first half year and slightly decreased in the second semester. *Avoidance* increased over time. Only the increase of *Independent search for conceptual information* and *Developing views/ideas through discussion* support a development towards more independent meaning-oriented learning. On the other hand, the scales *Strong self-determination in performance improvement* and *Actively relating theory and practice*, which are also related to independent meaning-oriented learning, did not change over time. Analysis on the person-level outcomes in terms of the learning patterns showed that 37 per cent of the student teachers did not change their learning pattern throughout the programme. Thirty-four per cent of the student teachers changed their learning pattern in the direction of independent meaning-oriented learning, whilst 19 per cent moved away from it. An independent meaning-oriented learning orientation is regarded as essential in being prepared not only for academic learning but also for learning to teach and for further professional development (Bakkenes et al. 2010; Oosterheert 2001). This study showed that the majority of the student teachers did not change their learning towards this orientation during their programme.

Student teachers' learning patterns in relation to person-related variables

Oosterheert et al.'s (2002a) study also included several person-related variables. The 382 Dutch student teachers were also asked about several general characteristics and personality variables, such as the Big Five, their self-esteem and their tolerance of ambiguity. The student teachers with different learning patterns did not differ with respect to age, sex, the school discipline they taught, the number of hours they taught per week or their teaching experience outside the formal educational system. The fact that the amount of experience with independent teaching is *not* associated with a particular learning pattern suggests that learning patterns do not reflect different stages in the learning-to-teach programme (Oosterheert et al. 2002a).

Significant relations, however, were found when the learning patterns were related to the Big Five, self-esteem and tolerance of ambiguity. The outcomes showed that independent meaning-oriented learners scored highest on extraversion, emotional stability, openness to experience, tolerance of ambiguity and self-esteem. Dependent meaning-oriented learners scored lowest on extraversion, self-esteem, tolerance of ambiguity and emotional stability. Reproduction-oriented student teachers scored, together with their survival-oriented peers, lowest on openness to experience and they also scored low on tolerance of ambiguity. Survival-oriented learners scored average on most of these scales. No differences were found among the students with different learning patterns and their agreeableness and conscientiousness.

To further clarify the explanatory value of personal variables in relation to student teacher learning, Donche et al. (2009) explored whether individual differences in student learning are consistently associated with differences in academic motivation. In a cross-sectional study, 195 students from a university teacher education programme participated. In this study, dimensions of student teacher learning were measured by the ILTP and were related with differences in academic motivation. Academic motivation was assessed by means of the framework of self-determination theory (Deci and Ryan 2000), in which both the quality (autonomous and controlled motivation) and quantity of motivation as present in the construct a-motivation were taken into account. Structural equation modelling results show that a-motivation is a negative predictor for scales measuring meaning-oriented and reproduction-oriented aspects of teacher learning, such as developing one's own ideas based on discussions with others and using different sources of regulation (mentors and peers). Autonomous motivation positively predicts the extent to which students are using particular self-regulatory skills, such as searching for information in an independent way. Controlled motivation positively predicts aspects of preoccupation and avoidance behaviour. A-motivation was also found to be a positive predictor for avoidance behaviour. None of the estimated relationships between students' academic motivation and learning patterns were in conflict with theoretical expectations based on the self-determination theory. In this way, this study also provided more evidence of the construct validity of the ILTP. The findings support the relative importance of adding motivational aspects to the explanatory framework to further clarify why student teachers learn the way they do.

Student teachers' learning patterns in relation to context-related variables

Oosterheert et al.'s (2002a) study was the first to investigate the distribution of student teacher learning patterns across multiple types of teacher education programmes (cf. Oosterheert 2001): one-year postgraduate university programmes (UP) which prepare students for teaching in higher-level secondary schools; higher vocational education programmes (VP-sec) that prepare students for teaching in lower-level secondary schools; and higher vocational education programmes (VP-prim) that prepare students for teaching in primary schools. UP student teachers were more likely to have a dependent meaning or reproductive orientation when compared to the other student teachers. The four learning orientations were regularly distributed across the two types of VP students, with the exception being the independent meaning orientation, which was slightly more common among the VP-prim teachers. These differences may be related to the varying lengths of the programmes: the VP student teachers were in the last phase of a four-year programme whilst UP student teachers were about halfway through a one-year programme. The way in which UP student teachers learn may therefore be less consistent than the way VP student teachers learn. On the other hand, different pedagogies may have also have caused these differences.

Endedijk's (2010) study examined two different teacher education tracks within one university programme. Due to the shortage of teachers in The Netherlands, many student teachers following a university programme already have a job or have applied for a job when starting the teacher education programme. Therefore, the programme has a job track as well as an intern track. Student teachers who already have a job or applied successfully for a job follow the job track and start from the first day as a teacher at a secondary school. The other student teachers follow the internship track, in which they are gradually exposed to the teaching profession; they start observing their peer student teachers and experienced teachers, undergo their first teaching experiences and reflect on these together. In the second semester, the interns change schools and do the internship alone whilst taking on more responsibilities as a teacher, including an increase in the amount of lessons they teach. The content of the academic part of the programme is the same for both tracks. Differences were found between these two tracks: student teachers in the job track scored higher on actively relating theory and practice and developing views and ideas through discussion, scored lower on the learning conception that practising and testing is sufficient for learning to teach and they were less preoccupied with bad teaching experiences. Furthermore, student teachers with a job more often had a meaning-oriented learning orientation than interns, who were usually more reproduction oriented in their learning. On the other hand, students from the intern track were more likely to change their way of learning. Explanations for the differences found might point to the richness of the experience of student teachers with a job and the responsibilities they have and take on. In an internship, student teachers may, particularly in the first semester, not feel like a regular teacher but more like an observer whilst someone else is responsible for the pupils' learning (Endedijk 2010).

In Oosterheert et al.'s (2002a) study, student teachers were also asked about their perception of the teacher education programme. These results show very clearly that both types of meaning-oriented learners scored higher on the experienced 'constructive communicative press' and the extent to which the programme relates theory to practice. This means that these types of learners experience and appreciate more what the teacher education programme is doing to enhance their own learning.

Conclusion and discussion

In this chapter we aimed to provide a general overview of the main outcomes of past ILTP studies which have been carried out against the theoretical background of student teacher learning as described by Oosterheert (2001). These studies have shed further light on the ILTP as a valid tool for measuring student teacher learning and learning patterns and provided insights into (1) how student teachers' learning patterns are related to personal and contextual variables and (2) how these learning patterns develop over time. In what follows, we first summarise the most important conclusions and implications for further research in this field. We end this chapter with some reflections and suggestions for practice on how the ILTP can also be an important tool for enhancing student teacher learning and development.

Student teachers' learning patterns in relation to person, context and time

The set of studies presented in this chapter have shown that the ILTP is a valid tool for measuring student teacher learning in teacher education settings other than those in which the ILTP has been developed. However, not all learning patterns can always be found across all ILTP studies, including the independent meaning-oriented learning pattern. This may be due to contextual differences or sample size.

ILTP scale scores show meaningful relations with other measures such as student teachers' concrete learning activities, their preferences for their future teaching environments, their sense of self-efficacy of teaching and how they react to coaching interventions. This shows that the ILTP is a valid and reliable instrument to use, not only for further research, but also in helping practitioners predict how different types of learners behave in the various settings of their teacher education programmes. On the other hand, to determine the predictive validity of the ILTP, additional data about the quality of student teachers' teaching needs to be collected; for example, observation scores of their teaching behaviour in practice placements and the academic outcomes of their learning.

Two ILTP studies have clearly shown that learning to teach patterns are – just like academic learning patterns (Donche et al. 2010; Vermunt and Vermetten 2004) – not consistent over time. In general, student teachers appear to change towards more meaning-oriented learning during the programme but movement away from this learning pattern was also found. Most changes with respect to student teacher learning were found amongst survival-oriented students, which can be explained by the fact that this learning pattern can be regarded as a base level pattern; as soon as student teachers start developing their learning, they will change to another learning pattern. These two studies form only the first step in mapping the development of learning patterns in this context. Larger-scale studies in multiple programmes will hopefully make it possible to arrive at a deeper understanding of which personal and contextual factors evoke *changes* in learning patterns.

Several personal variables turned out to be related to the learning patterns. The personality variables as student teachers' motivation were different for the four types of learners. The differences between independent and dependent meaning-oriented learners in terms of their personality are particularly worth noting. Interventions for these student teachers to stimulate their quality of learning might therefore need to be adapted to their learning pattern in order to be effective.

The studies in which context-related variables were included showed that in different types of teacher education programmes different types of learners could be found. More research is needed to show whether this is related to the pedagogy of these programmes or that different types of learners enter these programmes. The results – that different types of learners perceive the same programme differently – is important information for teacher education institutes. Further research is needed to show to what extent student teachers actually benefit from dominant pedagogies within teacher education programmes and if more differentiation is needed.

In sum, we have pointed to the relevance of a selected set of empirical studies in which empirical evidence is mounting that shows the internal, external and concurrent validity of the ILTP. However, additional validation studies are needed to further determine the predictive validity of the ILTP. Also, the quality of the instrument in repeated measurements to measure changes over time in learning patterns should be further explored. Furthermore, a component that is not included in the ILTP is student teachers' motivation for learning to teach. The addition of this component might complete the picture of how and why student teachers learn to teach as they do. The ILTP is now focused on the individual learning process, whilst many teacher education programmes are presently using different forms of collaborative learning. How student teachers use various forms of informal and peer support might also be a valuable addition to the current framework. For practice, it would be helpful to develop a short version of the questionnaire that is easy to administer and to use in terms of follow-up of student teachers' quality of learning to teach. We hope that this overview will boost and inspire a next generation of studies with the ILTP. Currently, studies have been carried out using a German translation of the instrument and a translation in English has been made in order to test the validity of the ILTP in other cultural contexts. As has been said in the introduction, there is a general shortage of studies in contexts in which learning in practice is included. Therefore, we also see possibilities for adapting the ILTP framework for learning in medical education or other forms of professional higher education programmes.

Suggestions for practice

An important benefit of the ILTP framework is the small set of components and dimensions which enable important differences in learning of specific learner groups to be grasped. Very similar individual differences in student teacher learning, as measured with the ILTP, are consistently found in different teacher education contexts. The key dimensions of student teacher learning have been found to be associated with important outcome variables, such as concrete learning activities and student teachers' sense of self-efficacy in teaching. Also, the patterns appear to be subject to change. Therefore, it seems important to raise attention in teacher education programmes to the presence of these differences and to take these differences into account. Not all of the learning patterns are equally beneficial in becoming a teacher. Growing towards more active and meaning-oriented learning is necessary in becoming a teacher and in lifelong learning as a teacher (Bakkenes et al. 2010). Fortunately, learning patterns appear to be subject to change, which opens perspectives for all student teachers as they enter a teacher education programme. How can we address these differences? A common reaction is to think immediately of differential approaches to learning; different student teachers should be approached differently. We propose a three-step approach to addressing these differences. The first is to align education, the second is to design a curriculum in which there is some time to grow and the third is to help student teachers meet the expectations. We will close the chapter with making some remarks regarding the use of the ILTP in teacher education.

Aligning education

In an aligned curriculum there is a very strong relationship between the learning goals, the way student teachers are stimulated to learn and the way they are assessed (Biggs 1996). Within a year, topic or short period, the goals, instructions, means, feedback, guidance, lectures, assessment criteria and assessment forms are perfectly aligned. There is also full transparency for student teachers about this; they know where to strive for, how they can work towards it and they also know how assessors evaluate their knowledge and performance. As there is no greater impulse for learning than assessment (Biggs 1996; Frederiksen 1984), in an aligned curriculum the various learners will feel they *have to adapt* their learning behaviour in order to make progress. In meetings at the institute and in practice, they feel they have to learn to show new behaviour or engage in new activities (mental, emotional or physical) they would perhaps otherwise avoid or not initiate. So, the first step is to set the goals clearly (content *and* level!) and teach and assess accordingly; initial learning patterns of most student teachers will then be challenged without doing anything in particular for specific student teachers.

Time to grow

As they enter teacher education, not all student teachers show a meaning-oriented approach to their learning. A fully aligned meaning-oriented curriculum from the very start may therefore be too selective for potentially good teachers. Therefore, a certain gradual approach during the first year, for example, seems fairer. In curriculum design, the goals and standards should thus give room for different student teachers to still grow as learners. Meaning-oriented learning should be stimulated from the beginning but standards should not be too high immediately. To support student teachers in this growing process, they should be able to alternate practice and theory almost constantly; for example, in internships and from the very onset of the programme.

Differential guidance

What individual student teachers need in order to develop their skills and habits as learners depends on their initial predominant learning pattern(s). So, given a well-aligned curriculum and some time to grow as learners, the methods adopted to promote learning must vary from student to student. In our view, 'flexibility' and 'facilitation' should be the keywords for the approach of student teachers showing a predominantly independent meaning pattern. These student teachers are clearly virtually autodidactic and, as a result, do not need strong external regulation. They should not be obliged to follow strict rules with regard to the order in which they should think; reflection heuristics may impede their learning. What they do need is a wide variety of information sources, the opportunity to communicate with experts and the opportunity to teach. They need, like any other student teacher, encouragement and positive support from teacher educators and mentors during the process.

Student teachers with a dependent meaning pattern of learning typically need and welcome strong external support when it comes to sense-making activities such as the interpretation of their teaching experiences. As they do not (yet) rely sufficiently on their own insights, they need others to make them aware of their perceptions, interpret their perceptions and develop their perceptions of reality. They also need others to help them relate such information to their own experiences and thinking. Teacher educators must keep in mind that such student teachers often have low self-esteem and are relatively emotionally unstable. This calls for non-judgemental and positive communication which builds on and emphasises the strengths of such student teachers and encourages them to do more and more on their own accord. It is also then likely that these student teachers will develop into more independent thinkers and learners.

Student teachers with a reproductive learning pattern keep external resources at a distance when these are perceived as providing information which is not in accordance with their existing perceptions of reality or the goals they have stipulated for themselves. Teacher educators thus have the difficult task of carefully disrupting the comfortable equilibrium these student teachers have established for themselves. This can be done, for example, by confronting them with multiple perspectives on events, situations and developments. Given their personality characteristics, these learners need non-judgemental and cautious guidance. The use of a mixture of student teachers during constructive (institutional) activities can also be recommended for such student teachers. Immersed in these activities, their fellow students may unintentionally serve as role models when they overtly show their doubts and their struggles with interpretative dilemmas. Closed reproductive student teachers may also benefit from genuine (shared) responsibilities in a modern school and the alternative perspectives on reality such a school often provides.

The inactive/survival ways of learning can be understood both from their mental model of learning to teach as well as from other factors, such as personal situations (e.g. not enough time to study). When a student teacher does not think or cannot be 'permitted to' think that teaching must and can be learned, he or she must *experience* the opposite. Short and frequent tryouts in the classroom imposed by teacher educators accompanied with thorough observation and supportive feedback may be needed to give these student teachers the experience that shows them it makes a difference to make a real effort. They may first need to learn to change their practice without being concerned with knowledge construction beyond their existing frame of reference. Trying out something different in their teaching (without knowing beforehand if it will work well) is already a big step for these student teachers. Previously avoided situations may now cause feelings of uncertainty and anxiety. Extensive guidance is then needed for these student teachers, in particular in 'normalising' that experiments and tryouts will not all work out well. Also, guided discussions with these and other student teachers about their mental models of learning to teach and motivation for teaching may contribute to their change.

Using the ILTP in teacher education

Changing our way of learning is, in essence, changing our way of being in and approaching the world. It is a fundamental process. Therefore, in teacher education, it is of utmost importance to be clear on the one hand about what is needed to become a good teacher and on the other hand to be non-judgemental about the actual learning behaviour of student teachers. Learning behaviour should be seen as a first, dynamic adaptation of (most) students to a new learning context in which experiences are suddenly a valuable information source. In this respect, using individual ILTP scores as feedback information (in the context of assessment *for* learning) can have positive effects – it depends on how it is done and for what purpose. As the study of Donche et al. (2012) showed in the context of academic learning, the learning pattern of the student is also related to the kind of feedback the student prefers with respect to their quality of learning. In our view, the ILTP scores are not really *necessary* to know how individual student teachers learn (although handy as a starting point, just for teacher educators). More important is that teacher educators get to know student teachers as learners, from their weekly activities with them. The structure and dimensions of learning underlying the ILTP are a valuable framework for learning to recognise the behaviour of student teachers. During their activities with students, teacher educators can then detect mental models, activities, regulation patterns and emotion regulation in student teachers, so as to be able to say or do something 'just in time' to encourage or 'awaken' student teachers, possibly even without addressing individual student teachers explicitly. They can switch regularly from 'content' to 'how to learn this content', depending on what they see and hear (e.g. how to learn to recognise this theory in practice; what can you do). Also, then they can build on the underlying structure of the ILTP to discuss 'learning to teach as a process' with student teachers. *If ILTP scores are used to provide feedback or evoke some reflection on 'how do I learn at this moment?', then the feedback should be given non-judgmentally in the zone of proximal development of 'this student teacher at this moment'* (see above for a few suggestions).

Note

1 Originally, Oosterheert used the term 'learning orientations' to describe individual differences in student teacher learning. The concept of learning orientations, however, has also been used to refer to the motivational and volitional component of learning (Vermunt and Vermetten 2004). Nowadays, researchers have embraced the more neutral term of 'learning patterns' to refer to consistent relationships between cognitive, affective, regulative learning activities, beliefs about learning and learning motivations. Therefore, from this point forward we will also use the term 'learning pattern' for what Oosterheert called in her previous work 'learning orientations' (Oosterheert 2001; Oosterheert et al. 2002a, 2002b; Oosterheert and Vermunt 2001).

Appendix A

Examples of items of the Inventory Learning to Teach Report (Oosterheert, 2001)

Scale (number of items)	Example item
Learning conceptions	
Practising and testing (9)	Teacher educators should focus on giving practical tips and suggestions
Strong self-determination in performance improvement (3)	I am capable of signalling problems in my teaching
Raising consciousness under external control (7)	I appreciate it when teacher educators suggest which aspects of my teaching I should try to improve
Learning and regulation activities	
Proactive, broad use of the mentor (6)	I try to find out what information my mentor considers when deciding what to do in a specific situation

Independent search for conceptual information (5)	I try to find answers to my questions about teaching by consulting the literature on my own
Actively relating theory and practice (5)	I think I can do a lot with theory in my teaching experience
Developing views/ideas through discussion (5)	Through discussion with other teachers, I can further develop my ideas about education
Pupil-oriented evaluation criteria (3)	My satisfaction with a lesson is largely determined by the extent to which a good working climate occurs in the classroom

Emotion regulation	
Avoidance (recoded) (5)	When a lesson goes wrong, I prepare the next lesson more intensively
Preoccupation (4)	A lesson which went wrong keeps going through my head on at least the same day

References

Bakkenes, I., Vermunt, J. D. and Wubbels, T. (2010) Teacher learning in the context of educational innovation: Learning activities and learning outcomes of experienced teachers. *Learning and Instruction*, 20: 533–548.

Biggs, J. (1996) Enhancing teaching through constructive alignment. *Higher Education*, 32: 1–18.

Buitink, J. (2009) What and how do student teachers learn during school-based teacher education? *Teaching and Teacher Education*, 25: 118–127.

Cassidy, S. (2004) Learning styles: An overview of theories, models, and measures. *Educational Psychology*, 24: 419–444.

Darling-Hammond, L. and Snyder, J. (2000) Authentic assessment of teaching in context. *Teaching and Teacher Education*, 16: 523–545.

Deci, E. L. and Ryan, R. M. (2000) The 'what' and 'why' of goal pursuits: Human needs and the self-determination of behavior. *Psychological Inquiry*, 11: 227–268.

Donche, V., Coertjens, L. and Van Petegem, P. (2010) The development of learning patterns throughout higher education: A longitudinal study. *Learning and Individual Differences*, 20: 256–259.

Donche, V., Coertjens, L., Vanthournout, G. and Van Petegem, P. (2012) Providing constructive feedback on learning patterns: An individual learner's perspective. *Reflecting Education*, 8: 114–131.

Donche, V. and Van Petegem, P. (2005) Assessing preservice teachers' orientations to learning to teach and preferences for learning environments. *Scientia Paedagogica Experimentalis*, 17: 27–52.

Donche, V. and Van Petegem, P. (2007) *Developing student teacher learning: A longitudinal study.* Budapest, Hungary: European Association for Research on Learning and Instruction.

Donche, V. and Van Petegem, P. (2009) The development of learning patterns of student teachers: A cross-sectional and longitudinal study. *Higher Education*, 57: 463–475.

Donche, V., Van Petegem, P., Struyf, E. and Vanthournout, G. (2009) *The differential impact of motivation and approach to learning to teach on pre-service teachers' teaching efficacy.* Amsterdam, The Netherlands: European Association for Research on Learning and Instruction.

Endedijk, M. D. (2010) *Student teachers' self-regulated learning.* Utrecht: IVLOS, Utrecht University.

Endedijk, M. D. and Vermunt, J. D. (2013) Student teachers' learning patterns and their concrete learning and regulation activities. *Studies in Educational Evaluation*, 39: 56–65.

Endedijk, M. D., Vermunt, J. D., Meijer, P. C. and Brekelmans, M. (in press) Students' development in self-regulated learning in postgraduate professional education: A longitudinal study. *Studies in Higher Education.*

Entwistle, N. and McCune, V. (2004) The conceptual bases of study strategy inventories. *Educational Psychology Review*, 16: 325–345.

Frederiksen, N. (1984) The real test bias: Influences of testing on teaching and learning. *American Psychologist*, 39: 193–202.

Hagger, H., Burn, K., Mutton, T. and Brindley, S. (2008) Practice makes perfect? Learning to learn as a teacher. *Oxford Review of Education*, 34: 159–178.

Hooreman, R. W. (2008) *Synchronous coaching of trainee teachers – an experimental approach,* unpublished doctoral dissertation.

Korthagen, F. (2010) Situated learning theory and the pedagogy of teacher education: Towards an integrative view of teacher behavior and teacher learning. *Teaching and Teacher Education*, 26: 98–106.

Korthagen, F., Loughran, J. and Russell, T. (2006) Developing fundamental principles for teacher education programs and practices. *Teaching and Teacher Education*, 22: 1020–1041.

Lindblom-Ylänne, S. and Lonka, K. (2000) Dissonant study orchestrations of high-achieving university students. *European Journal of Psychology of Education*, 15: 19–32.

Lonka, K., Olkinuora, E. and Mäkinen, J. (2004) Aspects and prospects of measuring studying and learning in higher education. *Educational Psychology Review*, 16: 301–323.

Oosterheert, I. E. (2001) *How student teachers learn.* Groningen: UCLO.

Oosterheert, I. E., Vermunt, J. and Veenstra, R. (2002a) Manieren van leren onderwijzen en relaties met persoonsgebonden en contextuele variabelen [Orientations towards learning to teach and relations to personal and contextual variables]. *Pedagogische Studiën*, 79: 251–268.

Oosterheert, I. E. and Vermunt, J. D. (2001) Individual differences in learning to teach: Relating cognition, regulation and affect. *Learning and Instruction*, 11: 133–156.

Oosterheert, I. E. and Vermunt, J. D. (2003) Knowledge construction in learning to teach: The role of dynamic sources. *Teachers and Teaching: Theory and Practice*, 9: 157–173.

Oosterheert, I. E., Vermunt, J. D. and Denessen, E. (2002b) Assessing orientations to learning to teach. *British Journal of Educational Psychology*, 72: 41–64.

Richardson, J. T. E. (2011) Approaches to studying, conceptions of learning and learning styles in higher education. *Learning and Individual Differences*, 21: 288–293.

Tillema, H. H. (2009) Assessment for learning to teach. Appraisal of practice teaching lessons by mentors, supervisors, and student teachers. *Journal of Teacher Education*, 60: 155–167.

Tryggvason, M. T. (2009) Why is Finnish teacher education successful? Some goals Finnish teacher educators have for their teaching. *European Journal of Teacher Education*, 32: 369–382.

Vermunt, J. D. and Verloop, N. (2000) Dissonance in students' regulation of learning processes. *European Journal of Psychology of Education*, 15: 75–87.

Vermunt, J. D. and Vermetten, Y. J. (2004) Patterns in student learning: Relationships between learning strategies, conceptions of learning and learning orientations. *Educational Psychology Review*, 16: 359–384.

Part II

Measuring learning patterns and development

Chapter 7

Achievement goals, approaches to studying and academic attainment

John T. E. Richardson and Richard Remedios

Introduction

Interview-based research carried out in the 1970s demonstrated that students in higher education can adopt different approaches to their studies: a deep approach oriented towards the meaning of their course materials; a surface approach oriented towards being able to reproduce the materials for the purposes of assessment; and a strategic approach oriented towards obtaining the highest possible marks or grades. Subsequently, a wide variety of questionnaires have been devised to measure approaches to studying in larger numbers of students (see Richardson 2000 for a review).

Research has shown that the same students can exhibit different approaches to studying in different courses. This depends on their perceptions of the demands of different courses, the quality of the teaching and the nature of the assessment. Nevertheless, different students taking the same course may adopt different approaches to studying. This remains the case even when variations in their perceptions have been taken into account (see Sadlo and Richardson 2003). Perhaps students adopt one approach rather than another, depending on their motivation. In recent years, a specific theoretical framework has become influential in understanding motivation, that of achievement goals (see also Cano and Berbén, this volume).

This chapter is concerned with students' achievement goals and their relationships with approaches to studying and attainment. Most research on this topic has been concerned with young people who have recently gone straight from high school (secondary school) to college. However, as we shall explain, achievement goals may be different in adult learners. We are particularly interested in investigating achievement goals among adult learners taking courses of study by distance learning, for reasons that we discuss later.

Defining and measuring achievement goals

Diener and Dweck (1978, 1980) classified children as either mastery-oriented or helpless. Helpless children underestimated their own performance relative to that of mastery-oriented children and tended to ascribe their own failures to a lack of ability. Mastery-oriented children made fewer attributions but instead set about finding remedies for their failures. Failure led helpless children to devalue their performance but left mastery-oriented children undaunted.

Dweck and Elliott (1983; Dweck 1986) suggested that achievement motivation involved two kinds of goal: (a) learning goals (seeking to increase one's competence, understanding or mastery); and (b) performance goals (seeking favourable judgements or avoiding negative judgements of one's own competence from others). Dweck and Elliott argued that both kinds of goal could promote mastery-oriented behaviour. However, if confidence in one's ability was low, performance goals increased helpless behaviour and lowered motivation.

Ames and Archer (1988; Ames 1992) offered a similar account but referred to learning goals as 'mastery goals', which nowadays is the more common term. Grant and Dweck (2003) summarized the findings of early research as showing that 'those who adopt learning goals are found to engage in deeper, more self-regulated learning strategies, have higher intrinsic motivation, and perform better, particularly in the face of challenge or setbacks' (p. 543). Most of the early research on this topic was carried out with children, but this chapter is concerned with more recent research carried out with university students.

In the light of previous work on achievement motivation, Elliot and Harackiewicz (1996) divided performance goals according to whether they were oriented towards the attainment of success or the avoidance of failure, yielding three achievement orientations: mastery goals focused on the development of competence and task mastery; performance-approach goals focused on the attainment of favourable judgements of competence; and performance-avoidance goals focused on avoiding unfavourable judgements of competence. In experimental situations, Elliot and Harackiewicz found that performance-avoidance goals tended to reduce intrinsic motivation in comparison with the other two kinds of goal.

Elliot and Church (1997) carried out a further test of this model in the context of a course being taught at an American university. They found that mastery goals facilitated intrinsic motivation but not academic attainment; that performance-approach goals facilitated academic attainment but not intrinsic motivation; and that performance-avoidance goals impaired intrinsic motivation and academic attainment. Analogous results were obtained by Church et al. (2001), also in an authentic educational setting.

Elliot and McGregor (2001) applied the approach/avoidance distinction to mastery goals, leading to a 2 × 2 model of achievement goals. In this model, mastery approach goals represent the development of competence and task mastery, whereas mastery-avoidance goals represent a desire to avoid negative outcomes such as not completing a task fully. Performance-approach goals represent a desire to attain competence relative to others, whereas performance-avoidance goals represent the avoidance of demonstrating poor performance relative to others. Elliot and McGregor developed the Achievement Goal Questionnaire (AGQ) to measure the four kinds of goal. It contains three statements reflecting each kind of goal, and respondents are asked to indicate how true each item is of them on a seven-point scale from 'not at all true of me' (1) to 'very true of me' (7).

The relationships between achievement goals and approaches to studying

We identified 30 published studies that had investigated the relationships between students' achievement goals and their approaches to studying. Tables 7.1 and 7.2 summarize the findings with regard to deep and surface approaches to studying, respectively. The tables encompass studies that have adopted the dichotomous model, the trichotomous model, and the 2 × 2 model of achievement goals. They include studies that have employed measures of deep and surface processing, whether or not these were related to the specific concepts of deep and surface approaches. They also include research in both secondary and higher education.

Table 7.1 shows that there is a consistent relationship between students' adoption of mastery (approach) goals and their use of a deep approach to studying or deep processing. The study by Grant and Dweck (2003) found in addition that the adoption of mastery goals and the use of deep processing were both positively related to academic attainment. When variations in deep processing were statistically controlled, the relationship between mastery goals and attainment was no longer significant. Nevertheless, when variations in mastery goals were statistically controlled, the relationship between deep processing and attainment remained significant. Grant and Dweck inferred from this that the effect of mastery goals on academic attainment was mediated by variations in students' study strategies.

In other respects, however, the published studies do not yield a consistent picture of the relationship between achievement goals and approaches to studying. Why should this be the case? Hulleman et al. (2010) carried out a meta-analysis of the relationship between measures of achievement goals and academic attainment, and they concluded that different researchers were using the same labels for different constructs. For instance, some items that had been used to measure performance-approach goals focused on appearance (e.g. 'I feel successful if I show people I'm smart'), but others focused on normative evaluation (e.g. 'I try to do better in my courses than other students'). Again, some items that had been used to measure performance-avoidance goals included an affective component (e.g. 'My fear of performing poorly is what motivates me in this class'), whereas others did not.

Hulleman et al. found that the correlation coefficients among different achievement goals and between different achievement goals and measures of attainment depended on the kinds of items that were used to measure different

Table 7.1 The relationship between achievement goals and a deep approach to studying

Source	Mastery	Performance	Performance approach	Performance avoidance	Mastery approach	Mastery avoidance
Meece et al. (1988)	+					
Nolen (1988)	+	0				
Greene and Miller (1996)	+	0				
Miller et al. (1996, Study 1)	+	+				
Miller et al. (1996, Study 2)	+	0				
Wolters (1998)	+	−				
Fisher and Ford (1998)	+	−				
Dupeyrat et al. (1999)	+	0				
Elliot et al. (1999, Study 1)	+		0	−		
Elliot et al. (1999, Study 2)	+		0	−		
Somuncuoglu and Yildirim (1999)	+	0				
Harackiewicz et al. (2000)	+	0				
Vermetten et al. (2001)	+	0				
Elliot and McGregor (2001, Study 2)			0	−	+	0
Al-Emadi (2001)	+		+	0		
Zusho et al. (2003)	+	+				
Grant and Dweck (2003)	+	0				
Simons et al. (2004)	+					
Dupeyrat and Mariné (2005)	+	0				
Fenollar et al. (2007)	+		0	0		
Howell and Watson (2007)			+	0	+	0
Coutinho and Neuman (2008)			+	+	+	+
Sins et al. (2008)				0	+	
Liem et al. (2008)	+		+	0		
Senko and Miles (2008)	+		0	0		
Phan (2008)	+		+	+		
Phan (2009a)	+		0	0		
Phan (2009b)	+		0			
Phan (2009c)	+		0	0		
Phan (2010)	+		+	0		

Note: Studies are listed in chronological order of publication. +, statistically significant positive relationship with a deep approach; −, statistically significant negative relationship with a deep approach; 0, no significant relationship with a deep approach; blank, no relevant data.

Table 7.2 The relationship between achievement goals and a surface approach to studying

Source	Mastery	Performance	Performance approach	Performance avoidance	Mastery approach	Mastery avoidance
Meece et al. (1988)						
Nolen (1988)	+	+				
Greene and Miller (1996)	0	+				
Miller et al. (1996, Study 1)	+	+				
Miller et al. (1996, Study 2)	+	0				
Wolters (1998)	+	0				
Fisher and Ford (1998)	0	+				
Dupeyrat et al. (1999)	+	+				
Elliot et al. (1999, Study 1)	0		+	+		
Elliot et al. (1999, Study 2)	0		+	+		
Somuncuoglu and Yildirim (1999)	−	+				
Harackiewicz et al. (2000)	+	+				
Vermetten et al. (2001)	0	+				
Elliot and McGregor (2001, Study 2)			0	+	0	+
Al-Emadi (2001)	0		+	+		
Zusho et al. (2003)	+	0				
Grant and Dweck (2003)	0	+				
Simons et al. (2004)	−					
Dupeyrat and Mariné (2005)	0					
Fenollar et al. (2007)	0		+	0		
Howell and Watson (2007)			0	+	0	+
Coutinho and Neuman (2008)			+	+	+	+
Sins et al. (2008)				0	0	
Liem et al. (2008)	+		0	+		
Senko and Miles (2008)	+		0	0		
Phan (2008)	0		+	+		
Phan (2009a)	0		0	0		
Phan (2009b)						
Phan (2009c)	0		0	+		
Phan (2010)	+		+	0		

Note: Studies are listed in chronological order of publication. +, statistically significant positive relationship with a surface approach; −, statistically significant negative relationship with a surface approach; 0, no significant relationship with a surface approach; blank, no relevant data.

achievement goals. Nevertheless, Senko et al. (2011) subsequently found that the kinds of item did not seem to influence the correlation coefficients between different achievement goals and approaches to studying. Indeed, previous studies had yielded an inconsistent pattern of results, regardless of whether performance goals were measured using normative or non-normative statements.

An alternative explanation is that the inconsistencies in previous research are due to inadequate instrumentation. Indeed, many of the studies listed in Tables 7.1 and 7.2 used ad hoc measures of achievement goals and approaches to studying whose psychometric properties had not been adequately demonstrated. In the circumstances, it is unsurprising that the same studies failed to yield a consistent picture of the relationship between achievement goals and measures of attainment (most commonly, students' grade point averages), as Table 7.3 shows. In their meta-analysis, Hulleman et al. (2010) found that the correlation coefficients between achievement goals and attainment were statistically significant but small: mastery-approach, +0.11; mastery-avoidance, −0.12; performance-approach, +0.06; performance-avoidance, −0.13. More important, they were also markedly heterogeneous across different studies.

Another meta-analysis by Richardson et al. (2012) also found marked heterogeneity across different studies using the trichotomous goal framework. In addition, they examined the correlation coefficients between students' approaches to studying and their attainment. Once again, these were statistically significant but small: deep approach, +0.14; strategic approach, +0.23; surface approach, −0.18. A similar pattern had been found previously by Watkins (2001). Richardson et al. (2012) also found that the correlation coefficients between approaches to studying and attainment were markedly heterogeneous across different studies, suggesting that here, too, different instruments vary in their psychometric adequacy.

Evidence on achievement goals in adult learners

A major limitation of the research on students' achievement goals in higher education is that it was carried out with samples consisting predominantly of young people who had recently gone straight from high school to college. Indeed, in their meta-analytic review, Hulleman et al. (2010) did not use age as a mediator because it was confounded with educational level (C. S. Hulleman, personal communication, 17 August 2011). However, a few studies have considered achievement goals in older learners.

Eppler and Harju (1997) compared achievement goals in 207 'traditional' students (age range 17–22 years) and 48 'non-traditional' students (age range 22–53 years). The latter students were significantly more likely to endorse mastery goals and tended to be less likely to endorse performance goals than the former students. In both groups, the endorsement of mastery goals was significantly related to attainment, but the endorsement of performance goals was not. Sachs (2001) found that mastery goals seemed to facilitate intrinsic

Table 7.3 The relationship between achievement goals and measures of attainment

Source	Mastery	Performance	Performance approach	Performance avoidance	Mastery approach	Mastery avoidance
Meece et al. (1988)	0					
Greene and Miller (1996)	0	0				
Miller et al. (1996, Study 1)	+	+				
Miller et al. (1996, Study 2)	+	0				
Wolters (1998)	+	−				
Fisher and Ford (1998)	+	−				
Elliot et al. (1999, Study 1)	+		+	−		
Elliot et al. (1999, Study 2)	0		0	−		
Harackiewicz et al. (2000)	0	+				
Al-Emadi (2001)	0		0	−		
Zusho et al. (2003)	+	0				
Grant and Dweck (2003)	+	0				
Simons et al. (2004)	+					
Dupeyrat and Mariné (2005)	+	0				
Fenollar et al. (2007)	+		0	0		
Howell and Watson (2007)			+	0	+	−
Coutinho and Neuman (2008)			+	−	0	−
Sins et al. (2008)				0	+	
Liem et al. (2008)	−		0	−		
Senko and Miles (2008)	0		+	0		
Phan (2008)	+		0	0		
Phan (2009a)	+		0	0		
Phan (2009b)	+		0			
Phan (2009c)	0		0	0		
Phan (2010)	0		0	0		

Note: Studies are listed in chronological order of publication. +, statistically significant positive relationship with attainment; −, statistically significant negative relationship with attainment; 0, no significant relationship with attainment; blank, no relevant data. The studies are drawn from those listed in Tables 7.1 and 7.2. Only those studies that reported measures of attainment are included.

motivation but not attainment among part-time students aged between 25 and 40. However, Sachs argued that performance goals were often irrelevant for adult learners, and so he did not measure the adoption of performance goals in his sample of students.

Ng (2006, 2008) carried out two studies with older distance-learning students at the Open University of Hong Kong. The interactions of distance learners with other students are markedly reduced compared with face-to-face learners, and so they have fewer opportunities to demonstrate their abilities or to reveal their lack of ability to other students. It follows that they should be less likely to adopt performance-approach and performance-avoidance goals. Ng's first study involved 373 students and found that their endorsement of mastery goals was positively related to their academic attainment, whereas their endorsement of performance-approach goals was not. His second study involved 797 students and found that their endorsement of both mastery and performance-approach goals was positively related to their use of deep strategies in learning and negatively related to their use of surface strategies in learning. In this study, the endorsement of performance-approach goals was positively related to students' coursework marks, but the endorsement of mastery goals was not; the endorsement of mastery goals was *negatively* related to their examination marks, but the endorsement of performance-approach goals was not.

In distance education, there is an additional problem of student attrition at the course level. Kember and Harper (1987) found that the aspects of studying that were most important in predicting academic outcomes depended on the particular outcome being predicted (course completion versus final grade). It follows that academic attainment should not be regarded as a single continuum running from excellent to failure to non-completion. We therefore set out to examine whether the achievement goals that were reported by students at the beginning of a distance-learning course could predict the likelihood of their completing the course and the final level of attainment in those who completed the course (Remedios and Richardson in press). As part of our research, we also needed to assess the psychometric properties of the AGQ in the distinctive population of British adult learners.

We administered the AGQ in a postal survey to 1,140 students who were about to take one of three courses by distance learning with the UK Open University, each assessed by coursework and a final examination. The items in the AGQ were reworded to refer to 'this course' or 'my courses' rather than 'this class'. The students responded on the original seven-point scale from 'not at all true of me' (coded 1) to 'very true of me' (coded 7). We added three items. Two were: 'On the whole, I expect this course to be very interesting'; and 'On the whole, I expect this course to be very enjoyable'. The third asked the respondents to say whether they were studying to understand the material (intrinsic motive) or to obtain a good grade (extrinsic motive), using a seven-point scale from 'primarily understanding' (coded as 1) to 'primarily grades' (coded as 7).

Completed questionnaires were returned by 781 (or 68.5 per cent) of the participants. They consisted of 195 men and 586 women between the ages of 19 and 87. However, 41 students failed to respond to one or more of the 12 items in the AGQ, leaving 740 respondents with complete data. The majority expected their course to be both interesting and enjoyable (M = 6.43 and 6.19, respectively, on scales from 1 to 7), and they were evenly divided between intrinsic and extrinsic motives (M = 3.65 on a scale from 1 to 7).

Following Elliot and McGregor (2001), a principal components analysis was carried out on their responses to the AGQ followed by varimax rotation. This yielded four factors corresponding to the Mastery Approach, Master Avoidance, Performance Approach and Performance Avoidance scales. The values of Cronbach's (1951) coefficient alpha for the four scales were 0.69 or higher, and the scale scores were positively correlated with each other, implying that students can pursue several goals at the same time.

Of the 740 students with complete data, 547 went on to complete the course that they were taking, 189 withdrew and 4 deferred their assessment. Logistic regression was used to relate course completion to the respondents' AGQ scale scores. Out of the four scales, only Mastery Avoidance predicted course completion with an odds ratio of 0.85. In other words, an increase of one point in the scores on this scale reduced the odds of course completion by 15 per cent. Of the 547 students who completed their course, 444 had passed but 103 had failed. Logistic regression found that none of the scale scores significantly predicted whether or not students had passed their course.

The students who passed their course were marked on their performance both in their coursework and in the examination using a percentage scale with a pass mark of 40 per cent. Multiple regression analyses were used to determine whether the respondents' scale scores predicted their marks. Their scores on Performance Approach were positively related to their marks on both coursework and examination. Their scores on Mastery Avoidance and Performance Avoidance were negatively related to their marks on coursework and examination. However, their scores on Mastery Approach were not significantly related to their marks on either coursework or examination.

In short, the AGQ scales showed satisfactory internal consistency, and a principal components analysis identified the four constituent scales. In other words, the AGQ appears to be psychometrically as sound in adult British students as in traditional-age US students. Our students showed significant variation in the adoption of both mastery and performance goals, and so, contrary to Sachs's (2001) suggestion, performance goals are not irrelevant for adult learners. Nevertheless, when we compared the mean AGQ scores obtained by our students with those obtained by Elliot and McGregor's (2001) students, our students were more likely to endorse mastery-approach goals but were less likely to endorse performance-approach goals. This fits with the idea that adult learners and especially distance learners are more likely to be studying for intrinsic reasons rather than for extrinsic or instrumental reasons.

Moreover, the different kinds of achievement goal were related to students' academic attainment in different ways. Mastery-approach goals were unrelated to academic attainment. Performance-approach goals tended to facilitate attainment, whereas performance-avoidance goals tended to impair attainment. Mastery-avoidance goals tended to impair attainment and also increased the odds that students would drop out of a course. Our findings tend to support Elliot and McGregor's (2001) position that mastery-avoidance goals operate in many settings and have consequences for subsequent attainment. They suggest that the AGQ could provide a simple but useful diagnostic tool to identify students at risk of dropping out of their studies.

Achievement goals and approaches to studying in adult learners

Elliot and Murayama (2008) identified problems with the wording of the items in the AGQ. In particular, some of the items used to measure mastery-avoidance and performance-avoidance goals contained affective content ('My fear of performing poorly in this class is often what motivates me'), but the items that were used to measure mastery-approach and performance-approach goals did not (see also Hulleman et al. 2010). Elliot and Murayama addressed these problems by developing the AGQ-Revised (AGQ-R). In this version, any references to affective content were removed to focus on achievement.

We therefore used the AGQ-R in a survey of students who were about to take one of four distance-learning courses with the Open University. As in our previous study, the items in the AGQ-R were reworded to refer to 'this course' rather than 'this class'. The students responded on the original seven-point scale from 'not at all true of me' (coded 1) to 'very true of me' (coded 7). We also included an Approaches to Learning and Studying Inventory (ALSI) developed at the University of Edinburgh (Entwistle and McCune 2004). This contained 18 items measuring the use of a deep approach, a surface approach and two different aspects of a strategic approach (monitoring studying and organized studying). In this case, the participants were asked to indicate their agreement or disagreement with each of 18 statements on a scale from 1 ('definitely disagree') to 5 ('definitely agree').

Of the 2,000 participants, 1,211 (or 60.6 per cent) returned completed questionnaires. They consisted of 441 men and 770 women between the ages of 19 and 93. However, 109 students failed to respond to one or more of the 12 items in the AGQ-R, leaving 1,102 respondents with complete data. Following Elliot and Murayama (2008), a confirmatory factor analysis was carried out on the covariance matrix among the 12 items. The fit of the 2×2 model was generally satisfactory. The values of Cronbach's (1951) coefficient alpha for the four scales were 0.76 or higher, and the scale scores were positively correlated with each other, once again implying that students can pursue several goals at the same time.

Table 7.4 Correlation coefficients between AGQ-R scores and ALSI scores

Scale	Deep approach	Surface approach	Organized studying	Monitoring studying
Mastery approach	0.40*	−0.26*	0.29*	0.31*
Mastery avoidance	0.21*	−0.10*	0.15*	0.20*
Performance approach	0.11*	0.02	0.08*	0.14*
Performance avoidance	0.08*	0.09*	0.05	0.14*

* p < 0.05 (two-tailed tests).

Of the 1,211 respondents, 1,069 had complete data on both the AGQ-R and the ALSI. Table 7.4 shows the correlation coefficients between their scale scores on the two instruments. A canonical correlation analysis showed that the two sets of scale scores shared 23.0 per cent of their variance (Wilks' Λ = 0.770). The first two pairs of canonical variates were statistically significant, but only the first pair represented more than 10 per cent of shared variance (r = 0.45). The loadings on the first pair of canonical variates showed that scores on Mastery Approach and Mastery Avoidance were positively related to scores on Deep Approach, Organized Studying and Monitoring Studying but negatively related to scores on Surface Approach. Thus, the endorsement of mastery goals is related to the adoption of desirable approaches to studying, but the endorsement of performance goals is not.

Once again, the students' scores on Performance Approach were positively related to their marks in both coursework and examination, whereas their scores on Performance Avoidance were negatively related to their marks in both coursework and examination. These relationships were only slightly attenuated when the students' approaches to studying were taken into account. In other words, the relationship between achievement motivation and academic attainment was partly mediated but only to a small degree by variations in the students' approaches to studying.

In addition, their scores on Surface Approach were negatively related to their pass rate and to their marks in both coursework and examination. However, the students' scores on Deep Approach, Mastery Approach and Mastery Avoidance were unrelated to their completion rate, their pass rate or their marks in either coursework or examination. In short, neither the endorsement of mastery goals nor the adoption of adaptive forms of learning is rewarded by higher marks. This is apparently true of the assessment regime at the UK Open University, but the results summarized in Table 7.3 suggest that it is true at other institutions.

Finally, these results also suggest that the relationship between the scores on Mastery Avoidance and both course completion and attainment that we obtained in our previous study resulted from the affective content in the relevant items of the AGQ (e.g. 'I worry that I may not learn all that I possibly could in this class') rather than from students' achievement goals. In particular, worry and fear of failure rather than mastery avoidance per se seem to be linked to increased student dropout and lower attainment in distance education.

Conclusions and future directions

The results of our surveys demonstrate that the achievement-goal framework is as appropriate for understanding influences on attainment in adult learners as it is in younger students. The notion of 'learning patterns' in higher education might usefully be extended to include students' achievement goals and other indicators of motivation. These seem to be important predictors of students' approaches to studying and their subsequent academic attainment.

Nevertheless, the results of our second survey indicate that the effects of achievement goals on academic attainment are only mediated to a small degree by variations in approaches to studying. How then do achievement goals affect attainment? There is a separate literature on the achievement *strategies* that students adopt in academic environments and the impact of adopting different strategies on both students' attainment and their well-being (see, e.g. Eronen et al. 1998; Heikkilä and Lonka 2006; Heikkilä et al. 2011; Ning and Downing 2010). The role of achievement strategies in mediating the relationship between achievement goals and attainment remains to be explored.

There is also a distinct literature on the involvement of personality factors in student learning. In particular, the so-called 'Big Five' personality traits (Neuroticism, Extraversion, Openness, Agreeableness and Conscientiousness) appear to be related on the one hand to students' approaches to studying and on the other hand to their academic attainment (e.g. Chamorro-Premuzic and Furnham 2008, 2009; von Stumm and Furnham 2012). It is plausible that they are also related to students' achievement goals, but thus far this seems not to have been investigated. This would be worth considering in future research on student learning.

References

Al-Emadi, A.A. (2001) 'The relationships among achievement, goal orientation, and study strategies', *Social Behavior and Personality*, 29: 823–32. Available: http://dx.doi.org/10.2224/sbp.2001.29.8.823 (accessed 16 January 2013).

Ames, C. (1992) 'Classrooms: Goals, structures, and student motivation', *Journal of Educational Psychology*, 84: 261–71. Available: http://dx.doi.org/10.1037/0022-0663.84.3.261 (accessed 16 January 2013).

Ames, C. and Archer, J. (1988) 'Achievement goals in the classroom: Students' learning strategies and motivation processes', *Journal of Educational Psychology*, 80: 260–7. Available: http://dx.doi.org/10.1037/0022-0663.80.3.260 (accessed 16 January 2013).

Chamorro-Premuzic, T. and Furnham, A. (2008) 'Personality, intelligence and approaches to learning as predictors of academic performance', *Personality and Individual Differences*,

44: 1596–603. Available: http://dx.doi.org/10.1016/j.paid.2008.01.003 (accessed 16 January 2013).

Chamorro-Premuzic, T. and Furnham, A. (2009) 'Mainly openness: The relationship between the Big Five personality traits and learning approaches', *Learning and Individual Differences*, 19: 524–9. Available: http://dx.doi.org/10.1016/j.lindif.2009.06.004 (accessed 16 January 2013).

Church, M.A., Elliot, A.J. and Gable, S.L. (2001) 'Perceptions of classroom environment, achievement goals, and achievement outcomes', *Journal of Educational Psychology*, 93: 43–54. Available: http://dx.doi.org/10.1037/0022-0663.93.1.43 (accessed 16 January 2013).

Coutinho, S.A. and Neuman, G. (2008) 'A model of metacognition, achievement goal orientation, learning style and self-efficacy', *Learning Environments Research*, 11: 131–51. Available: http://dx.doi.org/10.1007/s10984-008-9042-7 (accessed 16 January 2013).

Cronbach, L.J. (1951) 'Coefficient alpha and the internal structure of tests', *Psychometrika*, 16: 297–334. Available: http://dx.doi.org/10.1007/BF02310555 (accessed 16 January 2013).

Diener, C.I. and Dweck, C.A. (1978) 'An analysis of learned helplessness: Continuous changes in performance, strategy, and achievement cognitions following failure', *Journal of Personality and Social Psychology*, 36: 451–62. Available: http://dx.doi.org/10.1037/0022-3514.36.5.451 (accessed 16 January 2013).

Diener, C.I. and Dweck, C.S. (1980) 'An analysis of learned helplessness: II. The processing of success', *Journal of Personality and Social Psychology*, 39: 940–52. Available: http://dx.doi.org/10.1037/0022-3514.39.5.940 (accessed 16 January 2013).

Dupeyrat, C. and Mariné, C. (2005) 'Implicit theories of intelligence, goal orientation, cognitive engagement, and achievement: A test of Dweck's model with returning to school adults', *Contemporary Educational Psychology*, 30: 43–59. Available: http://dx.doi.org/10.1016/j.cedpsych.2004.01.007 (accessed 16 January 2013).

Dupeyrat, C., Mariné, C. and Escribe, C. (1999) 'Mastery and challenge seeking: Two dimensions within learning goals?', *Swiss Journal of Psychology*, 58: 22–30. Available: http://dx.doi.org/10.1024//1421-0185.58.1.22 (accessed 16 January 2013).

Dweck, C.S. (1986) 'Motivational processes affecting learning', *American Psychologist*, 41: 1040–8. Available: http://dx.doi.org/10.1037/0003-066X.41.10.1040 (accessed 16 January 2013).

Dweck, C.S. and Elliott, E.S. (1983) 'Achievement motivation', in P.H. Mussen (gen. ed.) and E.M. Hetherington (vol. ed.), *Handbook of Child Psychology: Vol. IV. Social and Personality Development*. New York: Wiley.

Elliot, A.J. and Church, M.A. (1997) 'A hierarchical model of approach and avoidance achievement motivation', *Journal of Personality and Social Psychology*, 72: 218–32. Available: http://dx.doi.org/10.1037/0022-3514.72.1.218 (accessed 16 January 2013).

Elliot, A.J. and Harackiewicz, J.M. (1996) 'Approach and avoidance achievement goals and intrinsic motivation: A meditational analysis', *Journal of Personality and Social Psychology*, 70: 461–75. Available: http://dx.doi.org/10.1037/0022-3514.70.3.461 (accessed 16 January 2013).

Elliot, A.J. and McGregor, H.A. (2001) 'A 2 × 2 achievement goal framework', *Journal of Personality and Social Psychology*, 80: 501–19. Available: http://dx.doi.org/10.1037/0022-3514.80.3.501 (accessed 16 January 2013).

Elliot, A.J., McGregor, H.A. and Gable, S. (1999) 'Achievement goals, study strategies, and exam performance: A meditational analysis', *Journal of Educational Psychology*, 91: 549–63. Available: http://dx.doi.org/10.1037/0022-0663.91.3.549 (accessed 16 January 2013).

Elliot, A.J. and Murayama, K. (2008) 'On the measurement of achievement goals: Critique, illustration, and application', *Journal of Educational Psychology*, 100: 613–28. Available: http://dx.doi.org/10.1037/0022-0663.100.3.613 (accessed 16 January 2013).

Entwistle, N. and McCune, V. (2004) 'The conceptual bases of study strategy inventories', *Educational Psychology Review*, 16: 325–45. Available: http://dx.doi.org/10.1007/s10648-004-0003-0 (accessed 16 January 2013).

Eppler, M.A. and Harju, B.L. (1997) 'Achievement motivation goals in relation to academic performance in traditional and non-traditional college students', *Research in Higher Education*, 38: 557–73. Available: http://dx.doi.org/10.1023/A:1024944429347 (accessed 16 January 2013).

Eronen, S., Nurmi, J.-E. and Salmela-Aro, K. (1998) 'Optimistic, defensive-pessimistic, impulsive and self-handicapping strategies in university environments', *Learning and Instruction*, 8: 159–77. Available: http://dx.doi.org/10.1016/S0959-4752(97)00015-7 (accessed 16 January 2013).

Fenollar, P., Román, S. and Cuestas, P.J. (2007) 'University students' academic performance: An integrative conceptual framework and empirical analysis', *British Journal of Educational Psychology*, 77: 873–91. Available: http://dx.doi.org/10.1348/000709907X189118 (accessed 16 January 2013).

Fisher, S.L. and Ford, J.K. (1998) 'Differential effects of learner effort and goal orientation on two learning outcomes', *Personnel Psychology*, 51: 397–420. Available: http://dx.doi.org/10.1111/j.1744-6570.1998.tb00731.x (accessed 16 January 2013).

Grant, H. and Dweck, C.S. (2003) 'Clarifying achievement goals and their impact', *Journal of Personality and Social Psychology*, 85: 541–53. Available: http://dx.doi.org/10.1037/0022-3514.85.3.541 (accessed 16 January 2013).

Greene, B.A. and Miller, R.B. (1996) 'Influences on achievement: Goals, perceived ability, and cognitive engagement', *Contemporary Educational Psychology*, 21: 181–92. Available: http://dx.doi.org/10.1006/ceps.1996.0015 (accessed 16 January 2013).

Harackiewicz, J.M., Barron, K.E., Tauer, J.M., Carter, S.M. and Elliot, A.J. (2000) 'Short-term and long-term consequences of achievement goals: Predicting interest and performance over time', *Journal of Educational Psychology*, 92: 316–30. Available: http://dx.doi.org/10.1037/0022-0663.92.2.316 (accessed 16 January 2013).

Heikkilä, A. and Lonka, K. (2006) 'Studying in higher education: Students' approaches to learning, self-regulation, and cognitive strategies', *Studies in Higher Education*, 31: 99–117. Available: http://dx.doi.org/10.1080/03075070500392433 (accessed 16 January 2013).

Heikkilä, A., Niemivirta, M., Nieminen, J. and Lonka, K. (2011) 'Interrelations among university students' approaches to learning, regulation of learning, and cognitive and attributional strategies: A person oriented approach', *Higher Education*, 61: 513–29. Available: http://dx.doi.org/10.1007/s10734-010-9346-2 (accessed 16 January 2013).

Howell, A.J. and Watson, D.C. (2007) 'Procrastination: Associations with achievement goal orientation and learning strategies', *Personality and Individual Differences*, 43: 167–78. Available: http://dx.doi.org/10.1016/j.paid.2006.11.017 (accessed 16 January 2013).

Hulleman, C.S., Schrager, S.M., Bodmann, S.M. and Harackiewicz, J.M. (2010) 'A meta-analytic review of achievement goal measures: Different labels for the same constructs or different constructs with similar labels?', *Psychological Bulletin*, 156: 422–49. Available: http://dx.doi.org/10.1037/a0018947 (accessed 16 January 2013).

Kember, D. and Harper, G. (1987) 'Implications for instruction arising from the relationship between approaches to studying and academic outcomes', *Instructional Science*, 16: 35–46. Available: http://dx.doi.org/10.1007/BF00120004 (accessed 16 January 2013).

Liem, A.D., Lau, S. and Nie, Y. (2008) 'The role of self-efficacy, task value, and achievement goals in predicting learning strategies, task disengagement, peer relationship, and achievement outcome', *Contemporary Educational Psychology*, 33: 486–512. Available: http://dx.doi.org/10.1016/j.cedpsych.2007.08.001 (accessed 16 January 2013).

Meece, J.L., Blumenfeld, P.C. and Hoyle, R.H. (1988) 'Students' goal orientations and cognitive engagement in classroom activities', *Journal of Educational Psychology*, 80: 514–23. Available: http://dx.doi.org/10.1037/0022-0663.80.4.514 (accessed 16 January 2013).

Miller, R.B., Greene, B.A., Montalvo, G.P., Ravindran, B. and Nichols, J.D. (1996) 'Engagement in academic work: The role of learning goals, future consequences, pleasing others, and perceived ability', *Contemporary Educational Psychology*, 21: 388–422. Available: http://dx.doi.org/10.1006/ceps.1996.0028 (accessed 16 January 2013).

Ng, C. (2006) 'The role of achievement goals in completing a college assignment: Examining the effects of performance-approach and multiple goals', *Open Learning*, 21: 33–48. Available: http://dx.doi.org/10.1080/02680510500472189 (accessed 16 January 2013).

Ng, C.C. (2008) 'Multiple-goal learners and their differential patterns of learning', *Educational Psychology*, 28: 439–56. Available: http://dx.doi.org/10.1080/01443410701739470 (accessed 16 January 2013).

Ning, H.K. and Downing, K. (2010) 'The reciprocal relationship between motivation and self-regulation: A longitudinal study on academic performance', *Learning and Individual Differences*, 20: 682–6. Available: http://dx.doi.org/10.1016/j.lindif.2010.09.010 (accessed 16 January 2013).

Nolen, S.B. (1988) 'Reasons for studying: motivational orientations and study strategies', *Cognition and Instruction*, 5: 269–87. Available: http://dx.doi.org/10.1207/s1532690xci 0504_2 (accessed 16 January 2013).

Phan, H.P. (2008) 'Unifying different theories of learning: theoretical framework and empirical evidence', *Educational Psychology*, 28: 325–40. Available: http://dx.doi. org/10.1080/01443410701591392 (accessed 16 January 2013).

Phan, H.P. (2009a) 'Amalgamation of future time orientation, epistemological beliefs, achievement goals and study strategies: Empirical evidence established', *British Journal of Educational Psychology*, 79: 155–73. Available: http://dx.doi.org/10.1348/000709908X30 6864 (accessed 16 January 2013).

Phan, H.P. (2009b) 'Exploring students' reflective thinking practice, deep processing strategies, effort, and achievement goal orientations', *Educational Psychology*, 29: 297–313. Available: http://dx.doi.org/10.1080/01443410902877988 (accessed 16 January 2013).

Phan, H.P. (2009c) 'Relations between goals, self-efficacy, critical thinking and deep processing strategies: A path analysis', *Educational Psychology*, 29: 777–99. Available: http:// dx.doi.org/10.1080/01443410903289423 (accessed 16 January 2013).

Phan, H.P. (2010) 'Students' academic performance and various cognitive processes of learning: an integrative framework and empirical analysis', *Educational Psychology*, 30: 297–322. Available: http://dx.doi.org/10.1080/01443410903573297 (accessed 16 January 2013).

Remedios, R. and Richardson, J.T.E. (in press) 'Achievement goals in adult learners: Evidence from distance education', *British Journal of Educational Psychology*. Available: http://dx.doi.org/ 10.1111/bjep.12001 (accessed 16 January 2013).

Richardson, J.T.E. (2000) *Researching Student Learning: Approaches to Studying in Campus-based and Distance Education*. Buckingham, UK: SRHE and Open University Press. Available: http://labspace.open.ac.uk/course/view.php?id=3374&loginguest=true (accessed 16 January 2013).

Richardson, M., Abraham, C. and Bond, R. (2012) 'Psychological correlates of university students' academic performance: A systematic review and meta-analysis', *Psychological Bulletin*, 138: 353–87. Available: http://dx.doi.org/10.1037/a0026838 (accessed 16 January 2013).

Sachs, J. (2001) 'A path model for adult learner feedback', *Educational Psychology*, 21: 267–75. Available: http://dx.doi.org/10.1080/01443410120065478 (accessed 16 January 2013).

Sadlo, G. and Richardson, J.T.E. (2003) 'Approaches to studying and perceptions of the academic environment in students following problem-based and subject-based curricula', *Higher Education Research and Development*, 22: 253–74. Available: http://dx.doi.org/10.1080/0729436032000145130 (accessed 16 January 2013).

Senko, C., Hulleman, C.S. and Harackiewicz, J.M. (2011) 'Achievement goal theory at the crossroads: Old controversies, current challenges, and new directions', *Educational Psychologist*, 46: 26–47. Available: http://dx.doi.org/10.1080/00461520.2011.538646 (accessed 16 January 2013).

Senko, C. and Miles, K.M. (2008) 'Pursuing their own learning agenda: How mastery-oriented students jeopardize their class performance', *Contemporary Educational Psychology*, 33: 561–83. Available: http://dx.doi.org/10.1016/j.cedpsych.2007.12.001 (accessed 16 January 2013).

Simons, J., Dewitte, S. and Lens, W. (2004) 'The role of different types of instrumentality in motivation, study strategies, and performance: Know why you learn, so you'll know what you learn!', *British Journal of Educational Psychology*, 74: 343–60. Available: http://dx.doi.org/10.1348/0007099041552314 (accessed 16 January 2013).

Sins, P.H.M., van Joolingen, W.R., Savelsbergh, E.R. and van Hout-Wolters, B. (2008) 'Motivation and performance within a collaborative computer-based modeling task: Relations between students' achievement goal orientation, self-efficacy, cognitive processing, and achievement', *Contemporary Educational Psychology*, 33: 58–77. Available: http://dx.doi.org/10.1016/j.cedpsych.2006.12.004 (accessed 16 January 2013).

Somuncuoglu, Y. and Yildirim, A. (1999) 'Relationship between achievement goal orientations and use of learning strategies', *Journal of Educational Research*, 92: 267–77. Available: http://dx.doi.org/10.1080/00220679909597606 (accessed 16 January 2013).

Vermetten, Y.J., Lodewijks, H.G. and Vermunt, J.D. (2001) 'The role of personality traits and goal orientations in strategy use', *Contemporary Educational Psychology*, 26: 149–79. Available: http://dx.doi.org/10.1006/ceps.1999.1042 (accessed 16 January 2013).

Von Stumm, S. and Furnham, A.F. (2012) 'Learning approaches: Associations with typical intellectual engagement, intelligence and the Big Five', *Personality and Individual Differences*, 53: 720–723. Available: http://dx.doi.org/10.1016/j.paid.2012.05.014 (accessed 16 January 2013).

Watkins, D. (2001) 'Correlates of approaches to learning: A cross-cultural meta-analysis', in R.J. Sternberg and L.-F. Zhang (eds), *Perspectives on Thinking, Learning, and Cognitive Styles*. Mahwah, NJ: Erlbaum.

Wolters, C.A. (1998) 'Self-regulated learning and college students' regulation of motivation', *Journal of Educational Psychology*, 90: 224–35. Available: http://dx.doi.org/10.1037/0022-0663.90.2.224 (accessed 16 January 2013).

Zusho, A., Pintrich, P.R. and Coppola, B. (2003) 'Skill and will: The role of motivation and cognition in the learning of college chemistry', *International Journal of Science Education*, 25: 1081–94. Available: http://dx.doi.org/10.1080/0950069032000052207 (accessed 16 January 2013).

Chapter 8

Learning processes in higher education

Providing new insights into the effects of motivation and cognition on specific and global measures of achievement

Mikaël De Clercq, Benoît Galand and Mariane Frenay

Purpose of the chapter

The last three decades have witnessed an extensive investigation of learning processes in higher education. Four constructs seem to be at the core of this investigation: achievement goals, self-efficacy beliefs, self-regulation and learning strategies. The first two have provided some explanation of the processes that lead students to engage in learning tasks, whereas the last two have broadened our understanding of students' capacity to learn effectively and steer their own learning. According to the conceptual model of Phan (2009a, 2009b), each of these four specific constructs provides complementary information that allows for a global conceptualization of students' learning processes in higher education.

Research in a higher education context has evidenced intricate relations between goal orientation, self-efficacy beliefs, learning strategies and self-regulation (Diseth 2011; Galand, Raucent and Frenay 2010; Kaplan, Lichtinger and Gorodetsky 2009; Simons, Dewitte and Lens 2004; Zimmerman 1999). More specifically, some recent studies have looked, through path analysis and longitudinal design, at the direction of the effect between these factors (De Clercq, Galand and Frenay 2013; Phan 2009b). These authors have concluded that motivational factors (goal orientation and self-efficacy beliefs) are significant predictors of cognitive ones (learning strategies and self-regulation). The assertion that these four constructs are important predictors of academic performance is also supported by several studies in educational psychology (De Clercq, Galand, Dupont and Frenay 2012; Elias and MacDonald 2007; Minnaert and Janssen 1999; Pintrich and De Groot 1990; Simons et al. 2004; Valle et al. 2008, Vermunt 2005). However, some inconsistencies remain in the current literature concerning the link between these constructs and academic achievement, especially concerning goal orientations (Harackiewicz, Barron, Tauer, Carter and Elliot 2000) and learning strategies (Fenollar, Román and Cuestas 2007). From one study to another, the findings about the impact between these constructs and academic performance lack consistency with regard to both the significance and the direction of the effect.

These inconsistencies could be explained by the global nature of achievement measures. Following Vermunt's reasoning (2005), the relationship between the learning process and learning outcomes is highly dependent on the way they are measured. In this sense, aggregated achievement measures such as grade point average could be too global as a measure of achievement and might not accurately depict the impact of specific learning components. Such global measures aggregate several distinct evaluations with different requirements which do not draw systematically on the same learning process. Insofar as some factors are not of paramount importance in order to succeed in every evaluation task, their actual positive impact on academic achievement could be masked behind an aggregated measure of it. In that case, focusing on a more specific measure of achievement would provide us with an accurate and consistent understanding of the actual impact of the four constructs under investigation in this study.

Following this line of thought, this chapter is intended as a step forward in this important argument. To this end, we have developed a prospective study to investigate the impact of goal orientation, self-efficacy beliefs, learning strategies and self-regulation on different measures of learning. The purpose of this study was to determine which predictors are related to the global achievement at the end of the academic year and which are necessary to achieve specific tasks. Past performance was also introduced as a control variable in order to pinpoint the actual predictive power of factors under investigation. Therefore, our second aim is to assess the impact of the four above-mentioned factors when they are introduced together in a multivariate analysis, controlling for the impact of past performance on achievement outcomes.

In the following section, literature on goal orientation, self-efficacy beliefs, learning strategies and self-regulation will be reviewed. This section will emphasize the inconsistencies in the literature and the way these factors are related to academic achievement. Next we will introduce our hypothesis, the method used and the results. Finally this chapter will end with a discussion of our results, limitations, future prospects and a conclusion including practical implications of our work.

Why do I want to achieve?

A host of educational researchers have focused their work on understanding students' reasons for engaging in achievement tasks (Pintrich 2003). One of the most prominent theories in this conceptual framework proposed a model depicting two orthogonal goal orientations: mastery and performance goal orientation (Ames 1992; Dweck and Leggett, 1988; Nicholls 1984; Pintrich and De Groot 1990). Bong defines mastery as follows (2005, p. 656): 'When students pursue mastery goals, their primary purpose of engaging in academic activities is to develop their competencies. Mastery-oriented students welcome challenge and view occasional failures as a natural part of learning.' Mastery goal orientation can therefore be conceptualized as a focus on learning and mastering the task with a view to self-improvement. Conversely, performance-oriented students are mainly focused on the way they are evaluated against their peers, on attempting to surpass others, on proving their competence and on obtaining recognition for good performance (Bong 2005; Greene, Miller, Crowson, Duke and Akey 2004; Pintrich 1999; Simons et al. 2004). Performance goal orientation can therefore be conceptualized as focusing on documenting superior abilities relative to others or a high standard. The initial dichotomous model has recently been subject to revision in order to explain contradictory findings (Daniels et al. 2008). Three new models have flourished: the trichotomous model (Harackiewicz, Barron, Tauer and Elliot 2002), the 2 × 2 model (Elliot and McGregor 2001) and the 3 × 2 model (Elliot, Murayama and Pekrun 2011). However, empirical evidence concerning the validity of these new conceptualizations is still underdeveloped (Hulleman, Schrager, Bodmann and Harackiewicz 2010). For example, Pintrich (2003) questions the added value of using 2 × 2 perspectives. Other theorists such as Ames (1992) have provided evidence for a third goal orientation that may be relevant in the educational context: the work avoidance goal. Work avoidance-oriented students try to do the minimum necessary to succeed in a course (Fenollar et al. 2007). Theory about the relationship between work avoidance and other goal orientations is also underdeveloped. Nevertheless, the mastery goal is often considered the most adaptive achievement goal orientation and work avoidance the most maladaptive one (Kumar and Jagacinski 2011). In this chapter, we have conceptualized goal orientation according to the standard dichotomous mastery-performance perspective of Dweck and Leggett (1988).

This literature on goal orientation has consistently revealed that mastery goal orientation and academic achievement are positively correlated (Daniels et al. 2008; Dupeyrat and Mariné 2005; Greene et al. 2004; Harackiewicz et al. 2000; Simons et al. 2004). However, we may note that achievement has always been assessed by global measures. In studies with specific achievement measures, the results are different. These studies reveal mainly that mastery goals are not a direct predictor of academic achievement (Bong, 2005; Harackiewicz et al. 2002; Kennett, Young and Catanzaro 2009).

Moreover, studies on the effect of performance goal orientation on academic achievement have been less consistent, whether with global or specific measures of achievement. Some studies have highlighted a positive relationship between performance goals and achievement, whereas others have highlighted a negative one (Harackiewicz et al. 2002). Many studies also fail to find any link between achievement and performance goals (Bouffard, Boisvert, Vezeau and Larouche 1995; Dupeyrat 2000; Midgley et al. 1998; Nicholls 1989). These inconsistencies could be explained by the reasoning of Midgley and colleagues

(2001) that performance goal orientation is not itself adaptive, but can become a significant predictor of achievement if mastery goals are also high. Moreover, according to these authors, the effect of performance goal orientation on academic achievement is highly dependent on the circumstances of the context and on the characteristics of the students.

Do I expect to achieve?

Another line of research has focused on students' confidence in their ability or expectation of success (for a review see Bandura 1997 or Eccles and Wigfield 2002). These authors argue that academic self-efficacy beliefs/expectations are of the utmost importance for students' achievement in higher education. According to several authors, self-efficacy is of paramount importance because it enables the setting up of favourable motivational, cognitive, affective and behavioural processes that entail good adaptation to academic requirements (Brown et al. 2008; Elias and MacDonald 2007; Pintrich 2003; Robbins et al. 2004; Zimmerman, 2000). A large number of studies along these lines demonstrate that confidence in one's ability to succeed is strongly related to several adaptive variables such as goal orientation, intrinsic motivation, self-regulated learning, effort ratings, emotional competencies, social integration, intention to persist and deep processing strategies (Adeyemo 2007; Bong and Skaalvik 2003; Fenollar et al. 2007; Torres and Solberg 2001). Robbins and colleagues (2006) found in large-scale studies that academic self-efficacy beliefs were a strong predictor of global measures of achievement but not of results on specific courses. These results on self-efficacy beliefs could be explained by the specificity of the measure. As pointed out by Zimmerman (2000), self-efficacy beliefs are not an omnibus trait but rather a multidimensional construct differing on the basis of the domain of functioning. Global confidence in one's ability to succeed (as measured by Robbins and colleagues) therefore has to be considered as being essentially at the apex of the academic self-hierarchy. This would explain why global academic self-efficacy beliefs are less predictive of performance in specific tasks than domain-specific self-efficacy beliefs. In this study, we will attempt to replicate the results of Robbins and colleagues while controlling for past performance.

How am I going to achieve?

Students' learning processes are an ongoing subject of study in educational research. According to several authors (Busato, Prins, Elshout and Hamaker 2000; Entwistle and Ramsden 1983; Vermunt, 2005) we can define learning processes as thinking activities that students deploy to process subject matter in order to obtain certain learning results. In this vein, decades of research have investigated which cognitive processes determine students' effective learning in higher education. Hitherto, various overlapping theories of cognitive processes have been developed (for a review, see Vermunt and Vermetten 2004), making it difficult to rely on a consistent and rigorous theoretical framework. However, in line with our desire to create a clear path in this conceptual forest, we will refer to the most commonly used theories in learning literature. Moreover, in line with the review by Dinsmore and Alexander (2012), clear definitions of the constructs used are provided to avoid any misinterpretation or ambiguity. These theories make a distinction between two main learning strategies: deep and surface processing strategies (Biggs 1984; Busato et al. 2000; Marton 1988; Vermunt 1998). Surface processing consists of thinking activities such as rehearsing, rote processing or organizing (e.g. outlining or summarizing) that lead to the learning of the surface features of a study task. Conversely, deep processing can be understood as thinking activities leading the student to in-depth understanding of a task. For instance, deep processing strategies consist of relating, concretizing and critical processing (Kember and Gow 1994). Such learning strategies provide links with prior knowledge and provide better coding of information within the long-term memory store (Entwistle and McCune 2004).

Studies of the relationship between level of processing and academic achievement have also reported mixed findings. Some studies have found a positive association between deep processing strategies and achievement (Diseth 2011; Fenollar et al. 2007; Vermunt 2005; Ward and Walker 2008), while others have reported positive associations between achievement and both surface and deep processing strategies (Jakoubek and Swenson 1993), and others still have not found any significant correlations with achievement (Bruinsma 2004; Busato et al. 2000; Dupeyrat and Mariné 2005; Jansen and Bruinsma 2005). However, these studies did not assess academic achievement in the same way. The relationships between achievement and processing strategies were predominantly highlighted when using a specific measure of achievement, while global measures mostly failed to show a similar relationship. For instance, Jansen and Bruinsma (2005) measured academic achievement through aggregated grade point average of seven different courses, and did not find that processing strategies resulted in better achievement. Conversely, Diseth (2011) investigated academic achievement through results obtained by the students in a final examination composed of two essay-like questions and a multiple choice test. The results showed a significant positive impact of deep processing and a negative impact of surface processing on examination grade. Finally, Vermunt (2005) pointed out that the predictive power of processing strategies is not significant for every task. In his study, deep processing has an impact on achievement in econometry, sociology and psychology exams but not in economics, law and arts exams. Consequently, we can postulate that not all processing strategies are equally important for all academic tasks and that their actual impact on achievement is often hidden when using a global measure of academic achievement such as grade point average, number of credits or final percentage. Therefore, processing strategies will be predictive of achievement in particular tasks with specific requirements.

Am I still on the right track to achieve?

Beyond learning strategies, many researchers have devoted their energy to understanding how students manage their learning processes. Self-regulation is a core concept to resolve this issue. Self-regulation refers to the ways in which an individual monitors, regulates and controls his cognition (Elias and MacDonald 2007; Valle et al. 2008). When applied to a learning task, self-regulation consists of steering the learning process by using several strategies such as information-seeking, self-evaluation, monitoring, supervising or goal-setting strategies (Dahl, Bals and Turi 2005; Nota, Soresi and Zimmerman 2004). According to Howell and Watson (2007), the aforementioned strategies refer to the adaptive component of self-regulation. Conversely, strategies such as procrastination, susceptibility to distraction or lack of persistence would demonstrate students' difficulties in monitoring their learning processes. These strategies refer to the maladaptive component of self-regulation or the concept of lack of regulation (Boekaerts and Cascallar 2006; Vermunt 2005).

Prior work in cognitive psychology has accumulated consistent empirical evidence supporting the view that self-regulation is a crucial predictor of academic achievement (Nota et al. 2004; Perry, Hladkyj, Pekrun and Pelletier 2001; Pintrich and De Groot 1990; Valle et al. 2008). Moreover, Minnaert and Janssen (1999) have shown that adaptive self-regulation explains the same amount of variance in academic performance as intelligence test scores. The impact of self-regulation on academic achievement was consistent from specific (Nota et al. 2004) to global measures (Minnaert and Janssen 1999; Perry et al. 2001) of achievement. Finally, Nota and colleagues (2004) compared the impact of different self-regulation strategies on specific and global measures of achievement. The results of this study highlight a strong impact on both global achievement and specific course grades.

The present study: aims and hypotheses

The purpose of this study is to investigate the relationship between motivational and cognitive processes and several learning outcomes. On the one hand, goal orientations and self-efficacy beliefs were counted as motivational processes. On the other hand, learning strategies and self-regulation were considered as cognitive processes. Two learning outcomes were under investigation: a global (final average percentage) and a specific one (results in a test). According to the literature described above, three global hypotheses have been framed.

- First, the impact of general motivational factors on global measure of academic achievement will be significant, but their impact on specific measures will not be significant. Most of the literature on mastery goal and academic self-efficacy beliefs points in this direction (Kennett et al. 2009; Robbins, Allen, Casillas, Peterson and Le 2006). Finally, bearing in mind the inconclusive literature about performance goals, no specific hypothesis was formulated for this variable.

- Second, following the results of Diseth (2011), it is expected that cognitive processes will be predictive of achievement in specific learning outcomes.
- Third, it is assumed that self-regulation will have an impact on both measures of academic achievement (Nota et al. 2004).

Moreover, the investigations were set up while controlling for students' prior achievement. This control variable allows us to determine which factors remain significant predictors of achievement rather than being merely an indirect reflection of past performance. Our research therefore focused on individual differences that enhance the prediction of academic achievement over and above students' initial levels of content knowledge measured by prior achievement. Some results in the literature have already shown that self-efficacy beliefs could be incrementally predictive of academic achievement beyond the impact of past academic performance (e.g. Chemers, Hu and Garcia 2001; Valentine, DuBois and Cooper 2004), even if the relationship between past performance and self-efficacy beliefs appears to be reciprocal (Galand and Vanlede 2004; Huang 2011). However, this control was rarely undertaken for cognitive variables such as cognitive processing and self-regulation. Therefore, a control for past performance will corroborate that cognitive variables are not only an indirect measure of content knowledge but have an actual predictive power for academic achievement.

Method

Participants and procedure

The participants were 217 students from the engineering faculty at the Université catholique de Louvain in Belgium. The students were at the beginning of their third year of study. Self-report questionnaires were group-administered during a regular lecture at the beginning of the academic year (November). A test was also administered collectively during a regular lecture time later in the year (December). This test lasted 90 minutes and aimed to assess three specific learning outcomes through three distinct tasks.

Measures

The questionnaire was built on the basis of various international scales selected by educational experts and members of the engineering faculty through a broad review of the literature (Galand and Frenay 2005; Galand et al. 2010). The items of the questionnaire were rated on five-point Likert-type scales (achievement goal orientation: 1 = strongly disagree, 5 = strongly agree; self-regulation and learning process: 1 = never, 5 = very often). First- and second-order factor analyses using the oblimin rotation method were conducted to build strong and synthetic indicators of the motivational and cognitive factors. The factor solutions were extracted based on eigenvalues greater than 1. First-order factor solution, internal consistency, number of items and an example of the items are shown in Table 8.1. Final scales extracted from the second-order factor analysis are shown in Table 8.2 with factor loadings.

GOAL ORIENTATION

Nineteen items were selected and adapted from international literature on goal orientation (Bouffard et al. 1995; Dupeyrat 2000; Galand and Grégoire 2000; Midgley et al. 1998; Nicholls 1989). Using first-order exploratory factor analysis, goal orientation was divided into four factors: competition, self-image, work avoidance and learning goal orientation. Similar components of goal orientation have been identified by various authors supporting the notion that competition and self-image are two specific types of performance goal (Marsh, Craven, Hinkley and Debus 2003; Serra de Lemos and Gonçalves 2004; Young 1997). In view of the necessity to build strong and synthetic indicators of goal orientation, second-order factor analysis was conducted on the four goal orientation subscales, and two factors emerged from the analyses. These results are consistent with the study of Marsh and colleagues (2003) which pinpointed two higher-order goal orientations. Factor scores were extracted from the final factor solution, which explained 68 per cent of the variance.

Not surprisingly, competition and self-image subscales loaded on the same factor corresponding to performance goal orientation. The results also revealed that learning and work avoidance goal orientation subscales loaded on the same factor: positively in the case of mastery approach and negatively in the case of work avoidance. We therefore decided that these two subscales could be considered as the two extremities of the mastery goal orientation. Along these lines, a student with a high score on the mastery orientation scale will aim to maximize his understanding of a course, whereas a student with a low score will try to do the minimum necessary to succeed in the course. These results tally with previous studies highlighting that learning and work avoidance goal orientations are intricately related (Galand and Philippot 2002; Kumar and Jagacinski 2011; Shell and Husman 2008).

ACADEMIC SELF-EFFICACY BELIEFS

Ten items were selected and adapted from a previously validated scale (Galand and Philippot 2002) to assess self-efficacy beliefs. First-order factor analysis was conducted and revealed a two-factor solution referring to personal and comparative self-efficacy beliefs. A second-order factor analysis was

Table 8.1 Goal orientation, self-efficacy belief, learning strategies and self-regulation subscales

Subscales	Alpha	N	Example items
Goal orientation			
1. Learning	.74	5	Understanding the subject matter is more important to me than the grades I get
2. Work avoidance	.60	3	Understanding the subject matter is not important to me, as long as I get the right answers
3. Competition	.69	5	It's important for me to have better grades than other students
4. Self-image	.75	6	I work to prove to myself that I am able to succeed
Self-efficacy belief			
1. Comparative	.82	6	Compared to other students, I feel my abilities are lower (reverse score)
2. Personal	.68	4	I am sure I will be able to understand the subject matter in these courses
Learning strategies			
1. Criticizing	.67	4	I draw my own conclusions from the data presented by the teachers
2. Relating	.78	6	I try to see the connections between the content of several courses
3. Contextualizing	.77	4	I use what I learn at university in my activities outside university
4. Organizing	.64	4	I make a list of the main points to memorize
5. Rehearsing	.53	3	I try to learn word by word the content of the courses
Self-regulation			
1. Information-seeking	.72	4	If I don't understand part of the subject matter, I try to find relevant information from other sources
2. Supervising	.69	6	When I am having difficulty understanding part of the content, I try to analyze the nature of the problem in detail
3. Monitoring	.66	3	To test my progress in my studies, I try to answer questions I ask myself about the subject matter
4. Distraction vulnerability	.51	3	Most of the time, I wait till the last minute to do my work.
5. Lack of persistence	.54	3	If I don't understand something, I give up and do something else

Table 8.2 Second-order factorial analysis outcomes

	FI	FII
Goal orientation		
1. Learning	.83	
2. Work avoidance	−.83	
3. Competition		.82
4. Self-image		.81
Self-efficacy beliefs		
1. Comparative	.88	
2. Personal	.88	
Learning strategies		
1. Criticizing	.87	
2. Relating	.85	
3. Contextualizing	.78	
4. Rehearsing		.82
5. Organizing		.80
Self-regulation		
1. Information-seeking	.82	
2. Supervising	.79	
3. Monitoring	.54	
4. Distraction vulnerability		.81
5. Lack of persistence		.77

run, highlighting that these two subscales can be seen as two dimensions of a more global construct corresponding to academic self-efficacy beliefs and explaining 79 per cent of the variance. As for goal orientation, a factor score was extracted.

LEARNING STRATEGIES

Twenty-one items adapted from previous studies on the LASSI (Learning and Study Strategies Inventory) and ILS (Inventory of Learning Styles) were used to assess learning strategies (Vermunt 1994; Weinstein, Goetz and Alexander 1988). Five subscales emerged from the exploratory factorial analysis: relating, criticizing, contextualizing, rehearsing and organizing. Given the limited internal consistency of several scales, a second-order factorial analysis was conducted on the subscales in order to build more strongly on more synthetic indicators of learning strategies. Consistently with the literature (Entwistle and McCune 2004; Entwistle and Ramsden 1983), a two-factor solution that accounted for 69 per cent of the variance emerged from the analyses. Factor scores were extracted to create overall deep processing (relating, criticizing and contextualizing) and surface processing scales (rehearsing and organizing).

SELF-REGULATION

As for learning strategies, the nineteen items associated with self-regulation were adapted from the LASSI and ILS questionnaires. Exploratory factor analysis highlighted five subscales of self-regulation: information-seeking, supervising, monitoring, distraction vulnerability and lack of persistence. These five subscales were introduced in the second-order factor analysis. Two self-regulation factors were extracted from the analyses, explaining 59 per cent of the variance. Information-seeking, supervising and monitoring subscales loaded on the first factor, which can be considered as an adaptive regulation scale. Conversely, distraction vulnerability and lack of persistence subscales loaded on the second factor, named maladaptive self-regulation.

ACADEMIC ACHIEVEMENT

The overall measure of academic achievement was represented by students' average percentage for all courses at the end of the academic year, collected from department records. In the Belgian tertiary education system, 60 per cent is the overall pass mark. The final percentage from the preceding year was also collected and used as a measure of previous performance.

Specific measures of academic achievement were assessed through a test (Galand et al. 2010). In collaboration with teachers from the School of Engineering, the research team developed a criterion-referenced test to assess three learning outcomes that students should have mastered by the end of two years of studying engineering. According to the experts of the engineering faculty, these three tasks should assess the three levels of knowledge structure identified by Gijbels, Dochy, Van den Bossche and Segers (2005), namely acquisition of knowledge, understanding of principles and application of concept. The final version of the test was composed of three written tasks: (1) defining scientific concepts (acquisition of knowledge); (2) solving a mathematics problem (understanding of principles); and (3) solving a contextualized problem related to the functioning of an electro-mechanical system (application of concept). Test grades representing results in the three written tasks were retrieved and used as a specific and controlled measure of achievement.

Results

Preliminary analysis

Table 8.3 shows zero-order correlations between motivational (goal orientations and self-efficacy beliefs), cognitive (learning strategies and self-regulation) and achievement variables (final percentage and test grades). Taking this table into account, three preliminary statements can be made. First, academic achievement is highly correlated with past performance, highlighting that a student who passes the second year has a greater chance of passing the third one. More surprisingly, correlations between academic achievement and scores

Table 8.3 Correlations of the study variables

	1	2	3	4	5	6	7	8	9	10
1. Average final percentage	—									
2. Test grades	.38***	—								
3. Past performance	.68***	.34***	—							
4. Academic self-efficacy beliefs	.29***	.13	.39***	—						
5. Mastery goal	.23***	.11	.16**	.18**	—					
6. Performance goal	.00	.03	.07	.05	-.09	—				
7. Deep processing	.15*	.17**	.13*	.36***	.41***	.05	—			
8. Surface processing	-.03	-.24***	-.01	-.16*	.09	.04	.05	—		
9. Adaptive self-regulation	-.03	.13*	-.06	.01	.19**	-.02	.43***	.43***	—	
10. Maladaptive self-regulation	-.20**	-.08	-.09	-.14*	-.42***	.06	-.27***	-.14*	-.22***	—

*p < .05; **p < .01; ***p < .001

in the three written tasks were only moderate (r = .38). This second result suggests that the skills assessed by global and specific achievement measures are not entirely the same. Third, the main variables related to academic achievement differ from those related to the written tasks. Academic achievement was correlated mainly with academic self-efficacy beliefs (r = .29), mastery goal (r = .23), maladaptive self-regulation (r = −.20) and deep processing (r = .15). The three written tasks were negatively correlated with surface processing (r = −.24). Deep processing (r = .17) and adaptive self-regulation (r = .13) were also related to test grades.

From global to specific measures of achievement, while controlling for previous performance

The investigation of the impact of motivational and cognitive variables on global and specific measures of achievement was conducted by using hierarchical regressions. Based on previous studies (De Clercq et al. 2013), hierarchical regression analysis was performed in three steps. In order to control for the impact of past performance on the relationship between cognitive, motivational and achievement variables, this variable was introduced as step one. Second, motivational factors were introduced into the model. Third, cognitive factors were added. The results are presented in Table 8.4.

Predictors of final percentage

The results of the regression analyses with final percentage as dependent variable showed that mastery goal orientation was the only predictor remaining

Table 8.4 Hierarchical regression on the different achievement outcomes

	Average final percentage[a]			Test grades[b]		
	Step 1	Step 2	Step3	Step 1	Step 2	Step3
1. Past performance	.71***	.69***	.69***	.35***	.36***	.36***
2. Academic self-efficacy beliefs		.00	−.02		−.05	−.02
3. Mastery goal		.12*	.12*		.08	.03
4. Performance goal		−.04	−.04		.02	.02
5. Deep processing			.02			.24**
6. Surface processing			−.01			−.21**
7. Adaptive self-regulation			−.01			−.09
8. Maladaptive self-regulation			−.08			−.05

Notes
[a] R^2 = .51, p<.001 for Step 1; ΔR^2 = .02, p<.05 for Step 2; ΔR^2 = .00, p=.96 for Step 3.
[b] R^2 = .15, p<.001 for Step 1; ΔR^2 = .01, p=.61 for Step 2; ΔR^2 = .09, p<.001 for Step 3.
* p<.05; ** p<.01; *** p<.001

(β = .12; p < .05) when past performance was controlled for. Past performance had a significant positive impact on students' achievement (β = .69; p < .001). Self-efficacy beliefs also appeared to be a predictor of final percentage (β = .26; p < .001) but did not remain predictive of students' achievement when students' previous performance was controlled for. These results highlighted that only motivational factors have a significant impact on global measures of academic achievement over past performance. However, adding goal orientations to the model only increased the amount of variance explained in the final percentage by approximately 2 per cent, F (7, 210) = 3.11, p < .05.

Predictors of the three written tasks

The results of the regression analyses with specific learning outcomes as dependent variables revealed a consistent impact of cognitive factors on students' achievement. First, past performance had a significant positive impact on achievement in the test (β = .36; p < .001). Second, surface processing was found to be incrementally predictive of achievement (β = −.21; p < .01). Third, deep processing was highlighted as having a significant positive effect on test results (β = .24; p < .01). Results from the third step of this regression indicated that adding cognitive variables increased the amount of variance explained in test grades by approximately 9 per cent, F (7, 206) = 7.34, p < .01.

Analogous results are found when investigating the three tasks separately. Specifically, surface processing was incrementally predictive of achievement for defining scientific concepts (β = −.24; p < .001), solving a mathematics problem (β = −.17; p < .05) and solving a contextualized problem (β = −.21; p < .001). Deep processing was a significant predictor of achievement in solving a contextualized problem (β = .26; p < .001) and defining scientific concepts (β = .14; p < .05).

Discussion

This chapter was intended as a step forward in understanding the relationship between cognitive and motivational processes and different measures of academic achievement. Our findings have corroborated our assumption and provide two main results. These results provide an interesting entry point to undertake a general reflection on possible new directions in the field of learning in higher education.

Comparing 'apples and oranges': different levels of specificity with different predictors

The results highlighted that the impact of cognitive and motivational factors are not analogous from one achievement measure to another. Cognitive processes seem to have a significant impact on specific measures of achievement whereas motivational variables are more related to a global measure of achievement.

More precisely, test grades were positively predicted by deep processing and negatively by surface processing, whereas global final percentage was influenced by mastery goal orientation. In this respect, this study shows the necessity to identify carefully the underlying abilities assessed by the measure of achievement to avoid misinterpretation or inconsistent results in the literature. The inconsistencies in the extant literature could partially be explained by the lack of rigorous identification of underlying abilities evaluated by global and uncontrolled achievement measures such as grade point average and average final percentage.

In this line of thought, the use of a global measure of achievement could also be problematic in another way. Several authors argue that grades are modulated by specific requirements of the programme and vary significantly across faculties (Cliffordson 2008; Lekholm and Cliffordson 2008). In this vein, Vermunt (2005) highlighted that the link between students' learning patterns and achievements was not the same from one discipline to another. Therefore, grade point average does not always share the same underlying components and could reflect different kinds of learning, which could explain to some degree the inconsistent results. In other words, a global measure of achievement such as grade point average or final percentage could be a reflection of very different learning measures depending on exam content, faculty requirements or teachers' assessment (Lizzio, Wilson and Simons 2002). Accordingly, students in psychology may not have to meet the same requirements or master the same competencies as students in engineering. Therefore, students' uses of particular motivational and cognitive processes are benchmarked against the requirements of the programme. For instance, the adoption of deep processing could be of the utmost importance in some programmes, whereas this variable may play a secondary role in others. This reasoning questions the possibility of generalizing the results of a study to another educational context when we do not know what the specific requirements of this new context are. Without a rigorous description of the specificity of achievement measures (underlying tasks, requirements, educational context, etc.), the generalization of a factor's predictive power to another study could be very questionable. Further studies should examine this issue by investigating the effects of motivational and cognitive variables on achievement across different faculties. Multi-level analysis could be an effective way to reach this important issue.

The results also show that performance goal was a predictor neither of average final percentage nor of test grade. Moreover, if we take a close look at the correlation tables, we can clearly see that performance goal is not related to any adaptive variables such as deep processing or mastery goal. In the specific educational context of the study, our results substantiate the assertion of several authors (Dupeyrat and Mariné 2005; Fenollar et al. 2007; Kaplan et al. 2009; Phan 2009a) that there is no link between achievement and performance goal. Another explanation could be provided. According to Midgley and colleagues (2001), performance goal is a significant predictor of achievement when a high level of mastery goal and self-efficacy beliefs is also reported by the student. It follows that the actual effect of performance goal on achievement should be investigated taking students' self-efficacy beliefs and mastery goal orientation into account. This hypothesis is congruent with multiple goal theory (Pintrich 2003) and could be tested using a person-centered approach (Daniels et al. 2008).

Finally, despite some significant correlations, self-regulation was not incrementally predictive of achievement when past performance, goal orientation, self-efficacy beliefs and learning strategies were taken into account. Two hypotheses emerge from this conclusion. First, we can postulate that self-regulation has only an indirect impact on academic achievement (Dupeyrat and Mariné 2005). Second, we can also postulate that self-regulation is a strong predictor of achievement for students who have to adapt to a new learning context and new learning tasks. We can assume that the initiation of self-regulation ensures the mastery of the core competencies necessary to complete the first academic years successfully (Kaplan et al. 2009). However, when students have successfully completed the first academic years and are more acquainted with the context and the tasks (as is the case in our study), this construct could lose its predictive power on achievement.

Past performance, an important control variable

This study has also emphasized the necessity to take previous performance into account when assessing the predictors of achievement. In this regard, the factors that remain significant predictors of achievement after controlling for previous performance offer an effective entry point to promote student achievement. Our results revealed that self-efficacy beliefs, known to be a core predictor of achievement, lost their impact on achievement when controlling for students' previous performance. This result is not consistent with previous results of Chemers and colleagues (2001) which lent support for a direct and strong predictive power of academic self-efficacy beliefs for academic achievement above and beyond the impact of past academic performance. However, that study was conducted with first year university students, and could therefore suggest a different interpretation of past performance measures. Our study was undertaken with third year students. Thus, past performance was measured by final percentage obtained at the end of the second year. Therefore, strong past performance could be interpreted as demonstrating good adaptation to the academic world and its requirements, leading to mastery of the different subjects taught (content knowledge). Conversely, past performance in the first year of university is measured by high school grade. This second measure cannot be considered as demonstrating good adaptation to the academic world or a good knowledge of the programme content. Strong past performance in this context refers rather to students' general cognitive abilities (Richardson, Abraham and Bond 2012). Insofar as past performance can reflect two different underlying constructs (content knowledge and cognitive ability), its relationship with self-efficacy beliefs could also be specific from one measure to another.

Limitations and perspectives

Two limitations are particularly noteworthy. First, it is worth mentioning that the reliability of three subscales (rehearsing, distraction vulnerability and lack of persistence) was poor. This low reliability could qualify the validity of our results. Therefore, our studies need to be replicated to corroborate our findings. Second, although the analyses indicated a significant increase in the amount of variance explained in the final percentage, the strength of the relationship between mastery goal orientation and final percentage was low. This information has to be taken into account when interpreting the findings of this study.

Conclusion

This study sheds light on the differences emerging from the selection of two competing measures of achievement. Our hope is to pinpoint a gap in the educational literature that could, to a considerable extent, explain the inconsistencies in the current literature. The construct of academic achievement is often considered to be analogous from one study to another. However, the underlying content of achievement measures really depends on the context to which it belongs. The requirements, the courses and the tasks behind a global measure of academic achievement vary greatly from one programme to another, from one university to another and from one country to another. Therefore, it seems very important to take these variations into account when considering different studies together. A more in-depth depiction of the measures of achievement could yield more clarity in the literature about academic achievement. Moreover, the use of specific achievement measures designed to assess explicit abilities in higher education could also further our understanding of the actual impact of learning processes on achievement and broaden our understanding of this thorny issue.

From a practical point of view, the findings of this study substantiate the positive impact of deep processing and the negative impact of surface processing on specific tasks, over and above the influence of past performance. Thus, teaching practices in engineering faculties should foster the adoption of critical thinking and insist on the importance of relating the material taught with other courses and concrete applications. The study of Gibbs and Coffey (2004) shed light on some ways to develop teaching practices that could meet this specific need. Conversely, the caveat against the use of rote processing should be re-emphasized, even for learning tasks such as memorizing definitions of scientific concepts. Although rehearsal could be seen as the most adaptive and effective strategy for memorizing definitions, the results of this study refute this spontaneous assumption in engineering faculties. These two guidelines may help teachers to promote effective learning among students in engineering faculties, leading to the in-depth acquisition of the competencies required for academic achievement.

References

Adeyemo, D. A. (2007) Moderating influence of emotional intelligence on the link between academic self-efficacy and achievement of university students. *Psychology and Developing Societies, 19*, 199–213. doi: 10.1177/097133360701900204

Ames, C. (1992) Classrooms: Goals, structures, and student motivation. *Journal of Educational Psychology, 84*, 261–271. doi: 10.1037/0022-0663.84.3.261

Bandura, A. (1997) *Self-efficacy: The exercise of control.* New York: Freeman.

Biggs, J. B. (1984) Learning strategies, student motivation patterns, and subjectively perceived success. In J. R. Kirby (Ed.), *Cognitive Strategies and Educational Performance* (pp. 111–134). New York: Academic Press.

Boekaerts, M. and Cascallar, E. (2006) How far have we moved toward the integration of theory and practice in self-regulation? *Educational Psychology Review, 18*(3), 199–210. doi: 10.1007/s10648-006-9013-4

Bong, M. (2005) Within-grade changes in Korean girls' motivation and perceptions of the learning environment across domains and achievement levels. *Journal of Educational Psychology, 97*, 656–672.

Bong, M. and Skaalvik, E. M. (2003). Academic self-concept and self-efficacy: How different are they really?. *Educational Psychology Review, 15*(1), 1–40.

Bouffard, T. R. S., Boisvert, J., Vezeau, C. and Larouche, C. (1995) The impact of goal orientation of self-regulation and performance among college students. *British Journal of Educational Psychology, 65*, 317–329.

Brown, S. D., Tramayne, S., Hoxha, D., Telander, K., Fan, X. and Lent, R. W. (2008) Social cognitive predictors of college students' academic performance and persistence: A meta-analytic path analysis. *Journal of Vocational Behavior, 72*, 298–308.

Bruinsma, M. (2004) Motivation, cognitive processing and achievement in higher education. *Learning and Instruction, 14*, 549–568.

Busato, V. V., Prins, F. J., Elshout, J. J. and Hamaker, C. (2000) Intellectual ability, learning style, personality, achievement motivation and academic success of psychology students in higher education. *Personality and Individual Differences, 29*, 1057–1068. doi: 10.1016/s0191-8869(99)00253-6

Chemers, M. M., Hu, L. and Garcia, B. (2001) Academic self-efficacy and first-year college student performance and adjustment. *Journal of Educational Psychology, 93*, 55–64.

Cliffordson, C. (2008) Differential prediction of study success across academic programs in the Swedish context: The validity of grades and tests as selection instruments for higher education. *Educational Assessment, 13*, 56–75. doi: 10.1080/10627190801968240

Dahl, T. I., Bals, M. and Turi, A. L. (2005) Are students' beliefs about knowledge and learning associated with their reported use of learning strategies? *British Journal of Educational Psychology, 75*, 257–273. doi: 10.1348/000709905X25049

Daniels, L. M., Haynes, T. L., Stupnisky, R. H., Perry, R. P., Newall, N. E. and Pekrun, R. (2008) Individual differences in achievement goals: A longitudinal study of cognitive, emotional, and achievement outcomes. *Contemporary Educational Psychology, 33*, 584–608. doi: 10.1016/j.cedpsych.2007.08.002

De Clercq, M., Galand, B., Dupont, S. and Frenay, M. (2012) Achievement among first-year university students: An integrated and contextualised approach. *European Journal of Psychology of Education*, 1–22. doi: 10.1007/s10212-012-0133-6

De Clercq, M., Galand, B. and Frenay, M. (2013) Chicken or the egg: Longitudinal analysis of the causal dilemma between goal orientation, self-regulation and cognitive processing strategies in higher education. *Studies in Educational Evaluation*, 39, 4–13. doi: http://dx.doi.org/10.1016/j.stueduc.2012.10.003

Dinsmore, D. and Alexander, P. (2012) A critical discussion of deep and surface processing: What it means, how it is measured, the role of context, and model specification. *Educational Psychology Review*, 24, 499–567. doi: 10.1007/s10648-012-9198-7

Diseth, Å. (2011) Self-efficacy, goal orientations and learning strategies as mediators between preceding and subsequent academic achievement. *Learning and Individual Differences*, 21, 191–195. doi: 10.1016/j.lindif.2011.01.003

Dupeyrat, C. (2000) Conceptions de l'intelligence, orientation de buts et apprentissage auto-régulé chez des adultes en reprises d'études [Implicit theories of intelligence, goal orientations, and self-regulated learning among adult students], Unpublished doctoral dissertation, Université de Toulouse II, France.

Dupeyrat, C. and Mariné, C. (2005) Implicit theories of intelligence, goal orientation, cognitive engagement, and achievement: A test of Dweck's model with returning to school adults. *Contemporary Educational Psychology*, 30, 43–59. doi: 10.1016/j.cedpsych.2004.01.007

Dweck, C. S. and Leggett, E. L. (1988) A social-cognitive approach to motivation and personality. *Psychological Review*, 95, 256–273. doi: 10.1037/0033-295x.95.2.256

Eccles, J. S. and Wigfield, A. (2002) Motivational beliefs, values, and goals. *Annual Review of Psychology*, 53, 109–132.

Elias, S. M. and MacDonald, S. (2007) Using past performance, proxy efficacy, and academic self-efficacy to predict college performance. *Journal of Applied Social Psychology*, 37, 2518–2531. doi: 10.1111/j.1559-1816.2007.00268.x

Elliot, A. J. and McGregor, H. A. (2001) A 2 × 2 achievement goal framework. *Journal of Personality and Social Psychology*, 80, 501–519. doi: 10.1037/0022-3514.80.3.501

Elliot, A. J., Murayama, K. and Pekrun, R. (2011) A 3 × 2 achievement goal model. *Journal of Educational Psychology*, 103, 632–648. doi: 10.1016/s0361-476x(02)00043-7

Entwistle, N. and Ramsden, P. (1983) *Understanding Student Learning*. London and Canberra: Croom Helm.

Entwistle, N. and McCune, V. (2004) The conceptual bases of study strategy inventories. *Educational Psychology Review*, 16, 325–345. doi: 10.1007/s10648-004-0003-0

Fenollar, P., Román, S. and Cuestas, P. J. (2007) University students' academic performance: An integrative conceptual framework and empirical analysis. *British Journal of Educational Psychology*, 77, 873–891.

Galand, B. and Grégoire, J. (2000) L'impact des pratiques scolaires d'évaluation sur les motivations et le concept de soi des élèves [The impact of student evaluation practices on achievement motivation and self-concept among students]. *Orientation Scolaire et Professionnelle*, 29, 431–452.

Galand, B. and Philippot, P. (2002) Style motivationnel des élèves du secondaire: Developpement d'un instrument de mesure et relations avec d'autres variables pédagogiques [Achievement goals orientation in middle school: Validation of a scale for French-speaking students and its relationships with other motivational variables]. *Revue canadienne des sciences du comportement [Canadian Journal of Behavioural Science]*, 34, 261–275. doi: 10.1037/h0087179

Galand, B. and Vanlede, M. (2004) Le sentiment d'efficacité personnelle dans la formation: Quel rôle joue-t-il? D'où vient-il? Comment intervenir? [Self-efficacy beliefs in adult education and training: What are its effects? Where does it come from? How to intervene?] *Savoirs – Revue Internationale de Recherches en Education et Formation des Adultes*, 1, 'Autour de l'oeuvre d'Albert Bandura', 91–116.

Galand, B. and Frenay, M. (2005) *L'approche par problèmes et par projets dans l'enseignement supérieur: Impact, enjeux et défis [Problem and project based learning in higher education: Impact, issues, and challenges]*. Louvain-la-Neuve: Presses Universitaires de Louvain.

Galand, B., Raucent, B. and Frenay, M. (2010) Engineering students' self-regulation, study strategies, and motivational believes in traditional and problem-based curricula. *International Journal of Engineering Education*, 26, 523–534.

Gibbs, G. and Coffey, M. (2004) The impact of training of university teachers on their teaching skills, their approach to teaching and the approach to learning of their students. *Active Learning in Higher Education*, 5, 87–100.

Gijbels, D., Dochy, F., Van den Bossche, P. and Segers, M. (2005). Effects of problem-based learning: A meta-analysis from the angle of assessment. *Review of Educational Research*, 75(1), 27–61.

Greene, B. A., Miller, R. B., Crowson, H., Duke, B. L. and Akey, K. L. (2004) Predicting high school students' cognitive engagement and achievement: Contributions of classroom perceptions and motivation. *Contemporary Educational Psychology*, 29, 462–482.

Harackiewicz, J. M., Barron, K. E., Tauer, J. M., Carter, S. M. and Elliot, A. J. (2000) Short-term and long-term consequences of achievement goals: Predicting interest and performance over time. *Journal of Educational Psychology*, 92, 316–330. doi: 10.1037/0022-0663.92.2.316

Harackiewicz, J. M., Barron, K. E., Tauer, J. M. and Elliot, A. J. (2002) Predicting success in college: A longitudinal study of achievement goals and ability measures as predictors of interest and performance from freshman year through graduation. *Journal of Educational Psychology*, 94, 562–575. doi: 10.1037/0022-0663.94.3.562

Howell, A. J. and Watson, D. C. (2007) Procrastination: Associations with achievement goal orientation and learning strategies. *Personality and Individual Differences*, 43, 167–178. doi: 10.1016/j.paid.2006.11.017

Huang, C. (2011) Self-concept and academic achievement: A meta-analysis of longitudinal relations. *Journal of School Psychology*, 49, 505–528. doi: 10.1016/j.jsp.2011.07.001

Hulleman, C. S., Schrager, S. M., Bodmann, S. M. and Harackiewicz, J. M. (2010) A meta-analytic review of achievement goal measures: Different labels for the same constructs or different constructs with similar labels? *Psychological Bulletin*, 136, 422–449. doi: 10.1037//0022-0663.80.3.260

Jakoubek, J. and Swenson, R. R. (1993) Differences in use of learning-strategies and relation to grades among undergraduate students. *Psychological Reports*, 73, 787–793.

Jansen, E. P. W. A. and Bruinsma, M. (2005) Explaining achievement in higher education. *Educational Research & Evaluation*, 11, 235–252. doi: 10.1080/13803610500101173

Kaplan, A., Lichtinger, E. and Gorodetsky, M. (2009) Achievement goal orientations and self-regulation in writing: An integrative perspective. *Journal of Educational Psychology*, 101, 51–69. doi: 10.1037/a0013200

Kember, D. and Gow, L. (1994) Orientations to teaching and their effect on the quality of student learning. *The Journal of Higher Education*, 65, 58–74.

Kennett, D., Young, A. M. and Catanzaro, M. (2009) Variables contributing to academic success in an intermediate statistics course: The importance of learned resourcefulness. *Educational Psychology*, 29, 815–830. doi: 10.1080/01443410903305401

Kumar, S. and Jagacinski, C. M. (2011) Confronting task difficulty in ego involvement: Change in performance goals. *Journal of Educational Psychology*, *103*, 664–682. doi: 10.1037/a0023336

Lekholm, A. K. and Cliffordson, C. (2008) Discrepancies between school grades and test scores at individual and school level: Effects of gender and family background. *Educational Research & Evaluation*, *14*, 181–199. doi: 10.1080/13803610801956663

Lizzio, A., Wilson, K. and Simons, R. (2002) University students' perceptions of the learning environment and academic outcomes: Implications for theory and practice. *Studies in Higher Education*, *27*, 27–52.

Marsh, H. W., Craven, R. G., Hinkley, J. W. and Debus, R. L. (2003) Evaluation of the Big-Two-Factor Theory of academic motivation orientations: An evaluation of jingle-jangle fallacies. *Multivariate Behavioral Research*, *38*, 189–224. doi: 10.1207/s15327906mbr 3802_3

Marton, F. (1988) Describing and improving learning. In R. R. Scmeck (Ed.), *Learning strategies and learning styles* (pp. 54–82). New York: Plenum.

Midgley, C., Kaplan, A., Middleton, M., Urdan, T., Maehr. M. L., Hicks, L. et al. (1998). The development and validation of scales assessing students' achievement goal orientation. *Contemporary Educational Psychology*, *23*, 113–131.

Midgley, C., Kaplan, A. and Middleton, M. (2001). Performance-approach goals: Good for what, for whom, under what circumstances, and at what cost? *Journal of Educational Psychology*, *93*(1), 77–86. doi: 10.1037/0022-0663.93.1.77

Minnaert, A. and Janssen, P. J. (1999) The additive effect of regulatory activities on top of intelligence in relation to academic performance in higher education. *Learning and Instruction*, *9*(1), 77–91. doi: 10.1016/s0959-4752(98)00019-x

Nicholls, J. G. (1984) Achievement motivation: Conceptions of ability, subjective experience, task choice, and performance. *Psychological Review*, *91*, 328–346. doi: 10.1037/0033-295x.91.3.328

Nicholls, J. G. (1989). *The competitive ethos and democratic education.* Cambridge: Harvard University Press.

Nota, L., Soresi, S. and Zimmerman, B. J. (2004) Self-regulation and academic achievement and resilience: A longitudinal study. *International Journal of Educational Research*, *41*, 198–215. doi: 10.1016/j.ijer.2005.07.001

Perry, R. P., Hladkyj, S., Pekrun, R. H. and Pelletier, S. T. (2001) Academic control and action control in the achievement of college students: A longitudinal field study. *Journal of Educational Psychology*, *93*, 776–789. doi: 10.1037/0022-0663.93.4.776

Phan, H. P. (2009a) Amalgamation of future time orientation, epistemological beliefs, achievement goals and study strategies: Empirical evidence established. *British Journal of Educational Psychology*, *79*, 155–173. doi: 10.1348/000709908x306864

Phan, H. P. (2009b) Relations between goals, self-efficacy, critical thinking and deep processing strategies: A path analysis. *Educational Psychology*, *29*, 777–799. doi: 10.1080/01443410903289423

Pintrich, P. R. (1999) The role of motivation in promoting and sustaining self-regulated learning. *International Journal of Educational Research*, *31*, 459–470.

Pintrich, P. R. (2003) A motivational science perspective on the role of student motivation in learning and teaching contexts. *Journal of Educational Psychology*, *95*, 667–686.

Pintrich, P. R. and De Groot, E. V. (1990) Motivational and self-regulated learning components of classroom academic performance. *Journal of Educational Psychology*, *82*, 33–40.

Richardson, M., Abraham, C. and Bond, R. (2012) Psychological correlates of university students' academic performance: A systematic review and meta-analysis. *Psychological Bulletin*, *138*, 353–387.

Robbins, S. B., Lauver, K., Le, H., Davis, D., Langley, R. and Carlstrom, A. (2004) Do psychosocial and study skill factors predict college outcomes? A meta-analysis. *Psychological Bulletin, 130*, 261–288. doi: 10.1037/0033-2909.130.2.261

Robbins, S. B., Allen, J., Casillas, A., Peterson, C. H. and Le, H. (2006). Unraveling the differential effects of motivational and skills, social, and self-management measures from traditional predictors of college outcomes. *Journal of Educational Psychology, 98*(3), 598–616. doi: 10.1037/0022-0663.98.3.598

Serra de Lemos, M. and Gonçalves, T. (2004) Students' management of goals in the natural classroom setting: Methodological implications. *European Psychologist, 9*, 198–209. doi: 10.1027/1016-9040.9.4.198

Shell, D. F. and Husman, J. (2008) Control, motivation, affect, and strategic self-regulation in the college classroom: A multidimensional phenomenon. *Journal of Educational Psychology, 100*, 443–459.

Simons, J., Dewitte, S. and Lens, W. (2004) The role of different types of instrumentality in motivation, study strategies, and performance: Know why you learn, so you'll know what you learn! *British Journal of Educational Psychology, 74*, 343–360.

Torres, J. B. and Solberg, V. S. (2001) Role of self-efficacy, stress, social integration, and family support in Latino college student persistence and health. *Journal of Vocational Behavior, 59*, 53–63.

Valentine, J. C., DuBois, D. L. and Cooper, H. (2004) The relation between self-beliefs and academic achievement: A meta-analytic review. *Educational Psychologist, 39*, 111–133.

Valle, A., Núñez, J. C., Cabanach, R. G., González-Pienda, J. A., Rodríguez, S., Rosário, P. and Muñoz-Cadavid, M. A. (2008) Self-regulated profiles and academic achievement. *Psicothema, 20*, 724–731.

Vermunt, J.D. (1994) *Inventory of learning styles (ILS) in higher education*. Tilburg: University of Tilburg.

Vermunt, J. D. (1998) The regulation of constructive learning processes. *British Journal of Educational Psychology, 68*, 149–171.

Vermunt, J. (2005) Relations between student learning patterns and personal and contextual factors and academic performance. *Higher Education, 49*, 205–234. doi: 10.1007/s10734-004-6664-2

Vermunt, J. and Vermetten, Y. (2004) Patterns in student learning: relationships between learning strategies, conceptions of learning, and learning orientations. *Educational Psychology Review, 16*, 359–384. doi: 10.1007/s10648-004-0005-y

Ward, P. J. and Walker, J. J. (2008) The influence of study methods and knowledge processing on academic success and long-term recall of anatomy learning by first-year veterinary students. *Anatomical Sciences Education, 1*, 68–74. doi: 10.1002/Ase.12

Weinstein, C. E., Goetz, E. T. and Alexander, P. A. (1988) *Learning and study strategies*. New York: Academic Press.

Young, A. J. (1997) I think, therefore I'm motivated: The relations among cognitive strategy use, motivational orientation and classroom perceptions over time. *Learning and Individual Differences, 9*, 249–283. doi: 10.1016/s1041-6080(97)90009-1

Zimmerman, B. J. (1999) Commentary: Toward a cyclically interactive view of self-regulated learning. *International Journal of Educational Research, 31*, 545–551. doi: 10.1016/s0883-0355(99)00021-x

Zimmerman, B. J. (2000) Self-efficacy: An essential motive to learn. *Contemporary Educational Psychology, 25*, 82–91.

University students' achievement goals and approaches to learning in mathematics

A re-analysis investigating 'learning patterns'

Francisco Cano and Ana Belén García Berbén

Learning approaches and, in particular, the student learning patterns that can be identified, mainly in higher education, have attracted much interest from researchers in the last few decades (Meyer 2000; Vermunt & Vermetten 2004). The bulk of these studies are based on the student approach to learning (SAL) perspective, which refers to the way students go about the task of learning: their learning/study processes and related motivations (Biggs 2001; Entwistle & McCune 2004). Likewise, research on motivation has received particular attention in recent years, particularly the area of students' achievement goals (AG) and the different patterns of combination among them (i.e. multiple goal perspective) (Pintrich 2000, 2003). This has been the focus of an increasing number of theoretical and empirical studies. This AG perspective refers to the reasons or purposes students cite when engaged in academic work (Elliot & McGregor 2001).

Although both SAL and AG are related to students' motivations and perceptions of their learning environments and some analyses have been carried out to identify, separately, groups of individuals with similar SAL or AG patterns, there is a dearth of research examining the relationship between SAL and AG from a person-centred analysis (i.e. taking the individual as the unit of study). In the present investigation, we re-analyse data from an earlier investigation (Cano & Berbén 2009), this time using a combination of clustering procedures and discriminant analysis aimed at the identification of possible learning patterns constituted by the core variables of each of these research perspectives.

In what follows, we examine: (a) SAL patterns and changes in how they are analysed; (b) AG patterns; and (c) the interrelationship between SAL and AG. We then focus on the above-mentioned re-analysis, a discussion of the results and a comment on their theoretical and practical implications.

SAL patterns

Within the framework of the SAL perspective, research on student learning patterns has been extensive, including a wide variety of labels for apparently similar constructs that have evolved in different directions. In Chapter 2 of this book, Vanthournout, Donche, Gijbels and Van Petegem distinguished between the Biggs model and the Vermunt model (see also Vanthournout, Donche, Gijbels and Van Petegem 2009).

As we will describe later, authors within Biggs' theoretical framework have used labels such as patterns of learning or study orchestrations to describe the way in which (sub)groups of students approach their learning. The primary conceptual basis of Biggs' model (Biggs 2001) is his operationalisation of deep and surface SAL in terms of both a motive (why they learn) and a related learning strategy (what they do). The Revised Two Factor version of the Study Process Questionnaire (R-SPQ-2F) (Biggs, Kember & Leung 2001) aims to measure these (theoretically) opposed and mutually exclusive SAL (Biggs 1987; Entwistle, Hanley & Hounsell 1979). A deep approach to learning is associated with students' intrinsic motivation (e.g. intention to understand the author's intent) and their use of a meaningful strategy (e.g. integrating formal knowledge with experience). A surface approach is associated with students' extrinsic motivation (e.g. to avoid failure with the least personal effort) and their use of a repetitive strategy (e.g. memorising specific facts and accurately reproducing them). SAL are not stable traits, appear to be linked to both personological factors (e.g. conception of learning) and contextual factors (e.g. students' perceptions of their academic environment) (Baeten, Kyndt, Struyven & Dochy 2010; Biggs 1993; Biggs et al. 2001; Entwistle & McCune 2004), and generally influence learning outcomes (Biggs 2001; Marton & Säljö 1976a, 1976b). Thus, a constructive conception of learning or a cohesive experience of the subject matter they are studying (e.g. mathematics) and a positive perception of the academic environment (e.g. clear goals and standards, good quality teaching and appropriate assessment and workload) tend to be associated with a deep approach to learning, while the opposite tend to be linked to the adoption of a surface learning approach (e.g. Baeten et al. 2010; Crawford, Gordon, Nicholas & Prosser 1998; Trigwell & Prosser 1991a, 1991b).

Vermunt's model (Vermunt 1998) seems to be more integrative than Biggs' model, given its focus on the interplay between the various components of student learning: learning strategies (cognitive processing and regulative strategies), learning conceptions and learning orientations (motivational aspects). On the basis of a review of the components of learning and of phenomenographic analyses of how students go about learning (e.g. ways of learning, conceptions of learning, personal goals in their studies), Vermunt (1998) developed the Inventory of Learning Styles (ILS). Using principal component analysis, he found four factors or dimensions that delineated four different patterns (i.e. patterns of factor loadings of students on each of the components of the ILS), initially labelled as styles: an undirected style, a reproduction-directed style, a meaning-directed style and an application-directed style. However, admitting that these learning components were not stable and that they could be modified, he went on to use the term 'learning pattern'. This is the way students usually engage in learning and is characterised by a combination of different learning components. In recent publications it has been acknowledged that for learning pattern detection, cluster analysis is a better option than factor analysis, since while the former combines individuals in mutually exclusive categories, the latter combines variables (Donche & Van Petegem 2009). Moreover, factor analysis provides coordinates in an underlying multivariate space, but cannot indicate which entities go together (Gorman & Primavera 1983) and factor scores are not mutually exclusive variables.

Biggs and Vermunt 'use different but somewhat related concepts and dimensions to describe student learning . . . (and as Vermunt 1998, wrote) . . . "meaning-directed" and "reproduction-directed" learning patterns were to some extent related to what Biggs regards as "deep" and "surface" approaches to learning' (Vanthournout et al. 2009: 38).

Once these two models have been presented, an interesting question would be the following: what were the techniques used by researchers for detecting learning patterns? The answer to this would facilitate fulfilling the aim of this study.

Changes in the analysis of learning patterns

Basically, the way in which researchers have examined learning patterns has evolved in a direction of increasing complexity and improvement of analytical techniques.

On the basis of Biggs' model, some researchers detected, by means of cluster analysis, how students with similar learning patterns combine their learning approaches. Thus, Cano (2005, 2007) used k-means clustering and found that secondary and high school students could be put in four different groups: (a) surface: low scores on deep approach and high scores on surface approach; (b) deep: low scores on surface approach and high scores on deep approach; (c) high scores on both deep and surface approaches; and (d) low scores on both deep and surface approaches. Taking into account that deep and surface learning approaches are theoretically opposed and mutually exclusive (Biggs 1987; Entwistle et al. 1979), some of these patterns were congruent or coherent (e.g. a and b), whereas others were incoherent or dissonant (e.g. c and d). These groups differed from one another with regard to academic performance (Cano 2005, 2007): those who performed better displayed deeper and more congruent patterns, whereas those who manifested incoherent patterns and those who deployed congruent but surface patterns achieved least. Moreover, when comparing learning patterns in some other variables (e.g. metacognitive learning strategies, family's intellectual climate), worse scores were obtained by those who learned in a surface way or exhibited incoherent learning patterns (Cano 2007).

In this vein, Vanthournout, Gijbels, Coertjens and Van Petegem (2008), in a study on the development of the learning patterns of student teachers, identified by means of k-means cluster analysis five learning patterns: a high ambivalent profile (high scores in both deep and surface SAL); a deep approach profile; a surface approach profile; a moderate ambivalent profile (moderate scores in both approaches); and a fallen angels profile (low scores in both approaches).

The simple and apparently effective procedure followed in these studies seems, however, to have some theoretical and methodological limitations. First, only scores on the learning approaches subscales were included in the analysis, omitting some significant theoretical components of learning patterns (e.g. students' conceptions of learning and their perceptions of their learning environment). Second, they employed the k-means clustering technique, whose disadvantage is its use of a more or less arbitrary criterion to determine a globally optimal solution, which means (a) that there is no guarantee of convergence, (b) that it tends to obtain a degraded performance when the number of clusters is unknown (Steinley & Brusco 2011) and (c) that it may not yield consistent results (Richardson 2007).

Other authors, such as Prosser, Trigwell, Hazel and Waterhouse (2000) reduced some of these limitations by including in their analysis additional variables, such as students' perceptions of the learning context, and by using cluster techniques (e.g. Ward's hierarchical method) that are more valid in terms of both identification of the correct number of clusters (Milligan & Cooper 1985) and population recovery capabilities (Overall, Gibson & Novy 1993). Prosser et al. (2000) collected information focused on first-year participants: learning approaches, pre- and post-conceptual knowledge and perceptions of a specific course (physics). The latter were obtained by calculating the means of the grouping of the subscales of the Course Experience Questionnaire (CEQ; Ramsden 1991) into deep perception and surface perception. After submitting data to Ward's method, four clusters emerged: (a) the understanding cluster, characterised by deep perceptions, deep approach, well developed pre- and post-conceptual knowledge, and high academic achievement; (b) the reproducing cluster, characterised by exactly the opposite to the understanding cluster; (c) the disengaged cluster, characterised by students with low scores in both learning approaches, and in both deep and surface perceptions of the learning context, poor pre- and post-conceptual knowledge and average achievement; and (d) the disintegrated cluster, characterised by poor pre- and post-conceptual knowledge, disintegrated perceptions and approaches (they perceived their learning environment as affording both deep and surface learning approaches and reported adopting both approaches), and lowest achieving. The authors indicated that this disintegration or incoherence 'is structurally similar to Meyer, Parsons and Dunne's (1990) conception of disintegrated perceptions' (Prosser et al. 2000: 69), which is linked to 'study orchestration'; a construct, that although close to learning pattern, is not identical to it.

Meyer and colleagues (Meyer et al. 1990; Meyer 2000), who have used statistical techniques such as unfolding analysis and cluster analysis to detect study orchestrations, define it as a contextualised pattern of engagement in learning adopted by individual students or by a group of students, which is sensitive to students' conceptions of learning as well as to their perceptions of their learning context. While some study orchestrations are theoretically interpretable (i.e. they display 'conceptual consonance' between how the context and the content of learning are perceived and how learning takes place), others are theoretically un-interpretable (i.e. they display 'conceptual dissonance', between students perceptions of the learning context and their learning approaches). This notion was the theme of special editions of both the *European Journal of Psychology of Education* (vol. 15, no. 1) and *Studies in Higher Education* (vol. 28, no. 1), and has been the object of complex conceptualisations as has Meyer's 'interference model' (Meyer 2000), a measurement requiring '(a) two or more distinct and conceptually consonant but contrasting dimensions of variation and/or (b) at least one dimension of variation constituted in terms of conceptually "dissonant" sources of variation' (Meyer 2000: 10) that go beyond the scope of the current study, whose major focus will be the simple concept of learning patterns within Biggs' model. Nevertheless, it is worth mentioning that the study orchestration construct appears in some studies conducted within the framework of both Biggs' and Vermunt's models, and is related to the construct of self-regulation (e.g. Vermunt & Verloop 2000). An extensive review of learning pattern research inspired by Vermunt's model is also beyond the purpose of this work (see Donche & Van Petegem 2009; Richardson 2007; Vermunt 1998). There are, however, a few studies whose review would be useful because, although they could be improved by using clustering techniques other than k-means, their authors used some subscales related to both Vermunt's and Biggs' models.

Lonka and Lindblom-Ylänne published a series of investigations on study orchestrations. In the earlier one (Lonka & Lindblom-Ylänne 1996), they analysed them at the group level (forming a variable based on factor scores obtained from the principal components analysis of the different variables analysed). In the later one (Lindblom-Ylänne & Lonka 1999), however, they used the individual as the unit of study, according to Meyer's suggestions (Meyer et al. 1990; Meyer 2000). They measured different aspects of the learning of advanced medical students (e.g. learning approaches, learning conceptions, self-regulation, achievement motivation) and submitted them to a k-means cluster analysis. They identified four different study orchestrations: (a) meaning-oriented independent students, the typical good students (e.g. deep learning approach, constructivist conception of learning); (b) meaning-oriented students with a novice-like conception of knowledge (more dualistic than that of the others); (c) reproduction-oriented and application-directed students, who were professionally orientated but combined low scores on both achievement motivation and self-regulation, with high scores on surface approach; and (d) reproduction-oriented and externally regulated students, who displayed high scores on surface approach, lack of regulation and intake of knowledge (learning viewed as taking in knowledge provided by education through memorising and reproducing). When the academic success of these groups was compared, students of the first group obtained the highest grades, whereas students of the last group obtained the lowest grades. None of the remaining post hoc comparisons was statistically significant. Finally, they made a qualitative analysis of the four clusters by interviewing their members and found that 'dissonant study orchestrations may develop because of the mismatch between the demands of the learning environment and students' personal goals' (Lindblom–Ylänne & Lonka 1999: 1).

At this point it seems appropriate to ask if there is any evidence of the links between SAL and AG research. In the previous paragraphs, we found only scant references, such as those of Vermunt and Vermetten (2004) and Lindblom–Ylänne and Lonka (1999). The former included students' personal goals as part of learning orientations, inspired by Gibbs, Morgan and Taylor (1984), but this is a really broad notion that includes 'intentions, motives, expectations, attitudes, worries and doubts with regard to their studies' (Vermunt & Vermetten 2004: 362). The latter integrated achievement motivation in their analysis of study orchestrations but this subscale was taken from Entwistle and Ramsden (1983), and motivation theory in general and AG in particular have grown substantially in the past three decades (e.g. Hulleman, Schrager, Bodman & Harackiewicz 2010; Senko, Hulleman & Harackiewicz 2011).

AG patterns

AG theory 'has been one of the most prominent theories of motivation in educational research for more than 25 years' (Senko et al. 2011: 26) and has focused on the reasons students have for engaging in achievement-related behaviour and on evaluating their competence. These reasons have been considered as cognitive-dynamic 'representations rather than implicit needs or drives' (Hulleman et al. 2010: 423). Elliot and McGregor (2001) differentiate the way competence is defined: absolute/intra-personal (mastery) and normative (performance), and the way in which it is valenced: positive (approaching success) and negative (avoiding failure). This 2 x 2 framework results in four types of personal AG: (a) mastery-approach (focused on developing competence by gaining understanding and learning); (b) mastery-avoidance (focused on avoiding misunderstanding and intrapersonal incompetence); (c) performance-approach (focused on demonstrating competence and receiving public recognition); and (d) performance-avoidance (focused on avoiding failure, looking incompetent or doing badly relative to others). The types of goal endorsed lead to differential patterns of cognition, affect and behaviour (Ames 1992; Dweck & Leggett 1988; Elliot & McGregor 2001). Reliable and valid indices of each of these AGs can be obtained by means of the Achievement Goal Questionnaire (Elliot & McGregor 2001).

In addition to these personal goals, AG theorists have analysed two 'goal structures', that is, goals that are perceived in the learning environment (Wolters

2004). In a mastery goal structure, learning, understanding, effort and improvement are emphasised, whereas in a performance goal structure, emphasis is put on performing well, high ability relative to others, grades and test scores (Ames 1992; Ames & Archer 1988; Maehr & Midgley 1996).

Although much work has been done on the adoption of single separate goals, through using variable-centred analyses, the latest developments of AG theory have led to an examination of how students strive for multiple goals (Barron & Harackiewicz 2001; Pintrich 2000) by using person-centred analyses where individuals, rather than variables, are classified into categories (i.e. clusters of individuals who adopt similar multiple goals). Moreover, researchers have investigated how these different clusters of students differed on a variety of antecedents and consequences (e.g. Hulleman et al. 2010; Senko et al. 2011; Wolters 2004), and suggested that students' 'goals for a specific course rather than their goals for a given semester' be examined (Pastor, Barron, Miller & Davis 2007: 39).

Interrelationship between SAL and AG

For the purpose of the present research there is a tentative synthesis to draw from what has been explained so far: from a theoretical point of view AG and SAL seem to coincide in two aspects. First, AG and SAL both include some forms of motivation: demonstrating one's competence (performance goal orientation) and increasing one's competence (mastery goal orientation) in the case of AG (e.g. Elliot & McGregor 2001), and fear of failure and extrinsic (surface approach) versus intrinsic (deep approach), in the case of SAL (e.g. Entwistle, McCune and Walker 2001). Second, AG and SAL are linked to students' perceptions of their academic environment: AG are related particularly to perceived goals (goal structures) e.g. motives for effort, grading practices (e.g. Ames 1992; Wolters 2004), while SAL are related to their perceptions of their learning context in general, e.g. good teaching, assessment practices (e.g. Crawford et al. 1998; Richardson 2006). Furthermore, students learn neither in a deep nor a surface way exclusively, since these approaches can be combined; nor do they adopt only single goals since they can strive for multiple goals; approaches and goals that seem appropriate for a specific course are adopted. Are there, then, some traces of the possible links between multiple AG and multiple SAL? Could learning patterns (SAL perspective: Biggs' model) and multiple goals (AG perspective) be integrated?

One of the few studies where the interplay between SAL and AG perspectives was analysed (Cano & Berbén 2009), found a moderate association between them (canonical discriminant analysis) and detected four groups of students (Ward's clustering technique), enrolled on mathematics courses, who had distinctive multiple AG: (a) low AG, specifically on mastery goals (cluster 1); (b) low AG but moderately high mastery approach (cluster 2); (c) high AG but low performance approach (cluster 3); and (d) high AG, specifically on performance

approach (cluster 4). The students in these clusters showed statistically significant differences (MANOVA/Descriptive Discriminant Analysis) in different
variables. Thus, students in cluster 2, in particular, seemed the most adaptive because
they held a cohesive conception of mathematics, had a mastery-structured perception of their learning environment and adopted a deep learning approach. In
spite of using a suitable clustering technique, this study did not, however,
tackle the analysis of multiple SAL.

This limitation would be reduced by re-analysing these data, taking as
starting point a liberal definition of learning pattern: the way in which students usually engage in learning by blending both multiple AG and multiple
SAL. Therefore, consistent with Biggs' (2001) and Elliot and McGregor's
(2001) models and with the scant results of previous research, the aim of
this study will be to find support for a general rather than specific a priori
hypothesis: the existence of different groups of students characterised by different patterns of learning which include some core variables of SAL and AG
perspectives.

Method

Participants

To investigate the preceding hypothesis, data from students participating
in Cano and Berbén's (2009) research were re-analysed using a person-
centred method based on clustering techniques of accredited validity. The
data were from 680 first-year students recruited from 24 randomly selected
mathematics classes (e.g. algebra), these courses being offered in diverse
academic areas (e.g. mathematics, economics) at a major, state-supported
university. The overwhelming majority (97.1 per cent) volunteered to participate, and of these respondents, men constituted 56.2 per cent (382 men
and 298 women).

Measures

These, together with their psychometric characteristics, were described in
Cano and Berbén's study (2009: 139–140). They included the following.

> *Approaches to learning*: a modified version of the revised two-factor-SPQ
> (Biggs et al. 2001), that assessed deep and surface learning approaches.
> *Conception of mathematics*: the conception of mathematics questionnaire
> (Crawford et al. 1998), which assessed fragmented and cohesive concep-
> tions of mathematics.
> *Course experience*: a short form of the CEQ (Ramsden 1991) which com-
> prised five subscales (good teaching; appropriate assessment; clear goals;
> appropriate workload; and generic skills).

Achievement goals: the Achievement Goal Questionnaire (Elliot & McGregor 2001), which assessed mastery-approach, mastery-avoidance, performance-approach and performance-avoidance goals.

Goal structures: Urdan's (2004) scales of classroom goal structures, which assessed mastery goal and performance goal structures.

Academic performance: students' examination marks in mathematics, reported as a percentage.

Procedure

Students were informed about the research and instructed on how to fill in the questionnaires, which were worded to make students focus on their mathematics classes (see Cano & Berbén 2009: 139–140).

Results

The results are divided into three sections. The first section contains some preliminary analysis. The second section includes the results of two analyses: (a) a hierarchical cluster analysis, to identify groups of students who showed similar learning patterns and to determine the number of clusters, and (b) a non-hierarchical cluster analysis to optimise the preceding assignments. The third section consists of the results of discriminant analysis, carried out to differentiate which variables determine membership of the various clusters and to suggest a summary of the relevant predictors.

Preliminary analyses

First, following Prosser et al.'s (2000) proposal, the subscales of the CEQ (Ramsden 1991) were grouped into two subscales assessing students' deep and surface perceptions, but in an attempt to improve the procedure they followed (simple means), a factor analysis was carried out. Prior to this, taking advantage of the fact that all but one of the items on the subscales Appropriate assessment and Appropriate workload were negatively worded, students' answers were recoded in the opposite direction (Crawford et al. 1998 also modified the CEQ in order to obtain measures of Inappropriate Workload and Inappropriate Assessment), and these scores as well as those of the remaining subscales were submitted to principal factor analysis. Two factors with eigenvalues greater than the unit were identified and submitted to varimax rotation. They explained 40.81 per cent of the shared variance, were defined by their loadings as deep perception (good teaching, clear goals, and generic skills) and surface perception (inappropriate workload and inappropriate assessment), and their factor scores were saved for later use.

Second, hierarchical linear modelling (HLM; Bryk & Raudenbush 1992) was used to investigate the between-classroom variance for each of the variables used in this study. Adjusted intraclass correlation coefficients (ICCs) ranged between a minimum of 0.004 for performance avoidance and a maximum of 0.180 for fragmented conception of mathematics.

Thus, between-classroom differences accounted for a range between a minimum of 0.4 per cent of the total variance in performance avoidance and a maximum of 18 per cent of the variance in fragmented conception of mathematics. These figures indicate that much of the variance in all the variables was due not to systematic classroom-level differences, but rather to variability at the individual level (the variance between-students ranged, in fact, between 4.5 and 228 times that of the variance between-classroom differences). Therefore, it was not considered helpful to explore the relations between SAL and AG variables using multilevel analyses.

Table 9.1 presents descriptive statistics and zero-order correlations between the measured variables collected in this study.

Cluster analysis

Students' scores on the twelve subscales (six of the SAL set and six of the AG set) were standardised within the total sample and these standardised scores (mean of 0 and standard deviation (SD) of 1) served as the input variables for the analyses. A hierarchical cluster analysis was carried out on these scores with the aim of grouping the students into meaningful categories (clusters or subgroups), and determining the correct number of clusters in the data. Ward's method, with Euclidean distance, was preferred because it was used in a previous study, which made it easier to compare between research findings, and because after comparing the population recovery capabilities of 35 cluster analysis methods, Overall et al. (1993: 459) concluded that 'complete linkage and Ward's minimum variance methods, used with Euclidean or city block interprofile distance measures, performed best'. Moreover, according to Aldenderfer and Blashfield (1984), this method optimises the minimum variance within clusters, avoids the tendency to form elongated clusters and outperforms most other clustering methods in conditions of cluster overlap.

The optimal number of clusters to use was determined by following two procedures (see Wishart 2005, for a review) implemented in the ClustanGraphics program (Wishart 2006): tree/validate and Mojena's upper tail rule (Mojena & Wishart 1980). The former suggested that a partition of six clusters was optimal and the latter confirmed that this solution was statistically significant (t = 95.19, realised deviate = 3.65, df = 678, p < 0.05).

A limitation of hierarchical clustering, however, is that it tends to form nested series of mutually exclusive partitions or subgroups of the data, which may lead to inefficient assignments. Probably the most common optimisation method is to reallocate cases by applying k-means analysis, a type of non-hierarchical cluster analysis (Wishart 2005). Hence, the next step was to use the

Table 9.1 Descriptive statistics and zero-order correlations among the study variables

	1	2	3	4	5	6	7	8	9	10	11	12	13
SAL set													
1. Deep approach	—	-.43	.37	-.15	.38	-.01	.50	.30	.17	-.13	.33	.17	.15
2. Surface approach		—	-.15	.22	-.21	.16	-.34	-.08	.08	.39	-.24	.10	-.14
3. Cohesive			—	-.09	.28	.02	.28	.17	.14	-.03	.17	.05	.04
4. Fragmented				—	-.05	.04	-.02	.07	.00	.23	-.02	.04	-.17
5. Deep perception					—	-.17	.19	.08	.05	-.13	.55	.07	.04
6. Surface perception						—	-.01	.20	.03	.18	-.26	.34	-.03
AG set													
7. Mastery approach							—	.52	.15	-.01	.24	.10	.15
8. Mastery avoidance								—	.20	.21	.09	.19	.05
9. Performance approach									—	.18	.00	.22	.13
10. Performance avoidance										—	-.19	.14	-.03
11. Class mastery											—	.04	-.03
12. Class performance												—	-.03
13. Academic performance													—
Mean	2.70	2.55	3.59	3.21	.01	.01	3.68	3.28	2.21	3.33	2.98	2.87	5.98
Standard deviation	.61	.64	.64	.67	.81	.77	.76	.83	.98	.82	.53	.78	2.03

Focal-Point k-means procedure implemented in the ClustanGraphics program (Wishart 2005, 2006) by grouping the cases into six clusters.

Table 9.2 shows the Z scores (means) obtained by students in the six clusters on the twelve subscales. A multivariate analysis of variance (MANOVA) showed that students in the six clusters obtained significantly different scores (Wilks' Lambda = 0.53, F = 45.05; df = 60, 3103; p < 0.001; eta-square = 0.443), and the univariate analyses showed that they also produced significantly different scores on each of the twelve subscales. The differences among the six clusters were examined using the Newman-Keuls technique, which reduces the likelihood of type I errors (i.e. falsely rejecting the null hypothesis).

This six-cluster solution complied with both statistical (e.g. Mojena's upper tail rule, MANOVA) and substantive (e.g. ease of interpretability and match to theory) considerations.

Prior to describing the clusters, it is important to bear in mind, as Richardson (2007) warned: (a) that some of the variables that define the clusters may be correlated, (b) that it might have been an artefact resulting from confusion among these variables, and (c) that the univariate comparisons do not differentiate which variables determine membership of the various clusters. Hence, a discriminant analysis was conducted to summarise the relevant predictors.

Discriminant analysis

This was selected to predict cluster membership on the basis of the scores on the twelve scales and to identify which of these scales contributed the most to the differences among the six clusters. This analysis provided a 97.9 per cent hit rate of participants correctly identified and five statistically significant discriminant functions. However, as the last two presented only a marginal percentage of explained variance, only the first three functions, which explained 95.6 per cent of the between groups variance, were subjected to varimax rotation and used in the analysis: (a) Function 1, eigenvalue = 2.5080, percentage of variance = 51, and canonical correlation = 0.849; (b) Function 2, eigenvalue = 1.666, percentage of variance = 32, and canonical correlation = 0.790; and (c) Function 3, eigenvalue = 0.590, percentage of variance = 11.7, and canonical correlation = 0.609.

Table 9.3 shows the standardised structure coefficients or discriminant loadings, based on the rotated structure matrix. Function 1 showed the highest loadings on mastery goals (approach and avoidance) and on cohesive conception of maths. This seems to be a suitable combination of a mastery orientation (the pursuit of the development of competence, by approach or by avoidance) and a cohesive view of the subject matter being studied (conception of maths as a way of thinking and of understanding the world). Function 2 showed the highest loadings on class mastery, deep perception and deep approach. Together, these seem to refer to a combination of some appropriate learning

Table 9.2 Cluster analysis of Z-scores (means) in the twelve independent variables (the six SAL and the six AG)

Independent variables	Clusters						$F^{\dagger}$
	1 (n = 131)	2 (n = 92)	3 (n = 122)	4 (n = 96)	5 (n = 111)	6 (n = 128)	
SAL set							
Deep approach	-.04[b]	.02[b]	-.94[a]	-.81[a]	1.03	.64	136.63*
Surface approach	.34[a]	-.07	.26[a]	.96	-.46	-.86	69.28*
Cohesive	.13[a]	.24[a]	-.84	-.50	.59	.36[a]	46.30*
Fragmented	.54[b]	-.56[a]	-.15	.67[b]	.12	-.62[a]	42.32*
Deep perception	.43[b]	-.46[a]	-.35[a]	-.70	.47[b]	.44[b]	71.91*
Surface perception	-.20[a]	.19[b]	-.19[a]	.55	.32[b]	-.34[a]	26.89*
AG set							
Mastery approach	-.14	.39[a]	-1.10	-.35	.90	.38[a]	97.01*
Mastery avoidance	-.09[a]	.39[b]	-1.11	.32[b]	.89	-.14[a]	87.39*
Performance approach	-.02[a]	.74[c]	-.52[a]	-.10[b]	.54[c]	-.41[a]	34.53*
Performance avoidance	.41[a]	.24[a]	-.24	.73	.24[a]	-1.12	79.97*
Class mastery	.49[a]	-.68	-.43	-.90	.50[a]	.64[a]	80.27*
Class performance	-.12	-.28[a]	-.49[a]	.56	.96	-.45[a]	54.54*

Notes: Pairs of mean scores on the same scale with the same superscript are not significantly different according to post hoc (Newman-Keuls) tests. Different lettered superscripts for mean scores of the same variables indicate significant differences.
†df = 5, 674; p < .001.

Table 9.3 Rotated standardised discriminant function coefficients

Independent variables	1	2	3
Deep approach	.24	**.33**	−.24
Surface approach	.15	−.14	**.56**
Cohesive	**.50**	.13	.04
Fragmented	.02	.27	**.57**
Deep perception	−.09	.49	.03
Surface perception	.09	−.12	−.07
Mastery approach	**.48**	−.07	−.10
Mastery avoidance	**.57**	−.18	.20
Performance avoidance	−.16	.10	**.30**
Performance approach	.10	−.11	−.30
Class mastery	.02	**.54**	.02
Class performance	−.03	.06	.07

Note: Coefficients greater than .30 in absolute magnitude are shown in bold.

components: deep perception of the learning context (good teaching, clear goals, emphasis on understanding and effort) and deep learning approach. Function 3 showed salient loadings on fragmented conception of maths and surface approach, accompanied by performance avoidance (and negative performance approach). Together, these seem to refer to a combination of some inappropriate learning components: a conception of mathematics as a fragmented body of knowledge, a surface learning approach and an achievement goal of avoiding incompetence relative to others.

Table 9.4 shows the centroids (means) of the six clusters on the three discriminant functions. A MANOVA showed a significant effect of cluster membership on these functions (Wilks' Lambda = 0.103, F = 157.85; df = 15, 1855; p < 0.001; eta-square = 0.531). Follow-up univariate analyses revealed that they produced significantly different scores on each of the functions individually (F = 212.82, F = 160.06, and F = 145.9; df = 5, 674; p < 0.001, in each case). Newman-Keuls post hoc analyses showed statistically significant differences among the six clusters in the majority of the pairwise comparisons.

Function 1 separated clusters 5 and 2 from cluster 3. Function 2 discriminated clusters 5, 6 and 1 from clusters 4, 2 and 3. Function 3 separated clusters 4 and 1 from clusters 6 and 2.

The students in cluster 1 obtained moderately high scores on function 2 and function 3. These students tended to mix appropriate and inappropriate learning components, in a kind of disintegration between perceptions (deep), learning approaches (deep and surface) and personal goals (performance avoidance). This cluster is called the *disintegrated learning pattern*.

Table 9.4 Centroids of the six clusters on the three discriminant functions

Function	1 (n = 131)	2 (n = 92)	3 (n = 122)	4 (n = 96)	5 (n = 111)	6 (n = 128)	F[†]
1 MAV + cohesive conception + MAP	−.16[a]	.77	−2.23	−.39[a]	1.78	.49	212.82[*]
2 Class mastery + deep perception + deep approach	.87[a]	−1.17	−.85	−1.55	1.07[a]	1.00[a]	160.06[*]
3 Fragmented conception + surface approach + PAV	.80	−.61[a]	.27	1.71	−.47[a]	−1.52	145.91[*]

Notes: MAV = mastery avoidance; MAP = mastery approach; PAV = performance avoidance.
Pairs of mean scores on the function with the same superscript are not significantly different according to post hoc tests. All other differences between pairs of means in the same row are statistically significant.
[†]df = 5, 674; [*] = p < .001.

The students in cluster 2, however, scored moderately high on function 1 (mastery goals and cohesive conception of maths), but very low and moderately low on function 2 and function 3, respectively. This cluster is called *mastery-oriented with a cohesive conception of maths.*

The students in cluster 3 tended to have moderately low scores on function 2 and very low scores on function 1; that is, they showed neither appropriate nor suitable components of learning. This cluster is labelled *disengaged learning pattern.*

The students in cluster 4 obtained very low scores on function 2 and very high scores on function 3 (inappropriate learning components such as reproductive conceptions and approaches and performance avoidance AG). This cluster is labelled *reproduction and performance avoidance-oriented learning pattern.*

The students in cluster 5 tended to have very high scores on function 1 and moderately high scores on function 2. That is, they show a coherent integration between perceptions (deep), approaches (deep), conceptions of maths (cohesive) and goals (mastery goal orientation). This learning pattern cluster is labelled *mastery and meaning-oriented with a cohesive conception of maths.*

The students in cluster 6 performed similarly to those in cluster 5, with moderately high scores on function 2. However, the former obtained very low scores on function 3 and did not score in a salient way on function 1. That is, their way of experiencing and going about learning was close to a meaning orientation and far from a surface or reproductive orientation, but without a leading mastery goal like that of the students in cluster 5. This cluster is labelled *meaning-oriented learning pattern.*

Finally, to supplement the above, a univariate analysis of variance (ANOVA) was used to examine cluster differences on academic performance. Cluster

Table 9.5 One-way ANOVA of cluster scores on academic performance and post hoc comparisons

Outcome Variables	Clusters						$F^\dagger$
	1 (n = 131)	*2* (n = 92)	*3* (n = 122)	*4* (n = 96)	*5* (n = 111)	*6* (n = 128)	
Academic performance	−.30[a]	.31[b]	−.18[a]	−.12[a]	.19[b]	.17[b]	7.02*

Notes: Pairs of mean scores on the function with the same superscript are not significantly different according to post hoc tests. Differently lettered superscripts for mean scores of the same variables indicate significant differences.
$^\dagger df = 5, 674; ^* = p < .001$.

membership (taken as IV) showed a statistically significant effect (F = 7.02; df = 5, 674; p < 0.001; eta-square = 0.05) on academic performance (dependent variable) and, as can be seen in Table 9.4, Newman-Keuls post hoc analyses identified two kinds of cluster.

The results in Table 9.5 indicate that students in the *mastery and meaning-oriented with a cohesive conception of maths* (cluster 5) and *meaning-oriented* (cluster 6) learning patterns are those who achieve the best academic performance. On the other hand, students in the *disengaged* (cluster 3) and *reproduction and performance avoidance-oriented* (cluster 4) learning patterns show the worst performance.

Students in cluster 2 (*mastery-oriented with a cohesive conception of maths*), however, obtained an academic performance not statistically different from those of clusters 5 and 6, whereas students in cluster 1 (*disintegrated learning pattern*) exhibited the lowest academic performance scores.

Discussion

The findings of the present study confirm that SAL and AG are intertwined aspects of students' experience of learning mathematics at university, and provide evidence supporting a description of learning patterns based on SAL and AG, and consequently, a search for comprehensive models of how students learn, which would include students' reasons for competence-relevant behaviour (AG).

One main result of this study, consistent with Cano and Berbén (2009), is the confirmation that the SAL and AG research perspectives are related. However, in addition, our study is unique in two ways. First, this study reflects a first attempt to consider how the core variables of these research perspectives may generate patterns of motivation and learning. Second, in contrast to some of the previous research on learning patterns, we use an improved person-centred approach involving clustering procedures of acknowledged validity, followed by discriminant analysis. Arising from this, a *second main result* of this study is that maths students deploy learning patterns in which the core variables of the AG and SAL perspectives appear to be blended at an individual level, which constitutes a hitherto unpublished inference. A cluster analysis identifies six subgroups of students characterised by different learning patterns and a subsequent discriminant analysis allows for the interpretation of how these six subgroups can be differentiated in terms of their scores in three different dimensions. We will begin by interpreting these three dimensions, and in the light of this, we will interpret the six clusters.

Function 1 is the most powerful (in terms of explained variance and correlation with the clusters) and its coefficients could be interpreted as a kind of 'cognitive-dynamic representation' that includes a combination of a personal goal, the development of competence and a mature conception of mathematical knowledge. This is reminiscent of Vermunt and Vermetten's (2004) emphasis on the links between conceptions of learning and learning orientations, though it should be noted that the latter refers to a broad notion of motivation associated with Gibbs et al.'s (1984) work and tends not to be included in the latest studies because, unfortunately, it seems to exhibit weaker correlations with other components of learning patterns (Vanthournout et al. 2009). More specifically, some elements of this cognitive-dynamic representation appear in Lindblom-Ylänne and Lonka's (1999) research, where a cluster of meaning-oriented independent students was found, defined by their elaborate study practices and constructivist conceptions of learning and knowledge. These students, however, did not significantly differ in achievement motivation from those of the other clusters. This discrepancy with our results could be attributed to the different statistical techniques and/or the constructs used. More valid clustering techniques, followed by discriminant analysis to determine which variables best separate the clusters, are applied in the present study. In addition, achievement motivation in its original sense (Entwistle & Ramsden 1983; Biggs 1987: being competitive and confident to obtain the highest grades) seems to be only slightly related to the AG perspective. The latter is more focused on competence-relevant situations and also more complex, as it takes longer to account for four distinct personal goals and their different combinations (i.e. multiple goals) (Cano & Berbén 2009; Elliot & McGregor 2001; Linnenbrink 2005).

Function 2 also contributes to cluster differences providing the greatest discrimination after Function 1, and its coefficients suggest a coherent integration between students' perceptions (appropriate perceptions of both classroom goal structure, i.e. mastery, and learning environment, i.e. deep) and approaches (deep SAL). Whereas the first part of this combination, carried out with clustering techniques, is new in the research literature, the second part is systematically confirmed in a number of studies (Crawford et al. 1998; Prosser et al. 2000; Richardson 2007; Trigwell & Prosser 1991a, 1991b).

Function 3 is also useful, though to a lesser extent, in clarifying the cluster differences. Its coefficients seem to represent, partially at least, a kind of antithesis of function 1 (an immature view of mathematical knowledge, a sur-face approach and a non-positive personal goal, to avoid demonstrating low levels of competence). The first part of this combination is well known in the research literature, as one of the groups (clusters) of students detected in Crawford et al.'s (1998) research, who held fragmented conceptions of math-ematics and tended to approach learning in a surface way. Apparently, there are also some indirect traces of that combination in Lindblom-Ylänne and Lonka's (1999) investigation, since the cluster of reproduction-oriented and externally regulated students adopted a surface approach and had a conception of learning as intake of knowledge. Nevertheless, the second part is new in the studies in which clustering techniques have been applied.

Students' scores on these three functions helped to differentiate reasonably well the six clusters of learning patterns that emerged in the present study: (a) disintegrated; (b) mastery-oriented with a cohesive conception of maths; (c) disengaged; (d) reproduction and performance avoidance-oriented; (e) mastery and meaning-oriented with a cohesive conception of maths; and (f) meaning-oriented. Some of them, such as the meaning-oriented and the disengaged, had features that were in general akin to those reported in previous research, while the other clusters revealed features not found earlier. Moreover, an ancillary, but by no means negligible result of this study is the finding of a link between these learning patterns and study success.

Previous research has shown that some students tend to go through their studies without engaging in them in an appropriate or meaningful way. Thus, Cano (2005, 2007) and Vanthournout et al. (2008) mentioned clusters whose members showed low scores on their SAL, and Prosser et al. (2000) described a cluster of students characterised by a low profile on the different aspects of learning being assessed (e.g. deep and surface perceptions and approaches, pre- and post-conceptual knowl-edge). The disengaged learning pattern found in the present study is not identical to those mentioned, since those conforming to it scored not only moderately low on the appropriate learning components but very low on a new cognitive-dynamic representation (striving for the development of competence and having a cohesive conception of maths). However, this dimension was not relevant for defining the disintegrated learning pattern detected earlier in the research literature. In some cases the disintegration was defined by using scores on deep and surface SAL, as in Cano (2005, 2007), who reported an incoherent high–high pattern, labelled 'high ambivalent profile' in the study of Vanthournout et al. (2008). In other cases, such as Prosser et al.'s (2000) investigation, however, students' perceptions of the learning context were also included, as in the present research. In any case, students of the disengaged and disintegrated learning patterns showed the worst academic performance, which is in agreement with these authors' reports. Hence, our results are consistent with the earlier studies, but extend them by showing that not only students' views of the subject matter they are studying but also their personal goals and the goals they perceive in the learning environment are important components for defining learning patterns.

This appreciation is valid not only for the *meaning-oriented learning pattern*, which has been traditionally found in different investigations and labelled with similar names (Cano, 2005, 2007; Crawford et al. 1998; Lindblom-Ylänne & Lonka 1999; Prosser et al. 2000; Vanthournout et al. 2008), but also, in particular, for the learning pattern *mastery and meaning-oriented with a cohesive conception of maths*. This claim is supported by the fact that the latter seems to be a special type of meaning-oriented pattern that adds to the former, in terms of the most powerful first function, a cognitive-dynamic representation which apparently was not found earlier. Although Cano and Berbén (2009) detected a cluster of students who adopted both mastery approach and mastery avoidance goals, and Linbdlom-Ylänne and Lonka (1999) reported two different meaning-oriented clusters (differentiated by their conception of knowledge), none of these studies refers to the above-mentioned substantial relationship between SAL and AG. Hence, this finding sheds light on the dynamic of AG and SAL and emphasises the general impact of students' reasons for engaging in learning, beyond the typical extrinsic/intrinsic motivations analysed by SAL researchers. An in-depth comprehension of students' engagement and learning seems to require knowledge of not only 'what' students are trying to achieve, the personal context in terms of Marton, Dall'Alba and Beaty (1993), but also 'why' they are trying to do so. Generally, it might also be suggesting reflection on the possibility of refining and improving measurement of the motivational aspects involved in the theoretical models of learning patterns, perhaps taking into account, in an integrative way, those cognitive representations of what students want to achieve.

The theoretical significance of this cognitive-dynamic representation is based on two additional pieces of evidence. First, it is involved in defining, with moderately high coefficients, another learning pattern we call *mastery-oriented with a cohesive conception of maths*, which seems to be more linked to a kind of meta-goal (in this case the development of competence) and less related to both SAL and perceptions of the learning context. Other researchers have reported patterns of learning characterised by low scores on both deep and surface SAL, whether alone (e.g. Cano 2005, 2007; Vanthournout et al. 2008) or related to students' perceptions of the learning context (Prosser et al. 2000), but without including the component of representation mentioned above. Second, in spite of being less related to SAL and to perceptions of the learning context, the students included in this learning pattern obtained a similar academic performance to those belonging to the two types of meaning-oriented learning patterns. This is not easy to explain but could be potentially related to the beneficial effects of mastery goals on learning strategies and achievement outcomes (Elliot, McGregor & Gable 1999; Linnenbrink 2005; Wolters 2004), which in this case might be enhanced by the combined emphasis on mastery approach and mastery avoidance, a multiple-goal combination that in Cano and Berbén's (2009) study was strongly related to maths students' academic performance.

Finally, the reproduction and performance avoidance-oriented learning pattern seems to be the common surface or reproduction pattern mentioned in the research literature (e.g. Cano 2005, 2007; Lindblom-Ylänne & Lonka 1999; Prosser et al. 2000; Vanthournout et al. 2008), but improved due to the inclusion of aspects of both SAL and AG research perspectives (e.g. fragmented conception of maths, surface approach and performance avoidance). This seems to be in line with Biggs' (2001: 84) statement that 'Empirically, it is true that some people go through their university careers with a constant metagoal: to do enough work to avoid failure . . . and . . . develop a stable habit of selective rote learning of academic material.'

Implications

From a theoretical point of view, the finding of the present study (a) adds to the body of research on learning patterns, illustrating how helpful a combination of cluster and discriminant analysis is to identify the different ways in which students usually engage in learning, and (b) seems to suggest that integrating AG and SAL perspectives would provide a more complete picture of learning patterns, in line with the emphasis on integration of prevailing cognitive and affective components initiated by Biggs (1987) and broadened by Vermunt and Vermetten (2004) to learning strategies, learning conceptions and learning orientations.

From a practical point of view, it is important for teachers to become aware of the broad variety of learning patterns adopted by their students, some of which, e.g. mastery oriented, seem appropriate, whereas others, such as disintegrated and disengaged do not, with these students needing intensive assistance and support from the teacher. Although there are many reasons why students adopt these different learning patterns, our results point towards not only personological influences (e.g. views of mathematical knowledge, intentions, AG), but also contextual influences (e.g. students' perceptions of their learning environment, including perceptions of the goal structures), that seem to be intermingled with them. Hence, it may be inferred that learning and teaching are related, and that besides paying attention to the subject matter and its presentation, teachers should, as Crawford et al. (1998) suggest, take into account the ways students experience the total learning context.

Limitations and future research

This study has several limitations. First, this was a secondary analysis, exploratory in nature, of data collected for an earlier study and the results are pending replication, especially since the whole set of variables was used to develop a typology of learning patterns, and external cluster validity was not examined, except in the case of academic performance. Second, our participants were first-year maths students, and so the learning patterns detected may be more representative of this sector of the population than others, and may be affected by the fact that for some students maths is associated with anxiety (Pajares & Urdan 1996) and poor performance (Hembree 1990). It could be speculated that those AG focused on doing well or poorly relative to others would appear more in maths classrooms than in other subject areas. Recently, Elliot, Murayama and Pekrun (2011) presented a 3 x 2 AG model, where they argue for differentiation between three ways of defining competence: task (absolute), self (intrapersonal) and other (interpersonal), the latter being focused on the attainment of 'other-based' competence or on the avoidance of 'other-based' incompetence. Third, our data were correlational and we used a cross-section design, hence no causality links could be inferred.

Future research is needed to investigate the generalisability of our findings. First, it seems important to include new variables that could provide evidence regarding the construct validity of the different learning patterns detected and to gather data in other content areas. Second, a central issue that emerges from this research is the importance of the search for comprehensive models of how students learn and how appropriate it would be to pay attention to students' reasons for competence-relevant behaviour. Third, a more thorough examination of learning patterns, adding other instruments (e.g. Vermunt's ILS) and using longitudinal design and person-centred analysis (e.g. Bergman 2001; Bergman & Magnusson 1997) would greatly contribute to our understanding of these distinctive differences in the way students usually engage in learning.

References

Aldenderfer, M.S. and Blashfield, R.K. (1984) *Cluster analysis*, London: Sage Publications.

Ames, C. (1992) 'Classrooms: Goals, structures, and student motivation', *Journal of Educational Psychology*, 84: 261–271.

Ames, C. and Archer, J. (1988) 'Achievement goals in the classroom: Students' learning strategies and motivational processes', *Journal of Educational Psychology*, 80: 260–267.

Baeten, M., Kyndt, E., Struyven, K. and Dochy, P. (2010) 'Using student-centred learning environments to stimulate deep approaches to learning: Factors encouraging or discouraging their effectiveness', *Educational Research Review*, 5: 243–260.

Barron, K. and Harackiewicz, J. (2001) 'Achievement goals and optimal motivation: Testing multiple goal models', *Journal of Personality and Social Psychology*, 80: 706–722.

Bergman, L.R. (2001) 'A person approach to adolescence: Some methodological challenges', *Journal of Adolescent Research*, 16: 28–53.

Bergman, L.R. and Magnusson, D. (1997) 'A person-oriented approach in research on developmental psychopathology', *Development and Psychopathology*, 9: 291–319.

Biggs, J.B. (1987) *Student approaches to learning*, Hawthorn, Victoria: Australian Council for Educational Research.

Biggs, J.B. (1993) 'What do inventories of students' learning processes really measure? A theoretical review and clarification', *British Journal of Educational Psychology*, 63: 1–117.

Biggs, J.B. (2001) 'Enhancing learning: A matter of style or approach?', in R.J. Sternberg and L.F. Zhang (eds) *Perspectives on thinking, learning, and cognitive styles*, pp. 73–102, Mahwah, NJ: Lawrence Erlbaum Associates, Publishers.

Biggs, J., Kember, D. and Leung, D.Y.P. (2001) 'The revised two factor Study Process Questionnaire: R SPQ 2F', *British Journal of Educational Psychology*, 71: 133–149.

Bryk, A.S. and Raudenbush, S.W. (1992) *Hierarchical linear models: Applications and data analysis*, Newbury Park: Sage Publications.

Cano, F. (2005) 'Consonance and dissonance in students' learning experience', *Learning and Instruction*, 15: 201–223.

Cano, F. (2007) 'Approaches to learning and study orchestrations in high school students', *European Journal of Psychology of Education*, 22: 131–151.

Cano, F. and Berbén, A.B.G. (2009) 'University students' achievement goals and approaches to learning in mathematics', *British Journal of Educational Psychology*, 79: 131–153.

Crawford, K., Gordon, S., Nicholas, J. and Prosser, M. (1998) 'University mathematics students' conceptions of mathematics', *Studies in Higher Education*, 23: 87–94.

Donche, V. and Van Petegem, P. (2009) 'The development of learning patterns of student-teachers: A cross-sectional an longitudinal study', *Higher Education*, 57: 463–475.

Dweck, C. and Leggett, E. (1988) 'A social-cognitive approach to motivation and personality', *Psychological Review*, 95: 256–273.

Elliot, A. and McGregor, H. (2001) 'A 2 x 2 achievement goal framework', *Journal of Personality and Social Psychology*, 80: 501–519.

Elliot, A., McGregor, H. and Gable, S. (1999) 'Achievement goals, study strategies, and exam performance: A mediational analysis', *Journal of Educational Psychology*, 91: 549–563.

Elliot, A., Murayama, K. and Pekrun, R. (2011) 'A 3 x 2 Achievement Goal Model', *Journal of Educational Psychology*, 103: 632–648.

Entwistle, N., Hanley, M. and Hounsell, D. (1979) 'Identifying distinctive approaches to studying', *Higher Education*, 8: 365–380.

Entwistle, N. and McCune, V. (2004) 'The conceptual basis of study strategy inventories', *Educational Psychology Review*, 16: 325–345.

Entwistle, N., McCune, V. and Walker, P. (2001) 'Conceptions, styles, and approaches within higher education: Analytic abstractions and everyday experience', in R.J. Sternberg and L.F. Zhang (eds) *Perspectives on thinking, learning, and cognitive styles*, pp. 103–136, Mahwah, NJ: Lawrence Erlbaum Associates, Publishers.

Entwistle, N. and Ramsden, P. (1983) *Understanding student learning*, London: Croom Helm.

Gibbs, G., Morgan, A. and Taylor, E. (1984) 'The world of the learner', in F. Marton, D. Hounsell and N. Entwistle (eds) *The experience of learning*, pp. 165–188, Edinburgh: Scottish Academic Press.

Gorman, B.S. and Primavera, L.H. (1983) 'The complementary use of cluster and factor analysis methods', *Journal of Experimental Education*, 51: 165–168.

Hembree, R. (1990) 'The nature, effects, and relief of mathematics anxiety', *Journal of Research in Mathematics Education*, 21: 33–46.

Hulleman, C.S., Schrager, S.M., Bodman, S.M. and Harackiewicz, J.M. (2010) 'A meta-analytic review of achievement goal measures: Different labels for the same constructs or different constructs with similar labels?', *Psychological Bulletin*, 136: 422–449.

Lindblom-Ylänne, S. and Lonka, K. (1999) 'Individual ways of interacting with the learning environment – are they related?', *Learning and Instruction*, 9: 1–18.

Linnenbrink, E.A. (2005) 'The dilemma of performance-approach goals: The use of multiple goal context to promote students = motivation and learning', *Journal of Educational Psychology*, 97: 197–213.

Lonka, K. and Lindblom-Ylänne, S. (1996) 'Epistemologies, conceptions of learning, and study practices in medicine and psychology', *Higher Education*, 31: 5–24.

Maehr, M.L. and Midgley, C. (1996) *Transforming school cultures*, Boulder, CO: Westview Press.

Marton, F., Dall'Alba, G. and Beaty, E. (1993) 'Conceptions of learning', *International Journal of Educational Research*, 19: 277–300.

Marton, F. and Säljö, R. (1976a) 'On qualitative differences in learning - I: Outcome and process', *British Journal of Educational Psychology*, 46: 4–11.

Marton, F. and Säljö, R. (1976b) 'Learning processes and strategies', *British Journal of Educational Psychology*, 46: 115–127.

Meyer, J.H.F. (2000) 'The modelling of "dissonant" study orchestration in higher education', *European Journal of Psychology of Education*, 15: 5–18.

Meyer, J.H.F., Parsons, P. and Dunne, T.T. (1990) 'Study orchestration and learning outcome: Evidence of association over time among disadvantaged students', *Higher Education*, 20: 245–269.

Milligan, G.W. and Cooper, M.C. (1985) 'An examination of procedures for determining the number of clusters in a data set', *Psychometrika*, 50: 159–179.

Mojena, R. and Wishart, D. (1980) 'Stopping Rules for Ward's Clustering Method', in *COMPSTAT 1980 Proceedings*, pp. 454–459, Heidelberg: Physica-Verlag.

Overall, J.E., Gibson, J.M. and Novy, D.M. (1993) 'Population recovery capabilities of 35 cluster analysis methods', *Journal of Clinical Psychology*, 49: 459–470.

Pajares, F. and Urdan, T.C. (1996) 'Exploratory factor analysis of the Mathematics Anxiety Scale', *Measurement and Evaluation in Counselling and Development*, 29: 35–47.

Pastor, D.E., Barron, K.E., Miller, B.J. and Davis, S.L. (2007) 'A latent profile analysis of college students achievement goal orientation', *Contemporary Educational Psychology*, 32: 8–47.

Pintrich, P. (2000) 'Multiple goal, multiple pathways: The role of goal orientation in learning and achievement', *Journal of Educational Psychology*, 92: 544–555.

Pintrich, P. (2003) 'A motivational science perspective on the role of student motivation in learning and teaching contexts', *Journal of Educational Psychology*, 95: 667–686.

Ramsden, P. (1991) 'A performance indicator of teaching quality in higher education: The course experience questionnaire', *Studies in Higher Education*, 16: 129–150.

Prosser, M., Trigwell, K., Hazel, E. and Waterhouse, F. (2000) 'Students' perceptions of studying physics concepts: The effects of disintegrated perceptions and approaches', *European Journal of Psychology of Education*, 15: 61–74.

Richardson, J.T.E. (2006) 'Investigating the relationship between variations in students' perceptions of their academic environment and variations in study behaviour in distance education', *British Journal of Educational Psychology*, 76: 867–893.

Richardson, J.T.E. (2007) 'Mental models of learning in distance education', *British Journal of Educational Psychology*, 77: 253–270.

Senko, C., Hulleman, C.S. and Harackiewicz, J.M (2011) 'Achievement goal theory at the crossroads: Old controversies, current challenges, and new directions', *Educational Psychologist*, 46: 26–47.

Steinley, D. and Brusco, M, J. (2011) 'Evaluating Mixture Modeling for Clustering: Recommendations and cautions', *Psychological Methods*, 16: 63–79.

Trigwell, K. and Prosser, M. (1991a) 'Improving the quality of student learning: The influence of learning context and student approaches to learning on learning outcomes', *Higher Education*, 22: 251–266.

Trigwell, K. and Prosser, M. (1991b) 'Relating approaches to study and quality of learning outcomes at the course level', *British Journal of Educational Psychology*, 61: 265–275.

Urdan, T. (2004) 'Using multiple methods to assess students' perceptions of classroom goal structures', *European Psychologist*, 9: 222–231.

Vanthournout, G., Donche, V., Gijbels, D. and Van Petegem, V. (2009) 'Alternative data-analysis techniques in research on student learning: Illustrations of a person-oriented and developmental perspectives', *Reflecting Education*, 5: 35–51.

Vanthournout, G., Gijbels, D., Coertjens, L. and Van Petegem, P. (2008) 'The development of approaches to learning of student teachers with different study approach profiles', *Paper presented at the 13th Annual Conference of the European Learning Styles Information Network*, Ghent, 23–25 June.

Vermunt, J. (1998) 'The regulation of constructive learning processes', *British Journal of Educational Psychology*, 68: 149–171.

Vermunt, J. and Verloop, N. (1999) 'Congruence and friction between learning and teaching', *Learning and Instruction*, 9: 257–280.

Vermunt, J. and Verloop, N. (2000) 'Dissonance in students' regulation of learning processes', *European Journal of Psychology of Education*, 15: 75–87.

Vermunt, J.D. and Vermetten, Y.J. (2004) 'Patterns in student learning: Relationships between learning strategies, conceptions of learning, and learning orientations', *Educational Psychology Review*, 16: 359–385.

Wishart, D. (2005) 'Number of clusters', in B.S. Everitt and D.C. Howell (eds) *Encyclopedia of statistics in behavioral science*, vol. 3, pp. 144–1446, Chichester: Wiley.

Wishart, D. (2006) *ClustanGraphics primer: A guide to cluster analysis* (4th ed.), Edinburgh: St. Andrews.

Wolters, C.A. (2004) 'Advancing achievement goal theory: Using goal structures and goal orientations to predict students' motivation, cognition, and achievement', *Journal of Educational Psychology*, 96: 236–250.

Chapter 10

Exploring the use of a deep approach to learning with students in the process of learning to teach

Carol Evans

Introduction

In learning to teach in the 21st century, student teachers have to manage their own learning and support that of their pupils in increasingly challenging learning and teaching environments (Opfer, Pedder and Lavicza, 2010). In changing initial teacher education contexts (DfE, 2011), it is increasingly important for schools and higher education institutions (HEIs) to consider how they can best provide appropriate challenges, stimuli and support to student teachers to enable them to develop effective approaches to learning and to model these with their pupils (Burn, Hagger, Mutton and Everton, 2003; Gijbels, Segers and Struyf, 2008). A deep approach to learning is required in order to function effectively in complex learning environments and deal with supercomplexity described as the openendness of ideas, perspectives, values, beliefs and interpretations (Barnett, 2007). Student teachers need to have an increased awareness of their learning approaches if they are to make the best use of learning opportunities, self-regulate their own learning (Heikkilä and Lonka, 2006), and manage affordances and barriers within differing learning contexts more effectively (Evans and Kozhevnikov, 2011). Walker et al. (2009: 254) have argued that: 'student teachers need to understand that sometimes it is necessary to see knowledge as complex, evolving, effortful, tentative and evidence-based: these epistemological beliefs are at the very core of deep approaches to learning.' However, while approaches to learning research has strongly influenced practice in higher education, its influence and application to school settings has been limited (Evans and Waring, 2011). A better understanding is needed of what constitutes a deep approach to learning in the context of learning to teach. This is especially important given concerns surrounding whether the characteristics of a deep approach can be fully captured within existing measures of approaches to learning as a result of changes that have occurred in higher education and initial teacher education over the last ten years (Watters and Watters, 2007).

This chapter has two main aims: (a) to explore what a deep approach to learning is in the context of learning to teach within 21st century learning environments; and (b) to examine the factors impacting on student teachers' adoption of a deep approach in order to inform the development of practice. To ensure the study is contextually nuanced in order to engage with the complexities of location, time and context, an interpretivist phenomenological approach drawing on a range of theoretical constructs has been adopted (Marshall and Case, 2005).

Overview of approaches to learning

Defining approaches to learning

Approaches to learning refer to how students perceive themselves going about learning in a specific learning situation (Vanthournout, Donche, Gijbels and Van Petegem, 2011) and focus on how intention and process are combined in students' learning. The acknowledgement of deep and surface approaches to learning (Marton, 1975; Marton and Säljö, 1976; Walker et al., 2009) has been supported over a long period of time with many researchers noting similar distinctions (Biggs, 1993, 2003; Entwistle, McCune and Walker, 2001; Entwistle, Meyer and Tait, 1991; Entwistle and Ramsden, 1983; Trigwell and Prosser, 1991; Van Rossum and Schenk, 1984).

Characteristically a

> deep approach is associated with students' intentions to understand and construct the meaning of the content to be learned, whereas the concept of the surface approach refers to students' intentions to learn by memorisation and reproducing the factual contents of the study materials.
>
> (Gijbels, Coertjens, Vanthournout, Struyf and Van Petegem, 2009: 503)

Flexibility has been identified as an important characteristic of a deep approach, with those adopting deep approaches being more able to adopt versatile styles of learning using holistic and serialist approaches to understand content (Entwistle, 1981; Pask, 1988). This suggests a metacognitive element to a deep approach evidenced in students being consciously aware of their learning and how to adopt processes and strategies appropriate to the requirements of a specific learning context. Given that a deep approach interest in a subject and an intention to understand are linked to a student's selection of specific study strategies, it is feasible that in certain circumstances a deep approach may incorporate surface strategies where it is appropriate to the demands of the task as noted by Albergaria Almeida, Texeira-Dias, Martinho and Balasooriya (2011) who identified that the most successful students were those who knew how to use deep and surface approaches to achieve their end goal. Similarly, Peterson, Brown and Irving (2010) acknowledged that those with more advanced conceptions of learning were more able to select the most appropriate learning processes for a task which included both deep and surface approaches.

The later added strategic (or achieving) approach acknowledges the impact of the demands of assessment and has been described as well-organised and conscientious study methods linked to achievement motivation or the determination to do well (Entwistle et al., 2001). It is argued that a strategic approach differs from deep and surface approaches in its focus on the way students organise their studying rather than engaging in actual content (Lonka, Olkinuora and Mäkinen, 2004), although this division could be seen as pedantic within specific tasks.

Identification of a deep or surface approach was initially derived from collecting information from students on their attitudes towards learning, studying and motivation in university contexts (Heikkilä and Lonka, 2006). Information was evaluated from students undertaking a specific reading task (Marton and Säljö, 1976, 1984), with more recent information collected on a range of student tasks including student preparation for examinations (Entwistle and Entwistle, 2003; Entwistle and Ramsden, 1983) and using a variety of self-reported questionnaires (see Table 10.1) developed from different theoretical perspectives (Jungert and Rosander, 2009) including information processing theory (Marton and Säljö, 1984), cognitive psychology (Biggs, 1978), and sociological perspectives (Ramsden, 1992).

Relationship between approaches, conceptions and regulation of learning

Students' approaches to learning are related to conceptions of learning, motivational orientations, cognitive strategies and regulation of learning (Heikkilä and Lonka, 2006).

Conceptions of learning (views about the nature of learning: mental model of learning) and orientations (perceptions of what one is trying to achieve in learning) are thought to influence approaches to learning which in turn impact on choice of processing and regulation strategies. However, the nature and direction of such relationships has been identified as complex. It has been argued that patterns of learning appear to be less well defined at transfer points between educational environments indicating a period of acclimatisation and perhaps susceptibility to change. This finding is especially pertinent to the study of student teachers who have to navigate the different environments of schools and the transition from undergraduate or workplace to postgraduate study.

Deep approaches to learning are thought to be related to higher level conceptions of learning (abstracting meaning, interpreting information to understand the world, changing as a person), with surface approaches related to lower order conceptions of learning (increasing knowledge, memorising, acquiring facts) (Marton, Dall'Alba and Beaty, 1993; Säljö, 1979). The nature and direction of causal links between conceptions and approaches have been questioned. High order conceptions of learning do not necessarily imply an individual will use a deep approach. Behaviours can influence conceptions,

Table 10.1 Approaches to learning instruments

From cognitive psychology	
Schmeck, Geisler-Brenstein and Cercy (1991)	The Revised Inventory of Learning Processes
Pintrich, Smith, Garcia and McKeachie (1993)	The Motivated Strategies for Learning Questionnaire (MSLQ)

From educational research and Marton and Säljö's (1976) work	
Entwistle and colleagues	
Entwistle and Ramsden (1983)	Approaches to Studying Inventory (ASI)
Ramsden (1983)	Lancaster Approaches to Studying Questionnaire (LASQ)
Tait and Entwistle (1996)	Revised Approaches to Studying Inventory (RASI)
Tait, Entwistle and McCune (1998)	Approaches to Study Skills Inventory for Students (ASSIST)
Biggs	
Biggs (1987)	Study Processes Questionnaire
Biggs, Kember and Leung (2001)	Revised Two-Factor Study Process Questionnaire (R-SPQ-2F)
Vermunt and colleagues	
Vermunt and van Rijswijk (1988)	Inventory of Learning Strategies (LIS)
Vermunt (1994)	Inventory of Learning Styles in Higher Education (ILSHE)
Vermunt (1998)	the Inventory of Learning Styles (ILS)
Donche and Van Petegem (2008)	the ILS-SV
Meyer	
Meyer, Parsons and Dunne (1990)	Reflections of Learning Inventory (RoLi)
Makinen	
Makinen, Olkinuora and Lonka (2002)	Inventory of General Study Orientations (IGSO)

suggesting a two-way relationship between conceptions, approaches and cognitive processes, with conceptions being developed through experiences of teaching and studying and then influencing subsequent ways of studying (Evans and Kozhevnikov, 2011). Lowyck, Elen and Clarebout (2004) have made the important distinction between an individual's conception (their own response to an idea) and their instructional conceptions which include their beliefs about the learning environment.

Conceptions of learning (Marton et al., 1993) and approaches to learning are related to study strategies including regulation and processing strategies (Entwistle and Peterson 2004; Loyens, Rikers and Schmidt, 2008). Regulation strategies steer the processing of information (Ferla, Valcke and Schuyten, 2009) and can rely on the initiative of the learner or on external sources and take more account of the socio-cognitive and emotional aspects of learning. Combinations of these variables have been referred to as study orientations, learning styles or patterns (Lonka, 1997; Mäkinen, Olkinuora and Lonka, 2004; Vermunt and Vermetten, 2004) and/or orchestrations where combinations of approaches or orientations are involved. Vermunt's adoption of the term learning pattern stresses the potential for variability as well as stability of orientations defining the term as 'a coordinating concept, in which the interrelationships between cognitive, affective and regulative learning activities, beliefs about learning and learning motivations are united' (Vermunt and Endedijk, 2011: 295). It is generally believed that orientations are more stable across context than approaches to learning although evidence of both stability and variability is evident (Nijhuis, Segers and Gijselaers, 2006). A meaning orientation combining self-regulated learning, the deep approach to learning (Vermunt and van Rijswijk, 1988), and associated perceived control over learning (incorporating student cognitions about learning, strong self-efficacy beliefs, constructivist learning conceptions and attributions for academic performance) has been shown to be related to positive learning outcomes (Lonka and Lindblom-Ylänne, 1996). Further work exploring the relationship between self-regulation and external regulation has resulted in the identification of four key processing strategies (meaning directed, reproduction directed, application directed and undirected), with each pattern being associated with a characteristic mental model, learning orientation, affective process and regulation strategy (Vermunt, 1998). While Vermunt does not directly reference approaches to learning, a deep approach is implicated in the meaning directed strategy and a surface approach in the reproduction directed strategy. The implication is that a deep approach is related to high levels of metacognition and the ability to manage learning through development of self-regulation strategies over external regulation. The relationship between a deep approach to learning and self-regulation is also highlighted by Micari and Light (2009) who note that self-regulation coincides with the ability to know that one does not know.

Deep approach debates

It is known that approaches to learning are not characteristics of learners but are determined by a relation between the learner and the context (Evans and Kozhevnikov, 2011); that in practice, changing approaches is difficult (Gijbels et al., 2009); that changing the nature of instruction to facilitate a deep approach may have unintended consequences on student learning approaches (Balasooriya, Toohey and Hughes, 2009); and that learners do not pass through a series of developmental stages on the path to a deep approach (Marshall and Case, 2005). The modifiability of approaches to learning is an important area of discussion. Mattick, Dennis and Bligh (2004) have argued that approaches to learning are a phenomenon more influenced by the demands of a specific learning environment than by innate predispositions and therefore should be amenable to change. However, conceptions of learning, identified as impacting on approaches to learning, have also been identified as being difficult to change (Pedrosa-de-Jesus and da Silva Lopes, 2011). It is possible to identify both variability and stability in approaches to learning.

In reconceptualising a deep approach to learning it is important to address 21st century learning environment requirements within and across disciplines, where a deep approach may look markedly different in different contexts, as well as concerns about the most appropriate ways to measure dimensions of a deep approach. To meet the demands of 21st century learning environments, student teachers need to become more self-directed, have a good understanding of the core content of specific subject areas, the learning context and learning processes, and be able to collaborate effectively with others. These requirements in the context of learning to teach, emphasising individual identity development and interpersonal skills, require a broader definition of a deep approach. It has been suggested that descriptions of students' learning need to encompass emotional, vocational, collaborative and more discipline-specific elements of learning environments (Entwistle, 2009) including additional conceptions of learning focusing on sociability dimensions and the 'why' aspects of learning involving reasons for learning and the context of learning. Peterson et al. (2010) see these additional and more global conceptions regarding intentions and strategies as being of greater potential value in improving learning outcomes than the initially identified six focusing on the 'what' and 'how' of learning. The need to take greater account of social competence and cooperative study as a dimension of a deep approach is highlighted (Lonka et al., 2004); however, the extent to which cooperative learning is commensurate with a deep approach has been challenged by Lonka and Lindblom-Ylänne (1996) who showed that cooperation is not necessarily related to the deep approach to learning but, rather, can be interpreted as leaning on other students.

For Greasley and Ashworth (2007: 833) the 'superficial attractiveness of the deep/surface typology of approaches to learning masks its sensitivity to the actual lifeworld circumstances of the student'. Finer distinctions among different kinds of deep approaches which are more or less individualistic in focus are needed (Entwistle and McCune, 2004). The inherent assumption that taking a deep approach is desirable and equally achievable by all has been questioned (Struyven, Dochy, Janssens and Gielen, 2006). Links between a deep approach and positive learning outcomes are inconclusive and students may vary in their capacity and volition to adopt a deep approach and also change their approaches to learning depending on context. There are some assumptions that those who use surface strategies are less capable than those who engage in deep processes; however, to confirm this, a better understanding is needed of the learning context (Thompson, Pilgrim and Oliver, 2005) as, in certain situations, surface approaches can lead to successful learning (Haggis,

2003). As noted by Case and Marshall (2004) the original characterisation of deep and surface approaches has shifted to acknowledge that memorisation, originally thought of as a characteristic of a surface approach, can also be used effectively in a form of a deep approach (Marton, Dall'Alba and Tse, 1996). It may also be more useful to view a strategic approach as a dimension of a deep approach than as a separate construct in the context of certain tasks and outcomes (Lonka, Vesikansa and Lindblom-Ylänne 2000).

The extent to which a deep approach to learning always entails a given set of features is questioned, with Greasley and Ashworth (2007: 830) acknowledging 'that students may vary in the priority they give within an approach to learning which is generally "deep" to "seeking meaning" or "using evidence"'. The bipolarity of deep–surface has been highlighted in Meyer's identification of students' 'disintegrated approaches', in which elements of both deep and surface approaches are reported (Meyer, 2000; Meyer and Boulton-Lewis, 2003). Ramsden (2003) has described how students use a complex mixture of approaches to learning influenced by the learning environment and task demands. Thompson et al. (2005) also agreed that we need to think about approaches to learning in more complex ways. Rather than considering surface, deep and achieving as separate beliefs and strategies, it is more important to see how these are interconnected; the same argument can be applied to the relationship between deep approaches and regulation of learning strategies.

In reconceptualising a deep approach, McCune and Entwistle (2011: 305) identify what they perceive to be a relatively stable deep construct in the: '*disposition to understand for oneself.*' Stability is assumed given that it is unlikely that critical thinking is reversed (Barnett, 2007). The disposition to understand combines three elements compared to the two elements (motivation and learning strategies) of the traditionally defined deep approach. These three elements are: (a) *the knowledge and ability* to develop and use understanding in adopting a reasoned stance to complex issues; (b) continuing desire to adopt effortful, deep approaches across a range of contexts (willingness) and a readiness to monitor and discuss the process of learning and developing understanding within the discipline (*awareness* of process); and (c) *sensitivity to context* that makes students alert to opportunities to develop and apply their understanding whenever the situation allows. The extent to which an individual is able to activate all three elements, and consistently in practice, is important to explore, as is the question of what aspects of this disposition are most important for certain tasks and contexts. In practice, the interplay between affordances and barriers and how these impact on the development of dispositions are touched on by McCune and Entwistle (2011) who argued the importance of developing challenging, authentic curricula with a focus on personal understanding in order for dispositions to be developed.

To measure the complexity of a deep approach questions have been raised about the ability of measurement tools to capture the richness of student approaches and subtleties inherent in changes in approaches within and between students, suggesting the need for finer grained levels of analysis involving methods and measurement (Greasley and Ashworth, 2007). Inventories have been criticised for measuring general dispositions and not actual processes (Heikkilä and Lonka, 2006) and for focusing on consistencies in student behaviour rather than context sensitivity and thus failing to address situation specific variables (Boekaerts, 1996).

Methods

An interpretative phenomenological analysis approach was adopted (Smith, 2003) to explore student teachers' experiences of learning while training to teach during an intensive one year postgraduate certificate of education programme (PGCE) at one UK university. The training programme involved students undertaking 120 days of teaching experience in schools interspersed with training within the HEI throughout the year. This study aimed to investigate student teachers' experiences of managing a number of learning transitions (from specialist to professional programme; HEI to school in different roles as student and teacher, and from one school context to another) using a bottom-up, descriptive, phenomenographic approach adopting a second perspective (Rosenfeld and Rosenfeld, 2008) with students seen as active partners in the research process with explicit attention given to discussing student teachers' metacognition of their overall approaches to learning as well as in response to specific tasks.

The sample involving 14 student teachers (from a range of subject areas including modern foreign languages; religious education; English; music; science and history) was opportunistic and self-selected. There were 4 males and 10 females. Three of the students had come onto the programme from working in other professions and the remaining 11 had come straight from HEI undergraduate study. Student teacher perceptions of their experiences were explored via group and individual interviews both face to face and via the phone and email with the researcher at regular intervals during the one year training programme. The data collection process from an ethical perspective aimed to be as minimally disruptive to student teachers as possible given the intense nature of their study and was discussed and negotiated with each student teacher regarding contact times within the overall design of the project. Data were gathered via group (45–60 minutes duration) and individual interviews (60–90 minutes duration). Interviews followed a specific structure to be able to compare across four different strands of a Higher Education Academy funded larger project: facilitating transitions to master's-level learning to improving formative assessment and feedback processes (Scott et al., 2011). The four strands of the project considered the learning experiences of students on different master's pathways: students studying for a vocational and applied master's qualification (a postgraduate certificate in education), international students, students from non-traditional backgrounds, and part-time students.

The questions specifically asked students about: (a) their experiences of coming onto the programme and their reasons for doing so; (b) induction processes; (c) nature of programme materials; (d) teaching experiences; (e) writing experiences; (f) cultural, geographical and social differences – status, position, working with tutors, working with peers, knowledge acquisition and development; and (g) issues to do with specific transitions, usefulness of original disciplinary knowledge, relationships between disciplinary knowledge and practice-based knowledge, teaching practice, applied knowledge.

'To seek understanding of student teachers' situations via their own accounts of their perceptions' (Richards, 2009: 21), 48 individual and 5 focus group interviews and emails were collected. Six students were involved in four interviews and eight students were involved in three interviews lasting up to an hour each. The interviews took place at regular intervals throughout the year from December to July to ensure that student teachers were able to feed back on the two school placements that they experienced. The 42 emails and focus group meetings were used to gain feedback, to specifically share and verify with the student teachers the findings and to extend and develop understandings of the themes discussed in an iterative fashion. The data were analysed using content-analysis procedures (Braun and Clarke, 2006) to identify key themes, mindful of the literature on deep approaches to learning and underpinning relevant theoretical frameworks. All interview data was transcribed and subject to descriptive, topic and analytical coding (Richards, 2009). Attention was focused on individual comments within the interview transcripts rather than entire interviews with the aim to create a 'pool of meanings' discovered from the data (Marton, 1986: 43). The intention was to classify descriptions of experience and not to classify individuals (Micari and Light, 2009). Using a constant comparative method, newly collected data were constantly compared with existing data and theory and the codings were revised to ensure overall consistency (Arthur, Waring, Coe and Hedges, 2012). The data were checked and rechecked and cross-referenced on six separate occasions by the lead researcher to identify themes and to refine and review based on the reading and re-reading of the data. Throughout the process memos were generated to assist synthesis of the data including notations on transcripts identifying themes, field notes to assist the researcher in returning to the data, and theoretical notes looking at themes and links between them and underpinning theory (Waring, 2012).

Results and discussion

Developing an understanding of a deep approach in the context of learning to teach

It was possible to discern characteristics of a deep approach to learning in the context of learning to teach and to identify individual and contextual variables impacting on the adoption of a deep approach from analysis of individual and focus group data (interviews and emails), and triangulation of these with each other and the literature base. Characteristics of a deep approach discussed below included: (a) student focus on meaning making; (b) self-management skills; (c) perspective; (d) noticing; (e) resilience; (f) managing personal response to feedback; (g) proactive feedback-seeking behaviour; (h) adaptability, and (i) forward thinking. From these characteristics a number of higher order meta-themes could be discerned including a student teacher's collaborative, networking, emotional self-regulation, intuitive and boundary-crossing abilities.

Focus on meaning making

Identifying features included student teachers' use of research-informed approaches to learning and teaching in being able to apply theory within practice effectively; a critical engagement with subject pedagogy; a willingness to step back and critique their own approaches to learning; an ability to relate ideas and make connections; an enhanced awareness of the complexity of learning; and the ability to develop their own theories rather than blanket acceptance of others'. Those adopting a deep approach were able to cope with not knowing, understanding that it would take time to develop the necessary knowledge and skills. Student teachers discussed 'getting to grips' with the ambiguity and complexity of learning. Appreciating the ambiguity of learning can be seen as an important element of a deep approach as elaborated in McCune and Entwistle's (2011) discussion of a *disposition to understand for oneself*. The assumption is that learners have the knowledge and ability to manage their lack of knowing, see confusion as an important element of the learning process and are aware of the need for continuous interaction with, and critique of, information (Micari and Light, 2009). Four student teachers were able to discuss their own strategies to develop their learning environments seeing themselves as equal partners and not as legitimate peripheral participants. This correlates with Jungert and Rosander's (2009) ideas concerning the ability of individuals to influence their environments by adopting strategies to influence their study environment in order to change their institutions and to take control over their studies and professional practice. In developing deep approaches to learning, Silén and Uhlin (2008: 464) have argued that learners 'need to develop competencies for using their freedom and understanding of what the opportunities mean in relation to choices and decisions made on their own'.

Student teachers wanting to integrate theory into practice frequently discussed a tension between trying to implement an integrated approach to teaching (building connections, being creative, seeing learning holistically) and the procedural requirements of teaching within their schools and what they saw as a mechanistic approach to teaching. Much emphasis is placed within the initial teacher education (ITE) curriculum on supporting student teachers in developing behaviour management strategies; however, some student teachers perceived that this was often discussed in a technical and reductionist way without due consideration of pedagogy:

> I felt like looking into the pedagogy and looking at the theory was quite important for me in how I was shaping my teaching, and I felt like that, the assignment, is the only place that I've really been offered to do that . . . The assignment was kind of an aside . . . I wasn't happy with that shallow-ness . . . so I've gone on and tried to study it as much as possible myself. I felt that it has brought on a bit more maturity in how I think about it now, in terms of it helped shape how I view my lesson plans more and what I'm actually looking for in the class.
>
> (Student 1)

Working against meaning making were a number of related issues including: student teacher perceptions of the authenticity of assessment, their previous experiences of learning, how much agency student teachers perceived they were afforded within school contexts and their relative ability to relate to, and accept, school policies and practices. Here the 'hidden rules' of communities (Bergenhenegouwen, 1987) at a range of levels (discipline, year, faculty groupings) presented barriers in *coming to know* and tensions between student teachers' own goals and those of others. This may be especially problematic for student teachers trying to get to grips with institutional cultures within a short time frame and with limited frames of reference with which to establish norms.

Sensitivity to context was highlighted and the importance of soft skills for the kinds of work required in new learning environments were identified in the focus group and individual student teacher accounts. The notion of *project* (Greasley and Ashworth, 2007) in how the student teachers saw their own situation(s) and felt able to carry out core activities in meeting the needs of the school and their own learning was important.

Self-management skills

The link between the adoption of a deep approach and appropriate use of self-regulation strategies was evident. In considering a broader definition of a deep approach, it is important to consider how a student uses their self-regulatory capacity to operationalise a deep approach to learning. The metacognitive dimension is evident in student teachers' abilities to self-monitor, to identify priorities for development, and to manage the emotional dimension of learning. Student teachers were able to demonstrate a number of self-management skills linked to the adoption of a deep approach; these included: ability to process and filter information effectively; improvisation – thinking on their feet; flexibility in analysis of information; selectivity and criticality in how information was synthesised from different sources and integrated into their own teaching as opposed to an unthink-ing copying of ideas; adapting teaching to meet the requirements of the learning context; and compartmentalising and 'switching off' in order to recharge their own batteries. Those adopting a deep approach were more able to utilise opportunities within the learning environment and prioritise:

> And I do learn a lot, because everyone has their different styles, and I really enjoy trying to pick up bits from everyone else's different styles and trying to use them.
>
> (Student 4)

As part of self-management those evidencing a deep approach were more able to search out and integrate new information and to regulate their workload through balanced use of the schools' and their own learning resources. This resonates with McCune and Entwistle's (2011) requirement of a deep approach to include a will to learn (understanding of the learning process) and a will to offer (to put forward own ideas for critical consideration by others). In the context of learning to teach a deep approach exhibited by some student teachers was that of being able to offer ideas, develop their own ideas and integrate others' ideas to develop their own integrated style of teaching.

A key feature of a deep approach was the ability of some of the student teachers to focus on one thing at a time (one lesson, one class). This could be interpreted as a surface approach but in the context of learning to teach, the ability to adopt a disciplined and focused approach in order to fully consider what was needed at specific moments in time and in order to avoid distractions could be interpreted as a constituent of a deep approach.

> I think I've learnt to compartmentalise, and deal with the group that I'm in at the time . . . I think that you just have to deal with, you just have to respond to what you are given . . . you can't change things, you can't change who you are with, you've just got to work with what you've got.
>
> (Student 5)

Perceptions of high workloads and lack of confidence impacted negatively on the development of self-management skills for some student teachers. The trauma of being 'dumped in to a system and not being connected to it' was noted by five student teachers who articulated a real sense of desperation, feeling that they did not have the 'tools' and did not know how to access support. They talked of 'craving to be taught' and of 'scratching', 'scrabbling', 'fighting' and 'hunting down' support:

> You just get on with it, don't you? You work out what you've got to do. It's like any kind of situation where you're thrown in, where you have no support, basically . . . It was more like, muddle through, you'll be alright . . . I want . . . a more clever way to do what I am doing . . . but I am hoping that comes with practice and keeping my eye on the ball.
>
> (Student 7)

Most of the student teachers perceived that their self-management improved as they progressed through the year, from a position of 'climbing up that hill' and being on a 'constant treadmill' to one 'where the fear factor went away', where there was 'more space in my head to float ideas around and be more creative' (Student 5), 'could improvise more' (Student 13), 'could plan spontaneously better now than I could before' (Student 14) and felt 'more grounded' (Student 9). A key issue for teacher educators is working with student teachers to move them from a survival and containment mode to one that enables them to grow and develop the knowledge and skills and understanding of teaching (Haggar and McIntyre, 2006; Ure, 2009).

Perspective

Those exhibiting a deep approach were more able to see themselves from others' perspectives and evaluate their own performance objectively and dispassionately; they exhibited detachment where and when necessary:

> I didn't think I really appreciated how quickly schools change and the government, all new things coming in and I don't think I really appreciated how much that happened and how adaptable you have to be as teachers when something new is introduced. And I think I am able to – I think I have found a pragmatism that I didn't have before perhaps.
>
> (Student 9)

A deep approach in this context meant being able to see the bigger picture and balance the competing demands of academia and the school-based placement which often meant compromises to the ways that the student teachers had previously worked and to their own goals. It could be argued that such skills are of high value in learning to teach. Those adopting deeper approaches were very clear about what they could and could not tolerate and what the 'deal breakers' were for them within the learning context; they were more able to say no to requests when they needed to and at the same time more able to work with, rather than alongside, colleagues.

Limiting the development of perspective in the teacher training context was the level of compromise and openness of student teachers regarding their own goals and beliefs about learning compared to those of their colleagues. This was connected to their perceptions of agency, their views on the nature and quality of assessment of their own practice, awareness of their own weaknesses, and possessing the self-regulatory skills to being able to do something about them. As part of this, student teachers viewed the HEI tutor as extremely valuable in supporting them in being able to gain better perspective on their practice.

Noticing

The relational dimension of learning to teach can be seen as an important dimension of a deep approach to learning. Those adopting deeper approaches were able to make more effective use of school networks, had a good under-standing of the contexts that they worked in, were sensitive to the needs of others and were better able to manage their learning transitions compared to some student teachers who described existing in a separate vacuum to the com-munities that they were supposed to be part of:

> you are more involved in how the school does stuff, and . . . trying to run alongside what the school does, without interfering too much but also achieving the [teaching standards].
>
> (Student 12)

The ability to notice, build and function effectively within and across net-works is seen as an important social dimension of a deep approach to learning. Noticing includes making the most of opportunities and awareness and under-standing of contexts. It links to perceptual abilities and different forms of intui-tion (Sadler-Smith and Shefy, 2004). The ability to notice in this context meant being attuned to the nuances of the different cultures within schools (Volet and Chalmers, 1992), *sensitivity* to the needs of others (McCune and Entwistle, 2011), and *sociality* in being able to make the most of opportunities even if not easily accessible (Greasley and Ashworth, 2007). The relational aspect of learn-ing to teach is of paramount importance in learning to teach. Student teachers able to make the most of networks demonstrated a good understanding of *academic tribes* (social communities in to which individuals become socialised) (Becher, 1989) and their place within such tribes (Ylijoki, 2000) including a clear conceptualisation of which groups they wished to belong to, along with strategies for making this happen. However, some student teachers chose not to draw on resources in the school context; this could be characterised as positive where the student teacher had alternative networks to draw on and was self-sufficient, or negative where the student teacher was isolated and not developing the requisite knowledge and skills. A key tension some student teachers faced was not having the confidence to take ideas forward or having the confidence but being worried about upsetting the status quo, and for one student teacher: 'I think a lot of it's about finding the face that's going to fit with the people in the department or the school already'(Student 8).

Resilience

All student teachers in the study demonstrated relatively high levels of resil-ience, although in different ways. In individual and focus group interviews the student teachers evidenced how they had managed a number of difficulties they faced in learning to teach as noted by one student:

> Stubbornness, motivation, not giving up attitude . . . telling myself that this is going to be the hardest year and just get through this, but now I

know it is not, it is going to be hard for a couple of more years yet. Then it will get easier. But step at a time kind of thing, so get through this and then you have got the holiday, recharge and then take next year as it comes.

(Student 13)

Resilience was linked to high levels of self-efficacy (Bandura, 1997), confidence in their own ability, good self-understanding, ability to take risks and to learn from mistakes, and a repertoire of effective coping strategies. It could be argued that a key skill in 21st century learning environments is the ability to accurately assess one's own strengths and weaknesses and the ability to deploy effective strategies to compensate for these. Those adopting a deeper approach to learning were able to focus their efforts and also gain help, and delegate areas of work effectively to others to enable such a focus; in this context a re-evaluation is needed of what a self-directed approach encompasses. Ashworth and Greasley's (2009) notion of *embodiment*, involving the ability to identify with projects and remain committed to them, is also relevant in this context. A deep approach in the context of learning to teach would certainly include understanding of the self as a teacher in relation to how a student teacher comes to own their style by being open to and incorporating learning from a variety of sources to realise their own teaching style (Oosterheert and Vermunt, 2001):

> my first mentor . . . sat me down . . . and said . . . you can't just imitate what I am doing you have got to find your own way . . . I went and observed lots of other members of staff . . . so I then took all of that into [my second school] and . . . I was teaching lessons from five different members of staff [with] very different styles . . . they let me get on with it . . . I have developed my own teaching style. I am getting there it is not fully there . . . I have been in two schools that have been very keen on you developing your own style and lots of very good feedback and although that sometimes conflicts, it is just about experimenting and finding out what works for me.

(Student 10)

The nature and degree of support available to the student teacher, their ability to identify with the belief systems and procedures within the school, and conflicts associated with managing the dual role as learner and teacher impacted on some student teachers' ability to operationalise a deep approach.

Managing personal response to feedback

In 21st century learning environments, student teachers need to be able to manage information flows effectively. The ability to manage and take responsibility for seeking feedback are important elements of a deep approach. Manifestations of a deep approach were evidenced in student teachers being open to feedback, their ability to use, critique and apply feedback effectively, involving emotional self-regulation of feedback and their ability to filter feedback. Those adopting a deep approach were able to clearly articulate their feedback needs. Impacting on a deep response to managing feedback student teachers within individual and focus group meetings identified the following barriers: the relative quality of feedback, arguing that too much focus had been on personalised feedback compared to that related to the task and future performance (Hattie and Timperley, 2007); and inappropriate use of praise which was not authentic or warranted, and the need for more feedforward compared to feedback opportunities as well as the timing of feedback. Connected to this was student teacher lack of ability to articulate their feedback needs. Karagiannopoulou and Christodoulides (2005) have argued that students are more likely to engage in deeper processing when feedback involves reciprocal transactions between those engaged in the feedback dialogue. However, several student teachers highlighted that they did not feel able to question and engage in debate with mentors for a number of reasons (e.g. lack of experience of feedback dialogues, concerns about how they would be assessed, and lack of trust in the mentoring relationship).

Proactive feedback-seeking behaviour

Feedback-seeking behaviour was not well developed among the group of student teachers. Those demonstrating a deep approach felt more able to put across their own views, to challenge feedback, were more open to feedback and more proactive in seeking feedback from a variety of sources.

> Well, the first thing I did was try to find out about who were the advanced teachers . . . because I figured these guys obviously want to keep up to date with what's going on, whether through ambition, or just love of learning, or whatever, . . . It was kind of piggy backing on the systems that were in place. And I think, also, once you've been in school for a while you just sort of hear about these people. And I'm not, I don't have a problem just going up and saying this is me, would you mind if I come and watch your class? And I fully understand if you don't want me to, it's not a problem. I have never had anybody say no to me.
>
> (Student 10)

In developing a deep approach to feedback-seeking behaviours the ability to filter information effectively from a variety of sources is imperative. Some student teachers actively sought feedback from many sources but were unable to filter this successfully resulting in confusion and ineffective application of feedback. A key tension for some student teachers was a lack of perceived agency related to whether they felt the learning community open and accessible, and fundamentally a lack of experience of knowing how to manage feedback dynamics with colleagues:

it would be so helpful to have a session on just encouraging students to [ask for feedback] – maybe I am not particularly good at that but maybe other students have done that and been more successful. But for me that would have been brilliant . . . And to hear the challenges that mentors have – so from both sides.

(Student 9)

Adaptability

Student teachers varied considerably in their ability to manage transitions from one context to another. Importantly, those demonstrating a deep approach were able to apply what they had learnt to their teaching of pupils. Those more able to manage such transitions could be described as effective boundary-crossers in their ability to transfer and adapt what they had learnt from one context to another and contribute as full members of communities of practice (Wenger, McDermott and Synder, 2002). Ashworth and Greasley's (2009) notion of *spatiality* in relation to the student's picture of the geography of the places they need to go and act within affected by the limitations and affordances of the situation is relevant. For Richardson (2000) the level of integration of the learner within the context is fundamental to their relative success. Adaptable students had a clear idea of their own identity as a student teacher and preferred teaching styles but were also able to accommodate and adapt to the school's favoured styles. They managed unforeseen changes to their working conditions and demonstrated considerable ability to adapt their routines. It could be argued that such students demonstrated an open-mindedness thinking disposition (Elik, Wiener and Corkum, 2010) manifested in greater flexibility in their belief systems and ability to weigh new evidence against a favoured belief in making a decision.

Adaptability was influenced by student perceptions regarding their sense of agency in different settings with some student teachers feeling isolated from their school community. For some student teachers trying to find the balance between trying to fit in and develop their sense of self while being mindful of dominant styles of teaching within a school was difficult.

But when you go into the schools, if the school's not a good fit for you, if you're constantly battling with it, when your teaching skills aren't suitable for the pupils in that school . . . if I teach a certain way, but they're almost kind of conditioned to be taught a certain way, and if you don't teach them that way they go mental. So that would have been a useful thing.

(Student 12)

Forward thinking

Linked to resilience was the ability of some student teachers to visualise themselves in a teaching job and to be able to use the knowledge and skills they had learnt to move beyond what was seen by some as an 'inbetween phase':

> I was just making notes even though I realised that I wouldn't use them at that particular moment they would be useful in future . . . I can see myself in the next year trying to finish as much as I can at school, not take things home . . . I think a lot of the pressure that I've put on myself is because I've been in such a focus about getting everything perfect for my plan. So maybe in my next year that might be one of my targets, use resources that are available to me, be selective when I am trying to use them, and also save time so I can devote my energies elsewhere.
>
> (Student 3)

They were able to articulate what and how they would take ideas forward and took responsibility for their own development. This aligns with Greasley and Ashworth's notion of *temporality* in their ability to use the present to reassert the presence of the past and to anticipate what is to come. Linked to this was an alertness to new possibilities about how to apply ideas learnt to new contexts. This identifies with McCune and Entwistle's (2011) description of a moving approach as a component of a disposition to understand.

A key tension for these forward-focused student teachers was finding a job and remaining motivated in contexts where some did not feel they were being sufficiently challenged. Forward thinking was used in an expansive and creative way to develop new understandings and practices and in a reductionist way as a form of escapism from the present; however, both approaches had utility in addressing student teacher immediate concerns, although there is a question regarding the longer term impact of perceived restricted opportunities.

Conclusions

In summary, it was evident that some student teachers were more effective in managing their learning transitions than others, they were more effective boundary-crossers (Wenger, 2000), and were more able to manage their dual identities as learner and teacher. It was possible to identify those who demonstrated dissonant orchestrations in that they wanted to adopt a deep approach but because they found the context difficult were more likely to use more surface approaches. While a number of individual and contextual factors could be discerned, the way in which these affected student teachers was variable. Student teacher perceptions of context impacted on approaches to learning as identified in previous studies (Vermunt, Bakkenes, Wubbels and Brekelmans, 2008). The majority of student teachers highlighted their increased vulnerability when moving from one school context to another; careful induction into new practices was seen as of critical importance.

Contextual factors impacting significantly on student teachers' adoption of a deep approach were: (a) the nature and design of assessment including issues of alignment, authenticity and timing, and design of feedback including the relative balance of feedback and feedforward; (b) preparation and housekeeping issues (access to resources; clarity of information about processes and procedure); and (c) perceptions of agency within schools influenced by the nature of mentoring frameworks available within learning contexts, the degree of acceptance and accommodation of student teachers into communities of practice and accommodation of student teachers' styles of teaching. Contrary to many studies, workload in itself was not a key issue (Birenbaum and Rosenau, 2006); however, perceived freedom in learning was, and from two different perspectives (wanting to be able to innovate versus being scared to innovate).

Individual factors impacting on a student teacher's ability to adopt a deep approach to learning to teach included student teachers' (a) past experiences of learning and teaching and access to coping mechanisms; (b) flexibility in situations where style challenge was evident (mismatch between student teacher and school values, beliefs and/or teaching styles and where new understandings were needed); (c) emotional self-regulation capacity; (d) pre-existing knowledge and skills; and (e) priorities.

In considering the interaction of individual and contextual variables on student teacher ability to adopt a deep approach to teaching, student teachers' sense of self, their ability to connect with, and adapt to, the requirements of the learning environment and perceived 'personal fit' with the school were important. In being able to be part of a community of practice, their ability to use a deep approach in the selection of appropriate processing and regulation strategies was fundamental in enabling them to address areas of strength and weakness. To enhance effectiveness, it was noted by many that they needed training in navigating and negotiating relationships within school and HEI settings.

Implications for research and practice

In the context of learning to teach it is important to consider approaches to learning in more complex ways that also acknowledge the relational dimensions of a deep approach. A broader definition of a deep approach is advocated that takes into consideration the nature of the interrelationships between a number of variables impacting on a student's ability to realise a deep approach. Importantly, within this broader definition, strategic approaches to learning are seen as an integral part of a deep approach. Student teachers demonstrated attributes of a deep approach but enacted these in different ways linked to their own personal geographies and previous experiences of learning and teaching. Student teacher experiences need to be understood in context and not through the use of disconnected and decontextualised methods. Bipolar descriptions of approaches and strategies are too narrow to capture how learning approaches are enacted (Case and Marshall, 2004). To enable richer understandings of how deep approaches are developed and enacted, Ramsden has argued that we need to consider both *how* we organise, or structure, learning and *what* meaning we take from the learning experience. For Greasley and Ashworth (2007), phenomenographic descriptions would be enriched through a consideration of the '*actual lifeworld*' of the learner. Their framework incorporating notions of *selfhood, sociality, embodiment, temporarility, spatiality, project and discourse* provides a framework through which to explore student teachers' choices of approaches to learning within context. It does this by enabling a focus on the meaning of the learning situation to the individual in terms of agency, including social identity, issues of control, power, acceptance and authenticity. Lonka et al. (2004) have also suggested the need for a finer grained level of analysis to examine three different layers of context (the specific situation/task, the programme and the more general learning orientation of the student), the dominance of particular factors at each unit of analysis and the relationships between them. In this way, by considering deep approaches alongside related constructs we may learn more about the strategies student teachers use to influence their study environment (Jungert and Rosander, 2009).

While a one-size-fits-all approach is not appropriate, feedback from the student teachers' focus group interviews highlighted a number of key areas for attention. The impact of new environments on students' approaches to learning was considerable. In order to support student teachers to enhance their understanding of the learning process, close and early monitoring of students' approaches to learning and their development and use of self-regulatory skills and cognitive strategies are important (Vermunt and Endedijk, 2011). As part of this, there need to be opportunities for student teachers to explicate their own beliefs about learning and teaching (Evans and Kozhevnikov, 2011). It was notable in this study that none of the student teachers had discussed their beliefs about teaching with their school mentors.

To support student teachers in managing supercomplexity, and to effectively manage what they do and do not know, there needs to be more explicit attention given to learning processes. Practising ideas in non-threatening situations that approximate reality ('approximations of practice') provide one way of reducing complexity while also attending to core aspects and discrete components of complex practice (Grossman, Hammerness and McDonald 2009: 283). Being able to access, make sense of, synthesise, filter and apply different sources of information requires a greater focus on information processing strategies and the ability to use the right approach at the right time, including confidence to move away from established ways of thinking and doing.

Student teachers may require additional support in managing the relational dimension of their work and their own identity development in becoming a teacher, especially in negotiating entry and building relationships in new learning environments. Attention needs to be focused on student teacher strategy development to enable student teachers to engage as more than legitimate peripheral participants (LPP) within communities of practice. The LPP concept needs reframing and enriching to consider the ways in which student teachers can participate more centrally within such communities and *influence* practice given the range of expertise and new experiences they bring to new contexts. A mapping of student teacher networks of support and the strategies they use in order to develop successful interpersonal relationships is important (Karagiannonopoulou and Christidoulides, 2005).

To maximise opportunities for meaningful and authentic learning experiences, a number of recommendations can be made: (a) ensuring sufficient challenge and not removal of it (Silén and Uhlin, 2008); (b) providing staged learning opportunities (Ure, 2009); (c) co-teaching to assist in the development of cognitive insights about elements of teaching through shared action and discussion with experienced teachers (Ure, 2009); and (d) exposure to different ways of learning and teaching and tools to assist practice (Ellis, Goodyear, Prosser and O'Hara, 2006). As part of this, student teachers need to experience constructive friction in order to be aware of variation in ways of understanding knowledge in specific areas and enabled to focus on one area at a time to develop their practice change while ensuring other areas remain stable (Micari and Light, 2009).

Greater attention to the emotional dimension of learning through the provision of appropriate scaffolding and support for individual students (Balasooriya et al., 2009) is also required. Student teachers require greater opportunities for constructive, critical and focused feedback opportunities (Grossman et al., 2009). Student teachers also need to be supported to develop effective feedback-seeking behaviours and to manage their responses to feedback in order for them to move from being 'cue-deaf' (work hard to succeed without seeking support), to 'cue-conscious' (perceptive and receptive to cues) and ultimately to be 'cue-seekers' (more active in seeking out support) (Joughin, 2009). Student teachers need to be encouraged and empowered to critique their own and others' practice with the support of knowledgeable others. To do this, issues of power and agency need to be explicitly discussed in order to enable student teachers to adopt a deeper approach to their management of feedback both now and in the future; they need to be encouraged to review their own networks of support and the processes they use to manage feedback (Jakhelln, 2010).

To realise a deep learning approach to learning for themselves and their pupils, student teachers need to develop attributes to manage their own learning environments and need to be facilitated through the development of participatory pedagogies. We need to know more about how student teachers come to influence their study environment, to interact with colleagues, and how best they can be supported to develop sustained deep approaches to learning within and across contexts, and specifically in relation to subject specific demands. Student teachers, HEI and school-based tutors and mentors need to be open to explore beliefs about learning and teaching in order to develop and share a more complete understanding of what a deep approach constitutes in contemporary learning and teaching contexts.

References

Albergaria Almeida, P., Teixeira-Dias, J. J., Martinho, M. and Balasooriya, C. D. (2011) The interplay between students' perceptions of context and approaches to learning, *Research Papers in Education*, 26(2): 223–244.

Arthur, J., Waring, M., Coe, R. and Hedges, L (2012) *Research methods and methodologies in education*, London: Sage.

Ashworth, P. and Greasley, K. (2009) The phenomenology of 'approach to studying': The idiographic turn, *Studies in Higher Education*, 34: 561–576.

Balasooriya, C. D., Toohey, S. and Hughes, C. (2009) The cross-over phenomenon: Unexpected patterns of change in students' approaches to learning, *Studies in Higher Education*, 34(7): 781–794.

Bandura, A. (1997) *Self-efficacy: The exercise of control*, New York: Freeman.

Barnett, R. (2007) *Being a student in an age of uncertainty*, Berkshire: SRHE and Open University Press.

Becher, T. (1989) *Academic tribes and territories: Intellectual enquiry and the cultures of disciplines*, Milton Keynes: SRHE and Open University Press.

Bergenhenegouwen, G. (1987) Hidden curriculum in the university, *Higher Education*, 16(5): 535–543.

Biggs, J. B. (1978) Individual and group differences in study processes, *British Journal of Educational Psychology*, 48: 266–279.

Biggs, J. B. (1987) *Student approaches to learning and studying*, Melbourne: Australian Council for Educational Research.

Biggs, J. (1993) What do inventories of students' learning processes really measure? A theoretical review and clarification, *British Journal of Educational Psychology*, 63: 1–17.

Biggs, J. B. (2003) *Teaching for quality learning at university* (2nd ed.), Buckingham: SRHE and Open University Press.

Biggs, J., Kember, D. and Leung, D. Y. P. (2001) The revised two-factor study process questionnaire: R-SPQ-2F, *British Journal of Educational Psychology*, 71: 133–149.

Birenbaum, M. and Rosenau, S. (2006) Assessment preferences, learning orientations, and learning strategies of pre-service and in-service teachers, *Journal of Education for Teaching*, 32(2): 213–225.

Boekaerts, M. (1996) Personality and the psychology of learning, *European Journal of Personality*, 10: 377–404.

Braun, V. and Clarke, V. (2006) Using thematic analysis in psychology, *Qualitative Research in Psychology*, 3(2): 77–101.

Burn, K., Hagger, H., Mutton, T. and Everton, T. (2003) The complex development of student-teachers' thinking, *Teachers and Teaching: Theory and Practice*, 9(4): 309–331.

Case, S. and Marshall, D. (2004) Between deep and surface: Procedural approaches to learning in engineering education contexts, *Studies in Higher Education*, 29(5): 605–615.

DfE (2011) *Training our next generation of outstanding teachers*, London: HMSO.

Donche, V. and Van Petegem, P. (2008) The validity and reliability of the short inventory of learning patterns, in E. Cools et al. (eds), *Style and cultural differences: How can organisations, regions and countries take advantage of style differences* (pp. 49–59), Gent: Vlerick Leuven Gent Management School.

Elik, N., Wiener, J. and Corkum, P. (2010) Pre-service teachers' open-minded thinking dispositions, readiness to learn, and attitudes about learning and behavioural difficulties in students, *European Journal of Teacher Education*, 33(2): 127–146.

Ellis, R. A., Goodyear, P., Prosser, M. and O'Hara, A. (2006) How and what university students learn through online and face-to-face discussion: Conceptions, intentions and approaches, *Journal of Computer Assisted Learning*, 22: 244–256.

Entwistle, N. J. (1981) *Styles of learning and teaching*, Chichester, UK: John Wiley and Sons.

Entwistle, N. J. (2009) *Teaching for understanding at university: Deep approaches and distinctive ways of thinking*, Basingstoke: Palgrave Macmillan.

Entwistle, N. and Entwistle, D. (2003) Preparing for examinations: The interplay of memorizing and understanding, and the development of knowledge objects, *Higher Education Research and Development*, 22(1): 19–41.

Entwistle, N., and McCune, V. (2004) The conceptual bases of study strategy inventories, *Educational Psychology Review*, 16(4): 325–345.

Entwistle, N. J., McCune, V. and Walker, P. (2001) Conceptions, styles and approaches within higher education: Analytic abstractions and everyday experience, in R. J. Sternberg and L. F. Zhang (eds), *Perspectives on thinking, learning, and cognitive styles* (pp. 103–136), Mahwah, NJ: Lawrence Erlbaum Associates.

Entwistle, N., Meyer, J. H. F. and Tait, H. (1991) Student failure: Disintegrated patterns of study strategies and perceptions of the learning environment, *Higher Education*, 21: 249–261.

Entwistle, N. J. and Peterson, E. R. (2004) Conceptions of learning and knowledge in higher education: Relationships with study behaviour and influences of learning environments, *International Journal of Educational Research*, 41: 407–428.

Entwistle, N. J. and Ramsden, P. (1983) *Understanding student learning*, London: Croom Helm.

Evans, C. and Kozhevnikov, M. (2011) Styles of practice: How learning is affected by students' and teachers' perceptions and beliefs, conceptions and approaches to learning, *Research Papers in Education*, 26(2): 133–148.

Evans, C. and Waring, M. (2011) Application of styles in educational instruction and assessment, in L. F. Zhang, R. J. Sternberg and S. Rayner (eds) *The handbook of intellectual styles* (pp. 297–330), New York: Springer.

Ferla, J., Valcke, M. and Schuyten, G. (2009) Student models of learning and their impact on study strategies, *Studies in Higher Education*, 34(2): 185–202.

Gijbels, D., Coertjens, L., Vanthournout, G., Struyf, E. and Van Petegem, P. (2009) Changing students' approaches to learning: A two-year study within a university teacher training course, *Educational Studies*, 35(5): 503–513.

Gijbels, D., Segers, M. and Struyf, E. (2008) Constructivist learning environments and the (im)possibility to change students' perceptions of assessment demands and approaches to learning, *Instructional Science*, 36: 431–443.

Greasley, K. and Ashworth, P. (2007) The phenomenology of 'approach to studying': The university student's studies within the lifeworld, *British Educational Research Journal*, 33(6): 819–843.

Grossman, P., Hammerness, K. and McDonald, M. (2009) Redefining teaching, re-imagining teacher education, *Teachers and Teaching: Theory and Practice*, 15(2): 273–289.

Haggar, H. and McIntyre, D. (2006) *Learning and teaching from teachers: Realising the potential of school-based teacher education*, Maidenhead, UK: Open University Press.

Haggis, T. (2003) Constructing images of ourselves? A critical investigation into 'approaches to learning' research in higher education, *British Educational Research Journal*, 29(1): 89–104.

Hattie, J. and Timperley, H. (2007) The power of feedback, *Review of Educational Research*, 77: 81–112.

Heikkilä, A. and Lonka, K. (2006) Studying in higher education: Students' approaches to learning, self-regulation, and cognitive strategies, *Studies in Higher Education*, *31*(1): 99–117.

Jakhelln, R. (2010) Early career teachers' emotional experiences and development: a Norwegian case study, *Professional Development in Education*, *37*(2): 275–290.

Joughin, G. (2009) Assessment, learning and judgement in higher education: A critical review, in G. Joughin (ed.), *Assessment, learning and judgement in higher education* (pp. 13–29), New York: Springer.

Jungert, T. and Rosander, M. (2009) Relationship between students' strategies for influencing their study environment and their strategic approach to studying, *Studies in Higher Education*, *34*(2): 139–152.

Karagiannopoulou, E. and Christodoulides, P. (2005) The impact of Greek university students' perceptions of their learning environment on approaches to studying and academic outcomes, *International Journal of Educational Research*, *43*(6): 329–350.

Lonka, K. (1997) *Explorations of constructive processes in student learning*, Helsinki: Yliopistopaino.

Lonka, K. and Lindblom-Ylänne, S. (1996) Epistemologies, conceptions of learning, and study practices in medicine and psychology, *Higher Education*, *31*: 5–24.

Lonka, K., Olkinuora, E. and Mäkinen, J. (2004) Aspects and prospects of measuring studying and learning in higher education, *Educational Psychology Review*, *16*(4): 301–323.

Lonka, K., Vesikansa, S., and Lindblom-Ylänne, S. (2000) Finnish university students' study motivation. Paper presented at WATM Symposium, Leuven, Belgium, 12–15 May 2000.

Lowyck, J., Elen, J. and Clarebout, G. (2004) Instructional conceptions: Analysis from an instructional design perspective, *International Journal of Educational Research*, *41*: 429–444.

Loyens, S. M. M., Rikers, R. M. J. P. and Schmidt, H. G. (2008) Relationships between students' conceptions of constructivist learning and their regulation and processing strategies, *Instructional Science*, *36*: 445–462.

Mäkinen, J., Olkinuora, E. and Lonka, K. (2002) Orientations to studying in Finnish higher education: Comparison of study orientations in university and vocational higher education, in E. Pantzar (ed.), *Perspectives on the age of the information society*, Tampere, Finland: Tampere University Press.

Mäkinen, J., Olkinuora, E. and Lonka, K. (2004) Students at risk: Students' general study orientations and abandoning/prolonging the course of studies, *Higher Education*, *48*: 173–188.

Marshall, D. and Case, J. (2005) 'Approaches to learning' research in higher education: A response to Haggis, *British Educational Research Journal*, *31*(2): 257–267.

Marton, F. (1975) On non-verbatim learning: I. Level of processing and level of outcome, *Scandinavian Journal of Psychology*, *16*: 273–279.

Marton, F. (1986) Some reflections on the improvement of learning, in J. A Bowden (ed.), *Student learning: The Marysville symposium* (pp. 21–60), Melbourne: Centre for the Study of Higher Education, University of Melbourne.

Marton, F., Dall'Alba, G. and Beaty, E (1993) Conceptions of learning, *International Journal of Educational Research*, *19*: 277–300.

Marton, F., Dall'Alba, G. and Tse, L. K. (1996) Memorizing and understanding: The keys to the paradox? in D. A. Watkins and J. B. Biggs (eds), *The Chinese learner: Cultural, psychological and contextual influences* (pp. 69–83), Hong Kong: Comparative Education Research, Centre and Australian Council for Educational Research.

Marton, F. and Säljö, R. (1976) On qualitative differences in learning, outcome and process, *British Journal of Educational Psychology*, *46*: 4–11.

Marton, F. and Säljö, R. (1984) Approaches to learning, in F. Marton, D. Hounsell and N. Entwistle (eds), *The experience of learning* (pp. 36–55), Edinburgh, UK: Scottish Academic Press.

Mattick, K., Dennis, I. and Bligh, J. (2004) Approaches to learning and studying in medical students: Validation of a revised inventory and its relation to student characteristics and performance, *Undergraduate Medical Education, 38*: 535–543.

McCune, V. and Entwistle, N. (2011) Cultivating the disposition to understand in 21st century university education, *Learning and Individual Differences, 21*(3): 303-310.

Meyer, J. H. F. (2000) The modelling of 'dissonant' study orchestration in higher education, *European Journal of Psychology of Education, 15*: 5–18.

Meyer, J. H. F. and Boulton-Lewis, G. M. (2003) Editorial. Variation in dissonance in learning patterns: Towards an emerging theory?, *Studies in Higher Education, 28*: 3–4.

Meyer, J. H. F., Parsons, P. and Dunne, T. T. (1990) Individual study orchestrations and their association with learning outcome, *Higher Education, 20*: 67–89.

Micari, M. and Light, G. (2009) Reliance to independence: Approaches to learning in peer-led undergraduate science, technology, engineering, and mathematics workshops, *International Journal of Science Education, 31*(13): 1713–1741.

Nijhuis, J., Segers, M. and Gijselaers, W. (2006) Redesigning a learning and assessment environment: The influence of students' perceptions of the assessment demands and their learning strategies, *Studies in Educational Evaluation, 32*: 223–242.

Oosterheert, I. E. and Vermunt, J. D. (2001) Individual differences in learning to teach: Relating cognition, regulation and affect, *Learning and Instruction, 11*(2): 133–156.

Opfer, V. D., Pedder, D. G. and Lavicza, Z. (2010) The role of teachers' orientation to learning in professional development and change: A national study of teachers in England, *Teaching and Teacher Education, 21*(2): 1–11.

Pask, G. (1988) Learning strategies, teaching strategies and conceptual or learning style, in R. R. Schmeck (ed.), *Learning strategies and learning styles* (pp. 83–100), New York: Plenum Press.

Pedrosa-de-Jesus, M. H. and da Silva Lopes, B. (2011) The relationship between teaching and learning conceptions, preferred teaching approaches and questioning practices, *Research Papers in Education, 26*(2): 223–244.

Peterson, E., Brown, G. T. L. and Irving, I. S (2010) Secondary students' conceptions of learning and their relationship to achievement, *Learning and Individual Differences, 20*: 167–176.

Pintrich, P. R., Smith, D. A. F., Garcia, T. and McKeachie, W. J. (1993) Reliability and predictive validity of the Motivated Strategies for Learning Questionnaire (MSLQ), *Educational and Psychological Measurement, 53*: 801–813.

Ramsden, P. (1983) *The Lancaster approaches to studying and course perceptions questionnaire: Lecturer's handbook*, Oxford: Educational Methods Unit.

Ramsden, P. (1992) *Learning to teach in higher education*, London: RoutledgeFalmer

Ramsden, P. (2003) *Learning to teach in higher education* (2nd ed.), London: RoutledgeFalmer.

Richards, L. (2009) *Handling qualitative data*, London: Sage.

Richardson, J. T. E. (2000) *Researching student learning: Approaches to studying in campus-based and distance education*, Buckingham: SRHE and Open University Press.

Rosenfeld, M. and Rosenfeld, S. (2008) Understanding teachers with extreme individual learning differences (ILDS): Developing more effective teachers, *Teaching Education, 19*(1): 21–41.

Sadler-Smith, E. and Shefy, M. (2004) The intuitive executive: Understanding and applying 'gut feel' in decision-making, *Academy of Management Executive, 18*(4): 76–91.

Schmeck, R., Geisler-Brenstein, E. and Cercy, S. (1991) Self-concept and learning: The revised inventory of learning processes, *Educational Psychology*, *11*: 343–362.

Scott, D., Evans, C., Hughes, G., Burke, P .J., Watson, D., Walter, C. and Huttly, S. (2011) *Facilitating transitions to Masters-level learning – Improving formative assessment and feedback processes*, *Final Extended Report*, London, UK: Institute of Education. Retrieved from http://transitions.wlecentre.ac.uk/.

Silén, C. and Uhlin, L. (2008) Self-directed learning: A learning issue for students and faculty, *Teaching in Higher Education*, *13*(4): 461–475.

Smith, J. (Ed.) (2003) *Qualitative psychology: A practical guide to research methods*, London: Sage.

Struyven, K., Dochy, F., Janssens, S. and Gielen, S. (2006) On the dynamics of students' approaches to learning: The effects of the teaching/learning environment, *Learning and Instruction*, *16*(4): 279–294.

Tait, H. and Entwistle, N. J. (1996) Identifying students at risk through ineffective study strategies, *Higher Education*, *31*: 97–116.

Tait, H., Entwistle, N. J. and McCune, V. (1998) ASSIST: A reconceptualisation of the Approaches to Studying Inventory, in C. Rust (ed.), *Improving student learning: Improving students as learners*, Oxford: Oxford Centre for Staff and Learning Development.

Thompson, G., Pilgrim, A. and Oliver, K. (2005) Self-assessment and reflective learning for first year university geography students: A simple guide or simply misguided?, *Journal of Geography in Higher Education*, *2*(3): 403–420.

Trigwell, K. and Prosser, M. (1991) Relating approaches to study and quality of learning outcomes at the course level, *British Journal of Educational Psychology*, *61*: 265–275.

Ure, C. (2009) Reforming teacher education: A developmental model for program design and pedagogy. Unpublished report, London: Institute of Education.

Van Rossum, E. J. and Schenk, S. M. (1984) The relationship between learning conception, study strategy and learning outcome, *British Journal of Educational Psychology*, *54*(1): 73–83.

Vanthournout, G., Donche, V., Gijbels, D. and Van Petegem, P. (2011) Further understanding learning in higher education, in S. Rayner and E. Cools (eds), *Style differences in cognition, management and learning* (pp. 78–98), New York: Routledge.

Vermunt, J. D. (1994) Design principles of process-oriented instruction, in F. P. C. M. de Jong and B. H. A. M. C. Van Hout Wolters (eds), *Process-oriented instruction and learning from text* (pp. 15–26), Amsterdam: VU University Press.

Vermunt, J. D. (1998) The regulation of constructive learning processes, *British Journal of Educational Psychology*, *68*: 149–171.

Vermunt, J. D., Bakkenes, I., Wubbels, T. and Brekelmans, M. (2008) *Personal and contextual factors and secondary school teachers' adaptation of innovation*. Paper presented at the 11th International Conference on Motivation, Turku, Finland, 21–23 August.

Vermunt, J. D. and Endedijk, M. (2011) Patterns in teacher learning in different phases of the professional career, *Learning and Individual Differences Journal*, *21*(3): 294–302.

Vermunt, J. D., and van Rijswijk, F. A. (1988) Analysis and development of students' skill in self-regulated learning, *Higher Education*, *17*: 647–682.

Vermunt, J. D., and Vermetten, Y. J. (2004) Patterns in student learning: Relationships between learning strategies, conceptions of learning, and learning orientations. *Educational Psychology Review*, *16*: 359–384.

Volet, S. E. and Chalmers, D. (1992) Investigation of qualitative differences in university students' learning goals, based on an unfolding model of stage development, *British Journal of Educational Psychology*, *62*: 17–34.

Walker, S., Brownlee, J., Lennox, S., Exley, B., Howells, K. and Cocker, F. (2009) Understanding first year university students: Personal epistemology and learning, *Teaching Education*, *20*(3): 243–256.

Waring, M. (2012) Grounded theory, in J. Arthur, M. Waring, R. Coe. and L. Hedges (eds), *Research methods and methodologies in education* (pp. 297–307), London: Sage.

Watters, D. J. and Watters, J. J. (2007) Approaches to learning by students in the biological sciences: Implications for teaching, *International Journal of Science Education*, *29*(1), 19–43.

Wenger, E. (2000) Communities of practice and social learning systems, *Organization*, 7: 225–246.

Wenger, E., McDermott, R. and Synder, W. M. (2002) *Cultivating communities of practice*, Boston, MA: Harvard Business School Press.

Ylijoki, O. H. (2000) Disciplinary cultures and the moral order of studying: A case study of four Finnish university departments, *Higher Education*, *39*: 339–362.

Chapter 11

Understanding differences in student learning and academic achievement in first year higher education

An integrated research perspective

Vincent Donche, Liesje Coertjens, Tine van Daal, Sven De Maeyer and Peter Van Petegem

Introduction

Higher education in Flanders (Dutch speaking part of Belgium) is characterised by an open access system, and as many other countries, confronted with a growing heterogeneous student population in the first year which is paralleled by an increasing dropout rate of students in the first year. Empirical studies investigating why some students are more successful in their studies in the first year of higher education and other students not are needed to better understand the actual possibilities and boundaries of entry in higher education for students from different backgrounds. Studies based upon the theories of Spady (1970) and Tinto (1993) have put emphasis on the fact that many direct determinants of study success or persistence are still student characteristics, more specifically pre-entry factors such as gender, study delay, prior education and socio-economic and cultural status or capital (Reynolds and Walberg 1992; Tinto 1993). However, former research shows that other factors at the student level also play a significant role and have a direct impact on academic performance such as autonomous motivation (Deci and Ryan 2000), differences in student learning (Vermunt 2005) and academic self-confidence (Tinto 1993). In addition, factors such as academic motivation, perceptions of ability (e.g. Deci, Vallerand, Pelletier and Ryan 1991), self-efficacy (e.g. Bandura 1977) and learning strategies (e.g. Donche, Coertjens and Van Petegem 2010) are assumed not to be stable or trait-like characteristics of students and are relatively malleable or dynamic in nature.

It is, however, (too) often the case that in studies in which the impact of individual characteristics of students on academic achievement is assessed, attention is only given to those variables that can be influenced by interventions. Although we fully agree with the importance of assessing the impact of dynamic factors on academic achievement, it remains important to also take the direct effects of pre-entry factors into account and jointly investigate the interrelationships between pre-entry factors and dynamic factors on academic achievement. If not assessed in one integrated model (e.g. if the impact of for instance the socio-economic and cultural context in which students have grown up has not been taken into account), the size of the effects of dynamic factors such as, for instance, self-regulation and deep learning on academic achievement may be biased (e.g. Watkins 2001). The present study assesses the predictive power of both pre-entry factors and dynamic factors on academic achievement in one structural model. Particular attention is given to the following dynamic factors: academic motivation, academic self-confidence and learning strategies. A brief overview of the theory and research evidence of the selected constructs integrated in our explanatory model is given below.

Pre-entry factors

Former research has shown that pre-entry factors such as gender, age, prior education, and the socio-economic and cultural background of students are associated with academic achievement (e.g. Pascarella and Terenzini 1991; Richardson, Abraham and Bond 2012; Tinto 1993). Students' age has been found to be related to academic achievement, with older students shown to be less successful than younger students (e.g. Jansen 2004). In addition to age, students' study delay can have an impact on their success in higher education.

In previous longitudinal research, it was found that students who repeated one or more grades in secondary education were less successful in higher education (Pustjens, Van de Gaer, Van Damme and Onghena 2004). Students with a lower socio-economic status and disadvantaged background were repeatedly found likely to underachieve in the first year of higher education (Tinto 1993). Also cultural background (DiMaggio 1982) as well as linguistic ability (Sullivan 2001) has been investigated and is known to have a differential impact on educational outcomes.

In previous studies gender effects are also reported but studies reveal contradictory findings. In some studies, female students were repeatedly found to fail more in the first year of higher education (Tinto 1993). Other studies show that women achieve higher results in higher education (e.g. Richardson and Woodley 2003). Also students' prior education and, more specifically, prior achievement was found to have differential effects regarding dropout or persistence in higher education (e.g. Jansen and Bruinsma 2005; Reynolds and Walberg 1992; Tinto 1993).

In previous research pre-entry factors such as gender, age and prior education have not only been related to academic achievement but also to students' motivational orientations and learning strategies. Female students are likely to have more reproduction oriented learning characteristics (Severiens and Ten Dam 1997) and students who followed secondary education tracks preparing for higher education are less likely to be reproduction oriented or unregulated learners in higher education (Van Petegem and Donche 2006). From these studies we assume that the effects of pre-entry factors on academic achievement will be mediated by the effects of these dynamic factors.

Academic motivation

Motivation research based upon self-determination theory has shown that the quality and quantity of motivation has a differential impact on academic achievement (Deci and Ryan 2000; Vallerand et al. 1992). The quantity of motivation has been investigated by means of the concept of 'amotivation' (Deci and Ryan 2000), which was found to be a relevant predictor for lack of regulation (Ryan and Deci, 2000) and dropout (Vallerand et al. 1992). The quality of motivation, although basically distinguished as intrinsic or extrinsic, can be further refined according to self-determination theory by making a distinction between autonomous and controlled motivation. Studies investigating the effects of controlled and autonomous motivation on learning strategies and academic achievement have shown that controlled motivation goes with surface processing (Grolnick and Ryan 1987) and weak coping strategies in the case of failing (Ryan and Connell 1989). Autonomous motivation has been found directly and positively related to the use of more information processing, high concentration while studying and better time management, and indirectly to higher academic achievement (Vansteenkiste, Zhou, Lens and Soenens 2005). Based upon these studies we assume that the quality and quantity of motivation will be directly related to how students learn and will be associated with academic achievement.

Academic self-confidence

Not only differences in cognitive abilities or academic skills are valuable explanatory factors in explaining differences in academic achievement. This is also the case for students' positive academic self-confidence, realistic estimation of own competencies (e.g. Tinto 1993) and the related construct of self-efficacy (Bandura 1977; Richardson et al. 2012). A proxy of students' self-efficacy and academic self-confidence is their expectations about grade or study outcome. Research has shown that positive expectations facilitate academic performance, and increase motivation and persistence (Armor and Taylor 1998). Furthermore, success expectations have also been found to be negatively related to undirected learning and positively related to both self-regulated and deep learning and academic achievement (Heikkilä and Lonka 2006). Outcome expectations and related academic achievement can also be explained by students' past school success and prior achievement (Svanum and Bigatti 2006) as well as differences in adult identity (Lange and Byrd 2002). From these studies, we assume that after control for academic motivation, students' academic self-confidence will have a direct effect on how they engage in learning and on academic achievement.

Learning strategies

Empirical research into students' learning strategies has shown that the quality of student learning and learning strategies is related to academic achievement

(Dinsmore and Alexander 2012; Vermunt and Vermetten 2004). Learning strategies can be distinguished on the level of processing strategies and on the level of regulation strategies. Usually, a further distinction is made between deep and surface processing strategies. In theory it is often assumed that deep and surface processing strategies lead respectively to higher or lower achievement (Marton and Säljö 1976). Empirical research shows often only positive and weak to moderate correlations between deep processing and academic achievement measured by GPA or mean exam results (Richardson et al. 2012; Vermunt 2005; Watkins and Hattie 1981). In many studies, the expected negative relationship between surface processing and academic achievement does not appear or appears only very weakly (e.g. Vermunt 2005).

Research on regulation strategies found both self-regulation and external regulation to be related to higher achievement (Vermunt 2005). In particular the unregulated learning strategy or non-academic orientation has been repeatedly found related to lower academic achievement (Busato, Prins, Elshout and Hamaker 1998; Donche and Van Petegem 2011; Entwistle and Ramsden 1983; Vermunt 2005). A learning strategy often labelled as meaning oriented learning, combining self-regulation and deep information processing, has been found to be related to positive study success (Lindblom-Ylänne and Lonka 1999; Watkins 2001). In line with these studies we assume that both meaning oriented learning and unregulated learning will predict academic achievement.

This study

This study aims to explore and identify the relationships among the pre-entry factors, aspects of academic motivation, academic self-confidence and learning strategies in one integrated model and to assess the variance that can be explained in academic achievement (Figure 11.1).

Three research questions (RQ) are central in this study: RQ1: To what extent are students' academic self-confidence, academic motivation and learning strategies associated with pre-entry factors? RQ2: To what degree do students' academic self-confidence, academic motivation and learning strategies predict academic achievement? and RQ3: Is academic achievement influenced by the interplay between pre-entry factors, academic self-confidence, academic motivation and learning strategies?

Based upon previous research findings and theoretical expectations sketched above, we expect (hypothesis 1) that the included pre-entry factors in this study: gender (h1a), socio-economic status (h1b), cultural background (h1c), study delay (h1d) and prior education (h1e) will be associated with academic self-confidence, academic motivation and learning strategies. We also expect to find that both the quality and quantity of academic motivation (hypothesis 2a–b) and academic self-confidence (hypothesis 3) will be associated with students' learning strategies. After control for pre-entry factors, we expect (hypothesis 4) that dynamic factors such as autonomous motivation (h4a), academic self-confidence (h4b),

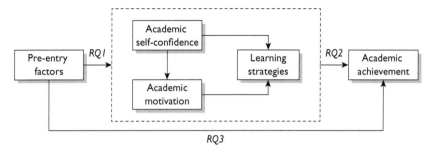

Figure 11.1 Path model for the prediction of academic achievement

self-regulated learning (h4c) and deep learning (h4d) positively predict academic achievement. In addition to these effects, we assume that controlled motivation (h4e), lack of motivation (h4f), unregulated learning (h5g) and surface learning (h5h) negatively predict academic achievement. In line with former research findings and theoretical expectations, we assume (hypothesis 5) that, after control for the dynamic variables, students' socio-economic status (h5a), cultural background (h5b), study delay (h5c) and the kind of prior education (h5d) students have followed will have a direct effect on academic achievement.

Methodology

Sample and procedure

In this study the data of two consecutive cohorts of first year full-time students of a university college in Flanders were used (N = 1594). Six hundred and forty-one students were male (40.2 per cent) and 953 students were female (59.8 per cent). The overall response rate was 70 per cent. Eight study disciplines were involved: communication sciences, social work, journalism, electromechanics, hotel management, office management, business management, and teacher education. In both cohorts, all students were invited to participate voluntarily. They completed an online survey during the first semester. The respondents were not rewarded for their participation.

Measurements

Pre-entry characteristics

Information about students' *gender, study delay* and *prior education* were obtained from enrolment data gathered by the student administration office. The indicator of prior education is the type of secondary education that students have followed in the fifth and sixth year of secondary education. In Flanders, higher education is characterised by an open access system and students can enrol from different secondary education tracks. Secondary education is provided for young people aged 12 to 18 in four branches: ASO (general secondary education), TSO (technical secondary education), KSO (artistic secondary education) and BSO (vocational secondary education), each divided into three two-year periods. Pupils come into contact with as many subjects as possible during the first two years of their secondary education. From the third and fourth year of secondary education on, pupils can opt for a certain branch of study within ASO, TSO, KSO or BSO. In the fifth and sixth years of secondary education pupils are offered either occupational training or higher education training. Students in our sample were spread across three secondary education categories: ASO (general), TSO (technical) and BSO (vocational). For use in further analyses the variables gender and prior education were coded: gender (0 = male, 1 = female) and prior education (0 = technical/vocational and 1 = general).

Students' *socio-economic status* (SES) was assessed by means of a student background questionnaire addressing the parents' educational level, level of employment, unemployment status and the amount of years of joblessness of the father. Based upon PRINCALS analyses, which is a categorical principal component analysis (see Gifi 1990), a SES continuum could be mapped. The fit of the model (.41) was adequate and revealed a one-dimensional structure. The strongest predictor for SES was the level of education of the mother (.71). Based upon the parameter estimates, each student was assigned a SES score reflecting the students' position on the continuum. For instance, students with a high SES are students whose parents both have a university degree and are active professionals and whose father has never been jobless. Students with a low SES are students whose parents have no secondary education degree and are jobless and whose father has been jobless for more than two years.

Students' *linguistic ethnic background* (LEB) was assessed by means of indicating parents' birth place and language spoken at home. A PRINCALS analysis showed an adequate fit of the LEB model (.88) and revealed a one-dimensional structure. The strongest predictors for LEB were the nationality of the father (.95) and mother (.96). Based upon the specific parameter estimates, students were positioned by means of their individual score on the LEB continuum. For instance, students with a high LEB were students whose parents were both born in Belgium and whose only language spoken at home (Dutch) is the language of instruction in the higher education institution. Students with a low LEB were students whose parents were both foreign-born, in particular born in Turkey, and who only speak Turkish at home.

Academic motivation

To assess the quality and quantity of students' motivation for studying in higher education, we used a self-report questionnaire: the 'Academic Motivation

Scale' (AMS; Vallerand et al. 1992). Students had to respond to the question stem 'Why are you following higher education?' The AMS contains seven subscales, reflecting one subscale of amotivation 'I once had good reasons for going to college, however, now I wonder whether I should' (four items, α = .85), three subscales of extrinsic motivation (external regulation, introjected and identified regulation), and three subscales of intrinsic motivation (intrinsic motivation to know, to accomplish things and to experience stimulation). In line with self-determination theory, we considered the three subscales of intrinsic motivation to be one scale measuring intrinsic motivation as a whole. All 12 items are scored, ranging from 1 (does not correspond at all) to 7 (corresponds exactly). In line with self-determination theory and the approach carried out by Vansteenkiste and others (2005), we combined the scales to form an autonomous motivation composite by averaging the scores for the general scale of intrinsic motivation and identified regulation (r (1594) = .55, p < .01; α = .91) and a controlled motivation composite by averaging the scores for external regulation and introjected regulation (r (1594) = .54, p < .01, α = .87). An autonomous motivation sample item is 'Because I experience pleasure and satisfaction while learning new things'. A controlled motivation sample item is 'to show myself that I am an intelligent person'.

Academic self-confidence

An indicator of academic self-confidence used in this study was the answer of students to the specific question 'How do you think about your study success?' Three answering categories were given: (1) I will pass after the first exam period, (2) I will pass after two exam periods or (3) I will not pass. As the answer to this question can be hierarchically ordered, a continuous variable was created ranging from −1 (low academic self-confidence) to +1 (high academic self-confidence).

Regulation and processing strategies

Students' regulation and processing strategies were assessed with six scales from the self-report questionnaire 'Inventory of Learning Styles' (ILS; Vermunt 1998). Three scales representing three different regulation strategies, that is, self-regulation (e.g. 'To test my learning progress, I try to answer questions about the subject matter which I make up myself'; 11 items; α = .77), external regulation (e.g. 'I study according to the instructions given in the course materials'; 11 items; α = .65) and lack of regulation (e.g. 'I notice that it is difficult for me to determine whether I have mastered the subject matter sufficiently'; 6 items; α = .71). Three scales representing three different processing strategies, that is, deep processing and, in particular, 'relating and structuring' (e.g. 'I try to combine the subjects that are dealt with separately in a course into one whole'; 5 items; α = .82), surface processing and, in particular, 'memorising' (e.g. 'I memorise lists of characteristics of a certain phenomenon'; 11 items; $\alpha = .72$) and concrete processing (e.g. 'I pay particular attention to those parts of the course that have practical utility'; 5 items; $\alpha = .67$). All items are scored, ranging from 1 (I never or hardly ever do this) to 5 (I (almost) always do this).

Academic achievement

Each student participated in one or two exam periods in the first year and obtained a grade point average (GPA), which is the students' average exam mark across all courses of their specific study discipline programme. If students participated in two exam periods only the second GPA was used.

Results

In a first step, the intercorrelations among the constructs under study were investigated by means of the calculation of Pearson Product Moment Correlations (Table 11.1). The table shows moderate to strong significant correlations between GPA on the one hand and LEB ($r = .19$), general secondary education ($r = .28$), academic self-confidence ($r = .39$) and unregulated learning ($r = -.25$) on the other hand. Weak to moderate significant correlations are found between GPA and SES ($r = .12$), study delay ($r = -.14$), controlled motivation ($r = -.15$), amotivation ($r = -.15$), external regulation ($r = .10$) and deep processing ($r = .14$). The results indicate in general that students' GPA is correlated to some extent with most of the included pre-entry and dynamic factors.

In a second step, structural equation modelling was applied to further investigate the relationships among these factors and academic achievement using Amos 6.0. Based on previous research findings and the theoretical assumptions we discussed about the interplay between all included variables predicting academic achievement and on the findings in the correlation matrix (Table 11.1), an initial model, containing all assumed relations, was tested by using structural equation modelling. In line with the exploratory goals of this study and in order to obtain a more refined model, non-significant paths within the initial model were omitted. The $\chi^2/df = 4.63$ in this adjusted model was fairly high and reached significance. Due to the large sample used in this study, this is not uncommon and therefore it is suggested to also take other fit indices into account to assess the quality of the model (Bollen 1989). The goodness of fit (GFI), adjusted goodness of fit (AGFI) and comparative fit (CFI) are alternative indices to identify a well fitting model when values are above .95. The Root Mean Square Error of Approximation (RMSEA) with values less than 0.05 is another index of a good model fit (Byrne 2010). The additional fit indices of our path model were: GFI = .98, AGFI = .95, CFI = .95 and RMSEA = .04. Based upon these indices we conclude that the resulting path model has a good

Table 11.1 Intercorrelations between constructs

	Gen	Ses	Leb	Sdl	Gse	Scf	Aut	Con	Amo	Self	Ext	Unr	Dp	Sp	Cp	GPA
Gen	—	.00	.04	*-.14*	*.12*	*-.15*	**.20**	-.01	**-.16**	.06	-.06	.04	.01	**.25**	-.04	.01
Ses		—	**.60**	*-.14*	*.11*	.04	.05	-.05	*-.10*	.02	-.03	-.03	.04	-.01	.06	*.12*
Leb			—	**-.23**	.05	.01	-.01	*-.14*	*-.09*	-.03	-.05	-.04	.01	-.03	.03	*.19*
Sdl				—	-.04	.01	.06	.01	.04	.07	-.05	.04	.06	-.03	.07	*-.14*
Gse					—	.05	.02	*-.09*	-.04	.01	-.08	*-.18*	*.09*	.06	-.04	**.28**
Scf						—	*.11*	.07	*-.18*	*.10*	*.13*	**-.29**	*.17*	-.06	.07	**.39**
Aut							—	**.45**	**-.44**	**.39**	*.19*	*-.09*	**.39**	**.21**	**.36**	.08
Con								—	*-.13*	-.09	-.10	**.27**	*-.18*	-.10	*-.13*	*-.15*
Amo									—	*-.09*	-.10	**.27**	*-.18*	-.10	*-.13*	*-.15*
Self										—	*.19*	-.03	**.65**	*.13*	**.53**	.04
Ext											—	*.10*	*.19*	**.30**	*.17*	*.10*
Unr												—	*-.16*	*.16*	.05	**-.25**
Dp													—	.08	**.55**	*.14*
Sp														—	.04	-.01
Cp															—	.04
GPA																—

Notes: *italics*: p < .05 (2-tailed), **bold italics**: p < .01 (2-tailed), Gen = gender, Ses = socio-economic background, Leb = linguistic ethnic background, Sdl = study delay, Gse = general secondary education, Scf = academic self-confidence, Aut = autonomous motivation, Con = controlled motivation, Amo = amotivation, Self = self-regulation, Ext = external regulation, Unr = unregulated/lack of regulation, Dp = deep processing, Sp = surface processing, Cp = concrete processing, GPA = grade point average.

fit. In what follows we describe the most important results of the structural equation modelling analyses with respect to the relationship between pre-entry characteristics, the dynamic variables under study and academic achievement.

Pre-entry factors, academic motivation, academic self-confidence and learning strategies

To what extent are the dynamic factors under study determined by pre-entry characteristics (RQ1)? Gender effects in the path model show that female students ($\beta = -.161$, p < .001) were less optimistic about their study success in higher education compared to male students. Although female students are likely to have a lower academic self-confidence, directional links in the model show that female students are less amotivated ($\beta = -.179$, p < .001) in their study than male students and are more autonomously motivated learners ($\beta = .212$, p < .001). On the level of learning strategies we found that female students engage more in surface processing than male students ($\beta = .246$, p < .001).

Prior education is an important explaining factor regarding students' expectations of study success and motivation. This indicates that students from more academically preparing study tracks in secondary education are more optimistic about their study success in higher education ($\beta = .075$, p < .001) and are less controlled in their study motivation ($\beta = -.088$, p < .001). These students are also less externally regulated ($\beta = -.063$, p < .001) and unregulated ($\beta = -.146$, p < .001) in their learning and engage more in deep processing activities ($\beta = .073$, p < .001). A minor effect was observed regarding the amount of years of study delay students experienced, indicating that older students are more amotivated in their studies in higher education ($\beta = .053$, p < .001). The results confirmed the hypothesised relationship between gender (h1a) and prior education (h1e) on students' academic self-confidence, academic motivation and learning strategies. This was also partially the case for the indicator of study delay (h1d). Students' SES and cultural background were not found to be directly associated with these dynamic variables.

Academic motivation, academic self-confidence, learning strategies and academic achievement

To what extent are the dynamic factors related to academic achievement after control for pre-entry characteristics (RQ2)? In general, the path model presented in Figure 11.2 confirms the assumed relationship between the quality and quantity of academic motivation and learning strategies (hypothesis 2a–b). Furthermore, the results indicate that students who are more autonomously motivated tend to be more self-regulated ($\beta = .437$, p < .001) and engage more in different processing activities, especially in deep and concrete processing (respectively, $\beta = .139$, p < .001 and $\beta = .218$, p < .001). Students who are more controlled in their motivation are more externally regulated ($\beta = .267$,

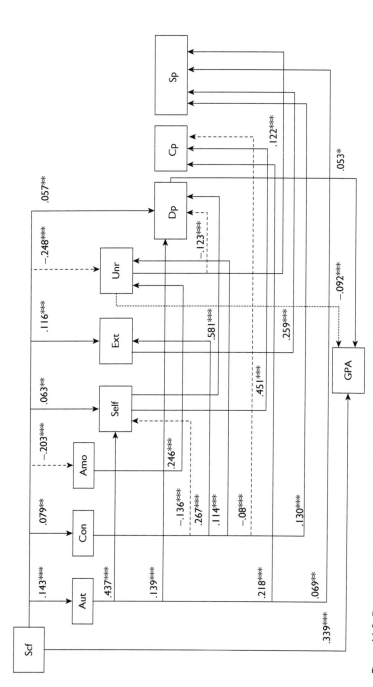

Figure 11.2 Directional links between academic self-confidence, academic motivation, learning strategies and academic achievement

Notes: Scf = academic self-confidence, Aut = autonomous motivation, Amo = amotivation, Con = controlled motivation, Self = self-regulation, Ext = external regulation, Unr = unregulated/lack of regulation, Dp = deep processing, Sp = surface processing, Cp = concrete processing, GPA = grade point average

p < .001) and engage more in surface processing activities (β = .130, p < .001). Not only the quality but also the quantity of motivation has an impact on students' learning strategies, indicating that amotivated students are more unregulated in their learning (β = .246, p < .001). Why students engage in studying in higher education goes along with their own expectations of study success. In general, it was found that students with high study expectations are less amotivated (β = −.203, p < .001) and more autonomously motivated learners (β = .143, p < .001). Furthermore, the study confirms the third hypothesis and clarifies that having more academic self-confidence is related with less unregulated learning (β = −.248, p < .001).

The study shows that as expected a proportion of the variance of GPA can be predicted by solely dynamic factors (17 per cent). Confirmation of three out of six hypotheses regarding the relationship between dynamic factors and academic achievement was found in this study (h4b, h4d and h4g). No associations were found regarding students' academic motivation, regulation strategies (self or external) and surface processing. Academic self-confidence and unregulated learning were far better predictors for academic achievement than deep learning which showed a weak relationship with academic achievement. In contrast with the variance of academic achievement (17 per cent), the variance of deep processing could be fairly well explained within this model (47 per cent). The study reveals, however, that after control for pre-entry factors a considerable amount of variance in academic achievement can be explained by variables which are relatively malleable or dynamic.

Pre-entry factors, academic motivation, academic self-confidence, learning strategies and academic achievement

To what extent do pre-entry factors have a direct effect on academic achievement if the additional effects of the dynamic factors are controlled for (RQ3)? Regardless of students' quality and quantity of motivation, amount of academic self-confidence and use of specific learning strategies, pre-entry characteristics such as study delay (β = 0.093, p < .01), prior education (β = .226, p < .001) and LEB (β = .146, p < .001) have a direct effect on academic achievement which is in line with some of our expectations (h5b–d). Generation students (i.e. students in a non-delayed study trajectory) who followed a general secondary education track and who have no foreign background obtain higher exam scores compared to students who experienced more study delay, followed a vocational secondary education study track and who have a more foreign cultural background. Pre-entry and dynamic factors explain together 26 per cent of the variance in academic achievement. Less than half of the proportion of explained total variance in our model (11 per cent) is contributed by pre-entry factors. This indicates that the measured pre-entry factors only partly determine but are nevertheless important factors to take into account when predicting academic achievement in the first year in higher education.

Conclusions and discussion

The assumed path model generated from our theoretical framework (Figure 11.1) was generally confirmed in the present study. Pre-entry factors, academic self-confidence, academic motivation and learning strategies were also found to be interrelated and have to some extent a differential effect on the academic achievement of first year students. In what follows we discuss the main findings and implications of this study.

The relevance of pre-entry characteristics

The study showed that gender and prior education are important explanatory variables regarding learning strategies and results are as reported in previous studies (Severiens and Ten Dam 1997; Van Petegem and Donche 2006). Female students engage more in surface processing and students from more academically preparing study tracks engage more in deep processing and are less externally regulated and unregulated. As expected, study delay, prior education and cultural or LEB have a differential effect on academic outcome. In this way, the study revealed a clearly disadvantaged group within the population of first year students. Students who experienced more study delay, who followed less academically preparing study tracks in secondary education and who have a foreign cultural background are clearly starting from a more disadvantaged position when entering higher education. They are likely to obtain lower study results. The LEB variable, indicating that students' parents are foreign-born and speak a language other than the language of instruction in higher education also explains variance in performance. A possible explanation may be that the LEB variable partially reflects students' literacy skills. Studies based on the PISA (Programme for International Student Assessment) 2000 database showed for instance that students with an immigrant background have poorer reading performance (e.g. Willms 2006). Although these students have successfully passed secondary education it might be the case that the literacy skills required in the first year of higher education are not fully mastered.

Another explanation could be that students with a foreign cultural background have more difficulties in getting socially and academically integrated in higher education. According to Tinto (1993) problems of integration explain why students drop out in the first year. According to Tinto's theory, the lack of social integration can be associated with a perception of incongruence between the values and norms, needs and interest of peers and the higher education institution and those of the student. The lack of academic integration can be associated with a lack of sufficient interaction between the student, the peers and the institution which hinders the student in terms of isolation from the new learning environment. Future research is, however, needed to investigate whether problems related to incongruence of perception and isolation in higher education contexts are indeed related to students' LEB and explain more why students with a foreign cultural background are likely to obtain lower academic achievement.

In this study we did not find direct effects of SES on academic achievement which is in line with research findings of Bruinsma and Jansen (2007) but not with earlier research (e.g. Pascarella and Terenzini 1991; Tinto 1993). A possible explanation is that the impact of SES has been removed by a selection effect. Although higher education in Flanders is characterised by an open access system, it is known that socio-economic background can have a differential effect on student achievement in secondary education (e.g. Marks, Cresswell and Ainley 2006) and that socially and economically disadvantaged groups are likely to be under-represented in the higher education student population, which could explain why the SES variable is not a direct explanatory variable in our model. The pre-entry factor prior education was a predictor for academic achievement. This finding suggests that students who followed general secondary education tracks are better prepared for academic education and as a consequence obtain higher exam results.

The relationship between dynamic variables and academic achievement

In line with former research findings different regulation strategies are associated with different processing strategies (e.g. Vermunt 1998). The structural equation model also reveals the expected negative relationship between unregulated learning and academic achievement, replicating earlier research findings based on regression analyses (e.g. Donche and Van Petegem 2011; Vermunt 2005). In line with former studies, the model showed only a weak relationship between deep processing and academic achievement (Vermunt 2005; Watkins 2001). A strength of the present study is that this weak correlation has been found after controlling for other mediating variables that were not included in previous research.

In line with previous research both the quality and quantity of motivation were found to be important predictors for the use of different learning strategies (e.g. Grolnick and Ryan 1987; Ryan and Deci 2000). The strength of our study is that the relationships are present after controlling for pre-entry factors. In addition, in our study we went beyond the often separate consideration of the effects of academic motivation and learning strategy on academic performance. In our model we could, in particular, identify that autonomously motivated students use self-regulated and active processing strategies like deep and concrete processing more frequently, while controlled motivation leads to more external regulated and reproduction oriented learning. In addition, amotivation was found to be a relevant predictor for unregulated learning. In line with former research, academic self-confidence is positively related to students' motivation and academic achievement and has a similar differential impact on the use of learning strategies (e.g. Lindblom-Ylänne and Lonka 1999).

Another important finding in this study is that the explanatory model, including pre-entry factors, academic motivation and self-confidence, is a better predictor for students' use of deep learning strategies than for academic achievement, respectively 47 per cent versus 26 per cent. Although the total explained variance in the model is not low, we do have to question why more variance in academic achievement could not be explained. As an indicator of academic achievement in this study, mean exam results could be contaminated by the assessment criteria teachers used. For instance, if assessment tasks put emphasis on reproduction of facts it is unlikely that a deep approach to learning can lead to higher grades (Vermunt 2005).

Implications for research and practice

In future research, it is important to replicate this study in other educational contexts within higher education in order to assess whether the research findings can be generalised. In addition to replication, adding more explanatory variables to the research model is important in order to better understand why and how students achieve in first year higher education. Although our research model explained a reasonable amount of variance in learning strategies and mean exam results, we are aware of the limitations of our model. In future research it is recommended examining whether integrating contextual variables into the model adds significantly to explanatory power. Based upon former research results, we expect that the integration of course-level factors such as teaching strategies (Donche, De Maeyer, Coertjens, van Daal and Van Petegem 2013), study load and the quality of assessment could additionally explain individual differences in student learning and academic achievement (Baeten, Kyndt, Struyven and Dochy 2010; Bruinsma and Jansen 2007).

This study revealed valuable insights regarding students starting from a more disadvantaged position in the first year in higher education. It has been made clear that not only student pre-entry characteristics are important indicators for academic achievement but also their motivational drive as well as their academic self-confidence and learning strategies. We cannot make statements about causality of effects in our study, but the investigated path model and found relationships suggest that when students are entering higher education their perceptions about their own ability and their own study drive should not be underestimated. Having more academic self-confidence as well as being more autonomously motivated seems to be an important lever for more academic performance in terms of more active learning engagement as well as obtaining higher study results. But the results also point in the other direction, as poor academic achievement seems to be related with lower levels of self-confidence and autonomous motivation and less active learning engagement. It seems important for educational practice that, in particular for those learners, specific feedback interventions regarding their own study drive and learning strategies might be fruitful (Donche, Coertjens, Vanthournout and Van Petegem 2012). It raises the importance of assessing students in the beginning of the first semester of higher education, in particular in terms of what students believe they can achieve as well as why they engage in studying in higher education. These insights are important to further understand why first year students learn the way they do, especially for those who are starting from a more disadvantaged position.

References

Armor, D.A. and Taylor, S.E. (1998) Situated optimism: Specific outcome expectancies and self-regulation, in M.A. Zanna (Ed.), *Advances in experimental social psychology*, (pp. 309–379), New York: Academic Press.

Baeten, M., Kyndt, E., Struyven, K. and Dochy, F. (2010) Using student-centred learning environments to stimulate deep approaches to learning: Factors encouraging or discouraging their effectiveness, *Educational Research Review 5*: 243–260.

Bandura, A. (1977) Self-efficacy toward a unifying theory of behavioural change, *Psychological Review 84*: 191–215.

Bollen, K. (1989) *Structural equations with latent variables*, New York: Wiley.

Bruinsma, M. and Jansen, E.P.W.A. (2007) Educational productivity in higher education: An examination of part of the Walberg Educational Productivity Model, *School Effectiveness and School Improvement 18*: 45–65.

Busato, V.V., Prins, F.J., Elshout, J.J. and Hamaker, C. (1998) Learning styles: A cross-sectional and longitudinal study in higher education, *British Journal of Educational Psychology 68*: 427–441.

Byrne, B.M. (2010) *Structural equation modeling with AMOS*, New York: Routledge.

Deci, E.L. and Ryan, R.M. (2000) The 'what' and the 'why' of goal pursuits: Human needs and the self-determination of behaviour, *Psychological Inquiry 11*: 227–268.

Deci, E.L., Vallerand, R.J., Pelletier, L.G. and Ryan, R.M. (1991) Motivation and education: The self-determination perspective, *The Educational Psychologist 26*: 325–346.

DiMaggio, P. (1982) Cultural capital and school success: The impact of status culture participation on the grades of U.S. high school students, *American Sociological Review 47*: 189–201.

Dinsmore, D.L. and Alexander, P.A. (2012) A critical discussion of deep and surface processing: What it means, how it is measured, the role of context, and model specification, *Educational Psychology Review 24*: 499–567.

Donche, V., Coertjens, L. and Van Petegem, P. (2010) The development of learning patterns throughout higher education: A longitudinal study, *Learning and Individual Differences 20*(3): 256–259.

Donche, V., Coertjens, L., Vanthournout, G. and Van Petegem, P. (2012) Providing constructive feedback on learning patterns: An individual learners' perspective, *Reflecting Education 8*(1): 114–131.

Donche, V., De Maeyer, S., Coertjens, L., van Daal, T. and Van Petegem, P. (2013) Differential use of learning strategies in first year higher education: The impact of personality, academic motivation and teaching strategy, *British Journal of Educational Psychology 83*(2): 238–251.

Donche, V. and Van Petegem, P. (2011) The relationship between entry characteristics, learning style and academic achievement of college freshmen, in M. Poulson (Ed.), *Higher education: Teaching, internationalisation and student issues* (pp. 277–288), New York: Nova Science Publishers.

Entwistle, N. and Ramsden, P. (1983) *Understanding student learning*, London: Croom Helm.

Gifi, A. (1990) *Nonlinear multivariate analysis*, Chichester: Wiley.

Grolnick, W.S. and Ryan, R.M. (1987) Autonomy in children's learning: An experimental and individual difference investigation, *Journal of Personality and Social Psychology 52*: 890–898.

Heikkilä, A. and Lonka, K. (2006) Studying in higher education: Students' approaches to learning, self-regulation and cognitive strategies, *Studies in Higher Education 31*: 99–117.

Jansen, E.P.W.A. (2004) The influence of the curriculum organization on study progress in higher education, *Higher Education 47*: 411–435.

Jansen, E.P.W.A. and Bruinsma, M. (2005) Explaining achievement in higher education, *Educational Research and Evaluation 11*: 235–252.

Lange, C. and Byrd, M. (2002) Differences between students' estimated and attained grades in a first-year introductory psychology course as a function of identity development, *Adolescence, 37*: 93–107.

Lindblom-Ylänne, S. and Lonka, K. (1999). Individual ways of interacting with the learning environment – are they related to study success? *Learning and Instruction 9*: 1–18.

Marks, G.N., Cresswell, J. and Ainley, J. (2006) Explaining socioeconomic inequalities in student achievement: The role of home and school factors, *Educational Research & Evaluation 12*: 105–128.

Marton, F. and Säljö, R. (1976) On qualitative differences in learning – I: outcomes and processes, *British Journal of Educational Psychology 46*: 4–11.

Pascarella, E.T. and Terenzini, P.T. (1991) *How college affects students: Findings and insights from twenty years of research*, San Francisco, CA: Jossey-Bass.

Pustjens, H., Van de Gaer, E., Van Damme, J. and Onghena, P. (2004) Effect of secondary schools on academic choices and on success in higher education, *School Effectiveness and School Improvement 15*: 281–311.

Reynolds, A.J. and Walberg, H.J. (1992) A structural model of science achievement and attitude: An extension to high school, *Journal of Educational Psychology 83*: 97–107.

Richardson, J.T.E. and Woodley, A. (2003) Another look at the role of age, gender and subject as predictors of academic attainment in higher education, *Studies in Higher Education 28*: 475–493.

Richardson, M., Abraham, C. and Bond, R. (2012) Psychological correlates of university students' academic performance: A systematic review and meta-analysis, *Psychological Bulletin 138*: 353–387.

Ryan, R.M. and Connell, J.P. (1989) Perceived locus of causality and internalization: Examining reasons for acting in two domains, *Journal of Personality and Social Psychology 57*: 749–761.

Ryan, R.M. and Deci, E.L. (2000) Self-determination theory and the facilitation of intrinsic motivation, social development and well-being, *American Psychologist 55*: 68–78.

Severiens, S.E. and Ten Dam, G.T.M. (1997) Gender and gender identity differences in learning styles, *Educational Psychology 17*: 79–93.

Spady, W. (1970) Drop-outs from higher education: An interdisciplinary review and synthesis, *Interchange 1*: 64–85.

Sullivan, A. (2001) Cultural capital and educational attainment, *Sociology 35*: 893–912.

Svanum, S. and Bigatti, S. (2006) Grade expectations: Informed or informed optimism, or both? *Teaching of Psychology 33*(1): 14–18.

Tinto, V. (1993) *Leaving college: Rethinking causes and cures of student attrition*, Chicago, IL: The University of Chicago Press.

Vallerand, R.J., Pelletier, L.G., Blais, M.R., Brière, N.M., Senécal, C. and Vallières, E.F. (1992) The academic motivation scale: A measure of intrinsic, extrinsic, and amotivation in education, *Educational and Psychological Measurement* 52: 1003–1017.

Van Petegem, P. and Donche, V. (2006). Learning environment research in higher education: Assessing constructivist approaches to learning, teaching and learning to teach, in D.L. Fisher and M.S. Khine (Eds.), *Contemporary approaches to research on learning environments: World views* (pp. 93–124), Singapore: World Scientific Publishing.

Vansteenkiste, M., Zhou, M., Lens, W. and Soenens, B. (2005) Experiences of autonomy and control among Chinese learners: Vitalizing or immobilizing? *Journal of Educational Psychology* 97: 468–483.

Vermunt, J. (1998). The regulation of constructive learning processes, *British Journal of Educational Psychology* 68: 149–171.

Vermunt, J. (2005). Relations between student learning patterns and personal and contextual factors and academic performance, *Higher Education* 46: 205–236.

Vermunt, J.D. and Vermetten, Y. (2004) Patterns in student learning: Relationships between learning strategies, conceptions of learning and learning orientations, *Educational Psychology Review* 16: 359–384.

Watkins, D. (2001) Correlates of approaches to learning: A cross-cultural meta-analysis, in R.J. Sternberg and L.F. Zhang (Eds.), *Perspective on thinking, learning, and cognitive styles*, (pp. 165–195), Mahwah, NJ: Lawrence Erlbaum Associates.

Watkins, D. and Hattie, J. (1981) The learning processes of Australian university students: Investigations of contextual and personological factors, *British Journal of Educational Psychology* 51: 384–393.

Willms, J.D. (2006) Variation in socioeconomic gradients among cantons in French- and Italian-speaking Switzerland: Findings from the OECD PISA, *Educational Research and Evaluation* 12: 129–154.

Chapter 12

Challenges in analysing change in students' approaches to learning

Sari Lindblom-Ylänne, Anna Parpala and Liisa Postareff

Introduction

Our research reported in this chapter has its roots in the student's approaches to learning (SAL) tradition (Lonka, Olkinuora, & Mäkinen, 2004; Vanthournout, Donche, Gijbels, & Van Petegem, 2013). Students' approaches to learning and studying reflect the objectives they attempt to reach as well as their study processes in specific learning contexts. Previous research has roughly divided the approaches to learning into two qualitatively different categories: 'deep' and 'surface' (e.g. Biggs, 1979; Entwistle & Entwistle, 1992; Entwistle & Ramsden, 1983; Marton & Säljö, 1976, 1997). Students applying a surface approach concentrate on the text itself, whereas those applying a deep approach focus more on the meaning of the text. Researchers have also identified a 'strategic' approach (Biggs, 1987; Entwistle, McCune, & Walker, 2001; Entwistle & Ramsden, 1983). Originally this approach reflected students' attempts to achieve the highest grades through effective studying and by applying organised study methods, as well as students developing an awareness of current assessment methods and criteria. Recently, however, this approach has been modified to cover organised studying and effort management without such a clear focus on attaining the highest grades (Entwistle & McCune, 2004; Entwistle & Peterson, 2004). The 'organised' approach has been described as an approach to studying rather than learning, because it measures how students go about their everyday studying, how they organise it, and how they manage their time (Entwistle, 2009). In the present chapter, however, we apply the *approach to learning* concept to cover three approaches to learning and studying: the deep approach, the surface approach, as well as organised studying and effort management (referred to hereafter as *organised studying*).

Exploring changes in approaches to learning with follow-up designs in various contexts is highly important because previous research has shown contrasting evidence of the contextual versus stable nature of approaches to learning. In the mid-1970s Marton and Säljö (1976) suggested that students are likely to adjust their approaches depending on the study context and the requirements they face. However, contradictory evidence has also been presented: some studies claim that the approaches are relatively stable (e.g. Lietz & Matthews, 2010; Zeegers, 2001), whereas others claim that they are changeable and contextual (e.g. Nieminen, Lindblom-Ylänne, & Lonka, 2004; Vermunt, 1998). Recently, McCune and Entwistle (2011) have suggested that a deep approach to learning remains stable among some students who have a stable disposition to understand. The *disposition to understand for oneself* is a more consistent and stronger form of the 'intention to understand' found in a deep approach. Students with such a disposition aim at reaching a full and satisfying understanding of what they study.

In recent years we have explored university students' learning processes in different teaching–learning environments, and particularly the factors that contribute to changes in students' approaches to learning. We have repeatedly been confronted by challenges related to the creation of research designs and to the selection of methodological approaches. In order to meet these challenges, we have used a mixed methods approach combined with follow-up research designs. When referring to mixed methods research we follow the definition of Johnson, Onwuegbuzie and Turner (2007: 123):

> Mixed methods research is the type of research in which a researcher or team of researchers combine elements of qualitative and quantitative research approaches (e.g., use of qualitative and quantitative viewpoints, data collection, analysis, inference techniques) for the broad purposes of breadth and depth of understanding and corroboration.

This chapter focuses on the challenges faced when analysing change in students' approaches to learning in different study contexts using various research methods. First, we report research results concerning changes in approaches to learning from follow-up designs in which the focus has been on student learning in their major subjects. Second, we describe changes in the approaches to learning at course level by using 'before and after the course' designs. Third, we report research results concerning changes in approaches to learning at the individual level by creating student profiles. Fourth, we present results of elements related to the changes in approaches to learning at the individual level by using qualitative interview data. For our analyses, we use our extensive inventory and interview data of bachelor-level students representing various disciplines. Thus the aim of this chapter is to provide an overview of our research on changes in students' approaches to learning by presenting examples from different methodological designs and different disciplines.

Exploring group-level changes in approaches to learning by applying follow-up designs

There is a long tradition of exploring the changes in approaches to learning at group level by applying quantitative methods and 'before and after' designs. Different types of factor analyses followed by comparisons of mean changes using t-tests or analyses of variance have been widely employed to measure changes in approaches to learning over a particular period of time. Furthermore, the use of only two measurement points has been very common. Our own research does not make an exception to this 'before and after' design. In most cases, a longitudinal data setting with many measurement points is not possible due to student dropouts and other difficulties in having students answer the same questionnaires many times (Verbeke & Molenberghs, 2009). We argue that by using a group-level analysis only, especially in a data setting with two measurement points, one is not able to make the most of the data, nor is one able to see the rich variation of change processes that occur within the students.

Changes in the approaches to learning during bachelor studies

We have explored changes in approaches to learning in follow-up designs where the focus has been on students' learning in their major subjects during the bachelor years. Here we present results from two disciplines, namely veterinary medicine and bioscience. In both faculties the students answered a questionnaire twice during their major studies: at the end of both their first and third study years. They completed a modified version of the Experiences of Teaching and Learning Questionnaire (ETLQ) (Entwistle, McCune, & Hounsell, 2003) entitled LEARN (Parpala & Lindblom-Ylänne, 2012), which contains scales measuring students' approaches to learning. The LEARN questionnaire has been developed over many years on the basis of extensive statistical analyses as well as student and expert interviews held across the University of Helsinki. The questionnaire's current version is called the LEARN questionnaire. It consists of two sections of the original ETLQ: a modified Approaches to Learning and Studying Inventory (ALSI) with 12 items and the other the same with 22 items measuring students' experiences of the teaching–learning environment. The deep approach scale consists of four items, the surface approach scale four items, and the organised studying scale four items. It appears that the instrument is relatively reliable as, for example, the reliabilities concerning the scales measuring the approaches to learning vary from .720 to .797 (Parpala & Lindblom-Ylänne, 2012). For the results presented here, we have used the three scales from the LEARN questionnaire that measure approaches to learning.

The group-level changes in students' approaches to learning from the first to the third year of studies were examined with a paired samples t-test which would give results similar to those of repeated measures' analysis of variance (ANOVA), because there were only two measurement points. The paired samples t-test showed no statistically significant changes in veterinary students' approaches to learning; more precisely, in their deep approach, surface approach and organised studying and effort management. However, in the second measurement the bioscience students scored statistically significantly higher in both the deep approach (t = 2.96, p = .004, partial η^2 = .078) and surface approach (t = 2.31, p = .023, partial η^2 = .044), but the effect sizes of the changes remained small.

On the basis of these results it is difficult to speculate about the reasons for the changes, and their direction (either an increase or decrease), particularly when the magnitude of the effect seems rather low. Furthermore, practical implications for academic development are not clear. In addition, the lack of more than two measurement points give us no further information about the actual trends in the change processes, and the selected method yielded no information that could be used to explain the slight or no changes in students' approaches to learning, or whether the changes only reflect a regression to the mean effect. Regression to the mean (RTM) is a statistical phenomenon that can make natural variation in repeated data appear as real change (e.g. Furby, 1973; Mee & Chua, 1991; Smith & Smith, 2005). According to Zhang and Tomblin (2003), research designs that use multiple measurements for documenting change are vulnerable to an important threat to their validity. RTM will only occur when the normality of distribution holds (Zhang & Tomblin, 2003). RTM takes place when unusually high or low scores tend to be followed by scores that are closer to the mean (Barnett, van der Pols, & Dobson, 2005; Furby, 1973; Smith & Smith, 2005). Very high scores therefore tend to decrease closer to the average and, respectively, very low scores tend to increase closer to the average, both on the second measurement when considered as a group (Barnett et al., 2005; Zhang & Tomblin, 2003).

Only a few studies have focused on change in students' approaches to learning in which students have answered the same questionnaire more than twice and where the trends in the change processes were quite visible (e.g. Vanthournout, 2011). However, to understand the reasons for group-level changes, especially in situations with two measurement points, we must search for new tools when elaborating the longitudinal data settings.

Measuring group-level changes in the approaches to learning at the course level

We have recently explored the use of change variables to create a more detailed picture of changes at the group level, because the use of t-tests to compare mean scale scores before and after a course does not capture variation in the change processes, nor does it deepen our understanding of changes that take place during a specific course. By exploring variation in the approaches to learning separately for students who scored the highest, above and below average, and the lowest on approaches to learning at the beginning of the courses, we hoped to be able to avoid making erroneous inferences about changes due to the RTM effect.

Below we will show an example of using change variables and change groups, which we consider a helpful way to create a more thorough picture of group-level variation in approaches to learning in a specific teaching–learning context. We computed the change variables for the three approaches to learning by subtracting the students' scale scores after the course from their scale scores at the beginning of the course in order to explore the extent of individual changes in their approaches to learning. The magnitude and the direction of the change served to create five groups according to type of change: strong increase, increase, no change, decrease and strong decrease. The distributions of the change variables were explored in detail in order to decide upon the best cutting points for the change groups. The creation of the change groups was based on Likert-scale point changes of greater or less than half a Likert-scale point. However, for the 'no change' group, we used a quarter of a Likert-scale point similar to the procedure previously used by Lindblom-Ylänne, Trigwell, Nevgi, and Ashwin (2006). We could have also created a 'no change' group of only those students whose change variable was zero, but then the criteria for no change would have been very strict and not have allowed any changes. Thus in order to leave some space for very small changes we decided to use a quarter of a Likert scale as the criterion. We also considered categorisation on the basis of median split, but that would have rendered a comparison of the changes between the three approaches impossible. In addition, forming the change variables enabled us to explore individual changes throughout the study process. Our choice of applying the change groups can be criticised for losing the actual variation in the approaches to learning. However, the examination of distributions of the change variables showed a greater concentration on certain values. Therefore the use of the change groups was justifiable.

Table 12.1 shows changes in mathematics students' (N = 89) deep and surface approaches to learning and in organised studying and effort management in a compulsory bachelor-level mathematics course by using change groups instead of the comparisons of mean scores before and after the course. The mean scores of the scales measuring the deep approach to learning and organised studying declined significantly during the mathematics course measured by paired samples t-test, but the smaller decline in the mean score of the surface approach to learning was non-significant. The mean scores of the deep approach scale declined from 3.42 (standard deviation (SD) = 0.69) to 3.07 (SD = 0.83; t = 4.86, p = 0.001) showing a medium effect size (Cohen d = 0.458), and the mean scores of the organised studying scale declined from 3.09 (SD = 0.81) to 2.75 (SD = 0.86; t = 5.17, p = 0.001) showing an almost medium effect size (Cohen d = 0.407). As can be seen in Table 12.1, the use of the change groups shows a much more detailed view of the change processes. Even though the mean scores declined, an increase was not rare in the three approaches to learning. In addition, approximately every fifth or even every fourth student showed no changes in scores measuring their approaches to learning.

Table 12.1 The distribution of mathematics students into the five change groups on the basis of their scores in deep and surface approaches to learning and in organised studying (N = 89)

Change during the course	Approach to learning		
	Deep F (%)	Surface F (%)	Organised studying F (%)
Strong increase	6 (7)	14 (15)	7 (8)
Increase	11 (12)	15 (16)	10 (11)
No or slight change	24 (27)	16 (18)	20 (22)
Decrease	30 (34)	26 (29)	25 (27)
Strong decrease	18 (20)	20 (22)	29 (32)

Table 12.2 shows an example of the same mathematics course as in Table 12.1, but this time the changes were explored using a ranking of students and by creating four ranked percentile groups. However, to simplify the results, Table 12.2 presents changes only in the deep approach during the course. For Table 12.2, we ranked the students on the basis of their mean scores on the scale measuring the deep approach to learning at the beginning and at the end of the course, and we then divided their 'before and after' rankings into four groups of equal size. Ranking the students enabled us to explore the changes in a particular approach to learning *in relation* to the other students who participated in the same course. In addition, by grouping the students and widening the range of their scores, the ranking procedure diminished the RTM effect. The students' rankings in the approaches to learning before and after the course were categorised into four groups of equal size (percentiles): highest, above average, below average and lowest rankings. Finally, we compared the ranking groups of each student before and after the course to determine whether he/she remained in the same ranking group or whether his/her scale scores changed in relation to the other students during the course. The use of the percentile ranked groups can also be criticised for losing the actual variation in the approaches to learning. Similar to the change variables, a concentration on certain values in the rankings of the students was noted. Therefore, we also consider the use of the percentile ranked groups as justifiable.

Table 12.2 shows that the highest-ranking group of the deep approach remained stable: of these, approximately 77 per cent remained in the same ranking group. The other ranking groups showed more relational changes, because roughly only half of the students remained in their original ranking group. None of the students shifted from the lowest-ranking group to the highest, or vice versa.

These two examples from the same compulsory mathematics course show that both research methods − the use of change variables and the use of ranked percentile groups − provided more insight into the change processes of the student groups in a specific teaching–learning context representing a variety

Table 12.2 Tabulation of the ranked percentile groups of the deep approach at the beginning and end of the mathematics course, showing the number of students, means and standard deviations of average change in each cell (N = 89)

Before \ After	Lowest n = 21 M (SD)	Below average n = 23 M (SD)	Above average n = 22 M (SD)	Highest n = 23 M (SD)
Lowest n = 22	11 −0.43 (0.41)	6 0.29 (0.27)	5 0.07 (0.29)	0 –
Below average n = 24	6 −0.69 (0.19)	13 −0.26 (0.17)	4 0.09 (0.12)	1 0.50 (–)
Above average n = 21	4 −1.34 (0.48)	2 −0.88 (0.00)	10 −0.34 (0.17)	5 0.2 (0.11)
Highest n = 22	0 –	2 −0.75 (0.00)	3 −0.88 (0.45)	17 −0.01 (0.35)

of disciplines (e.g. Lindblom-Ylänne, Parpala, & Postareff, 2011; Lindblom-Ylänne, Postareff, & Parpala, 2013: Postareff, Lindblom-Ylänne & Parpala, 2013a). Importantly, even though comparisons of the mean scores according to the t-tests showed a decline in each approach to learning, the use of change groups or ranked percentile groups captured in greater detail the variation in changes during the mathematics course. And although we have provided evidence from only one course here, we have obtained similar results from several bachelor-level courses: that the t-tests show only the average trends at group level, but hide the variation which occurs in different directions. Our conclusion is that the t-tests are not fully capable of exploring the contextual variation in the approaches to learning, because the changes in different directions cancel each other out.

For the next example presented in Table 12.3 the change groups and ranked percentile groups were combined to explore changes in theology students' (N = 79) deep approach to learning during a compulsory bachelor-level theology course (Lindblom-Ylänne et al., 2013). By combining the two methods of analysing change, we aimed to give a detailed illustration of the different change paths during a specific course, taking into account the relational 'starting level' of the students in terms of their scores in the deep approach scale. We ranked the students on the basis of their deep approach scores at the beginning of the course and categorised the rankings into four percentile groups. We are aware that the results must be interpreted with caution, because of the RTM effect. However, by exploring the variation in the deep approach separately for students who scored the highest, average and lowest on the deep approach at the beginning of the course, we hope to be able to avoid drawing erroneous conclusions about the changes. Finally, we cross-tabulated the ranked percentile groups and the change groups of the

Table 12.3 Distribution of the change variables and group-level average changes before and after the theology course across the ranked percentile groups (N = 79)

Ranked percentile group of the deep approach	Group-level average changes				Distribution of the change variable		
	Before M (SD)	After M (SD)	Change (M)	Change Min – Max	Decrease (n = 32) f (%)	No change (n = 7) f (%)	Increase (n = 15) f (%)
Lowest (n = 22)	2.80 (0.35)	3.0 (0.58)	0.18	−1.5 – 1.75	7 (31.8)	3 (13.6)	12 (54.6)
Below average (n = 15)	3.37 (0.13)	3.23 (0.62)	−0.13	−1.25 – 0.75	6 (40)	2 (13.3)	7 (46.7)
Above average (n = 19)	3.87 (0.13)	3.51 (0.36)	−0.36	−1.00 – 0.25	13 (68.4)	4 (21.1)	2 (10.5)
Highest (n = 23)	4.48 (0.27)	4.10 (0.53)	−0.38	−1.75 – 0.25	13 (56.5)	7 (30.4)	3 (13.1)

deep approach in order to explore whether the students' relational level of the deep approach at the beginning of the course was related to the direction and magnitude of change in the deep approach during the course (Lindblom-Ylänne et al., 2013). At group level, the theology students' mean scores in the deep approach declined significantly, from 3.66 (SD = 0.7) to 3.48 (SD = 0.69; t = 2.69, p = 0.009). The effect size of the decline measured by Cohen's d was small (Lindblom-Ylänne et al., 2013).

Table 12.3 shows that during the course the lowest-ranked students' mean deep approach scores increased, whereas the mean scores for the three higher-ranked student groups decreased. In addition, a large individual variation in the amount and direction of change during the course is evident (Lindblom-Ylänne et al., 2013).

Tabulating the ranked percentile groups with the change groups enabled us to create an accurate picture of the change processes at the course level compared to analysing mean scores changes with t-tests or using only change variables or ranked percentile groups. We are aware that by grouping the students into either the change or ranked percentile groups we reduce the actual variation in the deep approach. However, as mentioned earlier, when we investigated the distributions of both the change variables and ranked scores we discovered a high degree of concentration on certain values. Therefore we consider the use of change and ranked percentile groups as justifiable (Lindblom-Ylänne et al., 2013). To conclude, the group-level mean changes 'neutralise' the variation in the approaches to learning, because change seems to occur equally frequently in opposite directions (Lindblom-Ylänne et al., 2013). It is therefore important to search for new ways of exploring group-level changes, which can better capture students' change processes.

Creating bachelor students' change profiles for each approach to learning, to allow for individual-level analyses

The need for individual-level analyses emerged from our results of the group-level analyses. On one hand, the comparisons of the mean scores showed no or only slight changes in students' approaches to learning and, on the other, it appeared that the use of change variables and ranked percentile groups revealed large individual variation. However, these group-level analyses do not give us the tools to further investigate differences between the student groups or individual students. Therefore we decided to analyse individual variation among the veterinary medicine and bioscience students by separately examining each scale measuring the approaches to learning and by looking at individual variation at the scale level by using ranked percentile groups. By doing this, we were able to form scale profiles of individual students for each scale measuring the approaches to learning. The students' scores from the first and the third study year in the three approaches to learning were ranked, and three groups of equal size were separately formed for each approach to learning. The number '1' was given to the lowest-ranked group and '3' to the highest. We then formed the scale profiles by combining the two numbers of each student in the following way: for example, in the scale profile '11' a student belonged to the lowest-ranked group in both measurements, in the scale profile '13' a student belonged to the lowest-ranked group in the first and to the highest-ranked group in the second measurement; and in the scale profile '22', a student belonged to the average group in both measurements. Nine different combinations emerged in each approach to learning, and each of these combinations was represented in both the bioscience and veterinary data.

The analyses of the veterinary students' scale profiles showed that even though there were no statistically significant group-level changes in the students' approaches to learning from the first to the third study year, one fifth of the students showed a decrease in their deep approach scores and one third scored higher on the deep approach in the second measurement. Although half of the students belonged to the same ranked group in both measurements, the same number changed their ranking group. Similar results were also found when we explored changes in the surface approach and in organised studying. Table 12.4 presents the direction of change and percentage of students representing each change profile of the approaches to learning.

We found similar results in the bioscience data in terms of the changes in students' approaches to learning. The group-level comparisons of the mean scores showed a statistically significant increase in both the deep approach ($t = 2.96$, $p = .004$, partial $\eta^2 = .078$) and surface approach ($t = 2.31$, $p = .023$, partial $\eta^2 = .044$). However, examining the scale profiles in these two approaches revealed that in the second measurement only one third of the bioscience students scored higher on the deep approach and that one

Table 12.4 The scale profiles for each approach to learning, and students representing these profiles in veterinary medicine

The change direction	Deep approach	Surface approach	Organised studying
No change	**51%**	**46%**	**62%**
11 (remains low)	19%	24%	22%
22 (remains average)	13%	6%	23%
33 (remains high)	19%	16%	17%
Decrease	**22%**	**29%**	**17%**
21 (average to low)	10%	9%	4%
32 (high to average)	8%	14%	11%
31 (high to low)	4%	6%	2%
Increase	**27%**	**25%**	**21%**
12 (low to average)	11%	11%	11%
13 (low to high)	8%	7%	2%
23 (average to high)	8%	7%	8%

third scored higher on the surface approach. Thus there were more students whose scores on the deep and surface approaches either remained the same or decreased despite the fact that the group-level analyses showed a significant increase in both approaches. Table 12.5 presents the scale profiles of the deep and surface approach to learning which changed in the group-level analysis, and presents the percentages of students representing these scale profiles. Students' scores in the organised studying scale are excluded in order to focus on the two scales, which showed a statistically significantly increase at the group level.

Some of the changes described above might reflect the RTM effect. Yet in both data sets there were students whose scores in the different approaches to learning changed from the lowest ranking group to the highest, and vice versa. In these cases the change is clear, and not only caused by the RTM. By using the scale-level profiles we were able to see the richness in individual variation in the change processes even though we did not explore student profiles in which the changes in all three approaches were combined. For larger data sets, the use of the student profiles is too complex to create a clear picture of changes in a specific teaching–learning process. For example, in the data of the 141 veterinary students, 123 student profiles emerged when the results from the three scale profiles were combined. However, the use of scale profiles enabled us to examine individual students' change processes in more detail and to analyse the differences in relation to students' perceptions of their teaching–learning environments and study success. The use of the scale profiles also showed that a very simple method could capture the variation in individual change processes.

Table 12.5 The scale profiles of the deep and surface approaches to learning, and the percentages of bioscience students representing these profiles

The change direction	Deep approach	Surface approach
No change	**49%**	**36%**
11 (remains low)	20%	16%
22 (remains average)	14%	9%
33 (remains high)	15%	11%
Decrease	**22%**	**32%**
21 (average to low)	13%	1%
32 (high to average)	3%	21%
31 (high to low)	6%	10%
Increase	**29%**	**32%**
12 (low to average)	7%	17%
13 (low to high)	7%	8%
23 (average to high)	15%	7%

Explaining individual changes in the deep approach by qualitative methods

We now move to analysing changes in approaches to learning at the individual level by using qualitative interview data. Although we used no more than two measurement points in our quantitative studies, we collected an extensive set of data through the mixed methods approach. Our data include teacher and student interviews, video recordings, and observations from the courses for the purpose of analysing both the approaches to learning and the changes deeply and broadly from different perspectives. The student interviews were conducted soon after the courses ended and thus provided a retrospective view of individual students' study paths and processes during the course. The interviews were thorough and open in nature and focused on the students' descriptions of their intentions and goals with respect to studying and learning at the university, as well as their learning processes and practices both in general and during the course they had just completed, along with their experiences of studying and learning in the specific course they had recently attended. We therefore argue that the interviews can be applied to compensate for the missing third measurement point.

We now give examples from two qualitative interview studies, which focused on analysing students' learning and their experiences of studying in a specific course. The data were collected from four bachelor-level courses from four disciplines (Postareff, Parpala & Lindblom-Ylänne, 2012; Postareff et al., 2013a; Postareff, Parpala, & Lindblom-Ylänne, 2013b). We analysed how the students described their learning both in their university studies generally and in the specific course, as well as their study experiences during the specific course.

In addition, elements related to the students themselves and to the context, which might explain an increase, decrease or stability in their deep approach scores during the courses were explored. Content analysis was selected as the analysis method. The first and third authors analysed the interviews separately, and the outcomes were compared and discussed. The inter-rater agreement was high, although some cases needed to be discussed carefully.

For the first study (Postareff et al., 2013b), we analysed interviews of students showing an increase, decrease or no change in their deep approach measured by the ETLQ described above. We concentrated on exploring the elements explaining change or stability in the students' deep approach. The qualitative analysis revealed that the increase in their deep approach was related to aiming at a deep understanding of the course content and at high grades, good self-regulation skills and investing time and effort in studying regularly throughout the course. Most of the students showing an increase in their deep approach were satisfied with the teaching but interestingly the level of interest varied between the students, with not all showing a specific interest in the course content. Despite this lack of interest, the students did invest time and effort in studying, as the following interview quotation shows:

> I think the content did not interest me that much . . . The lectures did not include much activation so I did not get myself involved . . . I spent quite a lot of time reading, and I focused a lot on the course books and made notes. I started reading for the exam at a very early stage although it felt quite uncomfortable.
>
> (Female student, educational sciences)

The results further showed that the elements related to a decrease in the students' deep approach were mainly the same as the elements related to an increase in it, but that they were opposite in nature. Thus, aiming to only pass the course instead of aiming at a high grade, problems with self-regulated learning, low activity during the course, problems with time management, and having difficulty understanding the course content were typical of students whose scores in the deep approach decreased. In addition, all of the students described a lack of interest in the course content. Furthermore, overly easy course content and not enough challenges, or conversely, overly challenging course content, were often experienced by these students. The experienced lack of challenges is described in the following way by a theology student:

> I think it was quite surprising that there was not that much new information. The teacher emphasised that we should strengthen or shape our own opinions about things. I could have invested more in studying during the course. But I felt that I would remember these things well anyway, and that there was no need to write a learning diary during the course; instead I did it right before the deadline.
>
> (Female student, theology)

Stability in the deep approach during the course was found to be related to the use of effective and functional study strategies that students had developed for themselves. This result is in line with those of Lindblom-Ylänne and Lonka (1999, 2001), who showed that some students are 'immune' to the effects of their teaching–learning environment. For these students, clear aims, individual ways of learning and studying, and self-assessment were more valuable than study advice from the teachers, instructions included in the study material and assessment results. Some students whose deep approach scores remained stable during the course, therefore described having studied in a similar way in all their courses, as the following interview quotation illustrates:

> I usually read the course material intensively and try to understand it. I study until I understand. If the lectures are good, it takes less time to understand, but if they are not, the process takes more time.
>
> (Male student, biosciences)

Our second qualitative study (Postareff et al., 2013a) analysed interviews of students who scored extremely highly on the deep approach. We were particularly interested in the students whose deep approach remained at a high level, or even increased, during the course. They described their studying and learning in a very similar manner. These students' interviews clearly reflected the high level of their deep approach as well as their self-regulated learning: their intention was to learn deeply and form a coherent whole from the subject matter, and they used strategies which enabled deep-level learning. Moreover, good self-regulation skills were evident when the students described setting goals for their own learning and studying regularly instead of only before deadlines or exams, as well as assuming responsibility for their learning. They were all intrinsically motivated, they described using well-developed study strategies and they devoted much time and effort to studying the course content. In addition, they showed an emotional commitment to their studies, although they expressed different levels of interest in the course content. Furthermore, the courses had positively challenged these students to study deeply, although they described their experiences of the course teaching in somewhat neutral terms. Thus the results suggested that a high level of interest in the course content, or positive experiences of the teaching, were not necessary for these students to apply a deep approach throughout an entire course. These students' interviews therefore reflected similarities with what McCune and Entwistle (2011) call the 'disposition to understand for oneself', in that the students used effective learning strategies, had a desire to acquire a deep understanding of the course content, and showed an emotional commitment towards their studies. This is reflected in the following interview quotation:

> . . . I hugely enjoy studying and learning. I am very attached to my own major subject, but I would also like to explore what else I can learn outside

my major subject because I want to learn things deeply and broadly. I want to gain thinking and writing skills as well, and absorb information from all possible sources.

(Male student, educational sciences)

The results of the qualitative analysis supported those of our quantitative analysis in that the students' descriptions of their own learning were in line with their questionnaire scores. Furthermore, the interviews deepened our understanding of the quantitative results in that the students' descriptions of their learning and study practices during the course as well as their course experiences provided explanations for the changes identified in their deep approach during the quantitative analysis.

Conclusions

This chapter dealt with the challenges we confronted when analysing change in students' approaches to learning within various study contexts. We provided examples of different methodological designs for analysing change. Our examples showed that at the individual level, the change in students' self-reports was much richer than at the group level, and that these changes took place in both directions: an increase and a decrease. Our conclusion is that by using group-level analyses only, we lose the possibility of detecting the rich variation of change processes occurring among individual students.

Our examples further showed that while some students displayed variation – either an increase or decrease – in their approaches to learning, others in the same teaching–learning environment showed no change in approach. These findings seem to empirically support both the view that students' approaches to learning are contextual and dynamic (Marton & Säljö, 1976; Nieminen et al., 2004; Vermunt, 1998) and the view that they are relatively stable (Lietz & Matthews, 2010; Zeegers, 2001). The previous contrasting results can be explained both by the effects of the methodological approaches applied and by individual students' characteristics, aims and different reactions to the dimensions of the teaching–learning environment on the basis of their perceptions of that environment. Furthermore, we were able to identify a stable disposition to understand for oneself (McCune & Entwistle, 2011) in some students who scored highly on their deep approach and showed no change in it. However, not all students who scored highly showed a disposition to understand for oneself. Some might have evaluated themselves as applying a deep approach *in theory*, but in practice the expected study processes were not implemented. Some students might have lacked the metacognitive skills to evaluate their aims and study processes, and therefore may have overestimated their commitment to a deep approach.

We wish to highlight the critical role of the method that is selected to analyse change in students' approaches to learning. In our view, not enough attention has been focused on the method's effect on the results. Contradictory results in previous studies may have occurred due to a narrow selection of methods for exploring these changes. Thus we emphasise here the importance of a mixed methods approach. It is crucial to look at students' change processes by applying a rich variety of research methods. By combining inventory data with student interviews it is possible to form a deeper understanding of the factors and processes that explain the changes which take place. Furthermore, we wanted to demonstrate that simple analytical methods are sometimes enough to show the variation in students' change processes and to enable researchers to proceed further with their analyses. We therefore argue that the use of more sophisticated analyses are not necessarily a solution to the problem raised in this study.

We hope this chapter can be used in research methodology courses. In addition, we hope it sends a message to researchers in the field of educational psychology and the educational sciences in general to become more aware of the effect of methodological choices on research results and to understand the importance of carefully planning research designs. Our results imply that supporting students' self-regulated learning and requiring students to invest time and effort in studying, as well as appropriately adjusting the level of challenges, are important elements to consider if we want to promote deep learning in students. University teachers should be made aware of these important elements through pedagogical training. We also argue that the research instrument used for measuring changes in approaches to learning could be used to detect changes in student learning, for example at the course level. The instrument could also be used as a counselling tool for individual students as it appears to capture the individual changes as well (Parpala & Lindblom-Ylänne, 2012). However, the use of the instrument should be combined with counselling processes where students would have an opportunity to discuss the results.

References

Barnett, A.G., van der Pols, J.C., & Dobson, A.J. (2005). Regression to the mean: What it is and how to deal with it. *International Journal of Epidemiology*, *34*(1), 215–220.

Biggs, J. (1979). Individual differences in study processes and the quality of learning outcomes. *Higher Education*, *8*, 381–394.

Biggs, J. (1987). *Student approaches to learning and studying.* Camberwell, Victoria: Australian Council for Educational Research.

Entwistle, N. (2009). *Teaching for understanding at university: Deep approaches and distinctive ways of thinking.* Basingstoke, Hampshire: Palgrave Macmillan.

Entwistle, A., & Entwistle, N. (1992). Experiences of understanding in revising for degree examinations. *Learning and Instruction*, *2*, 1–22.

Entwistle, N., & McCune, V. (2004). The conceptual base of study strategies inventories in higher education. *Educational Psychology Review*, *16*(4), 325–345.

Entwistle, N., McCune, V., & Hounsell, J. (2003). Investigating ways of enhancing university teaching-learning environments: Measuring students' approaches to studying and perceptions of teaching, in E. De Corte, L. Verschaffel, N. Entwistle & J. van Merrienboer (Eds.) *Unravelling basic components and dimensions of powerful learning environments.* Oxford: Elsevier Science.

Entwistle, N., McCune, V., & Walker, P. (2001). Conceptions, styles and approaches within higher education: Analytic abstractions and everyday experience, in R.J. Sternberg & L.F. Fang (Eds.) *Perspectives on thinking, learning and cognitive styles* (pp. 103–136). London: Lawrence Erlbaum.

Entwistle, N., & Peterson, E.R. (2001). Conceptions of learning and knowledge in higher education: Relationships with study behaviour and influences of learning environments. *International Journal of Educational Research, 41,* 407–428.

Entwistle, N., & Ramsden, P. (1983). *Understanding student learning.* London: Croom Helm.

Furby, L. (1973). Interpreting regression toward the mean in developmental research. *Developmental Psychology, 8*(2), 172–179.

Johnson, R.B, Onwuegbuzie, A.J., & Turner, L.A. (2007). Toward a definition of mixed methods research, *Journal of Mixed Methods Research, 1*(2), 112–133.

Lietz, P., & Matthews, B. (2010). The effects of college students' personal values on changes in learning approaches. *Research in Higher Education, 51,* 65–87.

Lindblom-Ylänne, S., & Lonka, K. (1999). Individual ways of interacting with the learning environment: Are they related to study success? *Learning and Instruction, 9*(1), 1–18.

Lindblom-Ylänne, S. & Lonka, K. (2001). Students' perceptions of assessment practices in a traditional medical curriculum. *Advances in Health Science Education, 6,* 121–140.

Lindblom-Ylänne, S., Parpala, A., & Postareff, L. (2011). *Measuring students' approaches to learning using different methods.* A paper presented at the Learning in Transition seminar, Antwerp, Belgium, 1–2 December 2011.

Lindblom-Ylänne, S., Postareff, L., & Parpala, A. (2013). *Exploring variation in students' deep approach to learning in four disciplinary contexts.* A manuscript under review.

Lindblom-Ylänne, S., Trigwell, K., Nevgi, A., & Ashwin, P. (2006). How approaches to teaching are affected by discipline and teaching context. *Studies in Higher Education, 31*(3), 285–298.

Lonka, K., Olkinuora, E., & Mäkinen, J. (2004). Aspects and prospects of measuring studying and learning in higher education. *Educational Psychology Review, 16*(4), 301–323.

Marton, F., & Säljö, R. (1976). On qualitative differences in learning: I. Outcome and Process. *British Journal of Educational Psychology, 46,* 4–11.

Marton, F., & Säljö, R. (1997). Approaches to learning, in F. Marton, D. Hounsell & N. Entwistle (Eds.) *The experience of learning* (2nd ed., pp. 39–58). Edinburgh, UK: Scottish Academic Press.

McCune, V., & Entwistle, N. (2011). Cultivating the disposition to understand in 21st century university education. *Learning and Individual Differences, 21,* 303–310.

Mee, R.W., & Chua, C.T. (1991). Regression toward the mean and the paired samples t-test. *The American Statistician, 45*(1), 39–42.

Nieminen, J., Lindblom-Ylänne, S., & Lonka, K. (2004). The development of study orientations and study success in students of pharmacy. *Instructional Science, 32,* 387–417.

Parpala, A., & Lindblom-Ylänne, S. (2012). Using a research instrument for developing quality at the university. *Quality in Higher Education, 18*(3), 313–328.

Postareff, L., Lindblom-Ylänne, S., & Parpala, A. (2013a). *The relation of individual and contextual elements to a strong commitment to understand.* A manuscript under review.

Postareff, L., Parpala, A., & Lindblom-Ylänne, S. (2012). *The change in students' deep approach to learning in four courses.* Paper presented at the EARLI Sig Higher Education conference, Tallinn, 14–17 August 2012.

Postareff, L., Parpala, A., & Lindblom-Ylänne, S. (2013b). *Factors contributing to changes in a deep approach to learning.* A manuscript under review.

Smith, G., & Smith, J. (2005). Regression to the mean in average test scores. *Educational Assessment, 10*(4), 377–399.

Vanthournout, G. (2011). *Patterns in student learning: Exploring a person-oriented and a longitudinal research-perspective.* Antwerpen-Apeldoom: Garant.

Vanthournout, G., Donche, V., Gijbels, D., & Van Petegem, P. (2013). (Dis)similarities in research on learning approaches and learning patterns, in D. Gijbels, V. Donche, J.T.E. Richardson & J.D. Vermunt (Eds.) *Learning patterns in higher education in the 21st century: Dimensions and research perspectives.* London: Routledge.

Verbeke, G., & Molenberghs, G. (2009) *Linear mixed models for longitudinal data* (2nd ed.). New York: Springer.

Vermunt, J.D. (1998). The regulation of constructive learning processes. *British Journal of Educational Psychology, 68,* 149–171.

Zeegers, P. (2001). Student learning in science: A longitudinal study. *British Journal of Educational Psychology, 66,* 59–71.

Zhang, X., & Tomblin, J.B. (2003). Explaining and controlling regression to the mean in longitudinal research designs. *Journal of Speech, Language, and Hearing Research, 46,* 1340–1351.

Chapter 13

Students' approaches to learning in higher education

The interplay between context and student

Eva Kyndt, Filip Dochy and Eduardo Cascallar

Rationale for the study

Several characteristics and evolutions of our contemporary society such as continuously changing and rapid evolving (technological) innovation and growing (global) competitiveness (Kyndt, Dochy, Michielsen and Moeyaert, 2009) have led to the fact that both organisations and individuals experience the need for lifelong learning (Baert, 2002; Beck and Achtenhagen, 2007; Pillay, Boulton-Lewis and Wilss, 2003). Lifelong learning is understood as

> a process, in which both individuals and organisations, in all contexts of their functioning, acquire the needed knowledge and competences to be able to realise all their professional, economic, social and cultural responsibilities in a rapid changing society and to be able to adopt a critical, meaning giving and responsible attitude.
>
> (Baert, 2002)

Although research has shown that the educational degree obtained by an individual is an important predictor for participation in lifelong learning (Brooks and Everett, 2008; Fitzgerald, Taylor and LaValle, 2003; Kyndt, Michielsen, Van Nooten, Nijs and Baert, 2011), higher education has been criticised for not developing competences, such as critical thinking, self-management, the ability to solve novel and complex problems, etc. needed for professional expertise in this society (Boyatzis, Stubbs and Taylor, 2002; Kember, Charlesworth, Davies, MacKay and Stott, 1997; Neilsen, 2000; Segers, Nijhuis and Gijselaers, 2006; Tynjälä, 1999). Although these are the main aims of higher education today, it seems that graduates frequently lack these qualities (Kember et al., 1997).

Problem statement

In the study of Brooks and Everett (2008), higher education graduates indicated that their (lifelong) learning process was foremost influenced by the fact that they had to study independently in higher education. They reported that independent study gave them the necessary skills and motivation to engage in future learning through formal and informal routes. During the past decade, a wide range of teaching methods that emphasise the independence of the student have been implemented and investigated under the common denominator of student-centred teaching methods or learning environments. Their origin lies within the constructivist theory of learning that understands learning as an 'active process in which learners are active sense-makers who seek to build coherent and organised knowledge' (Mayer, 2004, p. 14). Students are expected to take responsibility and actively seek information to build their own knowledge. Characteristics of these student-centred learning environments are: a student who is active and independent, a coaching role of the teacher, and knowledge, that is considered a tool instead of an aim (Dochy, Segers, Gijbels and Van den Bossche, 2002). Some examples of student-centred learning environments are problem-based learning (Dochy, Segers, Van den Bossche and Gijbels, 2003), project-based learning (Dekeyser and Baert, 1999) and case-based learning (Ellis, Marcus and Taylor, 2005). Such learning environments are mostly variations of discovery learning (Mayer, 2004) and cooperative or collaborative learning (Decuyper, Dochy and Van den Bossche, 2010; Slavin, 1995). A reoccurring and principal aim of all these learning environments is fostering a deeper level of learning and understanding (Hannafin, Hill and Land, 1997; Lea, Stephenson and Troy, 2003; Mayer, 2004), which can be expressed by a deep approach to learning. This deep approach to learning has in turn been associated with competences such as problem solving, self-management and critical thinking, needed for professional expertise and beneficial for participation in lifelong learning (Biggs, 2001; Brooks and Everett, 2008; Kember et al., 1997).

Student-centred learning environments aim at fostering a deep approach to learning in students (Hannafin et al., 1997; Lea et al., 2003; Struyven, Dochy, Janssens and Gielen, 2006). Moreover, educational literature expected positive effects and showed promising results (Tiwari et al., 2006; Wilson and Fowler, 2005). However, the specific conceptual origin of this research lies in the finding that student-centred learning environments do not always push students towards a deep approach to learning (Gijbels, Van de Watering, Dochy and Van den Bossche, 2005; Nijhuis, Segers and Gijselaers, 2005; Segers et al., 2006; Struyven et al., 2006). Research results even showed an increase in students' surface approaches to learning after experiencing a student-centred learning environment (Gijbels et al., 2005; Nijhuis et al., 2005; Segers et al., 2006; Struyven et al., 2006). These results confirmed Marton and Säljö's (1997) statement that inducing a deep approach to learning seems to be quite difficult in contrast to inducing a surface approach to learning. The goal of this research project was to investigate why students did not adopt a deeper approach to learning. Therefore several factors that could encourage or discourage the adoption of a deep approach to learning were investigated.

Student learning: investigating students' approaches to learning

This research project conceptualised student learning starting from the theory of Marton and Säljö (1976) on students' approaches to learning. They described approaches to learning as a combination of the intention of the student when starting a task and the learning strategies applied to fulfil this intention (Marton and Säljö, 1976). Approaches to learning are not stable psychological traits but are determined by a 'relation' between a learner and a context. Students adjust their approaches to learning depending on the requirements of the task (Laurillard, 1984; Marton and Säljö, 1976; Struyven et al., 2006). In their research, Marton and Säljö (1976) identified two approaches to learning: deep and surface. This study also focused on the distinction between these two approaches and used the revised two factor study process questionnaire (R-SPQ-2F; Biggs, Kember and Leung, 2001) as a measurement of students' approaches to learning.

The *surface approach to learning* is based on an intention that is extrinsic to the real purpose of the task. The task is seen as a hurdle to be cleared with as little time and effort possible to meet the requirements (Biggs, 2001). Rote learning content without understanding in order to subsequently reproduce the material (Struyven et al., 2006; Trigwell and Prosser, 1991), is one of the most common strategies for the surface approach (Biggs, 2001). The surface approach is generally related to lower quality outcomes of learning (Trigwell and Prosser, 1991).

A *deep approach* is based on a perceived need, such as an intrinsic interest to engage the task appropriately and meaningfully. The focus is on the underlying meaning rather than on conceptually unsupported specifics (Biggs, 2001). This approach is associated with an intention to comprehend, to engage in active conceptual analysis and, if carried out thoroughly, generally results in a deeper level of understanding (Entwistle, McCune and Walker, 2001; Trigwell and Prosser, 1991). The essence of the deep approach is that the student adopts learning processes that are appropriate to completing the task at hand satisfactorily (Biggs, 2001). Examples of possibly appropriate strategies are reflecting, using various information sources, relating ideas and looking for patterns.

Selecting encouraging and discouraging factors

At the start of this research project, a systematic literature review was undertaken to identify the encouraging and discouraging factors when inducing a deep approach by means of student-centred learning environments (Baeten, Kyndt, Struyven and Dochy, 2010). This literature review yielded a lot of possible factors that can influence the adoption of a deep approach. In general these variables could be grouped in three categories: contextual variables, perceived contextual variables and individual characteristics. A selection of variables was made for the empirical studies based on their relevance for a student-centred learning environment, their relative importance and their innovative character in the field of students' approaches to learning.

Perceived workload and task complexity were chosen to be the investigated perceived contextual variables since students commonly associate both variables with student-centred learning environments (Perkins, 1991; Struyven et al., 2006). The hypothesis is that these student-centred learning environments demand too much from the students in terms of workload and task complexity. Besides the two perceived contextual variables workload and task complexity, three student characteristics were investigated: two relatively stable traits of students, *working memory capacity* and *attention*, and one state or variable characteristic, namely *motivation*.

The choice to investigate the cognitive capacities of students in relation to their approaches to learning was advanced by the ongoing 'state versus trait' debate in the field of approaches to learning (Watkins, 2001). Recent research has found that although student approaches to learning are not stable psychological traits (Marton and Säljö, 1997) the variability seems to be more limited than initially assumed (Gibbs, 1992; McParland, Noble and Livingston, 2004; Nijhuis, Seger, and Gijselaers, 2008; Vermetten, Vermunt and Lodewijks, 2002; Wilson and Fowler, 2005). Biggs (1993) suggests that students have a predisposition towards one of the approaches. The study of Trigwell, Hazel and Prosser (1996) described a dissonant group of students, whose learning approaches were not influenced by the learning environment, suggesting that there are indeed some groups of students who have relatively stable learning approaches. The study of Nijhuis et al. (2008) also investigated this issue. Their aim was to identify different groups of students who differ in the degree of variability of learning strategies. They were able to identify two clusters: a variable cluster and a restricted cluster and found that the variability was related to the characteristics of the course such as workload (Nijhuis et al., 2008). Apparently, some students experience more impact from a specific course than others (Nijhuis et al., 2008). The question that arises is whether this variability or lack of variability is related to certain student characteristics. Students' working memory capacity and attentional processes are relatively stable characteristics (Klein and Fiss, 1999) that could account for the limited variability in approaches to learning in student groups. Both working memory capacity and attention have been shown to play an important role in a variety of learning situations (Unsworth and Engle, 2005).

The final variable that was included in the research was motivation for learning. Previous research has argued that the inclusion of motivational aspects would give a better insight into the understanding of learning approaches (Marton, Watkins and Tang, 1997). Papinczak, Young, Groves and Haynes (2008) have stated that motivation is one of the personal factors that possibly played a role in the shift away from deep towards surface approaches to learning in students after experiencing a problem based learning (PBL) environment. Several other authors investigating the influence of a student-centred learning environment on students' approaches to learning have also stressed the importance of motivation in a learning environment that students experience as more demanding (e.g. Herington and Weaven, 2008; Struyven et al., 2006; Tiwari et al., 2006).

The selection of these five variables (i.e. perceived workload, perceived task complexity, working memory capacity, attention and motivation) in this research made an interesting mix of perceived context, traits and states of students. This selection of variables allowed us to investigate students' approaches to learning as a result of the interplay between student and context.

Theoretical background

The goal of this theoretical background is to define the variables selected for the empirical part of the research and present prior research on the relationship of these variables with students' approaches to learning.

The context

Workload

In the literature concerning workload, there is a tendency to differentiate objective and subjective or perceived workload. On the one hand, objective workload is commonly measured as the number of hours that students objectively spend on studying. Perceived workload, on the other hand, can be described as a combination of the demands placed upon the student, and the effect of these demands on the student, such as effort and frustration as a result of this perceived workload. Students experience a heavy workload as a feeling of pressure or stress (Kember, 2004). The distinction between objective and subjective workload is supported by the fact that the objective workload explains only 4 per cent of the variance of perceived workload (Kember and Leung, 1998).

There are two main reasons why this difference between objective workload and perceived workload should be emphasised. First, a paradox exists: when students evaluate teachers, the award-winning teachers are not the ones whose demands are low but, in fact, the opposite (Kember and Leung, 2006). Second, the relationship between time and learning is not illogical. Learning takes place within the available time of students. Despite individual differences in perceptions of time, a lack of an objective amount of time leads to the fact that nothing can be achieved. Karjalainen, Alha and Jutila (2006) also mentions that '. . . even an infinite amount of time does not guarantee learning, although the existence of time is an essential condition to learning, it is not sufficient itself, other factors are needed as well' (p. 13).

More specifically, Kember and Leung (1998) state that how students respond to the situation they perceive can differ, and that this perception is not necessarily the same as the situation that has been defined by their teachers or curriculum designers. In addition, research on student learning has shown that students are more influenced by how they perceive their learning environment, rather than by the objective context itself (Prosser and Trigwell, 1999).

When looking at the research on students' approaches to learning and perceived workload, several empirical research studies have argued that a perceived excessive workload is positively associated with surface approaches to learning (Entwistle and Ramsden, 1983; Kember, 2004; Nijhuis et al., 2005; Prosser and Trigwell, 1999; Ramsden, 1992; Sand-Jecklin, 2007; Segers et al., 2006; Struyven et al., 2006). Kember (2004) stated that a perceived excessive workload can have a tendency to encourage surface approaches to learning since students resort to shortcuts and undesirable study approaches to cope with the perceived excessive demands (Kember, 2004). Entwistle and Ramsden (1983) also found that a perceived heavy workload related to a reproduction orientation or surface approach. Other research came to the conclusion that an appropriate perceived workload has a positive significant relationship with a deep approach to learning (e.g. Diseth, Pallesen, Hovland and Larsen, 2006; Lizzio, Wilson and Simons, 2002; Wilson, Lizzio and Ramsden, 1997) and a significantly negative relation to a surface approach to learning (Diseth et al., 2006; Wilson et al., 1997).

Research studies investigating the influence of student-centred learning environments also propose the influence of workload as a possible explanation for their results. The results of Nijhuis et al. (2005) indicate that students' negative perceptions of the high workload of the PBL environment have acted as an inhibiting factor for the expected positive influence of the PBL environment on students' deep learning strategies. In interviews, students have also pointed out that a high workload is a problem associated with student-centred settings. They indicate that a high workload forces them to employ surface learning strategies (Segers et al., 2006; Struyven et al., 2006).

Perceived task complexity

Perceived task complexity was also selected as a variable due to its association with student-centred learning environments. Perkins (1991) states that a constructivist mode of instruction very often requires students to cope with complex situations. He states that the gap between the entry behaviour of the students and what is demanded of them could be too great (Perkins, 1991). A complex task can be seen as a task with multiple paths to a solution and multiple (not necessarily, but possibly equally valuable) solutions. Expertise can help but may not be sufficient and an uncertainty of outcome remains (Glouberman and Zimmerman, 2002; Haerem and Rau, 2007). In higher education an example of a complex assignment is asking students to apply a theoretical model to practice. Theoretical models are rarely found as they are in practice; students always have to choose between several likely correct outcomes, which leave them with an uncertainty about the solutions despite the fact they might have studied the model very well.

Perceived task complexity and objective task complexity are not identical but are strongly related (Campbell, 1988; Mangos and Steele-Johnson, 2001; Maynard and Hakel, 1997). Perceived task complexity is a reaction to task characteristics that may be evoked for reasons other than the task characteristics themselves (Braarud, 2001; Campbell, 1988), such as familiarity with the task, assessed cognitive resources, availability of tools and information (Mangos and Steele-Johnson, 2001). Therefore it is important to consider the subjective task's complexity, the individual's perception of how complex the task is (Braarud, 2001; Mangos and Steele-Johnson, 2001) when studying the influence of task complexity on human performance and behaviour.

Task complexity has been investigated in relation to performance (Campbell, 1988; Haerem and Rau, 2007; Mangos and Steele-Johnson, 2001; Maynard and Hakel, 1997; Salthouse, 1992; Szafran, 2001). Research has identified a main effect of subjective task complexity on performance (Mangos and Steele-Johnson, 2001). Maynard and Hakel (1997) specified this relation as a negative one in that when subjective task complexity increases, the quality of performance decreases. To our knowledge, task complexity has not been taken into account in the research regarding approaches to learning. But former research has shown that approaches to learning are related to qualitative learning outcomes and the performance of students (Trigwell and Prosser, 1991). Moreover, the research study of Stahl, Pieschl and Bromme (2006) showed that students acknowledge task complexity and plan their goals and strategies accordingly. This research project investigates whether student approaches to learning are influenced by the way in which they perceive task complexity.

The student

Motivation

Since the concept of approaches to learning contains a specific intentional component itself, we chose to focus on the more general reasons why students engage in learning-related behaviours or why they are studying a specific course. The focus lies on the quality rather than the quantity of motivation. Therefore we chose to describe motivation for learning from the perspective of the Self Determination Theory (SDT; Ryan and Deci, 2000). SDT has proven to be a very useful framework when looking at the influence of motivation on learning (Deci and Ryan, 2004). SDT researchers are concerned with examining the quality of the learner's motivation; this quality refers to the type or kind of motivation that underlies the behaviour (Vansteenkiste, Lens and Deci, 2006). Traditionally, a distinction between intrinsically and extrinsically motivated learners was made (Gagné and Deci, 2005). An intrinsically motivated learner undertakes learning for its inherent interest and enjoyment. An extrinsically motivated learner engages in learning to attain an outcome that is separable from the learning, like a reward or a good grade for example (Ryan and Deci, 2000; Vansteenkiste et al., 2006). SDT reconceptualised the continuum between extrinsic and intrinsic motivation by differentiating extrinsic motivation into types of regulation that vary in their degree of relative autonomy (Ryan and Deci, 2000; Vansteenkiste, Simons, Lens, Sheldon and Deci, 2004; Vansteenkiste et al., 2006). An important aspect of SDT is the proposition that extrinsic motivation can vary in the degree to which it is internalised (Gagné and Deci, 2005). The primary focus shifted to autonomous motivation versus controlled motivation. Autonomous motivation involves the experience of choice and volition, while controlled motivation involves the experience of being pressured or forced (Vansteenkiste et al., 2006). The research on motivation has concluded that to a certain extent motivation is a variable concept in terms of context and subject areas (Heikkilä and Lonka, 2006).

Both motivation for learning and students' approaches to learning have been widely applied when explaining student learning. In general, results show that autonomously motivated students thrive in educational settings (Deci and Ryan, 2004). More autonomous motivation was associated with more engagement, better performance and higher quality learning (Ryan and Deci, 2000). 'Within SDT, learning is seen as an active process that functions optimally when students' motivation is autonomous (vs. controlled) for engaging in learning activities and assimilating new information' (Vansteenkiste et al., 2004, p. 247). The same was found for deep approaches to learning; a deep approach to learning relates to study success and a high quality of learning outcomes (Trigwell and Prosser, 1991).

Working memory capacity

The working memory capacity of a person is in general described as the ability to process and maintain information while performing another task or being distracted (Conway et al., 2005; Jarrold and Towse, 2006). 'Working memory measures capture individuals' ability to combine maintenance and processing demands in a manner that limits information loss from forgetting or distraction' (Jarrold and Towse, 2006, p. 39). For example, the ability to remember your grocery list while talking on the phone to a colleague. It is a system for processing and storing information during cognitive tasks. It differs from short-term memory that refers only to short-term storage (Conway et al., 2005). Working memory has a limited capacity and is crucial in information processing.

Working memory capacity has been shown to be a good predictor of academic achievement (e.g. Grimley and Banner, 2008; Lehto, 1995; Riccio, Lee, Romine, Cash and Davis, 2002). Research in the area of learning disabilities has indicated that working memory processes underlie individual differences in learning ability (Swanson, Cochran and Ewers, 1990). Moreover, working memory capacity has been shown to influence the strategy selection of students; students with high working memory capacity tend to use more resource-demanding strategies than low working memory capacity individuals (e.g. Beilock and DeCaro, 2007; Hinze, Bunting and Pellegrino, 2009).

Attention

The conceptualisation of attention that was used throughout this research project has its roots in the research by Posner and Petersen (1990). In general, attention can be described as a cognitive process of selectively concentrating on one aspect of the environment while ignoring other aspects. However, human cognitive capacities are limited in their ability to process information simultaneously (Gazzaniga, Ivry and Mangun, 2002). A shifting of attention allows us to redirect our attention to other aspects of the environment we wish to focus on. A prominent theory in attention research that has attempted to explain how attention shifts is the moving-spotlight analogy. The primary idea is that attention is like a movable spotlight that is directed towards the intended targets, focusing on each target in a serial manner. When information is illuminated by the spotlight, hence attended to, processing proceeds in a more efficient manner (LaBerge, Carlson, Williams and Bunney, 1997; Sperling and Weichselgartner, 1995). Posner and Petersen (1990) proposed that attention can be further broken down into three networks. These three attentional networks have been defined in anatomical and functional terms (Fan, McCandliss, Sommer, Raz and Posner, 2002). The alerting network carries out the function of achieving and maintaining an alert state, the orienting network is responsible for the selection of information from sensory input and the executive control is defined as resolving conflict among responses (Fan et al., 2002). The executive control is responsible for the 'shifts' of the focus of attention. The efficiency of these three networks can be quantified by reaction time measures (Fan et al., 2002).

Earlier research found that attention is positively related to academic performance (Fernandez-Castillo and Gutiérrez-Rojas, 2009; Gsanger, Wa, Homack, Siekierski and Riccio, 2002; Riccio et al., 2002) and that attention problems contribute negatively to academic achievement (Jimmerson, Dubrow, Adam, Gunnar and Bozoky, 2006). The close relationship between working memory capacity and attention, particularly executive attention, and the relationship between attention and academic performance made it useful and conceptually important to add attention to this research study. Both attention and working memory capacity are considered to be relatively stable traits (Klein and Fiss, 1999).

Methodology

For the purpose of this book chapter we will only briefly present the methodology of the empirical studies included in this research project. Two quasi-experimental studies were set up to collect the data. For the details concerning the research design, instruments and analyses, we refer to the articles that were published based on this research project (Kyndt, Cascallar and Dochy, 2012; Kyndt, Dochy, Cascallar and Struyven, 2011; Kyndt, Dochy, Struyven and Cascallar, 2011, 2012).

Study I

During the academic year 2008–2009 the first study took place. The experiment was set up within the framework of the university course 'Theory and practice of group work', which is a mandatory course for all second year bachelor students in educational sciences. During the pretest students' working memory capacity and attention, their motivation to study the course and their 'typical' approaches to learning (based on their experiences in the first year of the bachelor programme) were measured. After an introduction with the theoretical content of the course given in five lectures, students were administered four assignments. Each assignment represented one research condition. The four research conditions investigated were: high workload–high task complexity, high workload–low task complexity, low workload–high task complexity, and low workload–low task complexity. A detailed description of the manipulation check is presented in Kyndt, Dochy, Struyven and Cascallar (2011). After each assignment (also 'research condition') students were asked to complete a post-test that measured their perceived workload, perceived task complexity and their approaches to learning when completing that specific assignment. Complete data were collected from 128 students. To control the effect of gradually implemented conditions or cross-over effects on the one hand and the effect of the content on the other hand, the group was divided into two subgroups, groups A and B. Each group received the same four assignments regarding content and type of task, but group A had a different order of research conditions than group B (see Table 13.1). Students were randomly assigned to groups A or B.

Study 2

During the next academic year a second smaller study was conducted. The second study was conducted to take a closer look at some of the relationships found in the first study, and had a similar design. It was also conducted within the framework of the same university course, 'Theory and practice of group work', in the second bachelor year of educational sciences. Students that needed to repeat the course were excluded from the research. As in the previous year, students attended five lectures to introduce them to the theory after completing the same pretest (as in study 1) that measured their working memory capacity, attention, motivation and 'typical' approaches to learning. However, during this second year the variable task complexity was excluded

Table 13.1 Overview sequences studies

Study 1		Study 2
Group A (n = 64)	Group B (n = 64)	All students (n =108)
Prior knowledge test Introduction theory: 5 lectures + 2 day practical Pretest: E-prime ANT and Aospan, R-SPQ-2F and SRQ		
Assignment 1 Low WL and low TC	Assignment 1 High WL and high TC	Assignment 1 Low workload
Assignment 2 High WL and low TC	Assignment 2 Low WL and high TC	Assignment 2 High workload
Assignment 3 Low WL and high TC	Assignment 3 High WL and low TC	
Assignment 4 High WL and high TC	Assignment 4 Low WL and low TC	
Post-test after each assignment = R-SPQ-2F, NASA-TLX and Subjective complexity questionnaire		Post-test after each assignment = R-SPQ-2F, NASA-TLX, Appropriate workload scale CEQ
Focus group + individual interviews		

Notes: ANT = Attention Network Test; Aospan = Automated Operation Span Task; R-SPQ-2F = revised two factor study process questionnaire; SRQ = Self-Regulation Questionnaire; WL = workload; TC = task complexity; NASA-TLX = National Aeronautics and Space Administration Task Load Index; CEQ = Course Experience Questionnaire.

and the focus was directed towards the influence of workload because of the fact that it was very difficult for students to distinguish between the task complexity and workload of an assignment. We will elaborate on this observation based on the first study in the section concerning the findings of this research. During the second experiment, students were given two assignments; one with a high workload and one with a low workload. After each assignment they completed a post-test that measured their perceived workload and approaches to learning when completing that specific assignment. In total 108 students participated in this second study.

One of the core characteristics of the first study is that the relationships between students' approaches to learning and the perceived workload, perceived task complexity, motivation, working memory capacity and attention, were investigated under different experimentally manipulated conditions in terms of workload and task complexity. In the second study, students' perceptions were used to check the implementation of high and low workload (see Kyndt, Dochy, Struyven and Cascallar, 2012), and these conditions were compared to each other. Our findings focus on the interplay between the 'induced' context in terms of workload and task complexity, the students' reactions to this contexts and how this relates to their personal characteristics. We will describe which relationships are similar and which relationships differ across the different research conditions.

Instruments

In both studies (see also Table 13.1) students' approaches to learning were measured by means of the R-SPQ-2F questionnaire (Biggs et al., 2001). The perceived workload of the task was measured by means of an adapted version of the National Aeronautics and Space Administration Task Load Index (NASA-TLX) questionnaire (Braarud, 2001; Hart and Staveland, 1988). The perception of task complexity was measured by a newly developed questionnaire. The task complexity index developed by Braarud (2001) was used as starting point for the construction of our questionnaire. Motivation for learning was measured by means of an adapted version of the Self-Regulation Questionnaire (SRQ) (Ryan and Connell, 1989). Students' cognitive capacities were assessed by means of automatised computer tests. Working memory capacity was assessed by the use of the 'Automated Operation Span Task' (Aospan; Unsworth, Heitz, Schrock and Engle, 2005). Attention was measured using the 'Attention Network Test' (ANT; Fan et al., 2002). In study 2, the subjective task complexity questionnaire was replaced by the appropriate workload scale from the Course Experience Questionnaire (CEQ) (Ramsden, 1991).

Key findings of the research project

As mentioned before, this book chapter will focus on the findings that can be derived from the entire research project, rather than formulating specific research questions and specifying their answers. For these specific research questions we also refer the reader to the published articles. Within this chapter, we have the opportunity to report on the entire research project, which offers us the opportunity to integrate the results and draw novel conclusions across the entire research project in comparison with the different separate empirical studies.

Task complexity and motivation

When starting our analyses, one of the first findings was that task complexity collapsed into three factors: a lack of information, familiarity and the possibility of having multiple correct solutions. The factor analysis on our newly developed questionnaire identified these three components. A lack of information pertains to the perception of students that they did not have enough information (content and practical arrangements) to solve the assignment. The items that constituted the factor 'familiarity' asked if students already had experience with the content or type of assignment at hand. The final factor focused on the perception of students with regard to the fact that the assignment had multiple correct solutions.

It was expected that assignments with multiple possible solutions would encourage students to apply a deep approach to learning because a critical examination of these solutions would be appropriate. However, the results showed that this factor was not related to students' approaches to learning. Concerning a lack of information, the results were clear: a *lack of information* influenced students' approaches to learning in an undesirable way. It consistently increased students' surface approaches to learning regardless of the fact that workload and task complexity were higher or lower. Moreover, when both workload and task complexity were high or both were low, a lack of information also decreased students' deep approaches to learning. The less information students had access to, the more likely they are of adopting surface approaches and the less prevalent a deep approach will be.

In addition to being a discouraging factor, the influence of lack of information was mediated by the influence of *motivation*. It was found that autonomously motivated students experience a lesser influence of lack of information than their colleagues who are less autonomously motivated. It can be concluded that the negative impact of a lack of information was weaker for autonomously motivated students. This was a first finding that points towards the fact that approaches to learning are influenced by the interplay between student and context. Different students constituted by certain different characteristics, experienced and reacted differently to the same objective context as all students received the same assignments.

This autonomous motivation did not only influence students' approaches to learning in an indirect manner. It also contributed positively to students' utilising deep approaches to learning in a direct way (see Figure 13.1). The more autonomously motivated students were, the higher their deep approaches to learning were. However, this relationship was only significant in the two research conditions where workload was induced to be high. Apparently a certain threshold needs to be exceeded before students' use of deep approaches benefited from their autonomous motivation.

Familiarity

Regarding *familiarity*, this research found that it had a different influence on students' approaches to learning under different conditions. When workload and task complexity were low, familiarity increased students' surface approaches to learning; while when workload and task complexity were high, familiarity increased students' deep approaches to learning. These findings provided an explanation for the results of prior research that found that a student-centred learning environment increased students' surface approaches to learning. Students in general perceived these student-centred learning environments as having a high workload and high

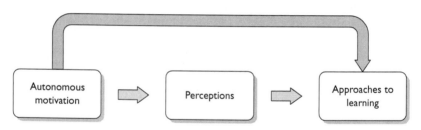

Figure 13.1 Direct and indirect relationship of autonomous motivation

task complexity (Hung, 2009; Perkins, 1991; Struyven et al., 2006). Moreover, these learning environments were investigated with students who experienced this new learning environment for the first time, which led to an unfamiliar situation for these students. This could have contributed to the fact that these learning environments did not enhance students' deep approaches to learning. A possible hypothesis for the differential influence of familiarity on students' approaches to learning is that familiarity plays a role in keeping a balance between challenging and 'overwhelming' students. On the one hand, when an assignment is not challenging enough, familiarity contributes even more to the lack of challenge leading to the fact that students might find it unnecessary to approach the material in a deep manner. While on the other hand, familiarity with a highly challenging assignment might help the student to feel confident enough to approach the assignment in a deep manner without feeling overwhelmed.

Cognitive capacities

The cognitive variables were introduced in this research project in order to be able to make a contribution to the 'state versus trait debate' and the issue of a limited variability of students' approaches to learning. The expectation concerning the relationships between working memory capacity and attention on the one hand and students' approaches to learning on the other hand were based on the *compensation hypothesis* of Chamorro-Premuzic and Arteche (2008). This hypothesis stated 'individuals who are quicker, more efficient, abstract thinkers (basically those capable of learning new things faster) are lower in achievement striving, order, and self-discipline' (Chamorro-Premuzic and Arteche, 2008, p. 570). Applied to the current research project, expectations were that students with high cognitive capacities would be less inclined to use deep approaches to learning because of its association with higher quality learning outcomes that could be considered as achievement striving. Based on the data of the first study, it was found that attention is negatively related to a deep approach and that having a higher working memory capacity showed a tendency towards adopting less deep approaches. These two findings seemed to support the compensation hypothesis. Unfortunately results were less clear-cut than that: working memory capacity was also found to be associated with less surface approaches to learning. Students with high cognitive capacities scored lower on both approaches to learning. Moreover, the relations of working memory capacity with students' approaches to learning as such were not confirmed by the data derived from the second study.

Student profiles

To explain these contradictory results, we argued that motivation could play an important role within the compensation hypothesis. We were able to confirm this statement based on the second study. By means of cluster analysis student profiles were constructed based on students' motivation and working memory capacities. The results yielded three clusters: students in cluster 1 are characterised by high working memory capacity. Regarding motivation, the mean scores are less extreme. On average, their autonomous motivation is higher than their controlled motivation. We will refer to this cluster as students with a high working memory capacity and average motivation. Cluster 2 has a low mean score for working memory capacity. These students also demonstrate average scores on both autonomous and controlled motivation. The third and final cluster demonstrates a working memory capacity that is comparable to the average of the entire sample. Students in cluster 3 are characterised by a high autonomous motivation and low controlled motivation (Table 13.2).

Regarding the role of motivation within the compensation hypothesis, our results showed that student profiles characterised by high working memory capacity and average motivation used more surface approaches to learning than their colleagues who had a distinct autonomous motivation. In addition to a profile characterised by high working memory capacity and a profile with obvious autonomous motivation, a profile characterised by a low working memory capacity and average motivation was also identified. Students who were characterised by obvious autonomous motivation applied more deep approaches than those students with profiles characterised by average motivation and high or low working memory capacity.

The relationship between stable student characteristics (working memory capacity and attention) and students' approaches to learning were a first indication that the variability of students' approaches to learning could indeed be

Table 13.2 Student profiles

	Cluster 1	Cluster 2	Cluster 3
Working memory capacity	High	Low	Average
Autonomous motivation	Average	Average	High
Controlled motivation	Average	Average	Low
Number of participants (Percentage of total N = 108)	36 (33.33%)	32 (29.63%)	35 (32.41%)

limited. Based on the identification of the above described student profiles (study 2) this issue was further explored. It was investigated whether the different identified *student profiles* (described above) were influenced in a different way by workload. For example, if some student profiles do not adapt their learning approaches due to higher or lower workload and others' profiles do. It was found that all of the student profiles were influenced by workload in the same direction; however, the differences between groups remained: autonomously motivated students consistently used more deep approaches to learning. These results did not confirm the results of Nijhuis et al. (2008) who found that the variability in learning approaches was related to the variability in the perception of workload. However, the constant differences between the groups under the influence of workload in this research does seem to indicate that student characteristics, especially a combination of them, can create a certain predisposition towards an approach to learning as was suggested by Biggs (1993).

Our results showed that high working memory capacity students use more surface approaches. A possible explanation is that their high capacity enables them to remain successful within the educational system although they are using an approach to learning that generally does not lead towards understanding the material. These students remain successful since they are very good in acquiring, processing and maintaining the materials they are studying (Conway et al., 2005). This statement was also supported by the finding that students with low working memory capacity and average motivation in general used less deep approaches than autonomously motivated students. In addition, they used as much deep approaches as their colleagues with high working memory capacity. However, when workload was induced to be high they used less surface approaches than the students with high working memory capacity. These low working memory capacity students probably failed when attempting to memorise everything, making them less successful (e.g. Gathercole, Pickering, Knight and Stegmann, 2004; Lehto, 1995; Riding, Grimley, Dahraei and Banner, 2003) and causing them to use alternative strategies and approaches.

Workload

The results regarding the influence of *workload* were not in line with the expectations. It was found that workload (perceived and induced) influenced students' deep approaches to learning in a positive way; however, the relationship was only significant in the condition that was created to induce a low workload and high task complexity. It was argued that this could be explained by the fact that there are two sides to perceived workload (Nijhuis et al., 2008). On the one hand you have the quantitative aspect of workload; this is for example the amount of literature, the hours spend on the assignment, the amount of required output, etc. When operationalising the workload conditions in the first study, the focus was on these aspects of workload. On the other hand, there is also the quality of workload which is linked to difficulty, stress, and resources coming from the students' prior knowledge, study habits and learning skills (Karjalainen et al., 2006). It is expected that the quantitative aspects of workload will encourage surface approaches to learning, while the qualitative aspects of workload have the potential to challenge students and give them a feeling of fulfilment, leading to the use of more deep approaches to learning. In this regard, a possible explanation for this result could be that the low workload and high complexity condition reflects a situation with low quantitative workload and high qualitative workload, hence the positive relationship between workload and deep approaches to learning under this condition that comes to the fore.

In the second study it was also found that students' deep approaches to learning were higher when workload was high. In addition to the statement about quantitative and qualitative workload, the high workload assignment could have been more interesting to students than the low workload assignment. The low workload assignment was theoretical and based on literature; while the high workload assignment required students to go into the actual practice they aspire to work in after graduation. This interest could have had a positive effect on their deep approaches regardless of the higher workload. Prior research has shown that interest is an important predictor for intrinsic motivation (Bye, Pushkar and Conway, 2007) and this research has shown that autonomous motivation contributes to students' deep approaches to learning, especially when workload is high.

Workload and task complexity

In this research, *workload* and *task complexity* were defined and operationalised as two different variables. However, our results in general but particularly the results on the influence of workload, have given rise to the question as to how separate these constructs actually are. A certain overlap seems to exist; when defining qualitative workload it is not unreasonable to argue that task complexity could be one of the factors influencing or constructing this perceived qualitative workload. However, if this is the case, can we then still say that qualitative workload should be defined as workload? It appeared that for students it was very difficult to distinguish between both concepts, especially in the mixed conditions; however, results seemed to indicate that both characteristics have different influences. A critical reflection and study about what constitutes and distinguishes perceived workload and task complexity not only in theory but also in the experience of students would benefit from carefully designed future research.

Future research

The findings of this research project confirm that students' approaches to learning result from an interaction between the context and the student and are therefore not to be considered as a stable trait (Marton and Säljö, 1997). In addition, the results also support the hypothesis that although these approaches are variable across contexts and subject areas, this variability seems to be limited (e.g. Nijhuis et al., 2008; Vermetten et al., 2002). More specifically these results indicate that students might have a predisposition towards a certain approach to learning (Biggs, 1993; Wilson and Fowler, 2005) and that their characteristics (i.e. motivation and cognitive capacities) are related to this predisposition. In addition, these characteristics are associated with how students perceive the learning environment and how they respond to it. When trying to induce deep approaches in students, for example by means of student-centred learning environments, it is important to bear this interplay between context and student in mind. When changing a learning environment in terms of workload and task complexity it is important to simultaneously consider the capacities of the student and to try to encourage their autonomous motivation by reinforcing their interest in the subject.

The main future research that we would like to propose is to focus more on what is happening at the individual level rather than the group level. Different individuals perceive and respond differently to the same learning environment. This is not a new research finding; prior researchers have stated that students' approaches to learning are primarily influenced by the students' perceptions of the context in comparison with the objective context (Hounsell, 1984; Laurillard, 1984; Prosser and Trigwell, 1999; Ramsden, 1992; Sadlo and Richardson, 2003). In addition, Kember (2004) for example found that objective workload only explained 4 per cent of the variance of perceived workload, which exemplifies that the objective learning context and perceived learning context can differ considerably. Future research could investigate more in depth why students' perceptions can differ so extensively and whether these differences can be related to the personal characteristics of students.

In the findings of this research project, students' thresholds seemed to play an important role for some influences to actually have an impact. For example, in the first study motivation was only significantly related to students' approaches to learning when workload was high. Future research is needed to determine what shapes students' thresholds, if it is necessary to change them and how this can be done. This research project also investigated different student profiles based on a combination of motivation and working memory capacity. Investigating both stable student characteristics and flexible or variable student characteristics offers the possibility to discover which students have more flexible students' approaches to learning and which students are more sensitive to the learning context. For example, we would expect that students with less obvious stable capacities would be more sensitive to the learning context, because they are less predetermined by these stable cognitive capacities. Future research can investigate whether this hypothesis is accurate and which other variables might be determining the flexibility and sensitivity of students in various learning environments.

In conclusion, we believe that a person-centred methodology provides the possibility to investigate the interplay between student and context. The main goal of this person-centred approach of analysing (e.g. cluster analysis) is to categorise individuals into groups whose members have similar profiles (Vansteenkiste, Sierens, Soenens, Luyckx and Lens, 2009). This person-centred approach is likely to yield more diagnostic and detailed information than the variable-centred approach, because it allows an examination of the additive or interactive effect of several variables (Vansteenkiste et al., 2009). It offers the possibility to explore which variables are important to consider when constructing student profiles. In addition, it can be investigated whether different student profiles are influenced differently by different contextual variables. Especially for the variables where the results of prior research (examining the group level) have not been univocal (e.g. influence of assessment and teaching methods or learning environments in general) this approach could yield interesting results (Segers et al., 2006; Struyven et al., 2006). Investigating student profiles can deepen our insight into students' approaches to learning, so that learning environments can be designed in a way that they enhance student learning for students with potentially different profiles.

References

Baert, H. (2002) 'Spanningsvelden in het discours van de officiële verklaringen over levenslang leren [Tension fields in the discourse of official statements on lifelong learning]', in H. Baert, L. Dekeyser and G. Sterck (Eds.), *Levenslang leren en de actieve welvaartstaat* [*Lifelong learning and the active welfare state*], Leuven: Acco.

Baeten, M., Kyndt, E., Struyven, K. and Dochy, F. (2010) 'Using student-centred learning environments to stimulate deep approaches to learning: Factors encouraging or discouraging their effectiveness', *Educational Research Review*, 5: 243–260.

Beck, K. and Achtenhagen, F. (2007) *Vocational education and training in a globalized world*, Göttingen: Georg-August-Universität Göttingen.

Beilock, S.L. and DeCaro, M.S. (2007) 'From poor performance to success under stress: Working memory, strategy selection, and mathematical problem solving under pressure', *Journal of Experimental Psychology: Learning, Memory, and Cognition*, 33: 983–998.

Biggs, J. (1993) 'What do inventories of students' learning processes really measure? A theoretical review and clarification', *British Journal of Educational Psychology*, 63: 3–19.

Biggs, J. (2001) 'Enhancing learning: A matter of style or approach?', in R.J. Sternberg and L. Zhang (Eds.), *Perspectives on thinking, learning, and cognitive styles*, Mahwah, NJ: Lawrence Erlbaum Associates.

Biggs, J., Kember, D. and Leung, D.Y.P. (2001) 'The revised two-factor study process questionnaire: R-SPQ-2F', *British Journal of Educational Psychology*, 71: 133–149.

Boyatzis, R.E., Stubbs, E.C. and Taylor, S.N. (2002) 'Learning cognitive and emotional intelligence competences through graduate management education', *Academy of Management Journal on Learning and Education*, 1: 150–162.

Braarud, P. (2001) 'Subjective task complexity and subjective workload: Criterion validity for complex team tasks', *International Journal of Cognitive Ergonomics*, 5: 261–273.

Brooks, R. and Everett, G. (2008) 'The impact of higher education on lifelong learning', *International Journal of Lifelong Education*, 27: 239–254.

Byc, D., Pushkar, D. and Conway, M. (2007) 'Motivation, interest and positive affect in traditional and non-traditional undergraduate students', *Adult Education Quarterly*, 57: 141–158.

Campbell, D.J. (1988) 'Task complexity: A review and analysis', *Academy of Management Review*, 13: 40–52.

Chamorro-Premuzic, T. and Arteche, A. (2008) 'Intellectual competence and academic performance: Preliminary validation of a model', *Intelligence*, 36: 564–573.

Conway, A.R.A., Kane, M.J., Bunting, M.F., Hambrick, D.Z., Wilhelm, O. and Engle, R.W. (2005) 'Working memory span tasks: A methodological review and user's guide', *Psychonomic Bulletin and Review*, 12: 769–786.

Deci, E.L. and Ryan, R.M. (2004) *Handbook of self-determination research*, Rochester, NY: University of Rochester Press.

Decuyper, S., Dochy, F. and Van den Bossche, P. (2010) 'Grasping the dynamic complexity of team learning: An integrative model for effective team learning in organisations', *Educational Research Review*, 5: 111–133.

Dekeyser, L. and Baert, H. (1999) *Projectonderwijs: Leren en werken in groep [Project based education: Learning and working in group]*, Leuven: Acco.

Diseth, A., Pallesen, S., Hovland, A. and Larsen, S. (2006) 'Course experiences, approaches to learning and academic achievement', *Education and Training*, 48: 156–169.

Dochy, F., Segers, M., Gijbels, D. and Van den Bossche, P. (2002) *Studentgericht onderwijs and probleemgestuurd onderwijs. Betekenis, achtergronden en effecten*, Utrecht: Lemma.

Dochy, F., Segers, M., Van den Bossche, P. and Gijbels, D. (2003) 'Effects of problem-based learning: A meta-analysis', *Learning and Instruction*, 13: 533–568.

Ellis, R., Marcus, G. and Taylor, R. (2005) 'Learning through inquiry: Student difficulties with online course-based material', *Journal of Computer Assisted Learning*, 21: 239–252.

Entwistle, N., McCune, V. and Walker, P. (2001) 'Conceptions, styles, and approaches within higher education: analytical abstractions and everyday experience', in R.J. Sternberg and L.-F. Zhang (Eds.), *Perspectives on cognitive, learning and thinking styles* (pp. 103–136), Mahwah, NJ: Lawrence Erlbaum Associates.

Entwistle, N.J. and Ramsden, P. (1983) *Understanding student learning*, London: Croom Helm.

Fan, J., McCandliss, B.D., Sommer, T., Raz, A. and Posner, M.I. (2002) 'Testing the efficiency and independence of attentional networks', *Journal of Cognitive Neuroscience*, 14: 340–347.

Fernandez-Castillo, A. and Gutiérrez-Rojas, M.E. (2009) 'Selective attention, anxiety, depressive symptomatology and academic performance in adolescents', *Electronic Journal of Research in Educational Psychology*, 7: 49–76.

Fitzgerald, R., Taylor, R. and LaValle, I. (2003) *National Adult Learning Survey 2002 [Research report 415]*, London: Department for Education and Skills.

Gagné, M. and Deci, E.L. (2005) 'Self-determination theory and work motivation', *Journal of Organizational Behavior*, 26: 331–362.

Gathercole, S.E., Pickering, S.J., Knight, C. and Stegmann, Z. (2004) 'Working memory skills and educational attainment: Evidence from national curriculum assessments at 7 and 14 years of age', *Applied Cognitive Psychology*, 18: 1–16.

Gazzaniga, M., Ivry, R. and Mangun, G. (2002) *Cognitive neuroscience: The biology of the mind* (2nd ed.), New York: W.W. Norton

Gibbs, G. (1992) *Improving the quality of student learning*, Bristol, UK: Technical and Education Services.

Gijbels, D., Van de Watering, G., Dochy, F. and Van den Bossche, P. (2005) 'The relationship between students' approaches to learning and the assessment of learning outcomes', *European Journal of Psychology of Education*, 20: 327–341.

Glouberman, S. and Zimmerman, B. (2002) *Complicated and complex systems: What would successful reform of Medicare look like?* Discussion Paper, Commission on the Future of Health Care in Canada. Available http://www.healthandeverything.org/files/Glouberman_E.pdf (accessed 4 January 2008).

Grimley, M. and Banner, G. (2008) 'Working memory, cognitive style, and behavioural predictors of GCSE exam success', *Educational Psychology*, 28: 341–351.

Gsanger, K., Wa, S., Homack, S., Siekierski, B. and Riccio, C. (2002) 'The relation of memory and attention to academic achievement in children', *Archives of Clinical Neuropsychology*, 17: 790.

Haerem, T. and Rau, D. (2007) 'The influence of degree of expertise and objective task complexity on perceived task complexity and performance', *Journal of Applied Psychology*, 92: 1320–1331.

Hannafin, M., Hill, J. and Land, S. (1997) 'Student-centered learning and interactive multimedia: Status, issues, and implications', *Contemporary Education*, 68: 94–99.

Hart, S.G. and Staveland, L.E. (1988) 'Development of NASA-TLX (Task Load Index): Results of empirical and theoretical research', in P.A. Hancock and N. Meshkati (Eds.), *Human mental workload*, Amsterdam: North-Holland.

Heikkilä, A. and Lonka, K. (2006) 'Studying in higher education: Students' approaches to learning, self-regulation, and cognitive strategies', *Studies in Higher Education*, 31: 99–117.

Herington, C. and Weaven, S. (2008) 'Action research and reflection on student approaches to learning in large first year university classes', *The Australian Educational Researcher*, 35: 111–134.

Hinze, S.R., Bunting, M.F. and Pellegrino, J.W. (2009) 'Strategy selection for cognitive skill acquisition depends on task demands and working memory capacity', *Learning and Individual Differences*, 19, 590–595.

Hounsell, D. (1984) 'Learning and essay-writing', in F. Marton, D. Hounsell and N. Entwistle (Eds.), *The experience of learning: Implications for teaching and studying in higher education*, Edinburgh: Scottish Academic Press.

Hung, W. (2009) 'The 9-step problem design process for problem-based learning: Application of the 3C3R model', *Educational Research Review*, 4: 118–141.

Jarrold, C. and Towse, J.N. (2006) 'Individual differences in working memory', *Neuroscience*, 139: 39–50.

Jimmerson, S.R., Dubrow, E.H., Adam, E., Gunnar, M. and Bozoky, I.K. (2006) 'Associations among academic achievement, attention, and andrenocortical reactivity in Caribbean village children', *Canadian Journal of School Psychology*, 21: 120–138.

Karjalainen, A., Alha, K. and Jutila, S. (2006) *Give me time to think: Determining student workload in higher education*, Oulu: Oulu University Press.

Kember, D. (2004). 'Interpreting student workload and the factors which shape students' perceptions of their workload', *Studies in Higher Education*, 29(2), 165–184.

Kember, D., Charlesworth, M., Davies, H., MacKay, J. and Stott, V. (1997), 'Evaluating the effectiveness of educational innovations: Using the study process questionnaire to show that meaningful learning occurs', *Studies in Educational Evaluation*, 23: 141–157.

Kember, D. and Leung, D. (1998) 'Influences upon students' perceptions of workload', *Educational Psychology*, 18: 293–307.

Kember, D. and Leung, D. (2006) 'Characterising a teaching and learning environment conducive to making demands on students while not making their workload excessive', *Studies in Higher Education*, 23: 185–198.

Klein, K. and Fiss, W.H. (1999) 'The reliability and stability of the Turner and Engle working memory task', *Behavior Research Methods, Instruments and Computers*, 31: 429–432.

Kyndt, E., Cascallar, E. and Dochy, F. (2012) 'Individual differences in working memory capacity and attention, and their relationship with students' approaches to learning', *Higher Education*, 64: 285–297.

Kyndt, E., Dochy, F., Cascallar, E. and Struyven, K. (2011) 'The direct and indirect effect of motivation for learning on students' approaches to learning through the perceptions of workload and task complexity', *Higher Education Research and Development*, 30: 135–150.

Kyndt, E., Dochy, F., Michielsen, M. and Moeyaert, B. (2009) 'Employee retention: Organisational and personal perspectives', *Vocations and Learning*, 2: 195–215.

Kyndt, E., Dochy, F., Struyven, K. and Cascallar, E. (2011) 'The perception of workload and task complexity and its influence on students' approaches to learning', *European Journal of Psychology of Education*, 26: 393–415.

Kyndt, E., Dochy, F., Struyven, K. and Cascallar, E. (2012) 'Looking at learning approaches form the angle of student profiles', *Educational Psychology*, 32: 493–513.

Kyndt, E., Michielsen, M., Van Nooten, L., Nijs, S. and Baert, H. (2011). 'Learning in the second half of the career: Stimulating and prohibiting reasons for participation in formal learning activities', *International Journal of Lifelong Education*, 30: 679–697.

LaBerge, D., Carlson, R.L., Williams, J.K. and Bunney, B.G. (1997) 'Shifting attention in visual space: Tests of moving-spotlight models versus an activity-distribution model', *Journal of Experimental Psychology: Human Perception and Performance*, 23: 1380–1392.

Laurillard, D. (1984) 'Learning from problem-solving', in F. Marton, D. Hounsell and N. Entwistle (Eds.), *The experience of learning*, Edinburgh: Scottish Academic Press.

Lea, S., Stephenson, D. and Troy, J. (2003) 'Higher education students' attitudes to student-centred learning: Beyond "educational boulimia"?', *Studies in Higher Education*, 28: 321–334.

Lehto, J. (1995) 'Working memory and school achievement in the ninth form', *Educational Psychology*, 15: 271–283.

Lizzio, A., Wilson, K. and Simons, R. (2002) 'University students' perceptions of the learning environment and academic outcomes: Implications for theory and practice', *Studies in Higher Education*, 27: 27–52.

Mangos, P.M. and Steele-Johnson, D. (2001) 'The role of subjective task complexity in goal orientation, self-efficacy, and performance relations', *Human Performance*, 14: 169–186.

Marton, F. and Säljö, R. (1976) 'On qualitative differences in learning: I. Outcome and process', *British Journal of Educational Psychology*, 46: 4–11.

Marton, F. and Säljö, R. (1997) 'Approaches to learning', in F. Marton, D. Hounsell and N. Entwistle (Eds.), *The experience of learning: Implications for teaching and studying in higher education* (2nd ed.), Edinburgh: Scottish Academic Press.

Marton, F., Watkins, D. and Tang, C. (1997) 'Discontinuities and continuities in the experience of learning: An interview study of high-school students in Hong Kong', *Learning and Instruction*, 7: 21–48.

Mayer, R. (2004) 'Should there be a three-strikes rule against pure discovery learning? The case for guided methods of instruction', *American Psychologist*, 59: 14–19.

Maynard, D.C. and Hakel, M.D. (1997) 'Effects of objective and subjective task complexity on performance', *Human Performance*, 10: 303–330.

McParland, M., Noble, L. and Livingston, G. (2004) 'The effectiveness of problem-based learning compared to traditional teaching in undergraduate psychiatry', *Medical Education*, 38: 859–867.

Neilsen, A.C. (2000) *Employer satisfaction with graduate skills: Research report. evaluations and investigation programme*, Canberra: DETYA, Higher Education Division.

Nijhuis, J., Segers, M. and Gijselaers, W. (2005) 'Influence of redesigning a learning environment on student perceptions and learning strategies', *Learning Environments Research*, 8: 67–93.

Nijhuis, J., Segers, M. and Gijselaers, W. (2008) 'The extent of variability in learning strategies and students' perceptions of the learning environment', *Learning and Instruction*, 18: 121–134.

Papinczak, T., Young, L., Groves, M. and Haynes, M. (2008) 'Effects of a metacognitive intervention on students' approaches to learning and self-efficacy in a first year medical course', *Advances in Health Sciences Education*, 13: 213–232.

Perkins, D.N. (1991) 'What constructivism demands of the learner', *Educational Technology*, 31: 19–21.

Pillay, H., Boulton-Lewis, G. and Wilss, L. (2003) 'Conceptions of work and learning at work: Impressions from older workers', *Studies in Continuing Education*, 25: 95–112.

Posner, M.I. and Petersen, S.E. (1990) 'The attention systems of the human brain', *Annual Review of Neuroscience*, 13: 25–42.

Prosser, M. and Trigwell, K. (1999) *Understanding learning and teaching: The experience in higher education*, Buckingham, UK: The Society for Research into Higher Education.

Ramsden, P. (1991) 'A performance indicator of teaching quality in higher education: The course experience questionnaire', *Studies in Higher Education*, 16: 129–150.

Ramsden, P. (1992) *Learning to teach in higher education*, London: Kogan Page.

Riccio, C.A., Lee, D., Romine, C., Cash, D. and Davis, B. (2002) 'Relation of memory and attention to academic achievement in adults', *Archives of Clinical Neuropsychology*, 18: 755–756.

Riding, R.J., Grimley, M., Dahraei, H. and Banner, G. (2003) 'Cognitive style, working memory and learning behaviour and attainment in school subjects', *British Journal of Educational Psychology*, 73: 749–769.

Ryan, R.M. and Connell, J.P. (1989), 'Perceived locus of causality and internalization: Examining reasons for acting in two domains', *Journal of Personality and Social Psychology*, 57: 749–761.

Ryan, R.M. and Deci, E.L. (2000) 'Self-determination theory and the facilitation of intrinsic motivation, social development, and well-being', *American Psychologist*, 55: 68–78.

Sadlo, G. and Richardson, J. (2003) 'Approaches to studying and perceptions of the academic environment in students following problem-based and subject based curricula', *Higher Education Research and Development*, 22: 253–274.

Salthouse, T.A. (1992) 'Why do adult age differences increase with task complexity?', *Developmental Psychology*, 28: 905–918.

Sand-Jecklin, K. (2007) 'The impact of active/cooperative instruction on beginning nursing student learning strategy preference', *Nurse Education Today*, 27: 474–480.

Segers, M., Nijhuis, J. and Gijselaers, W. (2006) 'Redesigning a learning and assessment environment: The influence on students' perceptions of assessment demands and their learning strategies', *Studies in Educational Evaluation*, 32: 223–242.

Slavin, R.E. (1995) *Cooperative learning: Theory, research, and practice* (2nd ed.), Englewood Cliffs, NJ: Prentice Hall.

Sperling, G. and Weichselgartner, E. (1995) 'Episodic theory of the dynamics of spatial attention', *Psychological Review*, 102: 503–532.

Stahl, E., Pieschl, S. and Bromme, R. (2006) 'Task complexity, epistemological beliefs and metacognitive calibration: An exploratory study', *Journal of Educational Computing Research*, 35: 319–338.

Struyven, K., Dochy, F., Janssens, S. and Gielen, S. (2006) 'On the dynamics of students' approaches to learning: The effects of the teaching/learning environment', *Learning and Instruction*, 16: 279–294.

Swanson, H.L., Cochran, K.F. and Ewers, C.A. (1990) 'Can learning disabilities be determined from working memory performance?', *Journal of Learning Disabilities*, 23: 59–67.

Szafran, R.F. (2001) 'The effect of academic load on success for new college students: Is lighter better?', *Research in Higher Education*, 42: 27–50.

Tiwari, A., Chan, S., Wong, E., Wong, D., Chui, C., Wong, A. and Patil, N. (2006) 'The effect of problem-based learning on students' approaches to learning in the context of clinical nursing education', *Nurse Education Today*, 26: 430–438.

Trigwell, K., Hazel, E. and Prosser, M. (1996) 'Perceptions of the learning environment and approaches to learning university science at the topic level', Paper presented at the HERDSA Conference, Perth, Western Australia, July.

Trigwell, K. and Prosser, M. (1991) 'Relating approaches to study and quality of learning outcomes at the course level', *British Journal of Educational Psychology*, 61: 265–275.

Tynjälä, P. (1999) 'Towards expert knowledge? A comparison between a constructivist and a traditional learning environment in the university', *International Journal of Educational Research*, 31: 357–442.

Unsworth, N. and Engle, R.W. (2005), Individual differences in working memory capacity and learning: Evidence from the serial reaction time task', *Memory and Cognition*, 33: 213–220.

Unsworth, N., Heitz, R.P., Schrock, J.C. and Engle, R.W. (2005) 'An automated version of the operation span task', *Behavior Research Methods*, 37: 498–505.

Vansteenkiste, M., Lens, W. and Deci, E.L. (2006) 'Intrinsic versus extrinsic goal contents in self-determination theory: Another look at the quality of academic motivation', *Educational Psychologist*, 41: 19–31.

Vansteenkiste, M., Sierens, E., Soenens, B., Luyckx, K. and Lens, W. (2009) 'Motivational profiles from a self-determination perspective: The quality of motivation matters', *Journal of Educational Psychology*, 101: 671–688.

Vansteenkiste, M., Simons, J., Lens, W., Sheldon, K.M. and Deci, E.L. (2004) 'Motivating learning, performance, and persistence: The synergistic effects of intrinsic goal contents and autonomy-supportive contexts', *Journal of Personality and Social Psychology*, 87: 246–260.

Vermetten, Y., Vermunt, J. and Lodewijks, H. (2002) 'Powerful learning environment? How do university students differ in their response to instructional measures', *Learning and Instruction*, 12: 263–284.

Watkins, D. (2001) 'Correlates of approaches to learning: A cross-cultural meta-analysis', in R. Sternberg and L. Zhang (Eds.) *Perspectives on thinking, learning, and cognitive styles*, London: Erlbaum.

Wilson, K. and Fowler, J. (2005) 'Assessing the impact of learning environments on students' approaches to learning: Comparing conventional and action learning designs', *Assessment and Evaluation in Higher Education*, 30: 87–101.

Wilson, K. L., Lizzio, A. and Ramsden, P. (1997) 'The development, validation and appreciation of the Course Experience Questionnaire', *Studies in Higher Education*, 22: 33–53.

Chapter 14

Do case-based learning environments matter?

Research into their effects on students' approaches to learning, motivation and achievement

Marlies Baeten,[1] Katrien Struyven and Filip Dochy

Theoretical background

Approaches to learning

Since Marton and Säljö, the pioneers in the 1970s (Marton 1976; Säljö 1975), the concept of approaches to learning has been a firmly established concept in the educational research literature for several decades now. Originally, Marton (1976) and Säljö (1975) used a phenomenographic research approach to reveal differences between students in how they approached a specific learning task. While some students made use of deep learning processes (e.g. relating ideas, using evidence and seeking for meaning) which were associated with an intention to understand and an intrinsic interest in the content to be learned, others used surface learning processes (e.g. rote memorisation and a narrow syllabus-bound attitude) in order to reproduce the learning materials (Biggs et al. 2001; Entwistle and McCune 2004). This combination of intention and related processes (deep versus surface) was called an 'approach to learning'.

Later, a third approach was defined, i.e. the strategic or achieving approach. Whereas the deep and surface approach describes ways in which students handle a learning task, the strategic approach indicates how students organise their learning (e.g. when, where, how long they learn). The intention of a strategic student is to achieve the highest possible grades. This student is aware of study requirements and tries to accomplish them by making effective use of space and time (Biggs et al. 2001; Entwistle and McCune 2004).

While the different approaches to learning were originally identified through phenomenographic research (Marton 1976; Säljö 1975), later on, in the 1980s, researchers started quantifying approaches to learning by means of self-report questionnaires (Biggs 1987; Entwistle and Ramsden 1983). Instead of qualifying students as taking one specific approach to learning, the questionnaires provide students' scores on the different approaches to learning. Since the development of these self-report questionnaires, a considerable amount of research has been conducted on the factors influencing the approach to learning a student adopts.

In view of the fact that approaches to learning are considered to be contextual in nature – a student can shift to the adoption of a different approach depending on the characteristics of the context and the student's interpretation thereof (Biggs 2001) – many studies have investigated whether students' approaches to learning can be enhanced by changing the learning environment. In this respect, it has been expected that student-centred learning environments inspired by the constructivist learning theory foster deep learning and understanding (Hannafin et al. 1997; Lea et al. 2003; Mayer 2004; Vermetten et al. 2002) and, as such, encourage students to adopt a deep approach to learning.

Student-centred learning environments

Due to the influence of the constructivist learning theory, there has been an increasing interest in developing learning environments that involve students in the learning process (Hannafin et al. 1997). The constructivist learning theory defines learning as an 'active process in which learners are active sense makers who seek to build coherent and organised knowledge' (Mayer 2004: 14). As such, it views learning as an active process of knowledge construction rather than as a passive reception of information (Mayer 2004; Tynjälä 1999).

Although the constructivist learning theory provides a view on learning and not on teaching, researchers began to think about appropriate learning environments to foster students' active knowledge construction. While some researchers indicate that active knowledge construction could take place irrespective of the learning environment, even while attending a lecture (Renkl 2008; Schelfhout et al. 2006), others argued that particular constructivist learning environments should be developed in order to achieve active knowledge construction (Loyens and Rikers 2011; Tynjälä 1999). These 'constructivist' learning environments have been frequently described as 'student-centred' since they emphasise the student's active role in the learning process (Elen et al. 2007; Loyens and Rikers 2011). Many different learning environments fall under the umbrella term of 'constructivist' or 'student-centred' learning environments, for instance problem-based learning and case-based learning.

In order to investigate the assumption that student-centred learning environments enhance the adoption of the deep approach to learning, a considerable number of studies have been conducted that investigated the dynamics in approaches to learning in a student-centred learning environment (e.g. Baeten et al. 2008; Gijbels et al. 2009) or that compared approaches to learning in different learning environments, among which were student-centred learning environments (e.g. Nijhuis et al. 2005; Struyven et al. 2006; Wilson and Fowler 2005). Nevertheless, these studies did not reveal unequivocal results. In 2010, an extensive literature study (Baeten et al. 2010) was conducted to explore the explanations for the diverging results. Explanations were found in the context, in the students' perceptions of the context and in the students' themselves (Figure 14.1).

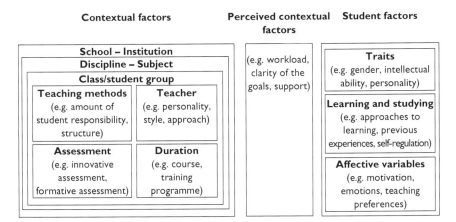

| Contextual factors | Perceived contextual factors | Student factors |

Figure 14.1   Factors of influence on students' approaches to learning

Source: Based on Baeten et al. 2010.

Empirical study

Based on this literature study (Baeten et al. 2010), a large-scale quasi-experimental study was conducted, in which one of the factors from Figure 14.1 was manipulated, i.e. structure. The amount of structure was manipulated by varying the number of lectures in a student-centred learning environment. Previous research (Struyven et al. 2006) showed that students in a student-centred learning environment had only fragmented knowledge; they were continuously looking up information in order to solve individual assignments and did not have an overview. Therefore, suggestions have been made to include lectures in a student-centred learning environment, which may provide structured support and ensure transparency in the coherence of the contents (Struyven et al. 2006). Other studies are also in support of this combination.

In this respect, Mayer (2004) argued that the constructivist view on learning should be supported by methods involving instructional guidance, because this combination seems to be more effective in helping students learn and transfer. Kirschner et al. (2006) emphasise the importance of direct instructional guidance (i.e. providing full explanatory information) especially for novice students. When these students have sufficiently high prior knowledge to provide internal guidance, the advantage of instructional guidance begins to diminish. Several authors indicate the importance of a gradual transition from direct instructional guidance towards a student-centred learning environment (e.g. Albanese and Mitchell 1993; Lake 2001) since students regularly encounter difficulties, discomfort and resistance when being confronted with a student-centred learning environment (Choi et al. 2009; Knight et al. 2008), for instance due to feelings of uncertainty about their new roles and responsibilities (Choi et al.

2009) or due to a lack of self-directed learning skills (Hung 2009). By means of a gradual introduction of a student-centred learning environment, there is a gradual transfer of control over student learning processes from the teacher to the student, which may help to promote meaning-directed learning patterns (Vermunt and Vermetten 2004), which are comparable to the deep approach to learning.

The student-centred learning environment under investigation in the present study is case-based learning (CBL). The roots of CBL lie in the case method as applied at the Harvard Business School at the beginning of the 20th century, where it was considered a problem-centred approach based on real-life situations (Merseth 1991). Since then, many definitions of CBL have arisen in the literature. At the core of these definitions is the fact that CBL tries to create a bridge between theory and practice (Engle and Faux 2006) by asking students to connect theories and concepts to real-life situations (Kurz et al. 2005).

In the present study, CBL is characterised by four features of student-centred learning environments, i.e. (a) an active involvement of the students in order to construct knowledge for themselves (Kirschner et al. 2006; Struyven et al. 2008a) by selecting, interpreting and applying information in order to solve assignments (Struyven et al. 2008a), (b) a coaching (Motschnig-Pitrik and Holzinger 2002) and facilitating (Beijaard et al. 2000) teacher, who is present to help students out with questions or problems and safeguards their learning process (Struyven et al. 2010), (c) the use of authentic assignments, for instance practical cases and complex vocational problems (Elen et al. 2007; Kirschner et al. 2006; Loyens et al. 2007; Struyven et al. 2008a), and (d) learning in cooperation with fellow students (Loyens et al. 2007; Tynjälä 1999).

Quasi-experimental research design

In the present study, a learning environment consisting of CBL was compared with three other learning environments (Table 14.1).

1   In the completely CBL environment, the course content was studied using CBL, in which students were challenged to construct knowledge by selecting and applying the information necessary to solve written, authentic cases. True/false and open-ended questions about the cases were solved in small student groups with the help of the course book. In solving these cases, the teacher's role consisted of scaffolding and supervising. The solutions to the cases were corrected by the students themselves using an answer key.

2   In the completely lecture-based learning environment, all content was provided through lectures, in which the teacher transmitted knowledge to the students by means of PowerPoint presentations and visual aids (i.e. pictures and videos). Together with the PowerPoint presentations, notes were provided to the teachers with example questions they could ask students so that teacher–student interaction could occur.

Table 14.1 Overview of the teaching methods used in each learning environment

Course content	LLLL	CCCC	LCLC	LLCC
Chapter 1: Introduction	Lecture	CBL	Lecture	Lecture
Chapter 2: Conception, birth, newborn	Lecture	CBL	Lecture + CBL	Lecture
Chapter 3: Baby	Lecture	CBL		Lecture
Chapter 4: Toddler	Lecture	CBL	Lecture + CBL	Lecture + CBL
Chapter 5: Kindergartner	Lecture	CBL	Lecture + CBL	Lecture + CBL
Chapter 6: School child	Lecture	CBL	Lecture + CBL	CBL
Chapter 7: Adolescent	Lecture	CBL	Lecture + CBL	CBL
Chapter 8: Synthesis	Lecture	Discussion in small groups	Lecture	Discussion in small groups

3   In the alternated learning environment, lectures and CBL were used in turn. The implementation of CBL was in accordance with the CBL as described in (1) above and the implementation of lectures was in accordance with the use of lectures as described in (2) above. Both lectures and CBL occurred in approximately equal amounts. Each case was preceded by a lecture, so that the goals of the lectures and CBL could constantly support each other.

4   In the gradually implemented CBL environment, lectures gradually made way for CBL. First, only lectures were provided; then, a combination of lectures and CBL was provided; and, in the end, only CBL was provided. The implementation of CBL was in accordance with the CBL as described in (1) above and the implementation of lectures was in accordance with the use of lectures as described in (2) above.

The study took place in the first year of the professional bachelor of teacher education during a course on child development. Twenty-six teachers participated with their student groups ($N_{Students}$ = 1098) and were assigned to one of the four learning environments. To guarantee standardised treatment, several measures were taken. First of all, standardised learning materials were developed, i.e. the same course book, PowerPoint presentations, case studies and correction keys. These materials were submitted to the participating teachers for preview. Their feedback was used in revising the materials. In addition, a meeting was organised with each teacher before the start of the research to ensure similar experimental protocols. Furthermore, each teacher was videotaped twice during the course with the aim of encouraging them to use the prescribed teaching methods as intended.

Research objectives

We were particularly interested in the effects of the four learning environments on students' *approaches to learning*. Furthermore, it was investigated how these learning environments influenced students' *motivation for learning* since approaches to learning have been frequently associated with motivation (Entwistle et al. 2002; Harris 2003).

In addition to students' approaches to learning and their motivation for learning, a 'hard' learning outcome, namely *achievement* (Lizzio et al. 2002), was studied in order to fully understand the effectiveness of the learning environment. Therefore, all students were assessed by means of the same written, open-book, case-based assessment, which took place after the entire set of classes during the regular examination period. The assessment consisted of a large, realistic case that students received about two weeks before the examination. During the examination, questions were asked about this case in relation to the theories and concepts of child development. As such, the assessment aimed to measure students' application of knowledge.

Since it is not necessarily the learning environment itself which influences students' (approaches to) learning, but the way in which students *perceive the (quality of the) learning environment and the teaching methods in particular* (Entwistle 1991), we also looked at students' perceptions, which may help to explain the effects of the learning environment. The main variables included in the research are presented in Table 14.2.

Finally, a person-oriented perspective (see Chapter 2) was taken in order to investigate whether *student profiles* (based on motivation and approaches to learning) influenced students' achievement and students' perceptions of the learning environment. The relationships under investigation are depicted in Figure 14.2.

Data analysis

As different teachers were involved in each of the four learning environments, multi-level analysis was conducted by means of the linear mixed model procedure in Statistical Package for the Social Sciences (SPSS) 16.0. In this way, the hierarchical data structure, i.e. students (level 1) nested within teachers (level 2), could be incorporated. For each dependent variable, a random intercept model was constructed. Effects were estimated through the maximum likelihood method. Post hoc Bonferroni comparisons were applied to identify significant differences between the four learning environments.

Table 14.2 Overview of the main variables in the empirical study

Name of the variable	Instrument	Scales
Approaches to learning	Approaches to Learning and Studying Inventory (Entwistle et al. 2002)	Deep approach Surface approach Monitoring studying Organised studying Effort management
Motivation for learning	Academic Self-Regulation Scale (Vansteenkiste et al. 2009)	Autonomous motivation Controlled motivation
Achievement	Case-based examination	
Perceptions of the learning environment	Course Experience Questionnaire (Wilson et al. 1997)	Good teaching Clear goals and standards Appropriate workload Generic skills
Perceptions of the teaching methods	Open-ended question	

Information about students' perceptions of the (quality of) teaching methods implemented in the learning environment was gathered by means of an open-ended question: 'How do you assess the instructional method you have experienced during the course on child development?' and analysed through quantitative content analysis. With the help of a coding scheme, answers were classified. The development of this coding scheme was data-driven. In the first phase, we ran through the transcripts in order to build a coding scheme. In the second phase, we applied this coding scheme to all the transcripts.

The student profiles, based on motivation and approaches to learning, were identified through K-means cluster analysis, in which the solution is derived

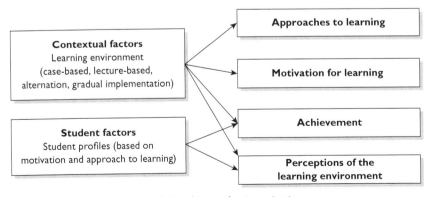

Figure 14.2 Depiction of the relationships under investigation

from an a priori determined number of clusters, in this case two. This number was based on theory, expecting that (1) autonomous motivation related to the deep approach and the strategic approach – which could be seen as a component of the deep approach, and that (2) controlled motivation related to the surface approach. Results of K-means clustering confirmed the expected cluster structure. The first cluster was labelled as autonomously motivated deep-strategic learners and the second cluster was labelled as little motivated and less pronounced deep-strategic learners.

The results concerning the effects of the learning environments on students' approaches to learning, motivation, achievement and perceptions of the learning environment have been published in international scientific journals (Baeten et al. 2011a, 2012, 2013a). In the following section, these results have been integrated. Similarities and differences between these studies were searched for, which allows the formulation of several main conclusions about the effects of case-based and lecture-based learning environments and suggestions for further research.

Main conclusions

There is a greater value in moving gradually from lectures to CBL

Although the literature suggested the inclusion of lectures in student-centred learning environments in order to provide structured support (Lea et al. 2003; Struyven et al. 2006) and enhance students' learning (Sivan et al. 2000), the large-scale quasi-experimental study confirms only the greater value of a gradual transition from lectures to a student-centred learning environment and not of alternating between the use of both. The results showed that, compared to the completely CBL environment, students in the gradually implemented CBL environment adopted less surface approaches to learning, worked in a more organised way, made a greater effort and concentrated better in a course on child development. They were more autonomously motivated for learning in that course, i.e. they studied because they enjoyed it or found it personally important, and they scored higher on the case-based assessment.

The benefits of the gradually implemented CBL environment can be explained by the gradual transition from lectures to CBL. The lectures, with which the course started, might have helped students to become familiar with the discipline and outline of the course (Albanese and Mitchell 1993) and might have helped them to acquire basic knowledge and appropriate schemas. Incrementally, as students progressed towards CBL, their basic knowledge and schemas might have taken over from the teacher's external instructional guidance (Kirschner et al. 2006). Students' perceptions of the (quality of the) teaching methods implemented in the learning environment also revealed the greater value of a gradual transition from lectures to CBL rather than simply alternating lectures and CBL. While students in the gradually implemented CBL environment were satisfied with the variation in teaching methods and the combination of lectures and CBL, students in the alternated learning environment disliked the lack of variation. Although these students were satisfied with the combination of lectures and CBL, they considered it to be always the same, repetitive pattern. In the gradually implemented CBL environment, on the other hand, there was more variation: first, only lectures; then, a combination of lectures and CBL; and, finally, only CBL. Moreover, there was an increase in student autonomy as the students progressed towards CBL in which they did not receive a lecture in advance, while, in the alternated learning environment, the case was always preceded by a lecture. An alternative explanation for the greater value of the gradually implemented CBL environment could be because of the teachers. Not only did the students gradually get used to the student-centred learning environments but so did the teachers. They gradually got used to offering support and guidance in a student-centred learning environment. This might have influenced student outcomes in a beneficial way.

While the prospect of solving cases without teacher preparation in the gradually implemented CBL environment might have stimulated students' learning, in the completely CBL environment, the exclusive use of cases without lectures might have caused the students to become lost and frustrated (Kirschner et al. 2006) because, for instance, they could not see the wood for the trees. This might have enhanced the adoption of surface approaches to learning (Struyven et al. 2006). Moreover, the exclusive use of cases might have frustrated students' need for competence, i.e. the need to feel effective in learning (Vansteenkiste et al. 2009), which may have led to the decrease in autonomous motivation. The students themselves mentioned the lack of lectures and teacher input as a disadvantage of the completely CBL environment. They suggested that a lecture could provide an overview and further explanation and could break the routine of solving and correcting cases. This demand for teacher input was supported by the study of McNaught et al. (2005) in which the students wanted the teachers to teach them the cases instead of the students taking personal responsibility for the CBL. Students felt safer in such learning environments where teacher input was greater (e.g. providing feedback, answering questions, giving direction) (Mitchem et al. 2008). Indeed, the findings showed that students were satisfied with a learning environment which included teacher input by means of lectures. In the completely lecture-based learning environment, students considered the lectures to be good and they appreciated the clarity, structure and overview provided by the PowerPoint presentations which made it easy for them to follow the course. Also, the videos and pictures clarified the course content. Nevertheless, the completely lecture-based learning environment differed only significantly from the completely CBL environment with respect to effort management and achievement.

Lecture-taught students showed significantly more effort and concentration when compared to students in the completely CBL environment. This might be explained by the fact that the lecturers directed students towards the most important course information. Consequently, these students might have shown more effort and concentration because it was clearer to them where to focus their efforts. On the other hand, students who were taught in the completely CBL environment might have become lost and frustrated (Kirschner et al. 2006). Consequently, they might have experienced difficulties showing effort and concentration since it was difficult for them to know on which matters they should focus. In view of the fact that assessment affects studying strongly (Entwistle and McCune 2004), the pre-assessment effect of the case-based assessment might be another relevant explanation (Gielen et al. 2003). Since lecture-taught students were less experienced in solving cases, the prospect of receiving this kind of assessment might have stimulated them to spend more effort and concentration in studying. Conversely, in the completely CBL environment, students, who were experienced in solving cases, might have felt at ease with the upcoming assessment and, therefore, because they know the drill, might have spent less effort and concentrated less.

In both the gradually implemented CBL environment and the completely lecture-based learning environment, in which effort management was significantly higher compared to the completely CBL environment, students scored significantly higher on the case-based assessment than students in the completely CBL environment. Subsequent analyses of our data (Baeten et al. 2011b) showed positive associations between effort management and achievement, as was also found in other studies such as, for instance, Schwinger et al. (2009). The highest assessment scores in the gradually implemented CBL environment and the completely lecture-based learning environment emphasised the importance of building a domain-specific knowledge base with the help of the structure and explanation which the teacher provided in the lectures (Kirschner et al. 2006) so that the students were able to apply this knowledge afterwards in cases (Albanese and Mitchell 1993). In the completely lecture-based learning environment, the focus was solely on building this knowledge base, whereas, in the gradually implemented CBL environment, a certain knowledge base had to be acquired before starting to solve cases. The significant difference in achievement between the gradually implemented CBL environment and the alternated learning environment supported the importance of firstly building a knowledge base. Students might need some time in order to acquire basic knowledge and develop adequate schemas through lectures before they can use their knowledge and schemas in order to solve cases appropriately.

In comparing the four learning environments, while clear differences were found in perceived quality of the teaching methods (e.g. variation in teaching methods, combination of lectures and CLB), no differences came across with respect to perceptions of good teaching, clear goals and standards, and appropriate workload. Instead of the learning environment, students' profiles, based on motivation and approaches to learning, were more important in explaining their perceptions (see below). Only in respect of generic skills were differences found between the learning environments. In the gradually implemented CBL environment, students scored higher on perceptions of generic skills as compared to students in the alternated learning environment. The latter group of students might have felt less need to adopt generic skills since they always received a lecture-based introduction before solving a case. They knew the routine and might have felt satisfied more quickly. Consequently, during the CBL, they might not have felt the need to study the contents in–depth and they might have perceived that the learning environment contributed less to the development of generic skills, compared to students in the gradually implemented CBL environment.

In conclusion, the large-scale quasi-experimental study showed the added value of gradually introducing students to CBL. Compared to the completely CBL environment, the gradually implemented CBL environment had more beneficial outcomes since students adopted less surface approaches to learning, worked in a more organised way, made more effort and concentrated better, were more autonomously motivated, achieved better assessment results, and were more positive about the teaching method. Compared to students in the alternated learning environment, students in the gradually implemented CBL environment perceived their learning environment as contributing more to the development of generic skills, were more positive about the teaching methods, and achieved better assessment results. The completely lecture-based learning environment had more beneficial outcomes compared to the completely CBL environment. In the completely lecture-based learning environment, students made more effort and concentrated better, were more positive about the teaching method, and achieved better assessment results. Figure 14.3 depicts these relationships concerning the effects of the learning environment.

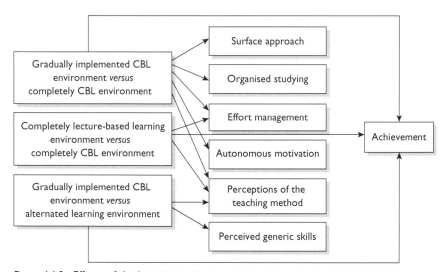

Figure 14.3 Effects of the learning environment

It is difficult to enhance the deep approach to learning

The findings from the large-scale quasi-experimental study confirm Marton and Säljö's (1997) statement that inducing a deep approach to learning seems to be quite difficult. The four different learning environments which included lectures and/or CBL did not have the power to enhance the deep approach. In these learning environments, the dynamics of approaches to learning between the first and final lessons revealed that the deep and strategic (organised studying and effort management) approaches decreased in the completely lecture-based, the completely CBL and the alternated learning environment. However, they remained the same in the gradually implemented CBL environment. The surface approach decreased in both mixed learning environments, with the greatest decrease found in the gradually implemented CBL environment. As regards the monitoring of studying, a decrease was found in all four learning environments, with the smallest decrease in the gradually implemented CBL environment. The repeated measures analyses (see, also, Baeten et al. 2013b) supported the gradually implemented CBL environment as being the most positive in terms of approaches to learning. However, at the same time, it confirmed the difficulty of enhancing students' deep approaches to learning.

Contrary to expectations, implementing a student-centred learning environment including lectures did not result in an increase in the deep approach. Moreover, no learning environment succeeded in enhancing the deep approach. The question remains how this can be explained. The literature review (see above) listed several encouraging and discouraging factors in the context, in the students' perceptions of the context and in the students themselves. Below, three arguments are discussed in-depth.

First, it could be that changes in the learning environment were not strong enough to induce changes in the deep approach to learning (Nijhuis et al. 2008). Several standardisation measures were taken in order to conduct quasi-experimental research. By standardizing the CBL format, its advantages might have been limited as the case solving process was rather structured: solving separate questions with the help of the course book. A CBL format, in which students had more freedom in determining the problem solving route and the use of resources, could possibly enhance students' deep approach to learning. Moreover, the study was limited to one course. Extending the CBL format over multiple courses or for a longer duration, for instance a complete training programme, might be more beneficial in enhancing students' deep approach to learning.

Second, the lack of increase in the deep approach might be explained by the fact that, at the beginning of the course, students might be more intrinsically motivated and might have good study intentions. This might have resulted in high(er) scores for the deep approach. However, by the end of the course, students might have experienced a higher workload due to, for example, deadlines for other courses and internships. This might have diminished their good intentions of adopting a deep approach and encouraged them to adopt a surface approach since a perceived high workload has been associated with the adoption of a surface approach to learning (e.g. Crawford et al. 1998; Diseth et al. 2006). At both the beginning and the end of the course, our sample of student teachers had rather high scores on the deep approach and lower scores on the surface approach. This supported the fact that there was a general trend in human sciences to adopt a deep approach to learning (e.g. Kember et al. 2008; Lawless and Richardson 2002). From the beginning of the course student teachers had already adopted a deep approach, so it was difficult to enhance it due to a ceiling effect.

A third explanation could be that the deep approach increased only in specific subgroups of students and did not result in a general increase in the whole sample of students (Lindblöm-Ylänne 2011). In respect to this explanation, it seems that in a student-centred learning environment students who had low scores on the deep approach adopted deeper approaches to learning (Vanthournout et al. 2009) or deeper learning strategies (Wilson and Fowler 2005). Accordingly, Gijbels et al. (2008) found that the stronger the students' initial deep approach, the less they changed this approach in a student-centred learning environment.

In addition to manipulating the teaching methods in order to enhance the adoption of the deep approach to learning, the large-scale quasi-experimental study made use of an innovative assessment mode, i.e. case-based assessment, on the assumption that it would help to increase students' deep approaches. However, this was not reflected in the data. Students' deep approaches did not increase and were unrelated to their scores in the assessment. The surface approach, on the other hand, had a significantly negative effect on the assessment scores (see also Baeten et al. 2011b). Therefore, adopting a surface approach was not beneficial since the assessment did not reward the surface approach.

In conclusion, the findings showed the difficulty of enhancing the deep approach to learning. Instead of the learning environment, other variables, which were mainly student characteristics, seemed to be more important (Figure 14.4). Age, prior knowledge, autonomous motivation, the initial deep approach and initial monitoring studying positively predicted the deep approach, whereas the initial surface approach negatively predicted the deep approach.

Students' motivational and learning profiles matter in explaining their perceptions of the learning environment

Since students may perceive the same learning environment differently (Struyven et al. 2008b) and since a certain teaching method may not work for all students (Ertmer et al. 1996), attention should be paid to the type of student entering the learning environment. Although no differences were found between the four learning environments in respect of perceptions of good teaching, clear goals and

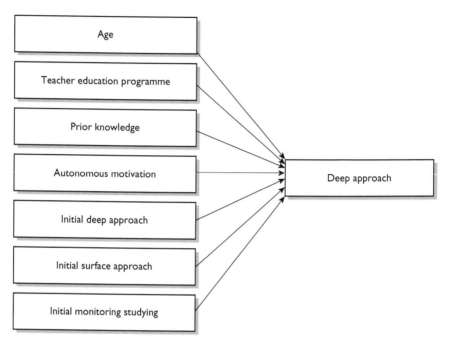

Figure 14.4 Variables influencing the deep approach to learning

standards, and appropriate workload, students' motivational and learning profiles mattered in explaining their perceptions of good teaching, clear goals and standards, appropriate workload, and generic skills. Autonomously motivated deep-strategic learners were more positive about each type of learning environment compared to little motivated and less pronounced deep-strategic learners. In each learning environment, the autonomously motivated deep-strategic learners were more positive about the quality of the teaching, clarity of the goals, the appropriateness of the workload and the development of generic skills. Since the autonomously motivated deep-strategic learners were the most positive, irrespective of the learning environment (either lectures, or CBL, or a combination of both), at first sight it seemed that this student profile was the most suited to higher education. However, when students' achievement on the case-based assessment was studied, no effects of the student profiles were found. Although perceptions were considered to be important in explaining learning (Entwistle 1991), a discrepancy between perceptions and performance was established here. The student profile with the most positive perceptions of the learning environment did not score better on the case-based assessment. Therefore, looking at student profiles, in terms of motivation and approaches to learning, tended to be important only in explaining the perceived quality of the learning environment.

Although perceived workload was a variable often used to explain the differential effects of the learning environment, there were no significant differences between the four learning environments in respect of perceived workload. Nevertheless, there was an interaction effect between the learning environment and the student profile. In all learning environments, except the completely lecture-based learning environment, few differences in perceived workload were found between autonomously motivated deep-strategic learners and little motivated and less pronounced deep-strategic learners. On the other hand, in the completely lecture-based learning environment, autonomously motivated deep-strategic learners perceived the workload to be more appropriate than little motivated and less pronounced deep-strategic learners. Consequently, particularly in this setting, the student profile mattered in explaining the perceived workload.

In conclusion, the large-scale quasi-experimental study showed that it was important to look at student profiles, based on motivation and approaches to learning, but only in respect of students' perceptions of the learning environment (Figure 14.5).

Suggestions for further research

Related to the three main conclusions, several suggestions for future research were formulated.

There is a greater value in moving gradually from lectures to CBL

While the large-scale quasi-experimental study shows the added value of gradually introducing students to CBL, there is a need to replicate this research with different participants in different contexts in order to strengthen the findings.

With regard to the *participants*, our findings related to first-year professional bachelor students in teacher education. Different results would be expected from

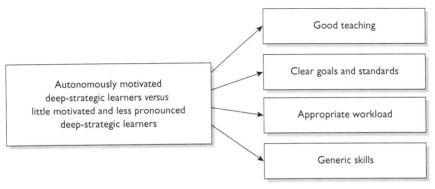

Figure 14.5 Effects of student profiles

samples of second and subsequent year students, who would be more familiar with and experienced in the discipline they were studying. Prior knowledge about the discipline or previous experiences could be helpful when confronted with student-centred learning environments. Perhaps, these students do not need a gradual transition towards a student-centred learning environment and can be directly presented with it. In addition, a sample of second or subsequent year students is more homogeneous since these students have passed the first-year selection. Different results can be also obtained for other student samples; for instance, students in other higher education (bachelor or master) programmes or students attending other levels of education (primary or secondary education). Furthermore, replicating the research with students from different disciplines could strengthen our findings.

As regards the *context*, several suggestions for further research are offered in relation to research design, group work, and assessment. In the research design of the mixed learning environments consisting of lectures and CBL, the lectures preceded CBL. Nevertheless, it would be interesting to let CBL precede the lectures so that, first, students have to acquire and apply the course content themselves before the teacher summarises the basic information, and provides structure and an overview. Such a learning environment appeals to students' active involvement and responsibility and still provides structure in order to prevent students from having fragmented knowledge. However, a repetitive pattern of constantly alternating CBL and lectures should be avoided. Students will not spend time and effort in acquiring the course content themselves if they know that the teacher will explain it later.

In addition to differences in the order of the teaching methods, it would be interesting to also look at different student-centred teaching methods or different forms of CBL. It seems more important to focus on the characteristics of the teaching methods (e.g. the use of realistic versus fictitious cases or different degrees of cooperation) rather than their name (e.g. CBL or problem-based learning) (Loyens and Rikers 2011) because a name can be used to refer to a diversity of teaching methods. For instance, the case-based method has been used to refer to cases used as an example in a lecture, to cases used as a preparation for a class discussion, and to cases used to encourage student inquiry (Maudsley 1999).

With regard to group work, it seems that more attention should be paid to group processes. Students reported several problems about the group work, for instance a lack of focus and unequal group contribution. A closer look at group processes, for instance by making use of concepts central to team learning in corporate settings such as group interdependence and psychological safety (Decuyper et al. 2010), could be useful in explaining the results of student-centred learning environments which make use of group work.

Finally, students experiencing CBL were not rewarded either by means of formative or summative assessment of the cases. Instead, with the help of correction keys, they had to correct cases themselves. In the completely CBL environment, students expressed a need for more teacher input or lectures, so providing teacher feedback on the solutions to the cases could be helpful for students' learning and, consequently, might lead to other results.

It is difficult to enhance the deep approach to learning

Several explanations for the lack of increase in the deep approach to learning were formulated (see above). Based on these arguments, a number of suggestions for future research are made.

First, increasing student-centred interventions (Nijhuis et al. 2005), in which students have more freedom to determine the problem solving route and resources used than was the case in this study, or interventions prolonged over time or broadened to several courses, could possibly enhance students' deep approach to learning.

Second, instead of measuring students' approaches to learning in the first lesson, it would be interesting to measure them in the second or third lessons when students better understand what the course is about. In this way, at the beginning of the course, initial strong deep approaches influenced by the fact that students may be more intrinsically motivated and may have good study intentions are more realistic.

Third, considering subgroups of students based on their approaches to learning and examining how the deep approach of these specific subgroups evolves over time is suggested. The findings have revealed that autonomously motivated deep-strategic learners were more positive about the teaching, workload, clarity of goals and standards, and generic skills present in the course. These positive perceptions may possibly enhance their deep approach to learning.

These three suggestions continue to take a quantitative approach to measuring approaches to learning, so considering what exactly students were doing when confronted with a case would complement this information. Making use of qualitative measures, for instance logbooks or think-aloud protocols in which students explain how they go about the case and which strategies they use, could help to give an insight into whether or not they attain a deep level of learning and understanding.

Finally, the findings show that it is difficult to realise the assumption of the constructivist learning theory to attain deep learning and understanding as conceptualised by means of the students' approaches to learning tradition. It seems necessary to also look at other variables, for instance self-regulation and transfer of learning.

Students' motivational and learning profiles matter in explaining their perceptions of the learning environment

The findings show that autonomously motivated deep-strategic learners have more positive perceptions of the learning environment than little motivated and less pronounced deep-strategic learners. However, the former group did not perform better on the case-based assessment.

Since students' achievement matter in higher education, it seems important to also consider other student profiles, for instance profiles based on cognitive capacities or prior knowledge, which may help to explain students' achievement. Kyndt's (2011) research provided additional arguments for basing student profiles on cognitive capacities. They found that the best and weakest academic performers were predicted by their cognitive capacities and not by their motivation and approaches to learning. Motivation and approaches to learning were important in explaining the performance of the majority of the students scoring around the middle. However, they did not improve the prediction of the group's best and weakest students, indicating that these top and bottom scoring students were regulated foremost by their cognitive capacities or lack of capacities.

Moreover, different learning environments may differently affect student profiles based on prior knowledge. In this respect, Berghmans' (2012) research showed that different approaches to tutoring had a differential impact on subgroups of students based on prior knowledge. Students with little prior knowledge performed better when being tutored by a facilitating tutoring approach (i.e. questioning and challenging students' thinking by means of questions and hints), compared to a directing tutoring approach (i.e. providing all the information and responding with cut-and-dried answers to students' questions).

Concluding remarks

This chapter was grounded in the research tradition of investigating students' learning in different learning environments. Making use of the suggestions for further research (see above) can broaden our knowledge about this topic. To date, the question central to this chapter, 'Do case-based learning (CBL) environments matter?', can be answered affirmatively. The main conclusions showed that CBL had a greater value when being implemented gradually, with lectures incrementally making way for it. Students in this learning environment adopted less surface approaches to learning, worked in a more organised way, made a greater effort and concentrated better, were more autonomously motivated, achieved better assessment results, and were more positive about the teaching methods compared to students who only received CBL. Translated to practice, this means that teachers should not present CBL or other student-centred teaching methods to students directly. Instead, they should start by means of lectures, which introduce students to the course content, before students have to explore new topics themselves by means of cases, problem tasks, etc.

Furthermore, the conclusions indicate that attention should be paid to the student profiles. The student audience is diverse and not every teaching method suits each student equally well. Therefore, implementing a variety of teaching methods might serve students' perceptions well.

As regards the deep approach, the effects of student-centred learning environments were not unequivocal. Several encouraging and discouraging factors were identified (Figure 14.4). Investigating these factors may help to further explore this complex research area.

Note

1 The contribution of Marlies Baeten is supported by an Aspirant FWO grant of the Fund for Scientific Research Flanders (FWO Vlaanderen).

References

Albanese, M. and Mitchell, S. (1993) 'Problem-based learning: A review of the literature on its outcome and implementation issues', *Academic Medicine*, 68: 52–81.

Baeten, M., Dochy, F. and Struyven, K. (2008) 'Students' approaches to learning and assessment preferences in a portfolio-based learning environment', *Instructional Science*, 36(5–6): 359–374.

Baeten, M., Dochy, F. and Struyven, K. (2011a) 'Using students' motivational and learning profiles in investigating their perceptions and achievement in case-based and lecture-based learning environments', *Educational Studies*, 38(5): 491–506.

Baeten, M., Dochy, F. and Struyven, K. (2011b) 'The effects of case-based and lecture-based learning on students' performance', poster presented at the Junior Researchers conference of the European Association for Research on Learning and Instruction, Exeter, United Kingdom, August.

Baeten, M., Dochy, F. and Struyven, K. (2012a now 2013a) 'Enhancing students' approaches to learning: The added value of gradually implementing case-based learning', *European Journal of Psychology of Education*, 28(2): 315–336.

Baeten, M., Dochy, F. and Struyven, K. (2012b now 2012), 'The effects of different learning environments on students' motivation for learning and their achievement', *British Journal of Educational Psychology*, doi:10.1111/j.2044-8279.2012.02076.x.

Baeten, M., Kyndt, E., Struyven, K. and Dochy, F. (2010) 'Using student-centred learning environments to stimulate deep approaches to learning: Factors encouraging or discouraging their effectiveness', *Educational Research Review*, 5: 243–260.

Baeten, M., Struyven, K. and Dochy, F. (2012 now 2013b) 'Student-centred teaching methods: Can they optimise students' approaches to learning in professional higher education?', *Studies in Educational Evaluation*, 39(1): 14–22.

Beijaard, D., Verloop, N. and Vermunt, J. (2000) 'Teachers' perceptions of professional identity: An exploratory study from a personal knowledge perspective', *Teaching and Teacher Education*, 16(7): 749–764.

Berghmans, I. (2012) 'Peer assisted learning: Unravelling approaches to peer tutoring and their effects on students' learning, experiences, and the dynamics of the tutored learning environment', unpublished doctoral dissertation, Faculty of Psychology and Educational Sciences, University of Leuven.

Biggs, J. (1987) *Study process questionnaire manual*, Melbourne: Australian Council for Educational Research.

Biggs, J. (2001) 'Enhancing learning: A matter of style or approach' in R. Sternberg and L. Zhang (eds.) *Perspectives on thinking, learning, and cognitive styles*, Mahwah, NJ: Lawrence Erlbaum.

Biggs, J., Kember, D. and Leung, D. (2001) 'The revised two-factor study process questionnaire: R-SPQ-2F', *British Journal of Educational Psychology*, 71(1): 133–149.

Choi, I., Lee, S. and Kang, J. (2009) 'Implementing a case-based e-learning environment in a lecture-oriented anaesthesiology class: Do learning styles matter in complex problem solving over time?', *British Journal of Educational Technology*, 40(5): 933–947.

Crawford, K., Gordon, S., Nicholas, J. and Prosser, M. (1998) 'Qualitatively different experiences of learning mathematics at university', *Learning and Instruction*, 8(5): 455–468.

Decuyper, S., Dochy, F. and Van den Bossche, P. (2010) 'Grasping the dynamic complexity of team learning: An integrative model for effective team learning in organizations', *Educational Research Review*, 5(2): 111–133.

Diseth, A., Pallesen, S., Hovland, A. and Larsen, S. (2006) 'Course experience, approaches to learning and academic achievement', *Education and Training*, 48(2–3): 156–169.

Elen, J., Clarebout, G., Léonard, R. and Lowyck, J. (2007) 'Student-centred and teacher-centred learning environments: What students think', *Teaching in Higher Education*, 12(1): 105–117.

Engle, R. and Faux, R. (2006) 'Towards productive disciplinary engagement of prospective teachers in educational psychology: Comparing two methods of case-based instruction', *Teaching Educational Psychology*, 1(2): 1–22.

Entwistle, N. (1991) 'Approaches to learning and perceptions of the learning environment. Introduction to the special issue', *Higher Education*, 22(3): 201–204.

Entwistle, N. and McCune, V. (2004) 'The conceptual bases of study strategy inventories', *Educational Psychology Review*, 16(4): 315–345.

Entwistle, N., McCune, V. and Hounsell, D. (2002) 'Occasional report 1: Approaches to studying and perceptions of university teaching-learning environments: Concepts, measures and preliminary findings', ETL Project, Universities of Edinburgh, Coventry and Durham. Available: http://www.ed.ac.uk/etl.

Entwistle, N. and Ramsden, P. (1983) *Understanding student learning*, London: Croom Helm.

Ertmer, P., Newby, T. and MacDougall, M. (1996) 'Students' responses and approaches to case-based instruction: The role of reflective self-regulation', *American Educational Research Journal*, 33(3): 719–52.

Gielen, S., Dochy, F. and Dierick, S. (2003) 'Evaluating the consequential validity of new modes of assessment: The influence of assessment on learning, including pre-, post-, and true assessment effects' in M. Segers, F. Dochy and E. Cascallar (eds.) *Optimising new modes of assessment: in search of qualities and standards*, The Netherlands: Kluwer Academic Publishers.

Gijbels, D., Coertjens, L., Vanthournout, G., Struyf, E. and Van Petegem, P. (2009) 'Changing students' approaches to learning: A two-year study within a university teacher training course', *Educational Studies*, 35(5): 503–513.

Gijbels, D., Segers, M. and Struyf, E. (2008) 'Constructivist learning environments and the (im)possibility to change students' perceptions of assessment demands and approaches to learning', *Instructional Science*, 36(5–6): 431–443.

Hannafin, M., Hill, J. and Land, S. (1997) 'Student-centered learning and interactive multimedia: Status, issues, and implications', *Contemporary Education*, 68(2): 94–99.

Harris, C. (2003) 'Understanding the role of epistemological beliefs in post-graduate studies: Motivation and conceptions of learning in first-year law students', unpublished doctoral dissertation, University of Texas at Austin.

Hung, W. (2009) 'The 9-step problem design process for problem-based learning: Application of the 3C3R model', *Educational Research Review*, 4: 118–141.

Kember, D., Leung, D. and McNaught, C. (2008) 'A workshop activity to demonstrate that approaches to learning are influenced by the teaching and learning environment', *Active Learning in Higher Education*, 9: 43–56.

Kirschner, P., Sweller, J. and Clark, R. (2006) 'Why minimal guidance during instruction does not work: An analysis of the failure of constructivist, discovery, problem-based, experiential, and inquiry-based teaching', *Educational Psychologist*, 41(2): 75–86.

Knight, J., Fulop, R., Márquez-Magaña, L. and Tanner, K. (2008) 'Investigative cases and student outcomes in an upper-division cell and molecular biology laboratory course at a minority-serving institution', *CBE-Life Sciences Education*, 7: 382–393.

Kurz, T., Llama, G. and Savenye, W. (2005) 'Issues and challenges of creating video cases to be used with preservice teachers', *TechTrends*, 49(4): 67–73.

Kyndt, E. (2011). 'Investigating students' approaches to learning. The role of perceived workload, perceived task complexity, working memory capacity, attention and motivation, and their predictive role of academic performance', unpublished doctoral dissertation, Faculty of Psychology and Educational Sciences, University of Leuven.

Lake, D. (2001) 'Student performance and perceptions of a lecture-based course compared with the same course utilizing group discussion', *Physical Therapy*, 81(3): 896–902.

Lawless, C. and Richardson, J. (2002) 'Approaches to studying and perceptions of academic quality in distance education', *Higher Education*, 44: 257–282.

Lea, S., Stephenson, D. and Troy, J. (2003) 'Higher education students' attitudes to student-centred learning: Beyond educational bulimia?', *Studies in Higher Education*, 28(3): 321–334.

Lindblöm-Ylänne, S. (2011) 'Approaches to learning – contextual or stable in nature?', keynote presented at the 16th Annual Conference of Education, Learning, Styles, Individual differences Network (ELSIN), Antwerp, June/July.

Lizzio, A., Wilson, K. and Simons, R. (2002) 'University students' perceptions of the learning environment and academic outcomes: Implications for theory and practice', *Studies in Higher Education*, 27: 27–52.

Loyens, S. and Rikers, R. (2011) 'Instruction based on inquiry' in R. Mayer and P. Alexander (eds.) *Handbook of research on learning and instruction*, New York: Routledge.

Loyens, S., Rikers, R. and Schmidt, H. (2007) 'The impact of students' conceptions of constructivist assumptions on academic achievement and drop-out', *Studies in Higher Education*, 32(5): 581–602.

Marton, F. (1976) 'On non-verbatim learning. II. The erosion of a task induced learning algorithm', *Scandinavian Journal of Psychology*, 17: 41–48.

Marton, F. and Säljö, R. (1997) 'Approaches to learning' in F. Marton, D. Hounsell and N. Entwistle (eds.) *The experience of learning: Implications for teaching and studying in higher education* (2nd ed.), Edinburgh: Scottish Academic Press.

Maudsley, G. (1999) 'Do we all mean the same thing by "problem-based learning"? A review of the concepts and a formulation of the ground rules', *Academic Medicine*, 74(2): 178–185.

Mayer, R. (2004) 'Should there be a three-strikes rule against pure discovery learning? The case for guided methods of instruction', *American Psychologist*, 59(1): 14–19.

McNaught, C., Lau, W., Lam, P., Hui, M. and Au, P. (2005) 'The dilemma of case-based teaching and learning in science in Hong Kong: Students need it, want it, but may not value it', *International Journal of Science Education*, 27(9): 1017–1036.

Merseth, K. (1991) 'The early history of case-based instruction: Insights for teacher education today', *Journal of Teacher Education*, 42(4): 243–249.

Mitchem, K., Fitzgerald, G., Hollingsead, C., Koury, K., Miller, K. and Tsai, H. (2008) 'Enhancing case-based learning in teacher education through online discussions: Structure and facilitation', *Journal of Interactive Learning Research*, 19(2): 331–349.

Motschnig-Pitrik, R. and Holzinger, A. (2002) 'Student-centered teaching meets new media: Concept and case study', *Educational Technology and Society*, 5(4): 160–172.

Nijhuis, J., Segers, M. and Gijselaers, W. (2005) 'Influence of redesigning a learning environment on student perceptions and learning strategies', *Learning Environments Research*, 8: 67–93.

Nijhuis, J., Segers, M. and Gijselaers, W. (2008) 'The extent of variability in learning strategies and students' perceptions of the learning environment', *Learning and Instruction*, 18: 121–134.

Renkl, A. (2008) 'Why constructivists should not talk about constructivist learning environments: A commentary on Loyens and Gijbels (2008)', *Instructional Science*, 37: 495–498.

Säljö, R. (1975) *Qualitative differences in learning as a function of the learner's conception of a task*, Gothenburg: Acta Universitatis Gothoburgensis.

Schelfhout, W., Dochy, F., Janssens, S., Struyven, K. and Gielen, S. (2006) 'Towards an equilibrium model for creating powerful learning environments: Validation of a questionnaire on creating powerful learning environments during teacher training internships', *European Journal of Teacher Education*, 29(4): 471–503.

Schwinger, M., Steinmayr, R. and Spinath, B. (2009) 'How do motivational regulation strategies affect achievement: Mediated by effort management and moderated by intelligence', *Learning and Individual Differences*, 19: 621–627.

Sivan, A., Wong Leung, R., Woon, C. and Kember, D. (2000) 'An implementation of active learning and its effect on the quality of student learning', *Innovations in Education and Teaching International*, 37(4): 381–389.

Struyven, K., Dochy, F. and Janssens, S. (2008a) 'Students' likes and dislikes regarding student-activating and lecture-based educational settings: Consequences for students' perceptions of the learning environment, student learning and performance', *European Journal of Psychology of Education*, 23: 295–317.

Struyven, K., Dochy, F. and Janssens, S. (2010) 'Teach as you preach: The effects of student-centred versus lecture-based teaching on student teachers' approaches to teaching', *European Journal of Teacher Education*, 33(1): 43–64.

Struyven, K., Dochy, F., Janssens, S. and Gielen, S. (2006) 'On the dynamics of students' approaches to learning: The effects of the teaching/learning environment', *Learning and Instruction*, 16: 279–294.

Struyven, K., Dochy, F., Janssens, S. and Gielen, S. (2008b) 'Students' experiences with contrasting learning environments: The added value of students' perceptions', *Learning Environments Research*, 11: 83–109.

Tynjälä, P. (1999), 'Towards expert knowledge? A comparison between a constructivist and a traditional learning environment in the university', *International Journal of Educational Research*, 31: 357–442.

Vansteenkiste, M., Sierens, E., Soenens, B., Luyckx, K. and Lens, W. (2009) 'Motivational profiles from a self-determination perspective: The quality of motivation matters', *Journal of Educational Psychology*, 101(3): 671–688.

Vanthournout, G., Donche, V., Gijbels, D. and Van Petegem, P. (2009) 'Alternative data-analysis techniques in research on student learning: Illustrations of a person-oriented and developmental perspectives', *Reflecting Education*, 5(2): 35–51.

Vermetten, Y., Vermunt, J. and Lodewijks, H. (2002), 'Powerful learning environments? How university students differ in their response to instructional measures', *Learning and Instruction*, 12: 263–284.

Vermunt, J. and Vermetten, Y. (2004) 'Patterns in student learning: Relationships between learning strategies, conceptions of learning, and learning orientations', *Educational Psychology Review*, 16(4): 359–384.

Wilson, K. and Fowler, J. (2005) 'Assessing the impact of learning environments on students' approaches to learning: Comparing conventional and action learning designs', *Assessment and Evaluation in Higher Education*, 30(1): 87–101.

Chapter 15

Students' learning patterns in higher education

Dimensions, measurement and change

Jan D. Vermunt, John T.E. Richardson, Vincent Donche and David Gijbels

As we stated in Chapter 1, the aim of this book was to further deepen current understanding of (1) the dimensionality of student learning patterns in higher education and (2) how differences and changes within learning patterns can be measured in a valid and reliable way. In this concluding chapter we will look back on the various chapters and try to bring together the understandings that have emerged from the various chapters in the light of this aim.

The dimensionality of student learning patterns

The concept of learning patterns

In comparison with related concepts, the concept of learning pattern is more a holistic notion. In Chapter 2, Vanthournout et al. discuss the similarities and differences between the concepts of student approaches to learning and learning patterns. Vermunt and Vermetten (2004: 362) define a learning pattern as 'a superordinate concept in which the cognitive and affective processing of subject matter, the metacognitive regulation of learning, conceptions of learning, and learning orientations are united'. Compared to earlier conceptualizations of student learning (e.g. Biggs, 1987; Entwistle and Ramsden, 1983), both metacognitive (regulation, conceptions) and affective elements are included in this broader concept of learning patterns. Recently, Vermunt and Endedijk (2011) depicted the elements of a learning pattern and their internal and external relations in a model of teacher learning.

Price (Chapter 4) likewise stresses the holistic nature of student learning patterns. Her 4P model tries to bring together a number of factors in university teaching and learning, based on the 3P models of Dunkin and Biddle and of Biggs. Her model focuses on the interplay between students' learning and teachers' teaching in explaining learning outcomes, and includes personal and contextual characteristics of both students and teachers in the form of presage variables. Although Price does not present new empirical data about the interrelations among the elements of the 4P model in this chapter, her contribution is of great theoretical value. For example, it would be interesting to study further the qualitatively different conceptualizations of 'learning outcomes' and how these different types of learning outcomes are related to earlier phases in the model.

Several chapters in this book highlight relations between elements of learning patterns. For example, in Chapter 11 Donche et al. present a path model concerning relations between motivation, regulation and processing. They found that students who are more autonomously motivated tend to be more self-regulated and engage more in deep and concrete processing activities. Students who are more controlled in their motivation are more externally regulated and engage more in surface processing activities, while students who are amotivated tend to be more unregulated in their learning. In Chapter 13 Kyndt et al. report their finding that high autonomous motivation is associated with the increased use of deep approaches to learning. In both chapters, the angle of self-determination theory (Deci and Ryan, 2000) was chosen to further understand differences in the motivational drive of student learning.

As Cano and Berbén observe in Chapter 9, the concept of learning patterns offers the possibility of integrating theories on student approaches to learning and achievement goal theory (Ames, 1992), thereby creating a more complete picture. All in all, the concept of learning patterns, with its focus on the interrelations among constituent learning components (e.g. learning strategies, conceptions of learning, regulation of learning, learning motivation), seems to be a more encompassing and holistic concept than the separate concepts it integrates.

Conceptions of learning and teaching

In Chapter 4 Price presented an integrated model of learning and teaching in higher education. At the core of this model are the conceptions of learning held by the students and the conceptions of teaching held by their teachers. These are supposed to be determinants of students' approaches to studying and their teachers' approaches to teaching. This is a fairly conventional account of conceptions of learning and teaching that tries to explain variations in students' and teachers' conceptions in terms of some objective reality. It seeks to interpret conceptions of learning and teaching as mental entities that provide causal explanations for variations in students' study behaviour and for variations in teachers' teaching behaviour. Similar assumptions can be found in previous models of teaching and learning as discussed by Gijbels et al. in Chapter 1 and by Vanthournout et al. in Chapter 2.

As Richardson (2013) pointed out, however, there is a flaw in this reasoning. Researchers who take this line of argument are only in a position to compare one kind of account (about students' conceptions of learning or teachers' conceptions of teaching) with another kind of account provided by the same informants (about students' study behaviour or their teachers' teaching behaviour). Uncritically accepting the idea that variations in study behaviour and teaching behaviour are the upshot of mental processes is a case, as Woolgar (1996) put it, of buying into a central precept of the 'natives' before setting foot in the field. Baxter Magolda (2001: 530) criticized the positivist assumption that the findings of research into students' epistemological development reflected an objective reality and were generalizable to other contexts. Instead, she argued that 'reality is local and context-bound' and that 'the issue of applicability of interpretations outside of their context hinges on transferability'.

Richardson (2013) suggested the more radical move of rejecting the idea that the accounts given by participants in interviews about their conceptions of learning and teaching counted as evidence for the ascription of mental processes. Instead, he suggested that these accounts should be regarded simply as examples of students' discursive practices. Indeed, he went further and argued that the entities that figured in these accounts were merely artefacts that were constituted in social situations and that had no independent existence. This view is known as 'social constructionism' (Gergen, 1994). More specifically, Richardson suggested that it was more appropriate to try to understand mentalistic notions such as 'conceptions of learning' or 'conceptions of teaching' in terms of the part that they play in social interactions and most especially in the idiosyncratic kinds of interaction that occur in research interviews about teaching and learning in higher education (for an extended argument along these lines, see Talmy, 2011).

Säljö (1988) had stressed the need for researchers to accept that the categories of description that they proposed were simply their own constructions and that other researchers might in principle arrive at different categorizations based on the same evidence. Richardson (2013) argued that it followed from this that such categorizations could not be taken to refer to some objective reality that would somehow be accessible through unbiased observations but should instead be regarded simply as forms of speech that happen to figure in people's interpretative practices concerning teaching and learning in higher education. Both Säljö (1997) and other writers have developed this constructionist reinterpretation of conceptions of knowledge, learning and teaching (e.g. Baxter Magolda, 2001).

As Richardson (2013) pointed out, on this kind of account, when students are asked, 'Well, what do you actually mean by learning?' (Säljö, 1979: 19), they do not consult mysterious entities in their heads but instead think about particular kinds of social interactions that would be described as 'learning', typically their experiences within particular educational institutions. These accounts would, he argued, exhibit qualitative variations depending upon the formal arrangements that are created by different kinds of institutions to facilitate 'teaching' and 'learning'. He concluded that pursuing the idea of conceptions of learning and teaching might therefore end up telling us less about what goes on in students' and teachers' heads and more about what goes on in their classrooms.

Motivation and affect

In Chapter 4, Price acknowledged a number of limitations of her model. One was that it focused primarily on the cognitive aspects of teaching and learning in higher education. Traditionally, human experience was divided into three domains: the cognitive (knowing), the conative (willing) and the affective (feeling). Price's model simply reflects the bias in previous research to consider the cognitive aspects of student learning. Nevertheless, there has always been a strong interest in the motivational aspects of student learning. Vermunt's (1998) model of the regulation of constructive learning processes incorporated a component concerned with students' motivation or 'learning orientations', and this has been taken over into contemporary discussions of learning patterns in higher education. The importance of motivational factors was discussed in contributions to this book by Raemdonck et al. in Chapter 5, by Endedijk et al. in Chapter 6, by Donche et al. in Chapter 11, by Kyndt et al. in Chapter 13, and by Baeten et al. in Chapter 14.

A particular theoretical framework for understanding students' motivation to achieve in higher education is that of achievement goals. This framework was approached from a variable-oriented perspective by Richardson and Remedios in Chapter 7 and by De Clercq et al. in Chapter 8, and from a person-oriented perspective by Cano and Berbén in Chapter 9. The advantage of this framework is that it has been investigated for more than 30 years, and there is now a wealth of evidence concerning both the determinants and the consequences of students adopting particular achievement goals. All three chapters showed an association between students' achievement goals and their approaches to studying, thus demonstrating the relevance of this framework for an understanding of students' learning patterns in higher education. Moreover, all three chapters showed an association between students' achievement goals and their attainment, thus demonstrating that the framework has practical relevance for predicting and improving student achievement in higher education.

In contrast, the affective domain has been neglected in previous research on teaching and learning in higher education, although Vermunt (1996) incorporated affective factors in his phenomenographic analysis of learning patterns. In Chapter 6, affective considerations were included in the analysis of student teachers' learning patterns by Endedijk et al. Moreover, in Chapter 7, Richardson and Remedios suggested that affective factors might be important determinants of student dropout from higher education. The role of affective factors in student learning is certainly worth exploring in future research.

Underlying dimensions in learning patterns

A different question is whether learning patterns are universal across cultures and contexts or whether different learning patterns emerge in different cultures and contexts. In Chapter 3, Vermunt et al. compared the results of principal components analyses with either varimax or oblimin rotation applied to students' scores on the Inventory of Learning Styles (ILS) in eight different countries. Most of the data sets yielded a meaning-directed learning pattern, a reproduction-directed learning pattern and an undirected learning pattern. However, these were construed somewhat differently in different countries, and other characteristics showed even greater variability. Even so, this supports the conclusion of a previous literature review by Richardson (1994) that the distinction between a meaning orientation and a reproducing orientation to learning emerges across all national systems of higher education but receives a specific interpretation in each system or culture.

Besides these similarities among students from different countries and cultures, the chapter by Vermunt et al. also yielded a deeper understanding of the differences. While meaning-directed learning, reproduction-directed learning and undirected learning seem to be universal patterns around the globe, three other patterns were found that seem to be more specific for certain countries and cultures. These are an application-directed pattern, a passive-idealistic pattern and a passive-motivated pattern. A striking underlying difference among students from different countries was the degree of association between the various learning components. In some countries, for example, strong associations emerged between students' conceptions, motives and strategies; in other countries these relations were different or much weaker. Findings such as these should make us aware that the value of a concept such as dissonance (see Chapter 9 by Cano and Berbén), meaning that the expected relations between conceptions, motives and strategies do not occur in some subgroups of students, may be limited to Western cultures.

Relations of learning patterns with personal and contextual variables and learning outcomes

Various chapters in this book shed new light on the relationships of learning patterns with personal, contextual and learning outcome variables. For example, Endedijk et al. (Chapter 6) present findings about relations between student teachers' learning patterns and several personal and contextual variables. Interestingly, they do not conceptualize students' learning motivation as a constituent element of their learning pattern, but view motivation instead as a student characteristic that influences students' learning patterns. Donche et al. found in Chapter 11 that older students tended to be less successful than younger students. In fact, there is a lot of evidence that older students tend to produce *better* achievement than traditional-age students. On the other hand, they also found that female students were more likely to use surface processing. We do not believe that there is any intrinsic difference between male and female students in their approaches to learning, although we do accept that differences in both directions can arise in particular contexts.

In Chapter 13, Kyndt et al. presented findings from a large research project in which they looked at relationships between students' perceived workload, perceived task complexity, motivation, working memory capacity and attention. One of their intriguing findings is that a higher working memory capacity is associated with less use of a deep approach, but also less use of a surface approach to learning. To explain this finding Kyndt et al. propose a compensation hypothesis, meaning that the use of any learning activity can be compensated by a good memory and the other way around, at least in some learning contexts. Another interesting notion Kyndt et al. put forward is the notion of 'thresholds'. They found for example that motivation was only significantly related to students' approaches to learning when workload was high.

An important issue in learning pattern research is how learning patterns are related to learning outcomes. Although the espoused aims of university education almost universally pertain to educating independent and critical thinkers, empirical evidence does not always support the realization of these aims. Vermunt (2005) for example found that students who used 'relating and structuring' learning activities in their studies (an important element of a deep approach) in general scored higher on examinations. However, the degree to which the use of critical learning activities (another important element of a deep approach) was associated with examination success varied greatly among different subject domains.

In this book, De Clerq et al. (Chapter 8) focused on relations between students' learning patterns and their test achievements. Interestingly, they found a difference between a general success measure (percentage end-of-year obtained) and specific tests in the relation with learning strategies and goal orientations. According to De Clerq et al., their findings indicate that self-regulation is especially important for explaining study success in the beginning of university studies. With a more advanced sample of engineering students in the third year of studies, they found that past examination performance was by far the best predictor of current examination performance. This finding is well documented in the research literature. The implication – take previous performance into account in explaining current performance – is, however, more or less clear-cut when considered from a practical or theoretical perspective. From a practical perspective, this fact is for example the basis of selective admission procedures to university studies based on previous examination achievements, which is defensible for practical reasons. From a theoretical viewpoint, one tends to end up in a circular argument: if past performance explains current performance, how should we explain past performance? When past performance represents subject domain knowledge, Kyndt et al.'s (Chapter 13) compensation hypothesis would predict that students' learning activities matter more when prior domain knowledge is less important (for instance, in novel and unfamiliar domains). This supports De Clerq et al.'s observation that self-regulation is especially important for study success in the first phase of university studies. Another explanation to take into account is that De Clerq's study was done with engineering students. Knowledge domains in the natural and technical sciences are often more hierarchically structured, initial knowledge and understanding being a prerequisite for later knowledge and understanding, more so than, for example, in the humanities (e.g. Entwistle and Ramsden, 1983). Another interesting finding of De Clerq et al. was that adopting a surface approach correlated negatively with remembering definitions.

Cano and Berbén (Chapter 9) bring forward the notion of dissonance in explaining study success, or actually study failure. In the context of learning patterns the idea of dissonance may be very interesting, meaning that for some groups of students the expected relations between their motives, conceptions and strategies do not occur. For example, some students may combine a constructive conception of learning with a surface approach to studying, or intrinsic, autonomous motivation with lack of regulation. In other words, students' motives, conceptions and strategies are not aligned. Previous research (e.g. Lindblom-Ylänne and Lonka, 2000; Meyer, 2000; Vermunt and Minnaert, 2003) has shown that these students are at risk in terms of examination achievements, at least within the boundaries of Western cultures (see above).

Learning patterns beyond the first years of Western higher education

Most research on learning patterns has been done with Western students in the first years of regular higher education, and this book is no exception. However, four chapters in this book have studied learning patterns with other populations, and therefore represent important extensions of learning pattern research. Raemdonck et al. (Chapter 5), for example, studied learning patterns in adult learners. They observed that little is known about learning patterns of older adults and argue that research should be broadened to include learning patterns across the lifespan. One of the implications is that informal learning should occupy a more prominent place in models and theories of learning patterns, which until now have been dominated by student learning in more formal educational settings. Raemdonck et al. compare theories of self-directed learning, typically prevalent in the literature on adult learning and education, with theories of self-regulated learning, which typically originated from research on children and adolescent students. Although at first sight these two concepts seem quite similar, the gap between the bodies of literature on both concepts is remarkable. Raemdonck et al. contribute to making this gap a little smaller by comparing instruments for measuring self-directed learning with those for measuring learning patterns.

Two chapters in this book examine student teachers' learning patterns in learning to teach: Chapter 6 (Endedijk et al.) and Chapter 10 (Evans). This means an extension beyond the most studied samples in two ways: first, the students are postgraduate (master's) students and, second, a considerable part of their learning takes place in practice (internships or placements in schools). Their challenging task is to combine the knowledge they gain from learning from their experiences in practice with the knowledge they gain from coursework at university. This proves not to be an easy task. Evans (Chapter 10) extensively interviewed student teachers about their learning experiences, in order to discover how a deep approach to learning looks like in learning to teach. Originally, the deep approach to learning was defined very much in terms of learning from texts (e.g. Marton and Säljö, 1984). Adopting an interpretative phenomenological analysis approach enables Evans to identify nine characteristics of a deep approach in the context of learning to teach.

Endedijk et al. (Chapter 6) describe a series of studies in which a new inventory was developed and used to tap students' learning to teach patterns, combining learning from theory and practice. A strong point of their approach was that they chose not to adapt an existing inventory for this different type of learning, but started from scratch interviewing student teachers about their learning activities, regulation and conceptions of learning. Subsequently, inventory items were based on these interviews, an approach similar to that followed in the construction of the ILS (Chapter 3, Vermunt et al.). In this way Endedijk et al. could identify learning patterns typical for learning to teach, in which combining theory and practice is so important. Recently, Bakkenes et al. (2010) studied experienced teachers' learning in the context of the introduction of educational innovations. Both of these studies show that a surface approach (rote learning, rehearsing) is irrelevant when learning to teach. Important dimensions emerging from both studies are a meaning-directed pattern (but now with a focus on thinking about relations between theory and practice), a pattern focused on trying to use what one learns immediately in one's classroom practice, and a problematic survival pattern, aimed at staying afloat in the classroom and surviving the day.

The chapter by Vermunt et al. (Chapter 3) extends the traditional samples by looking at studies carried out in countries and cultures other than Western ones and by comparing studies from Asia, Latin America and Europe. They discussed important findings with regard to the extension of the dimensions underlying student learning patterns in this chapter. Another relevant finding was that the inventory they used to measure student learning patterns (the ILS) proved to be a reliable instrument across cultures. They point to the importance of this kind of extended research from the perspective of understanding and improving international student mobility.

Research perspectives and analytic artefacts

In Chapter 2, Vanthournout et al. described three different perspectives in research on learning patterns in higher education: the variable-oriented perspective, the person-oriented perspective and the longitudinal perspective. Endedijk et al. also discussed these three perspectives in Chapter 6. It is worth pointing out that these different perspectives are associated with different methods of data analysis and that these encourage researchers to adopt different theoretical perspectives.

The variable-oriented perspective

The variable-oriented perspective normally consists of administering a range of instruments to a large sample of students and exploring the relationships among their scores on the scales contained in these instruments. The analytic technique most commonly used to explore these relationships is factor analysis using either confirmatory or exploratory methods. In Chapter 3, Vermunt et al. reviewed studies that had used factor analysis to investigate the constituent structure of the ILS. The critical choices to be addressed in using this technique are: the statistical model for extracting the relevant factors; the criterion for deciding how many factors to extract; and the method for rotating the extracted factors.

Makoe et al. (2008) pointed out that, when using factor analysis, each student's responses are represented as a point in a multidimensional space. Differences between students and changes within students are represented as quantitative variations within that space. Thus, an artefact of using factor analysis to analyse questionnaire data is that the results will accord with a theory that assumes continuous variation along one or more dimensions rather than a theory which assumes that students fall into discrete categories. Richardson (in press) noted that this artefact appeared to have beguiled a number of theorists into adopting multidimensional theories of epistemological development in higher education and rejecting the stage theories that had been derived from earlier interview-based research on epistemological development.

Having established a number of factor-based scales, researchers using the variable-oriented perspective then use regression techniques or structural equation modelling to investigate the relationships between students' scale scores, their background characteristics and outcome variables. Examples of this approach in the present volume are Chapter 7 by Richardson and Remedios, Chapter 8 by De Clercq et al. and Chapter 11 by Donche et al.

The person-oriented perspective

The person-oriented perspective also consists of administering a range of instruments to a large sample of students, but in this case researchers seek to identify subgroups of students with qualitatively different patterns of scores. The analytic technique that is most commonly used to identify these subgroups is cluster analysis. In Chapter 9, Cano and Berbén used cluster analysis to identify students with different patterns of achievement goals and approaches to studying. In Chapter 14, Baeten et al. used cluster analysis to divide students into two groups with different motivation and approaches to learning. The critical choices to be addressed in using this technique are: the metric used to define the similarity and dissimilarity among the students; the method used to identify the clusters; and the criterion for deciding how many clusters to extract.

The artefact in using cluster analysis is just the converse of that in using factor analysis: the results will accord with a theory which assumes that students can be assigned to a number of discrete categories rather than falling along one or more dimensions. It also tends to promote the assumption that students are heterogeneous across the relevant categories but relatively homogeneous within each of the categories, which may or may not be true in a specific case. However, latent profile analysis and certain forms of cluster analysis assign cases to clusters on a probabilistic rather than absolute basis, thus allowing for within-cluster variation as well as between-cluster variation.

Some researchers then use conventional multivariate techniques such as analysis of variance to analyse the differences among the clusters in their scale scores. However, since the point of cluster analysis is to maximize the variation among the clusters on the criterion variables, it is not surprising that the clusters will be significantly different on the majority of the scales. In addition, since the scale scores are also likely to be correlated and therefore confounded with one another, the results of such analyses will not be very informative. A better approach is to use discriminant analysis to determine the scales that contribute most to the differences among the different clusters. In Chapter 9, Cano and Berbén identified six clusters of students and then used discriminant analysis to determine which aspects of their achievement goals and approaches to studying predicted membership of the different clusters.

The results of certain studies using a person-oriented perspective are at odds with the results of those using a variable-oriented perspective. For instance, questionnaires on approaches to studying typically yield separate scales measuring a meaning orientation and a reproducing orientation that turn out to be roughly orthogonal to each other, so that an individual student might score high or low on both scales (for discussion, see Richardson, 2000: 186). However, in a study using a person-oriented perspective, Richardson (1997) gave a questionnaire to 98 students at two sessions 2 weeks apart. The questionnaire contained four scales measuring a meaning orientation and four scales measuring a reproducing orientation. A cluster analysis of their scores on all eight scales identified two distinct groups at both sessions: one group scored high on meaning orientation and low on reproducing orientation, and the other group showed the opposite pattern. This is consistent with the results of interview-based research, which suggest that the two orientations are mutually exclusive, not statistically independent.

However, rather different results were obtained by Vanthournout et al. (2013), who gave a questionnaire measuring a deep approach to studying and a surface approach to studying to 206 students. A cluster analysis of their scores on the two scales identified four groups: one group scored high on both scales; a second scored low on both scales; a third scored high on deep approach and low on surface approach; and the fourth scored low on deep approach and high on surface approach. These researchers noted that similar results had been found in previous research carried out in both Finland and Spain, suggesting that the pattern of results could be generalized across European systems of higher education. Nevertheless, Richardson (2013) suggested that this pattern might actually be a statistical artefact that would be generated by any data set based on two relatively independent variables.

To check on this, we constructed just such a data set consisting of 1,000 pairs of scores on two independent random variables following the standard normal distribution. The dissimilarity between any pair of cases was defined using the city-block metric as the sum of the absolute differences between their scores on the two variables. A cluster analysis was carried out on the scores using the method of complete linkage clustering (the 'furthest neighbour' method), and four clusters were extracted. One group scored high on the first variable and average on the second; a second group scored low on the first variable and average on the second; a third group scored average on the first variable and high on the second; and the fourth group scored average on the first variable and low on the second. This is quite different from the pattern of results obtained by Vanthournout et al., suggesting that the latter is a genuine finding and not merely a statistical artefact.

As Vanthournout et al. pointed out in Chapter 2, an important practical aspect of the person-oriented perspective is that in principle it can identify students who are at risk of dropping out or failing. To achieve this, however, students' progress needs to be monitored over time.

The longitudinal perspective

The longitudinal perspective is based on repeated surveying of the same sample of students using the same instruments over the course of time. Examples of longitudinal studies were described by Endedijk et al. in Chapter 6 and by Lindblom-Ylänne et al. in Chapter 12. The time interval in question can vary from a few weeks to several years. A major problem with longitudinal research is missing data due to students dropping out of their courses or declining to participate in follow-up surveys. However, neither Endedijk et al. nor Lindblom-Ylänne et al. reported the attrition rate in their studies.

Traditionally, the data from such investigations have been analysed using students' t-tests for paired samples or repeated-measures analyses of variance. However, these techniques make certain statistical assumptions that in practice may well not be met. In Chapter 12, Lindblom-Ylänne et al. used t-tests for paired samples at the group level, but they pointed out that these tests hid rather than revealed individual variation. They themselves plotted individual change scores and compared the results with the students' accounts in qualitative interviews. Other methods that could be used include cluster analysis (to identify different patterns of change over time) or latent growth analysis using structural equation modelling. The latter technique can be used to analyse group data or to identify changes over time in individual students.

A particularly interesting question is whether and how students' learning patterns change over the course of an entire programme of study in higher education. It is often assumed that students' adopt more desirable study behaviour as they progress through their programmes, as reflected in the idea of 'growth trajectories' (see Chapter 2). Vanthournout et al. (2011) reviewed longitudinal research mainly carried out in continental Europe and found that in general students did exhibit deeper, more concrete and more self-regulated study behaviour. However, both cross-sectional and longitudinal studies carried out in the United Kingdom, Australasia and Hong Kong find that students are *less* likely to show desirable approaches to studying as they proceed through a degree programme (for a review, see Richardson, 2000: 180). This is a paradox that needs to be resolved in future research.

Stability, variability, change and development

Stability versus variability in learning patterns

As Vanthournout et al. explained in Chapter 2, one basic question in learning patterns research is that of the stability versus the consistency of learning patterns over time. Vermunt and Vermetten (2004) summarized the findings of research on this matter up to that point:

> Research on a course-specific level showed that students do vary in their use of learning strategies for different courses, but that students are also consistent in their strategy use over different courses. Accordingly, there seems to be both a context-specific and an individual-bound component in the use of learning strategies. All in all, this points to the conclusion that learning patterns are rather stable within a constant educational context, but that they can be changed.
>
> (p. 379)

However, Richardson (2011) pointed out that this statement combined two quite different hypotheses:

> Stability or consistency in students' learning patterns across different courses might indicate some constant factor within the students themselves (an 'internal' or 'individual-bound' characteristic) or some constant factor within their educational context (an 'external' characteristic). After all, different courses taught within the same institution might well share many features in common and thus offer a 'constant educational context').
>
> (p. 291)

Subsequently, Richardson (2013) elaborated this argument:

> The important point is that the logical status of the hypothesis that students' learning patterns are stable over the course of time is akin to that of a universal affirmative: it cannot be confirmed, only refuted. . . . The proposition that students' learning patterns are stable over time is not confirmed by observing consistency in their study behaviour, because that might result from consistency in the educational context; it can only be refuted by observing variability in students' study behaviour over time. Even if students exhibit consistent learning patterns in the face of apparent variability in their context, this might merely indicate that the underlying features of their context are in fact consistent. These logical aspects of the stability hypothesis need to be carefully considered in the future.
>
> (p. 67)

Change and development in learning patterns

Related, but not equivalent to the issue of stability versus variability is the issue of change and development in student learning patterns. The chapters of Vanthournout et al. (Chapter 2), Endedijk et al. (Chapter 6), and Lindblom-Ylänne et al. (Chapter 12) are particularly relevant in this respect.

A basic finding in student learning research is that when a group of students is compared at two measurement occasions on one or more scales of a student learning inventory, often few changes emerge, even when the interval is a year or more (cf. Lindblom-Ylänne et al. in Chapter 12). At first sight such findings could be interpreted as a lack of change and development in learning patterns. However, as the authors of all three chapters argue, when one looks at the raw data many signs of change are evident on an individual level. Obviously, students do change but they change in different directions (decline, growth, no change) and on group level this often results in no change at all, averaging out individual growth patterns. In their chapter Lindblom-Ylänne et al. (Chapter 12) point to the limitations of quantitative analysis techniques in this respect and try to develop improved methods comparing individual growth patterns with group level analyses in a more qualitative way. Endedijk et al. (Chapter 6) and Vanthournout et al. (Chapter 2) point to another possible reason for the averaging effect, namely that with only two measuring points a researcher by definition can only detect linear changes. Real changes in learning patterns may also be curvilinear, quadratic or individual (Coertjens et al., 2013; Endedijk et al., in press; Vanthournout et al., 2012). To be able to detect these growth patterns multiple measuring moments are necessary.

Improving student learning

One of the most important practical applications of research on students' learning patterns is to find ways of improving the quality of student learning. Research on student learning has been dominated by the distinction between deep and surface approaches to learning, but, as Richardson (2000: 27) commented, this distinction is commonplace and has perhaps become a cliché in discussions about teaching and learning in higher education. In Chapter 10, Evans has performed the vitally important task of using interview-based data to explain what a 'deep approach' actually means to contemporary students. One criticism is that the students in question were engaged in teacher-training, and their interview responses seem to confound accounts of their own learning with accounts of improving learning in their students.

The model presented by Price in Chapter 4 was originally intended to explain why it was so difficult to enhance the quality of student learning in higher education. Price and Richardson (2004) had suggested that the quality of learning depended on a complex teaching–learning system, and that simply changing one component in this system (e.g. a teacher's approach to teaching) was unlikely to have any major effect. Using cases from the literature, Price and

Richardson showed that the effectiveness of interventions tended to vary with the number of components in the model that were subject to change. Both Chapter 13 by Kyndt et al. and Chapter 14 by Baeten et al. confirm that it is hard to induce more desirable approaches to learning. In the study by Kyndt et al., the researchers attempted to achieve this outcome by manipulating workload and task complexity, although this had only limited effects.

One of the implications of finding differences between students in their learning patterns is that *improving* students' learning patterns may need a differentiated approach as well. A one-size-fits-all approach to support students in their learning pattern development may well represent a contradiction in terms. In Chapter 6 Endedijk et al. in particular present a case for differential approaches to supporting student learning and provide us with many examples of how this can be achieved. Vermunt et al. in Chapter 3 argue that in an era of increasing student mobility, international students may profit from some kind of induction into the educational and learning cultures of their foreign host universities to boost the adaptation of their learning patterns to the new environment.

In the study by Baeten et al., the researchers attempted to induce more desirable approaches by introducing case-based learning, which was assumed to offer a more student-centred environment. Students who were taught in either a traditional lecture-based environment or through case-based learning demonstrated an increased tendency to adopt a surface approach, a decreased tendency to adopt a strategic approach and a decreased tendency to adopt a deep approach. The only exception to this pattern occurred when the students were gradually exposed to case-based learning after initially being taught in a lecture-based environment: in this case, the students showed a decreased tendency to adopt a surface approach, more autonomous motivation, higher scores on assessment, but no change in their use of a deep approach (see also Baeten et al., 2013).

The findings of Baeten et al.'s study support the notion of a process-oriented approach to learning pattern development: a gradual transfer of control from the educational environment to the learners themselves, a gradual transfer from external to internal regulation of learning. Immediate immersion into the novel case-based approach had adverse effects, very similar to what was described earlier as a destructive friction between teaching and learning (Vermunt and Verloop, 1999).

Among other things, these results show that to encourage a deep approach it is not sufficient to discourage a surface approach. In this study it would have been interesting to know more about the prevalent teaching practices to which the students had been previously exposed and hence their expectations about teaching. Experiences with international exchange students suggest that when the learning environment changes in a consistent, aligned and drastic way, students' capability to adapt their learning patterns to these new environments may be quite large.

To conclude

The different chapters in this volume aimed to further deepen our current understanding of the dimensionality of student learning patterns in higher education and how differences and changes within learning patterns can be measured in a valid and reliable way. Although all chapters contributed to this aim, there is considerable diversity in the book providing the reader with plenty of food for thought. In all of the different chapters a number of research issues and implications for practice are identified that invite the reader to participate in the debate.

References

Ames, C. (1992) 'Classrooms: Goals, structures, and student motivation', *Journal of Educational Psychology*, 84: 261–271.

Baeten, M., Struyven, K., and Dochy, F. (2013) 'Student-centred teaching methods: Can they optimise students' approaches to learning in professional higher education?', *Studies in Educational Evaluation*, 39: 14–22.

Bakkenes, I., Vermunt, J.D., and Wubbels, T. (2010) 'Teacher learning in the context of educational innovation: Learning activities and learning outcomes of experienced teachers', *Learning and Instruction*, 20: 533–548.

Baxter Magolda, M.B. (2001) 'A constructivist revision of the Measure of Epistemological Reflection', *Journal of College Student Development*, 42: 520–534.

Biggs, J. (1987) *Student approaches to learning and studying*. Melbourne: Australian Council for Educational Research.

Coertjens, L., van Daal, T., Donche, V., De Maeyer, S., and Van Petegem, P. (2013) 'Analysing change in learning strategies over time: A comparison of three statistical techniques', *Studies in Educational Evaluation*, 39: 49–55.

Deci, E.L., and Ryan, R. M. (2000) 'The "what" and "why" of goal pursuits: Human needs and the self-determination of behavior', *Psychological Inquiry*, 11: 227–268.

Endedijk, M., Vermunt, J.D., Meijer, P., and Brekelmans, M. (in press) 'Students' development in self-regulated learning in postgraduate professional education: A longitudinal study', *Studies in Higher Education*.

Entwistle, N., and Ramsden, P. (1983) *Understanding student learning*. London: Croom Helm.

Gergen, K.J. (1994) *Realities and relationships: Soundings in social construction*. Cambridge, MA: Harvard University Press.

Lindblom-Ylänne, S., and Lonka, K. (2000) 'Dissonant study orchestrations of high-achieving university students', *European Journal of Psychology of Education*, 15: 19–32.

Makoe, M., Richardson, J.T.E., and Price, L. (2008) 'Conceptions of learning in adult students embarking on distance education', *Higher Education*, 55: 303–320.

Marton, F., and Säljö, R. (1984) 'Approaches to learning'. In F. Marton, D. Hounsell and N. Entwistle (Eds.), *The experience of learning* (pp. 36–55). Edinburgh: Scottish Academic Press.

Meyer, J.H.F. (2000) 'The modeling of "dissonant" study orchestration in higher education', *European Journal of Psychology of Education*, 15: 5–18.

Price, L., and Richardson, J.T.E. (2004) 'Why is it so difficult to improve student learning?' In C. Rust (Ed.), *Improving student learning: Theory, research and scholarship*. Oxford: Oxford Centre for Staff and Learning Development.

Richardson, J.T.E. (1994) 'Cultural specificity of approaches to studying in higher education: A literature survey', *Higher Education*, 27: 449–468.

Richardson, J.T.E. (1997) 'Meaning orientation and reproducing orientation: A typology of approaches to studying in higher education?', *Educational Psychology*, 17: 301–311.

Richardson, J.T.E. (2000) *Researching student learning: Approaches to studying in campus-based and distance education*. Buckingham, UK: SRHE and Open University Press.

Richardson, J.T.E. (2011) 'Approaches to studying, conceptions of learning and learning styles in higher education', *Learning and Individual Differences*, 21: 288–293.

Richardson, J.T.E. (2013) 'Research issues in evaluating learning pattern development in higher education', *Studies in Educational Evaluation*, 39: 66–70.

Richardson, J.T.E. (in press). 'Epistemological development in higher education', *Educational Research Review*. Available: http://dx.doi.org/10.1016/j.edurev.2012.10.001 (accessed 6 February 2013).

Säljö, R. (1979) *Learning in the learner's perspective: I. Some common-sense assumptions* (Report No. 76). Göteborg, Sweden: University of Göteborg, Institute of Education.

Säljö, R. (1988) 'Learning in educational settings: Methods of inquiry', in P. Ramsden (Ed.), *Improving learning: New perspectives*. London: Kogan Page.

Säljö, R. (1997) 'Talk as data and practice: A critical look at phenomenographic inquiry and the appeal to experience', *Higher Education Research and Development*, 16: 173–190.

Talmy, S. (2011) 'The interview as collaborative achievement: Interaction, identity, and ideology in a speech event', *Applied Linguistics*, 32: 25–42.

Vanthournout, G., Coertjens, L., Gijbels, D., Donche, V., and Van Petegem, P. (2013) 'Assessing students' development in learning approaches according to initial learning profiles: A person-oriented perspective', *Studies in Educational Evaluation*, 39: 33–40.

Vanthournout, G., De Maeyer, S., Gijbels, D., Donche, V., and Coertjens, L. (2012, August) *The development of learning strategies in the first years of higher education: A multilevel study*. Paper presented at the EARLI SIG Higher Education Conference on Creativity and Innovation in Higher Education, Talinn, Estonia.

Vanthournout, G., Donche, V., Gijbels, D., and Van Petegem, P. (2011) 'Further understanding learning in higher education: A systematic review on longitudinal research using Vermunt's learning pattern model', in S. Rayner and E. Cools (Eds.), *Style differences in cognition, learning and management: Theory, research and practice* (pp. 78–96). London: Routledge.

Vermunt, J.D. (1996) 'Metacognitive, cognitive and affective aspects of learning styles and strategies: A phenomenographic analysis', *Higher Education*, 31: 25–50.

Vermunt, J.D. (1998) 'The regulation of constructive learning processes', *British Journal of Educational Psychology*, 68: 149–171.

Vermunt, J.D. (2005) 'Relations between student learning patterns and personal and contextual factors and academic performance', *Higher Education*, 49: 205–234.

Vermunt, J.D., and Endedijk, M.D. (2011) 'Patterns in teacher learning in different phases of the professional career', *Learning and Individual Differences*, 21: 294–302.

Vermunt, J., and Minnaert, A. (2003) 'Dissonance in student learning patterns: When to revise theory?', *Studies in Higher Education*, 28: 49–61.

Vermunt, J.D., and Verloop, N. (1999) 'Congruence and friction between learning and teaching', *Learning and Instruction*, 9: 257–280.

Vermunt, J.D., and Vermetten, Y.J. (2004) 'Patterns in student learning: Relationships between learning strategies, conceptions of learning, and learning orientations', *Educational Psychology Review*, 16: 359–384

Woolgar, S. (1996) 'Psychology, qualitative methods and the ideas of science', in J.T.E. Richardson (Ed.), *Handbook of qualitative research methods for psychology and the social sciences*. Leicester: BPS Books.

Index